Building Classroom Discipline

tenth edition

Building Classroom Discipline

C. M. Charles
Emeritus, San Diego State University

Collaboration by:

Gail W. Senter
California State University San Marcos

Contributions from:

Paula Cook
University of Manitoba

Eileen VanWie
New Mexico State University

Terrell Brown
University of Central Missouri

PEARSON

Boston   Columbus   Indianapolis   New York   San Francisco   Upper Saddle River
Amsterdam   Cape Town   Dubai   London   Madrid   Milan   Munich   Paris   Montreal   Toronto
Delhi   Mexico City   Sao Paulo   Sydney   Hong Kong   Seoul   Singapore   Taipei   Tokyo

Managing Editor: Shannon Steed
Editorial Assistant: Matthew Buchholz
Vice President, Director of Marketing: Quinn Perkson
Marketing Manager: Jared Brueckner
Production Coordinator: Mary Beth Finch
Editorial Production Service: Omegatype Typography, Inc.
Manufacturing Manager: Megan Cochran
Electronic Composition: Omegatype Typography, Inc.
Interior Design: Omegatype Typography, Inc.
Cover Designer: Linda Knowles

Credits and acknowledgments borrowed from other sources and reproduced, with permission, in this textbook appear on appropriate page within text or on page 322.

Library of Congress Cataloging-in-Publication Data

Charles, C. M.
  Building classroom discipline / C. M. Charles; collaboration by Gail W. Senter; contributions from Paula Cook, Eileen VanWie, Terrell Brown.—10th ed.
       p.   cm.
  Includes bibliographical references and index.
  ISBN-13: 978-0-13-703405-5 (pbk.)
  ISBN-10: 0-13-703405-9 (pbk.)
  1. School discipline. 2. Classroom management. I. Senter, Gail W.   II. Title.
  LB3012.C46 2011
  371.102'4—dc22

                                                                          2009035763

Printed in the United States of America.

10 9 8 7 6 5 4 3 2 1   RRD-VA   14 13 12 11 10

www.pearsonhighered.com

ISBN-10: 0-13-703405-9
ISBN-13: 978-0-13-703405-5

C. M. Charles was a public school teacher from 1953 to 1959, then moved into higher education and held positions at the University of New Mexico, Teachers College Columbia University, Pepperdine University, Universidade Federal do Maranhao (Brazil), and San Diego State University, where he is now professor emeritus. At San Diego State, Charles directed innovative programs in teacher education and five times received outstanding professor and distinguished teaching awards. He also served on several occasions as an advisor in teacher education and curriculum to the governments of Peru and Brazil. Charles has authored or co-authored numerous books that have attracted wide audiences in the United States and abroad, with translations into several foreign languages. Those dealing most directly with school discipline are *Teachers' Petit Piaget* (1972), *The Synergetic Classroom: Joyful Teaching and Gentle Discipline* (2000), *Essential Elements of Effective Discipline* (2002), *Classroom Management for Middle Grades Teachers* (2004), *Elementary Classroom Management* (5th edition, 2008), and *Today's Best Classroom Management Strategies: Paths to Positive Discipline* (2008). Charles, who resides in California and Australia, is married and has two children, both teachers.

CONTENTS

3 How Do I Recognize and Deal with Atypical Behavior That Is Neurological-Based?   41

---

6 How Do Harry and Rosemary Wong Use Responsibilities and Procedures to Establish Class Discipline?   101

7   **How Does Fred Jones Establish Class Discipline by Keeping Students Responsibly Involved?**   120

10　**How Does Marvin Marshall Establish Discipline by Activating Internal Motivation and Raising Student Responsibility?**　175

11   How Does Craig Seganti Use Positive Teacher Leverage and Realistic Student Accountability to Establish Class Discipline?   194

14 How Do C. M. Charles and Others Energize
Their Classes?   249

15 How Does Eileen Kalberg VanWie Build
and Maintain Democratic Learning Communities
in Technology-Rich Environments?   266

PART IV   What Remains to Be Done?   285

16   How Do I Finalize a System of Discipline Designed Especially for Me and My Students?   286

A pleasant classroom environment where students behave responsibly is essential for high-quality teaching and learning. Teachers, in their efforts to maintain such environments, work to help students show initiative, accept responsibility, and interact positively with others. The influence they exert—referred to as *discipline*—consists of a number of different strategies and tactics. In the past, discipline was often demanding and sometimes harsh. Although it helped students behave civilly and stay on task, it produced undesirable side effects such as student fearfulness, loss of motivation, and dislike for school. That earlier discipline has progressively been replaced with discipline that promotes self-control; responsibility; and positive attitudes toward school, teachers, and learning. The new approach to discipline relies on positive influence from teachers, and this book is designed to help you learn to exert positive influence effectively.

NEW TO THIS EDITION

New and promising approaches to discipline are appearing regularly that help educators work with students more humanely and productively. The best of those newer approaches have been incorporated into this edition, in some cases replacing material that was no longer at the forefront. Readers should find the following additions especially interesting and helpful:

- **MyEducationLab for Classroom Management** is integrated throughout the new edition. This new website features interactive simulations, classroom video, videos of discipline experts, assignments, and activities for students.
- Chapter 11 describes Craig Seganti's discipline approach that uses clear rules and positive leverage to ensure a calm, safe, and respectful environment focused on learning. Mr. Seganti is a teacher in inner-city Los Angeles.
- Chapter 12 presents suggestions from eight highly respected authorities on how outstanding teachers establish personal influence with students who are difficult to manage—a new approach for obtaining cooperation from troublesome students.
- Chapter 14 presents suggestions from various sources on ways of energizing classes to encourage enthusiastic student participation.
- Chapter 15 describes Eileen Kalberg VanWie's research and recommendations in establishing democratic learning environments in technology-rich environments. This topic is new to discipline. Professor VanWie is head of Distance Education at New Mexico State University.
- As new chapters were added, outdated material was deleted to keep the size of the book constant. Thus, although the book remains the same size as

previously, the chapters in this edition differ considerably from those in previous editions because they present new material and have been restructured to facilitate understanding.

- Chapter formats have been changed throughout to enhance readability. More scenarios, vignettes, and reflection questions are interspersed in the chapters, and more helpful suggestions are provided for applying given discipline strategies in the classroom. All the while, the clear, friendly reading style of the book has been maintained.

- The extensive references and glossary of terms have been updated for maximum usefulness to readers.

- The book is now organized into four parts, a change that enables readers to acquire a more comprehensive understanding of the nature, purpose, and practice of classroom discipline. Part One provides needed background in professionalism, ability to anticipate student behavior within the broad range of student traits, and knowledge of the great contributions that have revolutionized the practice of discipline. Part Two takes readers into an exploration and analysis of seven of the most effective programs of discipline available today. Part Three presents a range of additional discipline strategies that can be used to enhance any system of discipline. Lastly, Part Four guides readers through the process of designing a personal system of discipline suited to their preferences and the needs of their students.

THE PRIMARY PURPOSE OF THIS BOOK

Beginning with the first edition of *Building Classroom Discipline* almost three decades ago and continuing to today, the overriding purpose of this book has remained constant—to help teachers develop personal systems of discipline tailored to their individual philosophies and personalities and to the needs, traits, and social realities of their students. Many excellent commercial models of discipline are described herein; however, none is likely to provide a perfect match for the realities of any given classroom. For that reason, readers are urged to select elements from those approaches that can be organized into discipline systems tailored to their needs. Guidance for doing so is presented in Chapters 1 and 16.

   In recent years, many advances have been made in discipline, as outlined in the timeline of major contributions in discipline on page xxviii. Whereas earlier discipline was characterized by coercion, reward, and punishment, newer techniques encourage students to behave acceptably because they feel it is the right thing to do and see it as advantageous to themselves and their classmates. The tenth edition of *Building Classroom Discipline* describes a variety of such approaches set forth by leading authorities. These approaches show teachers how to work with students helpfully and respectfully to ensure learning while preserving student dignity and positive teacher–student relationships.

NATURE OF THIS BOOK AND PRIMARY AUDIENCES

The tenth edition of *Building Classroom Discipline* reviews and analyzes approaches to discipline that have been set forth by some of the most astute thinkers in the history of classroom discipline. Nine of those approaches, summarized in Chapter 4, review some of the best foundational contributions that underpin today's discipline. While no longer used in their entirety, those approaches provided groundbreaking strategies and their major components are still evident in today's finest models of discipline. Chapters 5 through 11 present seven prototypical approaches to discipline that can be used effectively in classrooms today. Although the seven approaches vary in nature, all are considered to be complete systems that give balanced attention to preventing misbehavior, supporting appropriate behavior, communicating effectively with students, and correcting misbehavior in a positive manner. Chapters 12 through 15 present a selection of concepts, strategies, and tactics that are at the cutting edge in discipline today and can help enhance virtually any system of discipline. Chapter 16 provides guidance to help readers formalize personal systems of discipline that meet their needs and those of their students.

This book, comprehensive enough to serve as a single or primary text yet compact enough for use with other texts, is designed for use in preservice courses in discipline and classroom management, learning and instruction, methods of teaching, and educational psychology. It is equally useful for teachers already in service who are seeking more effective and enjoyable ways of working with students. Instructors in school district training programs and teacher institutes will also find the book useful.

THE CHAPTERS AND HOW THEY ARE PRESENTED

Previous users of the book will notice that some changes in chapter structure have been made to involve readers more actively and present the material more clearly. As always, chapter organization and style of writing aim at maximum clarity, understanding, and applicability. Chapters 5 through 15, which describe various strategies and tactics of discipline, are structured as follows:

1. Brief biographical sketches of contributing authorities, including their principal publications
2. A preview of the chapter
3. Specific topics to look for in the chapter
4. A description of the particular authorities' views on discipline
5. Suggestions for implementing the approach in the classroom
6. Terms and concepts featured in the chapter

7. Application exercises that include one or more of the following: Activities, Concept Cases, and a "You Are the Teacher" scenario that calls on readers to consider how they would resolve real-life discipline situations

8. References

Following are the titles and contents of the 16 chapters that comprise this book.

Part One: How Do I Begin Organizing a System of Discipline That Meets My Needs?

Chapter 1: What Is Classroom Discipline and How Do I Encourage Productive Efforts in My Classroom?

This restructured chapter provides information to increase your sense of professionalism in teaching and discipline. It explains the nature of professionalism, indicates what is required of professional teachers, introduces an organizing structure to help you work toward a personalized system of discipline, and poses a number of questions about student behavior to expand your thinking about classroom behavior and how it is best managed.

Chapter 2: How Can I Anticipate My Students' Behavior and Deal with Factors That Promote Misbehavior?

This restructured chapter explores student behavior as influenced by maturation and socio-cultural experiences. Behavior is depicted as a product of inborn proclivities that are shaped by the social realities in students' lives. Several factors that tend to promote misbehavior in classrooms are described, along with suggestions for softening or otherwise dealing with those factors.

Chapter 3: How Do I Recognize and Deal with Atypical Behavior That Is Neurological-Based?

This updated chapter examines the sometimes baffling behavior of students with neurological-based behavior (NBB) and helps you understand why those students at times cannot control what they say or do. Authorities estimate that about 10 percent of students in school have NBB. This chapter provides information to help teachers work with these students more productively.

Chapter 4: What Are the Foundations That Underlie Today's Best Systems of Discipline?

This restructured chapter pinpoints the beginning of modern classroom discipline and traces its development up to the present day. The term *modern discipline* refers to comprehensive approaches that are designed to prevent misbehavior and to correct it through helpful tactics that do not treat students harshly. The chapter reviews some of the lasting contributions of great innovators in discipline whose influence is still evident in today's most advanced approaches to discipline.

Part Two: What Are Some of Today's Most Outstanding Approaches to Classroom Discipline?

Chapter 5: How Does Ronald Morrish Use Purposeful Teacher Guidance to Establish Class Discipline?

Morrish, a former teacher, calls his approach *Real Discipline*, which he describes as an organized set of tactics that good teachers have used for generations in helping students become well-mannered and self-directing.

Chapter 6: How Do Harry and Rosemary Wong Use Responsibilities and Procedures to Establish Class Discipline?

Harry and Rosemary Wong, authors of the all-time best-selling book in education, explain why and how students should be informed of classroom responsibilities and trained to follow procedures quickly and correctly. Their approach enhances learning and efficiency in all class activities and markedly reduces the incidence of misbehavior.

Chapter 7: How Does Fred Jones Establish Class Discipline by Keeping Students Responsibly Involved?

Jones, a psychologist, shows how to organize the classroom to enable teachers to "work the crowd," teach in a manner that keeps students actively involved in lessons, and use body language and incentive systems to help students conduct themselves responsibly.

Chapter 8: How Does William Glasser Use Choice Theory and Quality Education to Establish Class Discipline?

Glasser, a psychiatrist, emphasizes that we cannot successfully make students do anything— we must instead use legitimate influence that prompts students to choose to do the right thing. He explains how to exert such influence through quality communication and quality teaching.

Chapter 9: How Does Spencer Kagan Use Structures and Teacher–Student Same-Side Collaboration to Establish Class Discipline?

Kagan, a psychologist, shows teachers how to involve students in making collaborative decisions about classroom behavior and other matters, thus promoting calm, purposeful classrooms. He provides a number of *structures*, or sets of procedures, for teachers to use when students disrupt. The structures halt the disruption and provide acceptable ways for students to meet their needs in the classroom.

Chapter 10: How Does Marvin Marshall Establish Discipline by Activating Internal Motivation and Raising Student Responsibility?

Marshall, a former teacher and administrator, calls his approach *Discipline without Stress*. It uses four levels of social development to influence students to conduct themselves properly. At the highest level, students conduct themselves in accordance with what they believe to be the right thing to do.

Chapter 11: How Does Craig Seganti Use Positive Teacher Leverage and Realistic Student Accountability to Establish Class Discipline?

Seganti, a classroom teacher in inner-city Los Angeles, explains how to keep students actively engaged in lessons while conducting themselves in a courteous manner. In this new chapter Seganti describes the teaching style he has found effective and his system of benign leverage that keeps students well-mannered and on track.

Part Three: What Additional Strategies Might I Use to Enhance My Personal System of Discipline?

Chapter 12: How Do Top Teachers Establish Personal Influence with Students Who Are Difficult to Manage?

This new chapter describes the most effective tactics available for teachers to interact with students who are especially difficult to manage, thus establishing personal relationships that foster higher achievement and better behavior in the classroom. It includes the input of several highly respected authorities: Dave Hingsburger (on the use of power), Stephen R. Covey (on finding common frames of reference for empathetic listening), Haim Ginott (on congruent communication), Jane Nelsen and Lynn Lott (on relationship builders and barriers), William Glasser (on deadly habits and connecting habits), Tom Daly (on befriending students who are difficult to manage), Richard Curwin and Allen Mendler (on conferring dignity and restoring hope), and Ed Ford (on using the Responsible Thinking Process).

Chapter 13: How Do Leading Experts Engender Respect and Civility in the Classroom?

This reorganized chapter presents contributions from P. M. Forni, head of the Civility Initiative at Johns Hopkins University, Michele Borba, international author and consultant on building moral intelligence, and Diane Gossen, international authority on the role of restitution in bringing about long-term improvement in behavior.

Chapter 14: How Do C. M. Charles and Others Energize Their Classes?

This chapter presents strategies for increasing the levels of student involvement and classroom energy through activities that emphasize group spirit and sense of purpose. The chapter features the contributions of C. M. Charles, author of *The Synergetic Classroom*, and five teachers at various levels who share efforts they have found effective in energizing their classes.

Chapter 15: How Does Eileen Kalberg VanWie Build and Maintain
Democratic Learning Communities in Technology-Rich Environments?

This new chapter focuses on procedures for promoting democratic relations among
learners in classrooms that are richly endowed with technology, a topic new to discipline. The lead author, researcher and professor Eileen Kalberg VanWie, is one of
the first to become thoroughly conversant with the process of establishing group
purpose and camaraderie in classes that feature high levels of technology.

Part Four: What Remains to Be Done?

Chapter 16: How Do I Finalize a System of Discipline Designed Especially for Me and My Students?

This expanded chapter provides detailed guidance to help readers finalize an approach to discipline that is especially suited to their personal preferences and to the
needs and realities of the students they teach.

SUPPLEMENTS AND LEARNING AIDS

The following supplements provide an outstanding array of resources that facilitate
learning about classroom discipline. For more information, ask your local Pearson
Education representative or contact the Pearson Faculty Field Support Department
at 1-800-526-0485. For technology support, contact technical support directly at
1-800-677-6337 or http://247.pearsoned.com. Instructor supplements can be downloaded from the Instructor Resource Center at www.pearsonhighered.com/irc.

Resources for Instructors

Instructor's Manual

The Instructor's Manual includes a wealth of interesting ideas, activities, and test
items designed to help instructors teach the course. The Instructor's Manual is available for download from the Instructor Resource Center at www.pearsonhighered
.com/irc.

Resources for Students

MyEducationLab for Classroom Management

"Teacher educators who are developing pedagogies for the analysis of teaching and
learning contend that analyzing teaching artifacts has three advantages: it enables
new teachers time for reflection while still using the real materials of practice;
it provides new teachers with experience thinking about and approaching the
complexity of the classroom; and in some cases, it can help new teachers and

teacher educators develop a shared understanding and common language about teaching. . . ."[1]

As Linda Darling-Hammond and her colleagues point out, grounding teacher education in real classrooms—among real teachers and students and among actual examples of students' and teachers' work—is an important, and perhaps even an essential, part of training teachers for the complexities of teaching in today's classrooms. For this reason, we have created a valuable, time-saving website—MyEducationLab—that provides the context of real classrooms and artifacts that research on teacher education tells us is so important. The authentic in-class video footage, interactive skill-building exercises, and other resources available on MyEducationLab offer a uniquely valuable teacher education tool.

MyEducationLab is easy to use and integrate into assignments and courses. Whenever the MyEducationLab logo appears in the text, follow the simple instructions to access the interactive assignments, activities, and learning units on MyEducationLab. For each topic covered in the course you will find most or all of the following resources:

Connection to National Standards.   Now it is easier than ever to see how coursework is connected to national standards. Each topic on MyEducationLab lists intended learning outcomes connected to the appropriate national standards. And all of the Assignments and Activities and all of the Building Teaching Skills and Dispositions in MyEducationLab are mapped to the appropriate national standards and learning outcomes as well.

Assignments and Activities.   Designed to save instructors preparation time and enhance student understanding, these assignable exercises show concepts in action (through video, cases, and/or student and teacher artifacts). They help students synthesize and apply concepts and strategies they read about in the book.

Building Teaching Skills and Dispositions.   These learning units help students practice and strengthen skills that are essential to quality teaching. They are presented with the core skill or concept and then given an opportunity to practice their understanding of this concept multiple times by watching video footage (or interacting with other media) and then critically analyzing the strategy or skill presented.

---

[1] Darling-Hammond, L., & Bransford, J., Eds. (2005). *Preparing Teachers for a Changing World.* San Francisco: John Wiley & Sons.

IRIS Center Resources. The IRIS Center at Vanderbilt University (http://iris
.peabody.vanderbilt.edu), funded by the U.S. Department of Education's Office of
Special Education Programs (OSEP), develops training enhancement materials for
preservice and in-service teachers. The Center works with experts from across the
country to create challenge-based interactive modules, case study units, and podcasts that provide research-validated information about working with students in
inclusive settings. In your MyEducationLab course we have integrated this content
where appropriate.

General Resources on Your MyEducationLab Course. The Resources section on
MyEducationLab is designed to help students pass their licensure exams; put together effective portfolios and lesson plans; prepare for and navigate the first year
of their teaching careers; and understand key educational standards, policies, and
laws. This section includes:

- *Licensure Exams.* Contains guidelines for passing the Praxis exam. The *Practice
  Test Exam* includes practice multiple-choice questions, case study questions,
  and video case studies with sample questions.
- *Lesson Plan Builder.* Helps students create and share lesson plans.
- *Licensure and Standards.* Provides links to state licensure standards and national
  standards.
- *Beginning Your Career.* Offers tips, advice, and valuable information on:
  - Resume Writing and Interviewing. Expert advice on how to write impressive
    resumes and prepare for job interviews.
  - Your First Year of Teaching. Practical tips on setting up a classroom, manag-
    ing student behavior, and planning for instruction and assessment.
  - Law and Public Policies. Includes specific directives and requirements
    educators need to understand under the No Child Left Behind Act
    and the Individuals with Disabilities Education Improvement Act of
    2004.

Visit www.myeducationlab.com for a demonstration of this exciting new online
teaching resource.

REVIEW AND FEEDBACK FROM AUTHORITIES

Authorities whose work is featured in Chapters 5 through 15 have been invited to
interact with the author to ensure accurate depiction of their concepts, approaches,
and terminology. The ongoing cooperative liaison between discipline authorities and the author ensures that the information you read is accurate and up to
date.

TIMELINE OF MAJOR CONTRIBUTIONS IN DISCIPLINE

The following sequence shows when certain approaches were introduced that became important themes in classroom discipline. Included are the names of originating authorities and the titles of publications in which they set forth their contentions.

1951

Understanding Group Dynamics—Fritz Redl (psychiatrist) and William Wattenberg (educational psychologist)

In their book *Mental Hygiene in Teaching,* Redl and Wattenberg explain forces that cause students to behave differently in groups than they do when by themselves. Indicated are roles students assume and roles they expect of teachers. This work was the first systematic theory-based approach to discipline and inaugurated the movement toward modern discipline.

1954

Applying Reinforcement Theory in Teaching—B. F. Skinner (behavioral psychologist)

In his article entitled "The Science of Learning and the Art of Teaching," Skinner explains how behavior can be shaped through the process of reinforcement. Skinner set forth principles of reinforcement for teachers and provided the paradigm for positive reinforcement and behavior modification, both widely used today.

1969

Understanding Behavior as Student Choice—William Glasser (psychiatrist and educational consultant)

In his book *Schools without Failure,* Glasser makes two major contributions of lasting influence in classroom discipline:

- *Behavior as choice.* Glasser contends that students choose their behavior; they are not forced by circumstances to behave in particular ways. A major role of the teacher is therefore to help students make better choices.
- *Classroom meetings.* He advocates regularly scheduled meetings in which teachers and students discuss and jointly resolve behavior problems and other matters of concern to the class.

1971

Using Congruent Communication—Haim Ginott (teacher and psychologist)

In his book *Teacher and Child,* Ginott describes the use and value of teacher communication that is harmonious with student perceptions and emotions. This work, which urges teachers to address situations rather than the character of offending students, established a style of communication that is now advocated in all programs of classroom discipline.

1971   *Managing Students during Lessons*—Jacob Kounin (educational psychologist)

In his book *Discipline and Group Management in Classrooms,* Kounin reports his research into what teachers do to maintain proper student behavior. He concludes that management of classroom organization, lesson delivery, and attention to individual students were more effective than punishment or other known sanctions used to enforce proper behavior.

1972   *Emphasizing the Value of Democratic Classrooms*—Rudolf Dreikurs (psychiatrist and family counselor)

In a book entitled *Discipline without Tears,* co-authored with Pearl Cassel, Dreikurs explains the nature and value of classrooms operated in accordance with democratic principles, such as student involvement in making decisions about class matters, engaging in give and take with classmates and teachers, and having the opportunity to express personal ideas about class matters. He also identifies "gaining a sense of belonging" as a prime motive behind student behavior at school.

1976   *Assertively Taking Charge*—Lee Canter and Marlene Canter (teachers and consultants)

In their book *Assertive Discipline: A Take-Charge Approach for Today's Educator,* the Canters show teachers how to take charge of student behavior in their classrooms in a firm, yet kindly manner in which teachers' right to teach and students' right to learn are maintained without unnecessary disruptions. This approach revolutionized discipline in classrooms and was hugely popular for more than 20 years.

1986   *Applying the Principles of Choice Theory*—William Glasser (psychiatrist and educational consultant)

In his books *Control Theory in the Classroom* (1986) and *Choice Theory in the Classroom* (1990, 1998), Glasser strongly makes the points that we cannot control anyone's behavior except our own, and that teachers cannot successfully force students to do anything they don't want to do. What teachers can do is help students envision a quality existence in school and plan the choices that lead to it.

1987   *Keeping Students Actively Involved*—Fred Jones (psychologist and educational consultant)

In his books *Positive Discipline in the Classroom* and *Tools for Teaching,* Jones asserts that students seldom misbehave if they are kept actively involved in lessons. He shows teachers how to engage with students through body language; frequent personal interactions; working the crowd; and using Say, See, Do Teaching.

Discipline with Dignity—Richard Curwin (teacher educator) and Allen Mendler (school psychologist)

In their book *Discipline with Dignity*, Curwin and Mendler establish that a key principle in effective discipline is maintaining student dignity (allowing students to maintain self-respect), which reduces student defensiveness and helps promote positive relations between teacher and student.

Building Inner Discipline—Barbara Coloroso (educator and consultant)

In her book *Kids Are Worth It!: Giving Your Child the Gift of Inner Discipline*, Coloroso provides tactics for helping students develop self-control. Her plan urges teachers to establish classrooms that provide a climate of trust and responsibility, in which students are given power to make decisions about many of the problems they encounter and are required to manage the outcomes of their decisions.

The Value and Use of Classroom Roles and Procedures—Harry Wong and Rosemary Wong (teachers and consultants)

In their book *The First Days of School: How to Be an Effective Teacher*, the Wongs firmly state that the main problem in teaching is not poor discipline, but poor classroom management. They urge teachers to use all the time necessary to teach students how to fulfill their classroom roles, follow routines, and complete work assignments. They add that the most effective teachers spend most of the first two weeks teaching students those crucial matters.

2000

Building Synergy in the Classroom—C. M. Charles (teacher educator)

In his book *The Synergetic Classroom: Joyful Teaching and Gentle Discipline*, Charles describes how teachers can energize their classes through conditions and activities that interest and motivate students—as seen in athletic competitions, artistic productions, and displays of student work. Factors that tend to promote synergy include teacher charisma, topics and activities of high interest, competition, cooperative work with give and take, and recognition of accomplishment. During periods of synergy, little misbehavior occurs and students maintain a positive attitude toward school.

Implementing Realistic Discipline—Ronald Morrish (behavior specialist and consultant)

In his book *With All Due Respect,* Morrish describes three things he urges teachers to do in order to establish good discipline in the class: (1) train students through clear expectations and insistence on compliance to accept adult authority and automatically follow teacher directions; (2) teach students the skills, attitudes, and knowledge needed for cooperation, proper behavior, and responsibility; and (3) increasingly offer students opportunities to make choices that take into account the needs and rights of other students and school personnel. When students misbehave, they are asked to correct their misbehavior by redoing it properly.

2001 *Building Moral Intelligence*—Michele Borba (educator and consultant)

In her book *Building Moral Intelligence: The Seven Essential Virtues That Teach Kids to Do the Right Thing,* Borba describes moral intelligence as comprised of (1) the ability to distinguish right from wrong; (2) the establishment and maintenance of strong ethical convictions; and (3) the willingness to act on those convictions in an honorable way. Borba's program provides suggestions to strengthen students in these three areas, thus promoting better behavior in school.

2001 *Organizing Classrooms as Communities of Learners*—Alfie Kohn (educator and consultant)

In his book *Beyond Discipline: From Compliance to Community,* Kohn made the case for organizing classes to function as communities of learners. Kohn has soundly criticized teaching and discipline approaches that *do things to* students rather than involving them as partners in the process, where they can work cooperatively, support each other, and participate fully in resolving class problems.

2001 *Raising the Level of Student Responsibility*—Marvin Marshall (educator and consultant)

In his book *Discipline without Stress, Punishments, or Rewards: How Teachers and Parents Promote Responsibility & Learning,* Marshall describes his approach, called *Discipline without Stress,* in which students are taught, without coercion, to (1) understand four levels of social development and relate the levels to behavior and learning; (2) identify the level of their personal behavior at any given time; and (3) select better courses of action, when necessary, from self-perceptions or from *guided choices* the teacher provides if disruptions continue.

2001 *Understanding the Hidden Rules of Various Social Groups*—Ruby Payne (educator and consultant)

In her book *A Framework for Understanding Poverty,* Payne contends that each economic class has its own set of hidden rules that help it survive, rules that are seldom understood by people from other economic classes. Payne's depiction of the hidden rules of poverty greatly helps teachers understand the behavior of students from poverty and how to work with those students more effectively.

2002 *Establishing a Teacher–Student Same-Side Approach to Discipline*—Spencer Kagan (psychologist and educator), in collaboration with Patricia Kyle (teacher educator) and Sally Scott (school administrator)

In a website article entitled "What Is Win-Win Discipline?" Kagan introduced this approach in 2002. The Kagan, Kyle, and Scott book, *Win-Win Discipline*, followed in 2004 and explains how students and teachers can work together on the same side to help students develop long-term, self-managed responsibility. The approach emphasizes "three pillars," called *same side, collaborative solutions,* and *learned responsibility.*

2002 *Promoting Civility in the Classroom*—P. M. Forni (director of the Civility Initiative at Johns Hopkins University).

In his books *Choosing Civility: The Twenty-Five Rules of Considerate Conduct* and *The Civility Solution: What to Do When People Are Rude,* Forni reviews the rationale for civility in classrooms and society and provides many tactics for implementing civility in education.

2003 *Using the Responsible Thinking Process*—Ed Ford (director of Responsible Thinking Process, Inc.)

As described in his books *Discipline for Home and School, Book One* (3rd edition, 2003) and *Book Two* (revised edition, 1999), Ford advocates a noncontrolling discipline system that enables students to meet their needs without infringing on the rights or comforts of others.

2004 *Self-Restitution Theory*—Diane Gossen (educator and consultant)

In her book *It's All about We,* Gossen explains self-restitution as an activity in which students who have behaved inappropriately are encouraged, in a needs-satisfying environment, to reflect on their behavior, identify the need that prompted it, and create a new way of behaving as the responsible person they want to be. This is the first system to ask misbehaving students to make things right within themselves and improve from the experience.

2006 *Working Effectively with Students Who Are Difficult to Manage*—Tom Daly (teacher and teacher educator)

In his book *ADHD Solution for Teachers: How to Turn Any Disruptive Child into Your Best Student* and several website presentations, including "Eliminate Disruptive Behavior in your Classroom Forever," Daly shares techniques he has developed over many years in the classroom for working productively with all students, including the 15 percent who are most disruptive in classrooms.

Discipline through Teacher Leverage and Student Accountability—Craig Seganti (teacher)

In his electronic book *Classroom Discipline 101*, Seganti describes the techniques he has developed and tested in numerous classrooms over the past 20 years that serve to establish an ambience of respect, attention, and academic learning in classrooms. Principal among those techniques are benign teacher leverage that assists student compliance and student accountability, in which students take responsibility for learning and conducting themselves appropriately.

Building Democratic Communities in Technology-Rich Environments—Eileen Kalberg VanWie (teacher educator)

In her research, ongoing at the time of this writing, VanWie explains how a democratic sense of community can be established, maintained, and used to advantage in classrooms where students are heavily involved in the use of digital technology.

The author gratefully acknowledges the valuable contributions made to this and previous editions by the following teachers and administrators: Roy Allen, Constance Bauer, Linda Blacklock, Tom Bolz, Michael Brus, Gail Charles, Ruth Charles, Diana Cordero, Keith Correll, Tom Daly, Barbara Gallegos, Nancy Girvin, Kris Halverson, Leslie Hays, Charlotte Hibsch, Elaine Maltz, Colleen Meagher, Nancy Natale, Linda Pohlenz, David Sisk, Mike Straus, Deborah Sund, and Virginia Villalpando.

The author would like to thank the following reviewers of this edition for their comments: Gail Gregg, Florida International University; Malcolm Linville, University of Missouri–Kansas City; Susan Mintz, University of Virginia; and Alina Slapac, University of Missouri–St. Louis.

The author would also like to acknowledge other critical reviewers: Linda Albert, researcher; Dale Allee, Southwest Missouri State University; Michele Borba, researcher; Terrell Brown, University of Central Missouri; James D. Burney, University of North Alabama; Lee Canter and Marlene Canter, researchers; Barbara Coloroso, researcher; Paula Cook, University of Manitoba; Richard Curwin, researcher; Tom Daly, teaching specialist and author; Philip DiMattia, Boston College; Karen M. Dutt, Indiana State University; Carolyn Eichenberger, St. Louis University; Anne Rene Elsbree, California State University San Marcos; James D. Ellsworth, Northern Arizona University; Ed Ford, director of The Responsible Thinking Process, Inc.; P. M. Forni, director of Civility Initiative, Johns Hopkins University; Sara S. Garcia, Santa Clara University; Robert E. Gates, Bloomsburg University; William Glasser, researcher; Thomas Gordon (deceased), Effectiveness Training International; Diane Gossen, researcher; Marci Green, University of South Florida at Ft. Myers; C. Bobbi Hansen, University of San Diego; Fredric Jones and JoLynne Jones, researchers; David I. Joyner, Old Dominion University; Deborah Keasler, Southwestern Oklahoma State University; Spencer Kagan and associates, researchers; Alfie Kohn, researcher; Thomas J. Lasley, University of Dayton; Lawrence Lyman, Emporia State University; Bernice Magnus-Brown, University of Maine; Marvin Marshall, researcher; Vick McGinley, West Chester University; Janey L. Montgomery, University of Northern Iowa; Ronald Morrish, researcher; Janice L. Nath, University of Houston; Jane Nelsen and associates, researchers; Merrill M. Oaks, Washington State University; Jack Vaughan Powell, University of Georgia; Elizabeth Primer, Cleveland State University; Craig Seganti, teacher and author, Los Angeles City Schools; Gail Senter, California State University San Marcos; Mary C. Shake, University of Kentucky; Alma A. Shearin, University of Central Arkansas; Terry R. Shepherd, Southern Illinois University at Carbondale; JoAnne Smatlan, Seattle Pacific University; Kay Stickle, Ball State University; Marguerite Terrill, Central Michigan University; Sylvia Tinling, University of California, Riverside; Eileen VanWie, New Mexico State University; Bill Weldon, Arizona State University; Kathleen Whittier, State University of New York at Plattsburgh; and Harry Wong and Rosemary Wong, researchers.

Building Classroom Discipline

PART ONE

ONE

How Do I Begin Organizing a System of Discipline That Meets My Needs?

Modern discipline strives for three main goals: (1) to maintain productive learning environments, (2) to teach students to be self-directing and responsible, and (3) to promote civility among all members of the class. To the extent those goals are reached, classroom learning occurs well. Students will find school satisfying or even fun, teachers will feel rewarded and fulfilled, and parents will have positive feelings toward teachers and the school.

But how does one implement discipline so it accomplishes those important results? The answer is provided in this book, but it requires many things of you. In your approach to discipline, you must treat students as everyone wants to be treated; you must communicate with students respectfully and engagingly; you must make school as fun for students as possible while maintaining responsibility; you must teach them to behave as you expect them to and understand why; and when they misbehave, you must show them how to behave appropriately and require they do so.

The information you need for accomplishing those important results—and a great many others as well—is contained in the chapters that follow. There, you will find discipline approaches formulated by some of the greatest experts in education, psychology, and psychiatry. But you must do more than simply adopt what they advise. That brings us to the basic philosophy of this book—you want the best discipline approach possible for your students, and the best approach will almost certainly be one you modify or develop yourself. True, there are exceptionally good ready-made approaches available to you, but none of them fully recognizes or takes into account the particular conditions that affect you and your students. That is why you are urged to formulate a personal system of discipline, and why this book is organized to help you do so.

You are therefore urged to organize a discipline approach that is compatible with (1) your students' needs, (2) the social and cultural realities that affect your students, (3) the standards of the teaching profession, (4) your personality and philosophy, and (5) the best information on discipline available to you. To help you do so, this book provides a wealth of information from the world's foremost authorities on student behavior and discipline. Beyond that, the book will guide you in developing and implementing a personalized system of discipline that suits your situation and

1

meets your needs and those of your students. As you interact with the multitude of ideas herein, you will progressively move toward realizing that goal.

Now it is time to get underway. We will begin by reflecting on what you need to know about the following topics:

- Teacher professionalism and the nature and purpose of discipline
- The kinds of behavior you can usually expect from students
- Types of atypical behavior you sometimes encounter in students and how you can respond to them effectively
- The major changes that moved us from discipline of previous years to the *modern discipline* we have today

This first part of the book contains four chapters that provide the background information you need.

CHAPTER 1   What Is Classroom Discipline and How Do I Encourage Productive Efforts in My Classroom?

To help you answer those questions, this chapter explores the nature and value of professionalism in teaching and discipline. It indicates what is required of professional teachers, introduces an organizing structure to help you work toward constructing a system of discipline tailored to your needs and those of your students, and asks you to reflect on a number of questions about student behavior—an exercise to expand your thinking about classroom behavior and how it is best managed.

CHAPTER 2   How Can I Anticipate My Students' Behavior and Deal with Factors That Promote Misbehavior?

To help you answer those questions, this chapter summarizes typical behaviors of students at different levels of development, as influenced by genetic predispositions and social and cultural realities. Specific factors are identified that cause variations in behavior, and suggestions are provided for softening the effects of factors that lead to misbehavior.

CHAPTER 3   How Do I Recognize and Deal with Atypical Behavior That Is Neurological-Based?

This chapter examines the sometimes baffling behavior seen in students with NBB (neurological-based behavior), helps you understand why those students at times cannot fully control what they say or do, and provides suggestions for dealing with such behavior in an appropriate manner. (Authorities estimate that about 10% of students in school exhibit NBB.)

| CHAPTER 4 | What Are the Foundations That Underlie Today's Best Systems of Discipline? |

This chapter pinpoints the beginning of modern classroom discipline in 1951 and traces its development up into the twenty-first century. The term *modern discipline* refers to comprehensive approaches designed to prevent misbehavior and to correct it through tactics that are humane and helpful rather than harsh. The chapter reviews the lasting contributions made by nine great innovators whose influence helped form today's discipline.

1

What Is Classroom Discipline and How Do I Encourage Productive Efforts in My Classroom?

Teaching is indeed a complex endeavor, requiring that you attend to an astonishing number of different tasks. Your ability to carry out those tasks effectively is closely tied to **professionalism,** which refers to using the best and most ethical ways of fulfilling classroom duties. For example, professionalism requires that you have the following:

- Knowledge and understanding of students, including their background experiences, levels of maturity, psychological needs, favorite activities, present capabilities, how they are likely to react to various situations, and how they prefer to relate with others and conduct themselves in class
- Expertise in the curriculum for classes or subjects you teach, including a clear command of the major concepts and skills needed to help students learn
- Knowledge of classroom setup and management, instructional materials, and the procedures your students are expected to follow
- Ability to organize and conduct lessons and other class activities that promote learning and involve students willingly
- Effective communication with colleagues, students, and parents
- A positive influence on students to learn and conduct themselves responsibly
- The desire to give your best to teaching
- The desire and ability to act responsibly in regards to legal and ethical matters

Professionalism can strongly affect classroom discipline. If students always behaved nicely and did their best in school, there would be no need for discipline. But the reality is, a certain amount of misbehavior occurs in all classrooms. In some cases, the misbehavior is minor, with few adverse effects. In the majority of classrooms, misbehavior occurs frequently and interferes unnecessarily with teaching and learning. Dealing with that misbehavior consumes time that should be devoted to instruction and has a wearing effect on teachers and students. In the worst cases, classroom misbehavior is so extreme that teachers can hardly teach at all, and consequently students fail to reach acceptable levels of learning. As frustration grows, teachers in those out-of-control classes tend to make ever greater demands, but over time they draw into themselves, defeated and disillusioned, while students endure the classes without accomplishing much of value.

These realities point to a simple and undeniable fact: If you are to become a successful teacher, you must become able to keep student misbehavior within manageable limits. You cannot do so simply by asking or demanding that students comply with your wishes—coercion seldom achieves what you want, and frequently it makes matters worse. What you must do is learn to exert positive influence on students that motivates them to learn and behave properly. This book provides information to help you do so.

As to the kind of discipline that will serve you best, this book is based on the belief that your approach must be harmonious with your personality and your students' needs while making use of the best information and ideas available. Toward that end, instructions are provided in this chapter and Chapter 16 to help you organize a personal approach to discipline; the remainder of the book presents selected authoritative opinion and advice.

Patrick Traynor (2005) has pointed out that effective discipline depends on (1) teachers' ability to recognize maladaptive behavior in the classroom, (2) their skill in selecting and implementing effective intervention tactics, and (3) their positive can-do attitude toward any discipline procedure they try to use. We should add two more capabilities to Traynor's list: (4) their ability to prevent misbehavior from occurring, and (5) their ability to communicate effectively with students. Those five requirements can be satisfied in a variety of ways, but the method you use should be based on reliable information and made congruent with your preferences, your philosophy, and the social realities that impinge on the students you teach. As you proceed through this book, you will be advised to take notes of suggestions that you might wish to incorporate into your personalized approach.

A PREVIEW OF THIS CHAPTER

Professionalism in teaching and discipline, complemented with a personalized system of discipline, enables you successfully to meet one of your greatest challenges in teaching, which is to maintain an acceptable level of decorum in your classes.

WHAT TO LOOK FOR IN THIS CHAPTER

- The meaning of *teacher professionalism* and why it is important
- Seven things you can do to increase your level of professionalism
- The meanings of the terms *discipline* and *misbehavior*
- The purpose of discipline
- The 13 types of misbehavior you will encounter in the classroom
- How to develop a personalized system of discipline and why it is to your advantage to do so

PROFESSIONALISM IN TEACHING AND DISCIPLINE

To explore some of the opportunities and obstacles in a new teaching career, go to the Resources tab in the **MyEducationLab** for your course and click on Preparing for and Beginning Your Career.

Professionalism   Conducting oneself in accordance with the established standards and expectations of a given profession or line of work ■

A defining characteristic of professional teachers is that they focus first and foremost on promoting learning. That learning involves not only the usual knowledge and skills specified in the curriculum but, equally important, student growth in self-control, exercise of responsibility, and ability to relate effectively with others. In order for your students to learn these skills, they must pay attention, make an effort to learn, and show consideration for others, while you must devote yourself, helpfully and considerately, to ensuring that your students learn. It is your responsibility to establish and maintain that climate of learning, although it is difficult to do so without the willing assistance of students. As has been noted, teachers' efforts to maintain decorum and enlist student cooperation are called, collectively, **discipline** or **behavior management,** terms often used interchangeably. (The term *classroom management* is also often used in reference to discipline, but it more accurately has to do with establishing routines and organizing the classroom and materials of instruction.) Many years ago, discipline was thought of as something separate from teaching. Now it is acknowledged as a major and indispensable component of teaching.

Discipline   Teachers' efforts to maintain classroom decorum and secure students' cooperation in learning and exercising self-control ■

In teaching, professional conduct is concordant with the standards expected of teachers when carrying out their professional duties. It is revealed in teachers' highly skilled and ethical conduct that influences students' efforts to achieve, sense of responsibility, and love of learning. Teacher professionalism helps students prosper in classrooms free from disruptions and threats to personal safety. It also helps teachers avoid the burnout that so often results from struggling continually against disruptive students.

SEVEN SUGGESTIONS FOR MOVING TOWARD HIGHER LEVELS OF PROFESSIONALISM

No doubt you have already begun learning to think and conduct yourself as professional teachers do. Seven suggestions are presented here to further your professional growth. As you allow them to guide you, you will see a corresponding growth in your ability to promote the outcomes you desire in students. The suggestions also help open your thinking to the many strategies presented later in this book.

Suggestion 1: Align Yourself with the Established Standards of the Teaching Profession.   The National Education Association (1975) has set professional and ethical standards for educators that all teachers are expected to follow. The standards stipulate that the educator:

- Shall not misrepresent his or her professional qualifications in any way
- Shall not knowingly make false or malicious statements about a colleague
- Shall not accept any gratuity, gift, or favor that might impair or appear to influence professional decisions or action
- Shall not suppress or distort subject matter relevant to the student's progress
- Shall not intentionally expose students to embarrassment or disparagement
- Shall not disclose information about students obtained in the course of professional service unless disclosure serves a compelling professional purpose or is required by law

In addition to the NEA stipulations, professionalism in general requires that you:

- Dress professionally, as an adult in a professional situation
- Use appropriate language for the educational setting, with correct speech patterns and complete avoidance of obscenities
- Treat others respectfully and courteously

Suggestion 2: Commit to Abiding Unfailingly with the Ethics of Instruction.   Ethics of instruction have to do with teaching in a professionally proper manner, especially while interacting with students, presenting lessons, and managing behavior. Presented here are some of the major considerations that should guide your thinking.

- *Give your genuine best effort to the profession.* Your obligation is to do the best you can to help all students, without favoritism, to profit from their educational experience and find satisfaction in doing so. This best effort also applies to your relations with parents and colleagues.

- *Do your best to teach effectively.* Teach in a manner deemed most conducive to success for each of your students. This effort involves careful selection of subject matter, a focus on worthwhile learning, provision of interesting activities, effective and helpful relations with students, and insistence on considerate, humane treatment by and for everyone in the class.

- *Always do what you can to help students.* Helpfulness is an indispensable ingredient of effective teaching. You will see it emphasized and reemphasized in present-day approaches to discipline. As Haim Ginott (1971) said, always ask yourself what you can do, at a given moment, that will be most helpful to your students.

- *Treat students civilly, respectfully, and fairly.* Treat all students as your social equals. Give each of them some personal attention every day. Learn their names quickly and remember significant things about them. Give acknowledgment for work well done and for exemplary behavior. Smile and interact with them in a friendly manner, but don't single out any as your favorites. Spread your attention around evenly.

- *Emphasize cooperation with and among students.* Do what you can to help students understand that you and they must accept each other and work together in order to achieve class goals in a satisfying manner. Show that you have a plan for helping them learn and enjoy themselves. At the same time, reassure them you will be considerate of their desires and feelings. Invite their co-operation in helping making class enjoyable and productive. Do not attack their dignity or disparage them in any way. Instead, always treat them as you would like to be treated in similar circumstances.

■ *Communicate effectively.* Make sure students know what is expected of them. Take time to listen to their concerns. When you speak with them, be helpful and encouraging, but don't give too much advice, preach or moralize, grill them about their behavior, or otherwise put them on the defensive. When you ask for their input, try to see their perspective. When they explain, listen attentively. When you reply to what they say, indicate it is something for them to consider and is simply your opinion.

■ *Display a charismatic demeanor.* Charisma is a quality of attractiveness that draws attention and makes others want to be in your presence and interact with you. You acquire charisma by making yourself personally interesting to students. Be upbeat and pleasant, with a touch of wit (don't try to be overly witty—just a little bit works best). Share some of your interests, experiences, and talents. Let students know a bit about your family life and what you like to do outside of school. Use humor, without being silly. Never use sarcasm, which is too easily misinterpreted. Show personal interest, be helpful, and treat students considerately.

Suggestion 3: Understand Your Legal Responsibilities Concerning the Safety and Well-Being of Students.   School personnel operate under the doctrine of *in loco parentis*—"in place of parents." This doctrine requires that you watch over students as if you were their parent (actually, even more closely than that). It gives you and other school officials authority over students in school matters involving academics and discipline and permits you to take actions that a reasonable parent would take under similar circumstances. This doctrine includes specific requirements concerning due diligence, negligence, and physical contact with students. Very briefly, those requirements are as follows:

■ *Due diligence.* Teachers and other school personnel have a duty to oversee students at school and exercise reasonable care to protect them from harm (Goorian and Brown, 2002). Many teachers are not aware they are required to keep a diligent eye on all students under their supervision and may feel that their mere presence fulfills that duty. Diligence means taking reasonable care or giving reasonable attention to students you are overseeing. Legally, that means you must follow established policies and conduct yourself as would a reasonable and prudent professional in similar circumstances.

■ *Negligence and breach of duty.* If a student is injured emotionally or physically while at school and the teacher on duty did not exercise due diligence, the teacher and school may be sued for negligence (Drye, 2000). The following guidelines will help you make sure you are in a defensible position should questions arise about negligence and breach of duty:

1. Perform your assigned duties as directed by school policy, even those that seem boring and unnecessary.
2. Carefully oversee your students. Be attentive in monitoring their behavior. Do not leave students unattended in your classroom, shop, or instructional area.
3. Provide your students thorough instructions and teach them safety procedures before undertaking activities that involve risk.
4. Be vigilant for signs that students might harm themselves. Pay attention to what they do, say, and write. Observe them for changes in behavior. If you have concerns, speak immediately with your administrator or school counselor.
5. Report any suspicion that a student is being abused. Follow your school guidelines to familiarize yourself with signs of abuse. If you are suspicious, report your concerns to the school counselor or administrator, who will follow up.

■ *Concerns related to physical contact with students.* Don't allow yourself to be alone in the classroom with a student, unless you are in plain sight of others. Refrain from touching students, other than on the hands or arms or with pats to the head or shoulder. If students frustrate or anger you, never strike them or grab any part of their body, as it is very difficult to justify or defend physical contact motivated by anger. Also make sure you never throw pencils, pens, erasers, books, desks, or chairs, no matter how strongly you are provoked.

Suggestion 4: Recognize and Embrace the Understandings and Skills Deemed Necessary for All Teachers.   For years, many individuals, groups, and agencies have worked to specify the understandings and skills that lead to excellence in teaching. Today, much attention is given to competencies advocated by the Interstate New Teacher Assessment and Support Consortium (INTASC). All 10 of the competencies the consortium identifies are listed here, in abridged form. If you wish to see a fully detailed presentation with many examples, consult www.ccsso.org/projects/Interstate_New_Teacher_Assessment_and_Support_Consortium.

INTASC recommendations are stated as outcomes, as follows:

Outcome 1: The teacher understands the central concepts, tools of inquiry, and structures of the discipline(s) he or she teaches and can create learning experiences that make these aspects of subject matter meaningful for students.

Outcome 2: The teacher understands how children learn and develop, and can provide learning opportunities that support their intellectual, social and personal development.

Outcome 3: The teacher understands how students differ in their approaches to learning and creates instructional opportunities that are adapted to diverse learners.

Outcome 4: The teacher understands and uses a variety of instructional strategies to encourage students' development of critical thinking, problem solving, and performance skills.

Outcome 5: The teacher uses an understanding of individual and group motivation and behavior to create a learning environment that encourages positive social interaction, active engagement in learning, and self-motivation.

Outcome 6: The teacher uses knowledge of effective verbal, nonverbal, and media communication techniques to foster active inquiry, collaboration, and supportive interaction in the classroom.

Outcome 7: The teacher plans instruction based upon knowledge of subject matter, students, the community, and curriculum goals.

Outcome 8: The teacher understands and uses formal and informal assessment strategies to evaluate and ensure the continuous intellectual, social and physical development of the learner.

Outcome 9: The teacher is a reflective practitioner who continually evaluates the effects of his/her choices and actions on others (students, parents, and other professionals in the learning community) and who actively seeks out opportunities to grow professionally.

Outcome 10: The teacher fosters relationships with school colleagues, parents, and agencies in the larger community to support students' learning and well-being.

Suggestion 5: Learn as Much as You Can about Your Students' Experiences, Needs, and Typical Behaviors.   It is important that you recognize the behaviors typically displayed by your students and be able to identify the motivation behind those behaviors. Your knowledge of these matters allows you to anticipate

- What topics will interest your students
- How they are likely to conduct themselves
- How they are likely to react to various situations
- How you can interact with them most effectively
- How you can best work with them in a helpful manner

Suggestion 6: Organize Your Thoughts on How You Will Relate with Students and Provide the Support to Help Them Behave Responsibly.   Questions for you to keep in mind include the following:

- *Meeting students' needs.* What are students' prime needs and how can you attend to them in the classroom?
- *Relationships.* How will you relate to students and have them relate to you and each other?
- *Trust and responsibility.* How will you foster trust and responsible behavior in your classes?
- *Communication.* How can you communicate most effectively with your students?
- *Enjoyable teaching.* What will you do to make lessons interesting and worthwhile?
- *Your personality.* How can you make your personality work for you in teaching?
- *Partnerships with students.* How can you involve students as partners in maintaining responsible behavior?

■ *Your behavior.* How you will make sure you don't "misbehave" as a teacher?

Suggestion 7: Develop a Concise Discipline Strategy That Is Harmonious with Your Students' Traits and Needs and That Reflects Your Preferences in Promoting Desirable Behavior in Your Classes.   In Figure 1.1, you will find a planning rubric to help you organize a personalized system of discipline attuned to your needs and those of your students. (As used here, the word *rubric* means a set of planned procedures.) That rubric for organizing a personalized system of discipline gives attention to four aspects of discipline previously mentioned:

1. *Prevention of misbehavior.* Proactively prevent the occurrence of as much misbehavior as possible. This is done by identifying factors that lead to misbehavior and eliminating or reducing the influence of those factors. In Chapter 2, a number of causative factors are identified and suggestions are made for limiting or avoiding their effects.

2. *Support of proper behavior.* Support proper behavior by enhancing your instructional program. Make sure your curriculum is interesting to students and that you teach in a charismatic manner. Foster a class sense of purpose, togetherness, enjoyment, satisfaction, and personal responsibility. Suggestions for doing these things are presented throughout this book.

3. *Intervention when misbehavior occurs.* When misbehavior occurs, deal with it in a positive, helpful manner, rather than a negative one. Instead of scolding or nagging, help students remember how to behave acceptably or have them repeat the behavior in question until they are able to perform it properly. Ask them to reflect on their behavior and take personal responsibility for it. Suggestions for intervening in this manner are presented throughout the book.

4. *Communication with students.* Communicate with students in ways that build student dignity, help you relate better with students, clearly inform students of what they should and should not do, and influence students to behave civilly and responsibly.

Virtually all the discipline tactics presented in the chapters that follow have to do with prevention of misbehavior, support for positive behavior, positive intervention, and techniques for communicating with students. You will find that the prevent-support-intervene paradigm, overlaid with effective communication, can guide and coordinate all your efforts toward maintaining good discipline in your classes. Figure 1.1 will get you off to a productive start in discipline.

Miss Gusperson was one of the most popular teachers, if not *the* most popular teacher, on the faculty of Clines Middle School. Her elective classes were always filled to overflowing and students gravitated to her wherever she went on campus. They called her "Miss Gus," and she could often be seen "high-fiving" students and pretending to dance with them. On most days, she invited at least five students to have lunch with her in her classroom. Her usual attire was a dark sweatshirt, knee-length pants, and tennis

Figure 1.1   A Rubric for Planning a Personal System of Discipline

This rubric can be used to guide your efforts in conceptualizing and articulating a personal system of discipline. In this chapter and those that follow, you will find information pertinent to all aspects of this rubric. If you summarize what you encounter throughout the book, you will find it easy to compose a system of discipline that meets your requirements.

Professional and Philosophical Considerations

My Philosophy of Discipline
A philosophy of any topic summarizes one's beliefs about the overall nature and value of that topic. Your philosophy of discipline is revealed in your responses to two questions:

1. What is classroom discipline and why is it considered important?
2. What is the specific purpose of discipline—that is, what do we want it to accomplish?

My Theory of Discipline
Theories are attempts to describe the processes involved in given events or efforts. Your theory of discipline is made evident in your responses to the following two questions:

1. What are the necessary components of an effective system of discipline?
2. How do the various components affect behavior?

My Professional Demeanor
Include information here that shows understanding of and intent to abide by specifics of professionalism, ethics, and legalities in teaching.

Specifics of My Discipline Plan
Show what you will include in your discipline plan concerning the following:

- *Desired behavior.* The behavior you expect, and will endeavor to maintain, in the classroom
- *Rules of behavior.* A set of class rules that reflects the desired behavior
- *Prevention of misbehavior.* What you will do proactively to keep misbehavior to a minimum
- *Support of proper behavior.* How you will support proper student conduct during instruction
- *Intervention when misbehavior occurs.* How you will intervene when misbehavior occurs or is imminent
- *Communication with students.* How you will speak with students to influence proper behavior, including what you will say and how you will say it

Communicating My Discipline Plan to Students and Others
Indicate briefly how you will make students, administrators, and parents fully aware of your discipline plan, including its purpose and nature and the roles of teacher, students, and possibly parents.

shoes. She was conversant with students' slang expressions and used them liberally when interacting with students. She usually made time to talk with students about their personal and social concerns, and often used class time for doing so. Despite her popularity with students—or perhaps because of it—she was often the object of criticism. A few fellow teachers considered her to be too chummy with students. More than a few parents commented about her somewhat slovenly attire and grooming, and her principal, Mr. Clarke, was uneasy about her open reluctance to participate in groups working to update the school curriculum.

In view of this chapter's commentary about professionalism, what is your overall appraisal of Miss Gusperson's conduct at school? Can you identify strengths and areas of concern? If you could make anonymous suggestions to her and Principal Clarke, what might they be?

BEHAVIOR, MISBEHAVIOR, AND DISCIPLINE

Go to the Building Teaching Skills and Dispositions section of Topic #10: Maintaining Appropriate Student Behavior, in the **MyEducationLab** for your course and complete the activity entitled "Managing On-Task Behavior."

Behavior refers to the totality of what people do. In education, we are concerned mainly with behavior involved in learning certain information and skills, both academic and interpersonal. We have noted that in order to be successful, teachers must establish and maintain a level of decorum in their classes that does not interfere with learning. That means they must set **limits**, usually in the form of rules, separating acceptable behavior from unacceptable behavior. Acceptable behavior allows class activities to proceed smoothly with few disruptions. Unacceptable behavior disrupts teaching and learning and can make the educational experience unpleasant for everyone. When students (or teachers) violate behavioral rules or interfere with the well-being of others, their behavior is called **misbehavior**.

Behavior   The totality of one's physical and mental activities

Misbehavior   Student (or teacher) actions that disrupt teaching, interfere with learning, demean others, or otherwise violate the moral codes of society

Limits   The boundaries that separate acceptable behavior from unacceptable behavior in the classroom ∎

We all know that young people often misbehave in school. Much of their misbehavior seems innocuous, but even so, most authorities urge you to confront it. Even small amounts of misbehavior interfere with teaching and learning, and those small amounts can grow quickly to unacceptable proportions.

The information in this book will help you maximize appropriate behavior, minimize misbehavior, and deal effectively with misbehavior that occurs. Action taken in advance to minimize misbehavior is referred to as **preventive discipline.** Supporting students in staying on task with self-control is referred to as **supportive discipline.** Stopping misbehavior and helping students behave in a more suitable manner is called **corrective discipline,** and the act of applying corrective discipline is referred to as **intervention.** Teachers should strive to keep interventions positive, rather than using intervention tactics that denigrate or embarrass students. The intervention tactics presented in this book preserve student dignity without provoking resentment or rebellion.

> **?** What are the characteristics of preventive, supportive, and corrective discipline?
>
> What role does communication play in the discipline process?
>
> What does *intervention* mean, as applied to discipline?

Contrasting the Behavior in Two Classrooms

Now let's consider some real-life student behavior as once observed in two adjoining classrooms by educational anthropologist Frances Schwartz (1981). Although Schwartz conducted her study many years ago, her depictions remain accurate for classrooms today and help illustrate the sometimes subtle differences between appropriate and inappropriate classroom behavior.

The scene is an inner-city school. Classroom 314 is quiet as students listen attentively to the teacher's questions about a recent lesson. Suddenly, eager hands begin to wave and bodies twist out of their seats amidst shouts of "Aooh me! I know! Aooh-oh!" Quiet returns when one student is chosen to answer. As soon as she has responded, others begin to yell out refutations or additions and compete again for teacher recognition. When the questions end and seat work begins, most students work as directed. Some offer to help classmates who are unsure of how to proceed. A couple of them gaze out the window.

But across the hall in room 315, chaos reigns. The room is noisy with shouting, laughter, and movement. Though most students are seated, some are walking or running aimlessly around the classroom. Some stop at others' desks, provoke them briefly, and move on. Several students who are lining up textbooks as "race courses" for toy cars laugh when the teacher demands their attention. As the teacher struggles to ask a question over the noise, few if any students volunteer to answer. When one student does respond correctly, others yell out, "You think you're so smart." (Schwartz, 1981, p. 99)

What do you think of the behavior in the two classrooms? By most teachers' standards, the discipline in Room 314 is acceptable, while that in Room 315 is not. But what is the difference? In both rooms students are making noise and behaving spontaneously. Yet the teacher in Room 314 is probably satisfied with the lesson, while the teacher in Room 315 is not. Why?

The answer depends largely on the teacher's sense of whether or not learning is occurring productively. The students in 314 are showing initiative, but are still responsive to the teacher. Their personal interactions are positive and, for the most part, respectful. The teacher feels progress is being made and is happy to see students displaying reasonable manners while participating actively in the lesson.

In contrast, the students in 315 are barely in touch with the lesson. They are doing more or less what they want, disregarding what the teacher says and accomplishing little that is worthwhile. Their behavior is haphazard and their interactions are frequently disrespectful of the teacher and each other. The teacher should be concerned about the behavior in this class, for it is hindering student learning while encouraging habits that are self-defeating. An impartial judge would consider the lesson a failure.

If you were the teacher in Room 315, what would you like to see? How would you want students to respond to your lessons? How would you want them to relate to each other and to you? What would, or could, you do to make things as you'd like them to be? Suppose you developed what you considered an excellent lesson, only to find that students disregarded what you asked them to do. Then what? Questions such as these are difficult to answer, and in truth are more difficult to answer in real classrooms than when discussing these scenarios. But rest assured—by the time you have worked through this book, you will have answers to those questions and, moreover, you will have at your command effective procedures for promoting the kind of behavior that best serves your students and you.

A Closer Look at Student Misbehavior

As suggested earlier, student misbehavior is any behavior that, through *intent or thoughtlessness*

1. Interferes with teaching or learning
2. Threatens or intimidates others
3. Oversteps society's standards of moral, ethical, or legal behavior

In your work with students, you can expect to encounter 13 types of student misbehavior. Some of these types are far more serious than others, yet even those that seem benign require your attention because they can be disruptive or otherwise detrimental to group or individual progress. The 13 types, listed generally from less serious to more serious, appear below:

1. *Inattention.* Daydreaming, doodling, looking out the window, thinking about things irrelevant to the lesson
2. *Apathy.* A disinclination to participate, sulking, not caring, fear of failure, not wanting to try or do well
3. *Needless talk.* Chatting during instructional time about things unrelated to the lesson.
4. *Moving about the room.* Getting up and moving about without permission, congregating in parts of the room
5. *Annoying others.* Provoking, teasing, picking on, calling names
6. *Disruption.* Shouting out during instruction, talking and laughing inappropriately, using vulgar language, causing "accidents"

7. *Lying.* Falsifying to avoid accepting responsibility or admitting wrongdoing, or to get others in trouble
8. *Stealing.* Taking things that belong to others
9. *Cheating.* Making false representations for personal benefit or wrongly taking advantage of others
10. *Sexual harassment.* Making others uncomfortable through touching, sex-related language, or sexual innuendo
11. *Aggression and fighting.* Showing hostility toward others, threatening, shoving, pinching, wrestling, hitting, bullying
12. *Malicious mischief.* Doing intentional damage to school property or the belongings of others
13. *Defiance of authority.* Talking back to the teacher, ignoring the teacher, or hostilely refusing to do as requested

In Chapter 2, we will give attention to conditions that seem to foster these types of misbehavior and see what teachers can do to address them. For now, it is enough to be aware of the parameters of misbehavior and recognize the following:

- All of these types of misbehavior adversely affect teaching, learning, or personal feelings.
- Some of these types occur regularly and frequently, while others appear only occasionally. You are likely to encounter all of them sooner or later.
- Some of the misbehavior may occur inadvertently, but much of it will be intentional. Any behavior that is disruptive or self-defeating calls for positive change.
- Many of your students, including those who misbehave the most, are generally well-intentioned. On a personal level, they may treat you kindly, help you, and even befriend you.
- Most of your students, usually all of them, want your personal attention. Sometimes they misbehave in order to get it. For that reason, be generous with personal attention.
- All of these misbehaviors are prompted by underlying conditions that can usually be identified, such as a need to have fun, avoid failure, or gain the attention of teachers and other students. Often, by addressing the underlying need, you can reduce or eliminate the undesired misbehavior.

Two Vignettes

These vignettes were provided by Dr. Terrell Brown:

Anita is a seventh grader who is very eager to answer questions in Mrs. Asbury's classroom. Often, Anita's hand is raised before Mrs. Asbury finishes the question. However, when called on, Anita's answers tend to be incorrect and off topic. Most of the time, her responses are about personal experiences that have nothing to do with the topic at hand. If Mrs. Asbury doesn't call on her, Anita becomes visibly frustrated.

Anita shows great enthusiasm and she is also a pretty good student when she focuses on doing her work. When engaged, she is task oriented and productive. However, Mrs. Asbury has noticed that Anita's behavior and academic performance suffer when she is not called on in class. There are times that Anita tends to disrupt Mrs. Asbury's class when she is overlooked. Mrs. Asbury spends more time keeping her on task on those days.

Although Mrs. Asbury understands that she needs to teach her class without disruptions, she also feels that being too harsh with Anita will discourage her enthusiasm for learning.

Questions

1. What do you think might be the underlying motive for Anita's continual handraising?
2. Is this a discipline matter? What sort of action or attention from Mrs. Asbury do you believe Anita's behavior calls for—if any?

Thomas is an 11th grader in Mr. Spring's first period American History class. He is quiet, well-mannered, and does not disrupt class, but he often comes to class tardy and, once in his chair, he often falls asleep. When Mr. Spring wakes him, Thomas apologizes and tells him that he had to work late. He gives the same explanation for not turning in the majority of his assignments on time.

Mr. Spring is at a loss. When he contacted Thomas's parents to discuss this issue, they told him that they need him to help pay household bills. Mr. Spring has two concerns: Thomas will continue to get behind in his work if this behavior continues, and other students may begin to feel Thomas's actions are acceptable for them, too.

Question

1. Do Thomas's actions call for discipline intervention? Explain your point of view.

DEVELOPING A PERSONALIZED APPROACH TO DISCIPLINE

The major thrust of this book is to help you develop an approach to discipline that (1) suits your needs and those of your students, (2) remains compatible with your convictions about teaching and learning, and (3) always works in the best interests of your students, no matter what their backgrounds might be. This chapter and those that follow provide information and guidance to help you do so. Many excellent discipline programs are already available, as you will see in Part 2 and Part 3 of this book. You may find one there that suits you very well, although it is unlikely that any single one will address all your particular needs and contingencies.

Go to the Simulations section of Topic #4: Establishing Classroom Norms and Expectations, in the **MyEducationLab** for your course and complete the simulation entitled "Creating Classroom Behavioral Expectations."

Students differ from place to place and class to class. Their behavior is strongly affected by the realities of their social situations.

Moreover, you have your own distinct personality, philosophy, and preferred ways of teaching. For those reasons, the discipline approach that works best for you will probably be one you construct for yourself by choosing structures and strategies that fit your personal needs. Figure 1.1 is a planning rubric you can use in organizing a personal system of discipline that is well-rounded and effective; please refer to it continually as you proceed through the upcoming chapters. You will encounter it again in Part 4 of this book, where you will find guidance for completing your personal system of discipline.

> **?** What is your understanding of the rationale for composing a personalized system of discipline instead of using a ready-made approach?

FOR REFLECTION AND ORIENTATION: 20 TOPICS ABOUT DISCIPLINE

To help focus your attention further on practical questions about discipline, here are 20 topics for you to consider. You will find it helpful and enjoyable to exchange views on these questions with colleagues. As you progress through the book, you will become able to answer the questions more fully.

1. *Proper behavior.* How should students behave at school, and why? To what extent should you take into account students' natural behaviors that are part of their maturational process? To what extent should you insist that students behave in ways that do not come to them naturally?

2. *Misbehavior.* Why do students misbehave when they know they shouldn't? What is the attraction for doing so? What payoff do they expect? Do you believe most students from third grade upwards already know how to behave properly?

3. *Needs.* How do student needs affect discipline? What is meant by "needs"? How are needs different from "wants"? Should students' needs ever be resisted or denied? If so, to what extent and for what purpose?

4. *Students' realities.* How might discipline be affected by disability, poverty, or cultural realities? Should you have the same standards and expectations for all students? Why or why not? Do unequal expectations among students have any benefits? How would you justify to parents having different expectations among students in your class?

5. *Preventing misbehavior.* What can teachers do proactively to prevent student misbehavior? How much misbehavior do you think can be prevented? If it is true that we learn best from our mistakes, why try to keep students from making them? Should we encourage students to make mistakes in how they behave toward others, so as to learn better options?

6. *Responsibility.* What connection do you see between student behavior and responsibility? What does it mean to "accept responsibility"? Is that expression just jargon? Can all students learn to accept responsibility for their behavior? What if students willingly claim to accept responsibility for their misbehavior but don't change as a result?

7. *Promoting proper behavior.* What can teachers do to influence students from within to behave properly? That is, what might teachers do to get students to see a benefit in behaving properly?

8. *Personal connections.* What can you do to connect more closely with students on a personal level? Should you try to "be one of them"? What is the advantage of closeness? And how close is too close? Most teachers think a closer rapport with students is a good thing, but how do you accomplish it and where are the limits?

9. *Charisma.* How does teacher charisma affect student behavior? Do you like charismatic teachers? What does it take to be charismatic, and can it be overdone? How would you, personally, make yourself a bit more charismatic?

10. *Teaching style.* Do you think teaching style affects student behavior? If so, in what ways? What does teaching style mean? How would you characterize your natural style? Would you want to change it, or would you do better just being yourself?

11. *Physical environment.* In what ways can the physical environment of the classroom affect student behavior? What do you think *physical environment* means? Can you give examples of things in the environment that influence students to behave less acceptably or more acceptably?

12. *Psychosocial environment.* In what ways can the psychosocial environment (predominant emotions, feelings, attitudes) affect student behavior? How would you characterize the psychosocial environment you'd want in your classroom? Happy, fun, exciting, businesslike, task oriented, no nonsense? Toward what ends?

13. *Communication.* What does *communication* mean in relation to discipline? What are some different types of communication? What roles do they play and what effects can they have? What do you think you might say to a student who disrupts your lesson, and how would you say it?

14. *Parents.* How can parents or guardians assist, if at all, in matters of school discipline? How might you get them involved? How would you communicate with them? What would you expect them to do?

15. *Ethics and trust.* What do these terms mean? What do you see as their value in classrooms? How can teachers promote ethics and trust among students? Would you try to teach these things or would you just let them occur naturally?

16. *Intervening in misbehavior.* What should you do when students misbehave? What do you want to have happen? What would you say? Would you try to avoid offending the students? What could you do that would be most helpful to them, you, and other members of the class?

17. *Conflict.* What does *conflict* mean? How do you deal with a conflict between students? Between you and a student? Between you and a parent? Does conflict resolution necessarily result in a winner and a loser? Have you heard of win-win conflict resolution? How does it work, or how do you think it might work?

18. *Energizing your class.* How do you make your class energetic and lively? Have you experienced classes that were energetic and classes that were lethargic? What caused the difference? How did they affect you personally?

19. *Structured discipline.* How would you characterize a structured, consistent approach to discipline? What differences do you see between a structured approach and a "reactive" approach, in which teachers wait until students misbehave and then react to the situation? Which of the two approaches would you be most comfortable with? Why? Occasionally you see very good teachers who don't seem to use a well-organized approach to discipline—how do they get by with that?

20. *Support for your approach.* Would you like for parents and your administrator to know about and support your approach to discipline? What advantages would that bring? How would you communicate your program to them? How would you ensure their support? What would you do if they don't agree with your approach?

Terms and Concepts

behavior	*in loco parentis*	preventive discipline
behavior management	INTASC	professionalism
corrective discipline	intervention	supportive discipline
discipline	limits	
ethics of instruction	misbehavior	

Activities

1. In pairs or small groups, exchange personal views on questions presented in the 20 discipline topics. Share with the class if possible.
2. Begin keeping a journal to accompany this book. You might wish to make headings that correspond to the components shown in Figure 1.1. Leave several blank pages after each heading. As you proceed through this book, enter notations of ideas and tactics you'd like to remember and use. This will be of great help later as you construct a personal system of discipline.

References

Drye, J. 2000. *Tort liability 101: When are teachers liable?* Atlanta, GA: Educator Resources. www.educator-resources.com

Ginott, H. 1971. *Teacher and child.* New York: Macmillan.

Goorian, B., and Brown, K. 2002. *Trends and issues: School law.* ERIC Clearinghouse on Educational Management. http://eric.uoregon.edu/trends_issues/law/index.html

National Education Association. 1975. *Code of ethics of the education profession.* www.nea.org/about nea/code.html

Schwartz, F. 1981. Supporting or subverting learning: Peer group patterns in four tracked schools. *Anthropology and Education Quarterly, 12*(2), 99–120.

Traynor, P. 2005. *Got discipline? Research-based practices for managing student behavior.* Mansfield, OH: Bookmasters.

2

How Can I Anticipate My Students' Behavior and Deal with Factors That Promote Misbehavior?

You will find that teaching becomes easier and more effective—and your students benefit—as you learn how your students are likely to behave. A foundational understanding is that misbehavior is seldom random. Usually, it is caused (or prompted or fostered) by conditions within students as they react to given situations. This chapter will help you identify a number of those **causes of misbehavior** and situations that, for the most part, you can use to your advantage. As you do so, you will see a marked reduction in class misbehavior.

Human behavior is complex indeed, but a beginning point for understanding it better is to recognize that, aside from physical or psychological trauma, behavior is shaped through the interplay of three main factors: (1) *inborn propensities* encoded in our genes, (2) *experience* with the people, conditions, opportunities, customs, and values that exist within the groups of which we are members, and (3) our abilities to *think for ourselves and make decisions*. These three factors interact to determine how students conduct themselves in and out of school.

In this chapter we give attention to the influence of inborn traits and sociocultural experiences. In later chapters, especially Chapters 8 and 10, we will consider the roles that thinking and decision making play in behavior. The information presented here will help you pinpoint factors that often lead to classroom misbehavior and understand what you can do to curtail the effects of those factors.

A PREVIEW OF THIS CHAPTER

Inborn dispositions interact with personal experiences and decision-making abilities to produce what we call behavior—certain characteristics of which emerge notably at different levels of maturity and are motivated by student needs, wants, and preferences. Effective teaching depends in large measure on teachers' recognizing these factors, using them to advantage, and otherwise making accommodations for the influence they have on student behavior.

WHAT TO LOOK FOR IN THIS CHAPTER

In this chapter we briefly review typical student behavior, what motivates it, and how teachers can influence it. The chapter begins with depictions of behavior among students at different levels in school. It moves on to identify some of the needs, interests, habits, and social and economic realities that affect behavior. Finally, it sheds light on how student misbehavior is promoted or "caused" by certain factors and how teachers can address some of those causative factors. Information is provided to help you

- Recognize many of the specific conditions that motivate student behavior
- Anticipate more accurately how your students will behave at school
- Identify and curtail situations that prompt students to misbehave
- Understand better why some students often feel they are relatively powerless, misunderstood by teachers, and treated unjustly

Because the chapter is intended only to help you anticipate and understand student behavior, it does not offer specific methodology for teaching in diverse classrooms. It does, however, present suggestions for dealing with all students equitably and helpfully.
Please look for the following information in this chapter:

- Behaviors typical of students at various stages of maturation
- The meaning of "values" and how they may vary from group to group
- How socio-cultural and economic realities can affect student behavior
- Why some groups of students often feel undervalued and powerless, and what you can do to help
- How to recognize and respond to misbehavior caused by factors that reside within individual students, peers and groups, instructional environments, and teachers and other school personnel

TYPICAL BEHAVIORS AND INTERESTS OF STUDENTS AT FOUR LEVELS OF DEVELOPMENT

Go to the IRIS Center Resources section of Topic #10: Maintaining Appropriate Student Behavior, in the **MyEducationLab** for your course and complete the case study entitled "Encouraging Appropriate Behavior."

Throughout their lives, people display a variety of efforts and mannerisms in attempting to satisfy their desires and needs. Some of those efforts are motivated by inborn traits, while others are learned. The following paragraphs describe many of the traits typical of students at four levels of development. They summarize what you can generally expect of students and suggest curriculum topics and activities that serve students well. Keep in mind that these depictions are general and do not apply in their entirety to all students.

Primary Grades (Ages 5 to 8)

Children first come to school full of life and eager to learn. Most have a loving disposition. They are receptive to almost everything teachers introduce. They

especially enjoy stories, music, and rhythmic activities. Many—especially girls—develop proclivities in language that make them appear advanced beyond their years.

Until approximately age 7, students function intellectually at what Swiss psychologist Jean Piaget (1951) called the *preoperational stage*, where they reason not on the basis of logic but on impressions they obtain (see Piaget, 1951; Charles, 1974). Piaget (shown here) found that during the preoperational phase, students are poor at remembering the order of events, understanding rules, explaining relationships, comprehending number relationships, and understanding other speakers accurately, including the teacher. They get along reasonably well, although they squabble a great deal. They tire easily and get fussy, so they require frequent rest. They make little distinction between work and play.

At around age 7, on average, children begin to mature noticeably. Intellectually, they become able to consider the relationship of parts to whole and are thus able to reason logically in terms of cause and effect. Where previously they reasoned and explained on the basis of appearances or intuition (e.g., "The sun moves because the wind blows it along"), they can now understand number relationships and science concepts, such as the cause of day and night. They are learning to play well together.

By second grade, they are enjoying games such as tag and hide and seek. They like puzzles, riddles, and guessing games. Although they can learn rules for games, they are poor at following them. They accept adult authority with little question. They tell fabrications routinely but seldom in a malicious way. They are highly imitative of each other. For them, misbehavior is whatever adults don't like, and guilt is understood in terms of getting caught.

By the time they exit the primary grades, students are usually socialized to raising hands, standing in lines, taking turns, and waiting patiently. They continue to respond well to affection and personal attention. All the while, students at this level enjoy activities in science, especially those having to do with plants and animals.

Intermediate Grades (Ages 9 to 11)

Go to the IRIS Center Resources section of Topic #10: Maintaining Appropriate Student Behavior, in the **MyEducationLab** for your course and complete the module entitled "SOS: Helping Students Become Independent Learners."

As students move into grade 4, they become increasingly independent, although they still want attention and affection from teachers. Intellectually, their ability to think logically grows stronger. They use concrete language for thinking; they cannot yet think in terms of pure abstractions. Socially, students often become highly argumentative. Many are loud and abusive, yet there is increasing evidence of reason and efforts to persuade. They like to play group games and show a bent for competition. Losing is difficult to accept; many cry and throw temper tantrums. They recognize the need for rules and rule enforcement, both in games and class behavior. No longer is teacher authority blindly accepted. Students may argue with the teacher, talk back, and be uncooperative. They show a growing awareness of honesty and its importance in relationships. They see that the more a lie intends to deceive, the worse it is.

Conscience develops along with respect for others. A growing sense of right and wrong is evident. Students increasingly want to share each others' company. They like group names and begin to form gangs, clubs, and cliques. Their individual behavior begins to reflect peer norms. Their interest in the natural world continues strongly.

Middle School Grades (Ages 12 to 14)

Behavior becomes more diverse as students move into the middle school years, and teachers require great skill in order to teach well and build supportive relationships. Bodily changes worry, perplex, excite, and dismay these students. New realities associated with sex stir and baffle. Psychological weaning from parents leaves them feeling lost and cut off. They crave adult support, yet the emerging need for independence produces conflict with adults. These factors provide serious distractions to learning.

Meanwhile, students are becoming increasingly rebellious and disposed to probing at the boundaries of rules and customs. Their awe of the teacher has waned, but it has been replaced with respect and affection for teachers who show understanding and helpfulness. Intellectually, most of these students have acquired a great new power—the ability to think abstractly. Their minds work as quickly as do those of adults, although they lack adult wisdom. Students can make use of concepts such as love, hate, honesty, loyalty, negative numbers, force, speed, time, and atomic particles. They have become able to think about thought.

High School Grades (Ages 15 to 18)

Before entering high school, students have developed the capacity for deeper thinking. They now show a proclivity for theorizing. They try to find a cause, a purpose, and a place for everything. They think about the *possible* as much as the *actual* and have acquired a strong concern about right and wrong. Their rational power produces the idealism characteristic of adolescence. Propositional thinking emerges: "If I do so and so, then so and so will result." Interest in nature and society is growing rapidly.

Lies are now seen as anything intentionally false. Punishment must take into account factors such as intent to break a law, age of the violator, and previous record of behavior. Many rules and laws are seen as unfair or irrelevant, so breaking them is no longer seen as absolutely wrong. Socially, these students can see various groups' points of view, which they like to weigh, clarify, and evaluate against each other. They can't see why everything is not ideal—politics, institutions, human relations, and so forth—which makes them overly critical of the way institutions and people actually function. Students may scathingly reject existing social arrangements and values. Their behavior, however, usually indicates adherence to existing social norms.

As they near the end of high school, students begin to settle down emotionally. They understand themselves better and have reached a truce with their bodies and feelings. They have begun to think about what they hope to do in the future. Some, lamentably, become further alienated from the educational mainstream. A new relationship with adults emerges. The love–hate attitude of earlier years fades, while respect for adults grows as students recognize their own interdependence with the community. Teachers can interact with these students as fellow adults, while students see teachers as guides and role models.

> **?** Justin, whom teachers consider an average 12-year-old, cannot seem to grasp the rationale for dividing fractions by inverting the divisor and multiplying. Yet, by following the steps taught by his teacher, he can do the work correctly. What might you infer about his level of intellectual development?

NEEDS, INTERESTS, AND HABITS THAT MOTIVATE BEHAVIOR (AND MISBEHAVIOR)

Go to the Building Teaching Skills and Dispositions section of Topic #2: Understanding Students' Psychological Needs, in the **MyEducationLab** for your course and complete the activity entitled "Assessing Students' Basic Needs."

Go to the Building Teaching Skills and Dispositions section of Topic #9: Enhancing Student Motivation, in the **MyEducationLab** for your course and complete the activity entitled "Promoting Interest in Classroom Subject Matter."

We have noted that human behavior is seldom random or purposeless, but is prompted by innate needs and learned interests and habits. Need is a mental construct—an imaginary "something" that we use to help explain human motivation. We realize that something within us strongly motivates us persistently to seek out certain identifiable satisfactions. We call those persistent urges "needs." Psychologists generally agree we have inborn **basic needs** for safety, comfort, positive relations with others, and so forth. Abraham Maslow (1954) provided the first graphic model of needs, which he depicted hierarchically. Maslow contended that "lower-order" needs such as survival must be satisfied before "higher-order" needs such as creativity become activated. For teachers, the following list of needs is more useful than Maslow's hierarchy because it identifies what students require in order to benefit most from their educational program. This list of needs is drawn from suggestions set forth by William Glasser (1998) and C. M. Charles (2008), among others:

- *Security.* Feeling safe without worry
- *Association.* Being with and interacting with others
- *Belonging.* Feeling a part of things, being valued, having a place in the class
- *Dignity.* Feeling respected and worthwhile
- *Hope.* Feeling that school is worthwhile and success is possible
- *Power.* Having some control over and input into events in the class
- *Enjoyment.* Participating in activities that are interesting, pleasurable, or rewarding
- *Competence.* Being able to do many things well, including the expected schoolwork

Psychologists consider these to be needs because students continually attempt to satisfy them, and when they cannot do so, they become anxious or frustrated and unable to devote themselves fully to the instructional activities provided for them. Occasionally they may resist those activities and defy the teacher.

Needs contrast with wants that are more transient and far less necessary to our existence. Wants are mostly, if not entirely, learned. They are usually based on interests. Even though we may want something powerfully, we can still function fully (even happily and healthily) if we don't get it. For example, we may strongly want to eat a certain food or see a certain film, but if we miss out on them, we don't experience a long-lasting malaise.

Educators can help students meet basic needs by removing threat from class activities and social interactions, permitting students to work together, assigning meaningful tasks, insisting on courteous treatment of others, involving students in planning and decision making, ensuring that learning activities and personal interactions are enjoyable, and making sure students learn important information. As teachers do those things, they see that misbehavior declines while student satisfaction with school increases.

Discussing Needs, Interests, and Habits with Your Students

It is advisable to discuss behavior and its causes with your students, using language suited to their level of understanding. Point out that all of us have certain needs that are approximately the same for everyone. Those needs—along with interests, wants, and habits—prompt us to behave in certain ways. There is usually a reason behind what we do. When we act, it is usually because an inborn or acquired motive urges us to do so, perhaps to escape danger, avoid boredom, satisfy curiosity, associate with others, obtain pleasure, keep ourselves out of trouble, fulfill obligations, or make ourselves competent.

Using the list of needs previously presented, ask students what they think those needs mean and how they affect behavior. Ask them to give examples from personal experience. Ask if they can see how inability to meet a need produces discomfort and reduces enjoyment, learning, and willingness to try. Reassure your students that you will help them meet their needs in school by treating them with respect and providing interesting, worthwhile learning. Indicate you will also require they treat each other with respect and, further, that you will not tolerate anything in the class that threatens anyone's sense of safety and security, feeling of belonging, or sense of hope. Emphasize that you need to count on their cooperation in providing and maintaining those conditions.

In your discussions with students, explain that interests are strong attractions one feels toward certain topics, people, and activities. They are related to needs, but unlike needs they are learned from experiences that have brought us enjoyment, success, or satisfaction. We can also develop new interests when we encounter new topics, ideas, or activities that intrigue us. Teachers can use students' existing interests as springboards into new class activities, and they can also introduce puzzles or amazing facts that lead quickly to new interests. Further, students' interests provide a linkage you can use to establish closer relations with students.

Students need to know that habits also play strong roles in human behavior. Habits are learned procedures that we have repeated so often we can do them automatically, without having to think. They are central to our daily activities, and we use them regularly to save ourselves much time and effort. Learning in school can be greatly helped by habits, provided they are correct and productive. While habits can be useful, they sometimes work against us. Habits of that kind are usually referred to as "bad habits." Teachers recognize that bad habits underlie much of the misbehavior in their classes, such as undesirable language, inconsiderate actions toward others, and disinclination to accept responsibility. Fortunately, good habits can be taught and used to replace undesirable habits. Some of the foremost experts in school discipline, such as Ronald Morrish (2005) and Harry and Rosemary Wong (2004), urge teachers to help students establish successful habits they can rely on automatically.

> **?** Which of the following are most likely to be (a) needs, (b) wants, (c) habits?
>
> 1. To have a friend
> 2. To see a particular motion picture
> 3. To dress oneself quickly for school
> 4. To place completed homework in the proper location
> 5. To feel secure in the classroom
> 6. To gain the admiration of classmates

Exploring What Students Need and Want in Teachers and Schools

Go to the Simulations section of Topic #5: Creating Positive Student–Teacher Relationships, in the **MyEducationLab** for your course and complete the simulation entitled "Developing Positive Teacher–Student Relationships with All Students."

Even though students' behavior, attitudes, and interests vary from group to group and change steadily with maturation, students consistently do better in school and enjoy school more when they have the following:

- A teacher who is friendly, interesting, helpful, and supportive
- Camaraderie or enjoyable associations among classmates
- Interesting, worthwhile topics to learn about
- Awareness of the importance or value of what they are being asked to learn
- Enjoyable instructional activities
- Opportunity for and likelihood of success and accomplishment
- Attention drawn tactfully to student accomplishments and improvment

It is well to discuss these matters with students and emphasize that you will do your best to provide for them, and that students will need to help you do so at times.

Just as there are things students need and want from teachers, there are also certain things they dislike and try to avoid, such as the following:

- Sitting still for long periods
- Keeping quiet for long periods
- Working alone
- Not knowing why something is being taught or learned
- Memorizing facts for tests
- Completing lengthy reading and writing assignments
- Doing repetitive work
- Engaging in individual competition where there is little or no chance of winning
- Having little or no choice in activities, assignments, or assessment
- Not knowing how to improve the quality of their work

Discuss these negative situations or conditions with your students and tell what you will do to minimize them. Note, however, that some students do not object to all of these; ask their opinions about them and if they can see situations in which some of these conditions might be necessary or useful.

SOCIO-CULTURAL REALITIES THAT INFLUENCE BEHAVIOR

Today's rapidly changing demographics are increasingly bringing together students from many different economic and cultural groups. Each of these groups reflect values, outlooks, habits, customs, aspirations, and ways of interacting that are emphasized in their cultures. Those factors tend to differ, in some degree, from group to group. Teachers are often criticized for being insensitive to those differences, although virtually all teachers genuinely want to serve their students well and equitably. In their attempt to do so, they seek information that helps them understand the mannerisms of students from various backgrounds, particularly backgrounds different from their own.

Values That Are Usually Emphasized in Schools

The majority of schools and teachers in the Western world reflect beliefs and behaviors that stem from the Judeo–Christian ethic, influenced by a capitalistic outlook, future orientation, and interpersonal equality. Following are examples of such beliefs and behaviors:

- *Time orientation.* Promptness is valued; orientation is toward the future.
- *Planning ahead.* Plans are made ahead of time to serve as guides for action.
- *Relations with others.* A general sense of equality prevails; other people are to be treated with consideration and respect.
- *Personal achievement and competition.* Individuals are urged to aspire to personal achievement; it is considered good to compete and try to rise above the norm.
- *Child-to-adult relations.* Adults are shown respect but are not seen as infallible.
- *Adult-to-child relations.* Children require guidance but are not to be treated as subservient.
- *Opportunity.* Potential to advance in life is available to everyone; one has only to seize the opportunity and follow through.
- *Verbal learning.* Much learning in school is expected to occur verbally through listening, reading, and discussing.
- *Success.* Success in life is seen as performing well, getting a good job, providing a good home, and acquiring a degree of wealth.
- *Personal behavior.* We are all ultimately responsible for our own behavior; most people behave ethically; laws and regulations are to be obeyed.

Areas Where Values May Come into Conflict

While human behavior and values across all groups are far more similar than different, students from various cultural and economic groups may display some values and behaviors that conflict with expectations in school. Sometimes those differences are misunderstood by teachers, and sometimes teacher behavior is misunderstood by students. For example, some cultural groups do not prize individual achievement and recognition; although they want the group as a whole to do well, they consider it improper for individuals to stand out. Some groups place strong emphasis on traditions from the past. Some see little purpose in working at school activities that do not appear useful or are not inherently interesting. Students in some cultures adopt a subservient manner when interacting with teachers and are made uncomfortable by eye contact. Many do not want to voice opinions that show disagreement with the teacher. A failure to recognize and adjust to such differences can lead to misunderstandings between teachers and students, making teaching and learning more difficult than necessary.

Economic Realities That Impinge on Student Behavior

Today, large numbers of our students come from economically disadvantaged backgrounds. "Economically disadvantaged" is a term used synonymously with "living in poverty." *Students in poverty* are defined as students who are members of households that must spend more than one-third of their disposable income for food adequate to meet the family's nutritional needs. At present, about one-fourth of all students in the United States fall into that category (Payne, 2001). Karen Pellegrino (2005) has identified poverty as a major factor that limits student success in school. Ruby Payne (2001, 2003) maintains that poor children are much more likely than nonpoor children to suffer developmental delay and to drop out of school early.

Hidden Rules of Students in Poverty

Payne's investigations have led her to conclude that each economic class has its own set of **hidden rules** that help it survive. The hidden rules for schools, teachers, and about half of the school population are concordant with the predominant school values listed previously. But the hidden rules for students from *generational poverty* (meaning long-term poverty) are different. Payne urges teachers to learn those rules because they provide keys to understanding, communicating, and working productively with students.

Payne (2001) says that for people in poverty, the major driving life forces are survival, personal relationships, and entertainment. Students in poverty tend to value relationships more than achievement. It can be disquieting for an individual to acquire too much education because the educated person might leave the community. Conflict is often resolved by fighting, and respect is accorded to those who can defend themselves. School discipline is more about penance and forgiveness than behavior change, and students often save face by laughing when they are disciplined. One's sense of personal value is tied up with the ability to entertain others. Money is to be used and spent, not saved. Destiny and fate govern most matters; individuals feel they have relatively little control over their lives.

According to Payne, students in poverty often use a casual, informal style of speech that contrasts with the more formal style used in school and business. Teachers should clarify the difference between formal and informal speech and help students use the appropriate language for various situations. Noise level among people of poverty may tend to be high, with frequent displays of emotion. At home, the television may mix with participatory conversation, in which two or more people talk at the same time. The classroom, in contrast, is expected to be quieter, with speakers taking turns.

Why Some Students Feel Undervalued and Powerless

Quite often, some of the students in any given class feel slighted by the teacher, or feel they are not as highly valued as are other members of the class. Sometimes they believe they are treated unjustly. While most teachers attempt to treat all students equitably, a few fall short of this goal, or at least give the impression they do. Kimberley Alkins (2007) suggests this differing treatment may occur as a natural result of teachers' inadequate understanding of their students' backgrounds; their thinking is not synchronized with all their students' ways of looking at important life matters. She cites earlier work by P. C. Murrell (1991) who asserted that traditional teacher preparation programs fail to provide preservice teachers with the appropriate frameworks for interpreting the different developmental patterns of low-income urban students of color. Alkins and Murrell seem to agree, along with many other authorities, that the remedy for this condition lies in equipping future teachers with adequate information about the students they are teaching, including what to expect from these students in class settings. They would have teachers strive for understanding, not colorblindness, in which teachers consider all students the same and ignore cultural or racial differences. Marilyn Cochran-Smith (1995) states that colorblindness can be a barrier to the success of the student–teacher relationship. She explains that

> it is not advisable for teachers to mistake colorblindness for educational equity or to [only] learn "the characteristics" of people of various races and cultures . . . [because] these practices decontextualize teaching and often result in bolstering the very stereotypes they are intended to dispel. (p. 494)

Neither, she says, is it enough just to provide new teachers with lists of "best practices" in multicultural education. Instead, teachers should be called on to reflect on their own beliefs, understand the values and practices of cultures that are different from their own, and then teach in ways that take these realities into account. When able to do these things, teachers become better able to organize classroom environments that promote trust, safety, and respect, which are pivotal in establishing quality relationships with students.

General Suggestions for Working with Students from All Societal and Economic Groups

The following is a composite of suggestions from various authorities on working more effectively with students from various backgrounds.

- Learn as much as you can about the value systems of students from backgrounds different from your own, including what they consider important, how they relate to each other and to adults, and how they relate to teachers and school in general.

Go to the IRIS Center Resources section of Topic #13: Managing Special Groups, in the **MyEducationLab** for your course and complete the module entitled "Cultural and Linguistic Differences: What Teachers Should Know."

- Become knowledgeable about the hidden rules that regulate group and personal behavior.
- Show acceptance of your students, their families, and their lifestyles.
- Show solidarity with students and be eager to help them learn and find success.
- Emphasize the knowledge, skills, and values needed for school success and for a strong personal and cultural identity.
- Create a more hospitable environment by communicating the expectation that all students can succeed in school and will be helped to do so.
- Link curriculum content to students' out-of-school experiences.
- Attempt to mentor students; this is an especially effective tactic for improving motivation and good personal relations between student and teacher.
- Develop codes of class behavior that are sensitive to all cultures while emphasizing responsibility and respect. Demonstrate for students the kinds of behavior that helps them succeed in school and have them practice that behavior.
- Teach students how to speak and write in a formal manner.
- Keep family members informed about their child's performance and behavior and ask them to work with you for the child's benefit.

PERSONAL AND ENVIRONMENTAL FACTORS THAT PROMOTE MISBEHAVIOR

Go to the IRIS Center Resources section of Topic #12: Maintaining Problem Behaviors, in the **MyEducationLab** for your course and complete the modules entitled "Addressing Disruptive and Noncompliant Behaviors" (Parts 1 and 2).

You have probably wondered many times why people do undesirable things that seem to serve no useful purpose—why they are discourteous and disrespectful; why they try to harm each other; why they do not eagerly take advantage of the educational opportunities handed to them; and why at times they lie, cheat, and steal. Because we consider these behaviors undesirable (or worse), we call them misbehavior or bad behavior. Bad behavior, just like good behavior, is a product of ongoing interactions between psychological needs and socio-environmental influences that are part of the human condition. A need, such as that for affection, prompts us to take action. At the same time, social expectations put limits on how we are allowed to seek that affection. If we act in accordance with those expectations, our behavior is considered to be appropriate. If we violate those expectations, our efforts are deemed to be bad behavior or misbehavior, and unpleasant consequences often follow.

Effective teachers understand, sometimes intuitively, how the forces of need and civility both clash and support each other. They know that needs motivate behavior and that misbehavior occurs when something within the student or the environment pushes behavior outside the limits of acceptability. This realization shows us that teachers can have considerable influence on student behavior at four different points:

1. Before misbehavior occurs, we can soften factors that are known to promote misbehavior, thus reducing its incidence.
2. When misbehavior seems incipient, we can take steps to relieve fatigue, boredom, or distractions and thus help students keep their behavior within acceptable limits.

3. After misbehavior occurs, we can react in ways that help students replace misbehavior with appropriate behavior, thus leading to changes that improve students' lives.
4. We can communicate at all times in a manner that helps students conduct themselves appropriately while preserving their dignity.

We have at our disposal effective tactics for use at all four points, as you will see in the chapters that follow. In the past, the main discipline tactics were only applied at the third point, after misbehavior occurred. Now we know that it is easier to prevent misbehavior and support acceptable behavior than to correct it after it occurs (although corrections can and do accomplish important outcomes).

With that in mind, we now explore 26 conditions that often lead to misbehavior in school. You may find this material somewhat lengthy, but if you stick with it, you will learn how to reduce substantially the amount of misbehavior in your classes, the time required for correcting misbehavior, and much of the stress often associated with discipline. These 26 conditions that can lead to or cause school misbehavior are grouped in accordance with where they seem to reside, and suggestions are provided for removing or softening their effects.

Conditions That Reside in Individual Students

Ten conditions that often promote misbehavior reside within individual students: unmet needs, thwarted desires, expediency, urge to transgress, temptation, inappropriate habits, poor behavior choices, avoidance, egocentric personality, and neurological-based behavior (NBB).

- *Unmet needs.* Both in and out of the classroom, students continually try to meet strongly felt needs for security, belonging, hope, dignity, power, enjoyment, and competence. When any of these needs is not being satisfied, students become unsettled, distracted, and more likely to behave inappropriately.
  Suggestions: Acknowledge these needs and always try to see they are being met. By observing students and talking with them, you can usually identify and often remedy the needs that are prompting misbehavior.

- *Thwarted desires.* When students fail to get something they badly want, they may complain, become destructive, sulk, pout, or act out.
  Suggestions: When this happens, tell students you can see they are troubled or distracted. Ask if there is anything you can do to help. Be sympathetic, but don't dwell on the problem. Do something to draw their attention to the lesson, such as posing a challenge or creating a mystery.

- *Expediency.* All students look for ways to make their lives easier and more enjoyable. In doing so, they will sometimes take shortcuts, conveniently forget what they are supposed to do, look for ways to get out of work, and intentionally break rules.
  Suggestions: Expedient behavior is seldom a problem in classes that are interesting, but it appears often in classes students find boring. Hold discussions about expediency and its troublesome effects. Ask students why they sometimes take the easy way, such as reading book summaries or reviews rather than the as-

signed book, rushing through a writing assignment, or copying others' ideas. If they are comfortable enough to answer honestly, they will probably say they do so because they don't like the work, don't see the point in it, or don't want to spend time on it. Ask them what would encourage them to give their best effort. Listen to their suggestions and make use of them if you can.

■ *Urge to transgress.* Many of us have a natural aversion to rules imposed by others, and we seem to find it a challenge to break them, despite knowing there is a chance of getting caught or even harming ourselves or others. Students succumb to this urge frequently, especially when class activities are not appealing, and they cheat, take shortcuts, tell lies, break class rules, and annoy others.
Suggestions: Discuss this urge, its effects, and how it can be controlled sensibly. Discuss the reasons for rules, including how they reduce potential harm, equalize opportunity, and help us live together harmoniously. If students are old enough, ask if they understand what ethics, ethical conduct, and personal character mean. Ask why they think ethical people are so widely admired.

■ *Temptation.* Students regularly encounter objects, people, situations, and behaviors that are powerfully attractive. This phenomenon is evident in association with music and lyrics, ways of speaking, clothing fashions, lifestyles, and cheating on tests and assignments. Although pursuit of these temptations can result in mild or severe misbehavior, students nevertheless find them so attractive they will occasionally do, adopt, mimic, acquire, or associate with them, despite knowing they are forbidden to do so.
Suggestions: Conduct discussions with your students to analyze temptation and seek to understand why certain objects, styles, and opportunities are so seductive. Help students foresee the undesirable consequences of following disapproved styles and manners. Help them clarify the lines that separate appropriate behavior from inappropriate and urge them to resist involvement in activities that are likely to do them harm.

■ *Inappropriate habits.* Inappropriate habits are ingrained ways of behaving that violate established standards and expectations. Jason uses profanity at school. Maria is discourteous and calls others names. Larry shirks his assignments. Some of these habits are learned in school, but most become established outside of school.
Suggestions: Bring inappropriate habits to students' attention without pointing a finger at anyone. Discuss their harmful effects and, when desirable, have students practice acceptable alternatives to name-calling, teasing, verbal put-downs, cheating, lying, and showing disregard for others.

■ *Poor behavior choices.* The behaviors students use in attempting to meet their needs are sometimes acceptable, sometimes not. In most cases, students choose to behave as they do. For example, Alicia, when seeking attention, annoys others so much they avoid her. Alan, seeking to increase his sense of power, refuses to do what his teacher requests. Assuming those behaviors are under their control, we say that Alicia and Alan are making poor behavior choices.
Suggestions: Alicia and Alan need to understand that their choices of behavior are working against their success in school. To help them, you might address the class as a whole and pose the following questions:

"What are some of the things you have seen students do to (get attention, be acknowledged, get better grades than they deserve, get out of work, become members of certain groups)?"

"Does their behavior usually get them what they want?"

"What could those students do that would probably bring better results?"

- *Avoidance.* No one likes to face failure, intimidation, ridicule, or other unpleasant situations and treatment. One way to escape those things is to avoid activities or places where they might occur, or if that is not possible, simply refuse to participate. But in school, students' reasons for avoidance are often not evident to teachers. Consider Norona, who refuses to participate in a group assignment. Her refusal seems to show disrespect for the teacher, but her real reason is that she doesn't want to appear inept in front of her peers.
  Suggestions: To help students such as Norona, show them how to face unpleasant situations and work through them. Rather than singling out Norona, involve the entire class, perhaps first in pairs, then small groups, then large groups. You might ask the following questions:

"Are there things you try to avoid in school, such as people, events, or activities you find frightening or embarrassing?"

"Which of those things could best be dealt with through avoidance (e.g., a clique that is maligning other students)?"

"Which of those things cannot be dealt with through avoidance (e.g., giving an oral report in front of the class)?"

"What is the worst thing that can happen in class if we make a mistake?"

"Are mistakes valuable? Can they help us learn?"

"Could we agree as a class never to make others feel embarrassed when they make mistakes?"

"What might a person do to reduce his or her fear of mistakes or being involved in unpleasant situations?"

- *Egocentric personality.* Students with egocentric personalities focus primarily on themselves, believe they are superior to others, and usually think they can do no wrong. Most classes contain one or more students with such personalities.
  Suggestions: To help these students behave more appropriately, ask questions such as the following in class discussions:

"Are the needs and interests of all students important, or do only certain students deserve attention?"

"Is one person often entirely right and everyone else entirely wrong?"

"Is everyone entitled to an equal opportunity in the class? How should you and I react to a person who always wants to dominate, be first, be right, and quarrel with those who don't agree?" (Make sure the proffered suggestions are positive in nature, not negative.)

■ *Neurological-based behavior (NBB).* A few students behave undesirably not through intent or thoughtlessness but because their brains call forth behavior that they cannot fully control. NBB encompasses a number of different diagnoses—collectively called *mental health issues*—including learning disabilities, attention-deficit hyperactivity disorder (ADHD), sensory-processing disorder, fetal alcohol spectrum disorder, and autism spectrum disorder. Frequently, students with these diagnoses do not respond reliably to normal discipline tactics. Chapter 3 explains these conditions and provides information for working with students with NBB diagnoses.

Suggestions: Teachers who have students with NBB need help from specialists. That help will usually be provided by the school. But regular classroom teachers can do many things on their own, as indicated more comprehensively in Chapter 3. Mel Levine (2002) urges teachers to explain clearly to the class and others that some people function (are "wired up," if you prefer) in such a way that they lose control at times, more often than others do. Other authorities ask teachers to (1) always model the calm, soothing behavior we want students to display and make sure they feel loved and respected as human beings; (2) be careful about making eye contact, which stimulates upper-cortex activity and is often interpreted as a challenge or threat; (3) react to situations calmly (a raised voice tends to make students with NBB raise their voices in return); and (4) provide considerable structure to activities (meaning directions and procedures) because a lack of structure often makes learning difficult for students with NBB.

Conditions That Reside in Class Peers and Groups

Two significant causes of misbehavior reside in class peers and groups—provocation and contagious group behavior. Here are suggestions for dealing with them.

■ *Provocation.* A great amount of misbehavior results from students' provoking each through teasing, petty annoyance, put-downs, sarcastic remarks, and aggression or bullying. Heather is trying to study, but Art's incessant chatter frustrates her to the bursting point. Marty calls Jerry a name and Jerry responds hotly.

Suggestions: Provocation often produces strong emotions that overwhelm self-control and increase combativeness. Discuss this phenomenon with your class. Ask:

"Is provoking others or bullying them consistent with the class character we are trying to build?"

"Can you name some things people say or do that upset you so much you want to retaliate?"

"If you retaliate, what do you think will happen? Will that put an end to the conflict?"

"What are some positive things we can do to stop provocation in the class?"

- *Contagious group behavior.* Students sometimes succumb to peer pressure or get caught up in group emotion and as a result may misbehave in ways that would be out of character if they were by themselves. It is difficult for students to disregard peer pressure, easy to get swept up in group energy and emotion, and easy to justify one's misbehavior as "only what others were doing." Because Kerry and Lee want to look cool to their peers, Kerry defaces school property, and Lee bullies a weaker member of the class. Neither Kerry nor Lee would do those things if by themselves.
  Suggestions: Discuss this phenomenon with your class. For example, tell the class about some event in which a friend of yours, let's say Sarah, behaved badly just because others were doing so. Indicate that Sarah is now very embarrassed about her behavior and wishes no one knew about it. Ask your students if they know any stories like Sarah's they would be willing to share, without mentioning names the class might recognize. (Tell them they must not mention family matters or members—doing so is a sure way to get parents upset at you.) If they share stories, guide the class in analyzing one or two of them. If they don't contribute a story, have a fictional one ready for their consideration. After hearing or recounting the story, ask questions such as:

"Is the behavior something the person will be proud of later?"

"Why do you suppose the person behaved that way?" (e.g., fun, camaraderie, testing limits, being seen as clever or cool)

"What do you think the long-term results will be for the person?" (e.g., an unpleasant story to remember, regret, guilt, getting caught, being found out, worry, disappointing one's family, possible punishment, living with knowing you did the wrong thing)

"How do you think the possible benefits of the behavior compare with the probable dangers?"

"Once you do something you are ashamed of, is there any way to make amends and save your reputation?"

"How can you stay away from, or keep out of, group activities that are unlawful, unethical, or against the rules?"

Conditions That Reside in Instructional Environments

Four conditions that promote misbehavior reside in instructional environments. They are physical discomfort, tedium, meaninglessness, and lack of stimulation. All can be easily corrected.

- *Physical discomfort.* Students often become restless when made uncomfortable by inappropriate temperature, poor lighting, or unsuitable seating or workspaces.
  Suggestions: Attend to comfort factors in advance and ask students about them. Make corrections as necessary.

- *Tedium.* Students begin to fidget after a time when an instructional activity requires continued close attention, especially if the topic is not appealing.
  Suggestions: Break the work into shorter segments or add something that increases the interest level.

- *Meaninglessness.* Students grow restless when required to work at topics they do not comprehend or for which they see no purpose.
  Suggestion: Make sure the topic is meaningful to students—that they understand it and see its relevance and importance in their lives.

- *Lack of stimulation.* The topic and learning environment provide little that is attractive or otherwise stimulating. Students take no interest in the lesson.
  Suggestions: Select topics and activities in which students have natural interest. When that is not possible, introduce elements students are known to enjoy, such as novelty, mystery, movement, competition, group work, and role-playing.

Conditions That Reside in Teachers and Other School Personnel

We must face the fact that teachers and other school personnel sometimes misbehave in school, and in doing so they influence students to misbehave. Here are 10 examples of **teacher misbehavior** that sometimes contribute to student misbehavior:

- *Poor habits.* Personnel in the schools have sometimes unknowingly acquired counterproductive ways of dealing with students or each other, such as using bad language and speaking in a sarcastic or bossy manner.
  Suggestions: Reflect regularly on how you treat your students and speak to them. Self-monitor your behavior and make sure it is as you want it to be. If you see or hear colleagues treating students in an unprofessional manner, take the students aside at an appropriate time and casually mention the matter and ask students about the effect it had on them. If students are being adversely affected, speak in private with your school administrator and voice your concerns, then leave the matter in the administrator's hands. If you feel you must confront a colleague, do so tactfully. Your colleague is not likely to appreciate your comments.

- *Unfamiliarity with better techniques.* Some educators have not had occasion to learn some of the newer, more effective ways of teaching and relating with today's students.
  Suggestions: It is important that you keep yourself informed about topics and activities that are well-received by students. Don't be reluctant to approach popular teachers at your school and ask them what seems to work best for them. You can also find innumerable outstanding ideas and suggestions on the Internet and in professional books and journals that might be available at your school.

- *Presenting poor models of behavior.* At times all of us behave inconsistently and irresponsibly, especially on days when for whatever reason we are short on self-control. On those occasions we sometimes treat students discourteously. We can't expect to be perfect, but we must realize that when we treat students poorly—which is to say, in ways we would not want to be treated—we leave a lasting impression that not only damages relationships but also encourages students to imitate our unfortunate behavior.

Suggestions: Always be the best model you can for your students, who watch you very closely and often pattern their behavior after yours (especially when you misbehave). If you do anything inappropriate, call attention to it, explain why it was wrong, and apologize if necessary.

■ *Showing little interest in or appreciation for students.* We sometimes fail to show interest in students or appreciation for them as individuals, despite knowing they want our attention. If we disregard them repeatedly, students become hesitant to approach us or may seek our attention in disruptive ways.

Suggestions: Give each student as much personal attention as possible. Greet them by name, exchange a friendly word, and show you are open to discussing any challenges they might be facing in school. Try to help them feel at ease and acknowledge their accomplishments.

■ *Succumbing to personal frustration.* Some educators get beaten down from continually having to deal with misbehavior or inconsiderate parents. The stress may at times make it difficult for them to work with students in a kind, helpful manner.

Suggestions: Educators often try unsuccessfully to force students to comply with expectations. Force does not work. Replace it with encouragement and enticement and you will see your students become cooperative, considerate, and willing to make an effort. Go out of your way to communicate with parents and show appreciation for their child.

■ *Reacting badly to provocation.* Students may do and say things intentionally to get under your skin. You know you should react with composure, but instead you become upset and perhaps lose self-control.

Suggestions: When students try to provoke you, disregard their comments and actions and proceed as if nothing has happened. If you feel it necessary to respond, only say, "Something is causing violations of our agreement about being considerate of others. I don't like to see that in our class. Is there something we can do to fix the problem?"

■ *Providing ineffective guidance and feedback.* In the absence of guidance and feedback, students sometimes do not understand what is expected of them, how much progress they have made, or what they can do to improve.

Suggestions: Make sure students understand clearly what they are supposed to do and how they should go about it. During and after assigned activities, tell students what they have done well what they can do to improve. Ask them to give their appraisals of the activity and the efforts they have made.

■ *Using ineffective personal communication.* Some educators are not adept at communicating with students on a personal level. This may cause students to become uneasy and reticent about approaching their teachers.

Suggestions: Speak regularly with students in a friendly way. Students want you to know their names and exchange pleasantries with them. Often they want to tell you their views on various matters and would like to know yours. Speaking with students as social equals gives them a sense of personal validation. You just need to make sure you avoid comments that hurt feelings or dampen enthusiasm. Without exaggerating, say things that increase optimism and bolster confidence, and do so honestly.

■ *Failure to plan proactively.* Many educators do not adequately plan their instructional program in advance or anticipate problems that might arise. Then, when unexpected things happen, they are not prepared to respond as they would like.

Suggestions: Think carefully about your curriculum and instructional activities and how your students are likely to respond to them. By anticipating potential difficulties, you can avoid most problems and prepare yourself to deal with whatever might eventuate. Think through what you will do when people are injured or become suddenly ill, grow defiant, or get into fights. Decide what you will do and say if an unauthorized visitor approaches you, if a parent berates you, if the class groans when you make an assignment, and so forth. Determine how you can respond decisively to such eventualities, yet maintain your composure and ability to relate positively with others.

■ *Using coercion, threat, and punishment.* Students don't like to be threatened or forced to do anything. If you treat them abrasively, they keep a watchful eye on you—fearful of being scolded, embarrassed, or demeaned—and will very likely develop negative attitudes toward you and school.

Suggestions: Give up coercion and threat and replace them with considerate helpfulness, personal attention, and good communication. Explain to students how they should behave, demonstrate those behaviors, and have students practice the behaviors. When you see students behave responsibly, thank them for doing so. For older students, do this privately or express your appreciation to the class as a whole.

Terms and Concepts

basic needs	economically disadvantaged	teacher misbehavior
causes of misbehavior	hidden rules	

Activities

1. In pairs or with small groups of colleagues, refer to the values that are typically emphasized in school. Indicate to what extent your own values correspond to those typical of schools and refer to the general suggestions for working with students from all ethnic and economic groups. Select three of those suggestions that you feel would be most important to your students' success.

2. In pairs or small groups, review the 26 conditions that often promote misbehavior in school. Select five of them you believe most in need of attention in typical classrooms. Explain your choices.

3. Review the section on "conditions that reside in teachers and other school personnel." Have you experienced school personnel who misbehaved in any of those ways? What do you think they could have done to make conditions better for you? Share your conclusions with your classmates.

References

Alkins, K. 2007. AACTE proposal 2008. *Student-teacher relationships: Through the eyes of six beginning teachers.* www.allacademic.com/meta/p_mla_apa_research_citation/2/0/5/4/6/pages205469/p205469-4.php

Charles, C. M. 1974. *Teachers' petit Piaget.* Belmont, CA: Fearon.

Charles, C. M. 2008. *Today's best classroom management strategies: Paths to positive discipline.* Boston: Allyn & Bacon.

Cochran-Smith, M. 1995. Colorblindness and basket making are not the answers: Confronting the dilemmas of race, culture, and language diversity in teacher education. *American Educational Research Journal, 32*(3), 493–522.

Glasser, W. 1998. *The quality school: Managing students without coercion.* New York: HarperCollins.

Maslow, A. 1954. *Motivation and personality.* New York: Harper.

Morrish, R. 2005. What is Real Discipline? www.realdiscipline.com

Murrell, P. C., Jr. 1991. Cultural politics in teacher education: What's missing in the preparation of African American teachers? In M. Foster (Ed.), *Readings on equal education* (Vol. 11, pp. 205–225). New York: AMS Press.

Payne, R. 2001. *A framework for understanding poverty.* Highlands, TX: Aha! Process.

Payne, R. 2003. Quoted in Claitor, D. 2003. Breaking through: Interview of Ruby Payne. www.hopemag.com/issues/2003/SeptOct/breakingThrough.pdf

Pellegrino, K. 2005. The effects of poverty on teaching and learning. www.teachnology.com/tutorials/teaching/poverty/print.htm

Piaget, J. 1951. *Judgment and reasoning in the child.* London: Routledge & Kegan Paul.

Wong, H., and Wong, R. 2004. *The first days of school: How to be an effective teacher.* Mountain View, CA: Harry K. Wong Publications.

3

How Do I Recognize and Deal with Atypical Behavior That Is Neurological-Based?

In Chapter 2 we reviewed the behaviors typical of students at various levels of maturity. That information pertained to students who are able to control their behavior. But not all students can do so all the time. A few—estimated to be about one in 10—are notably erratic in selecting what they say and do. Behavior such as theirs, occurring outside the usual boundaries of self-control, is called **neurological-based behavior (NBB)**. NBB poses special challenges for teachers and students— challenges that are addressed herein.

The lead author of this chapter is Paula Cook, a specialist in teaching students who have NBB. Dr. Cook works in highly specialized programs for students with behavioral, emotional, and psychiatric disorders, with mild to moderate cognitive impairment. Her responsibilities involve curriculum modifications and adaptations, individualized educational planning, advocacy, behavior management, social skills, and life skills education. She also teaches at Red River Community College and the University of Manitoba. She has made numerous presentations at regional, national, and international conferences and was a 2003 recipient of the Council for Exceptional Children's Outstanding Educator of the Year award.

A PREVIEW OF THIS CHAPTER

About 10 percent of students cannot reliably control what they say or do. These students, real people struggling for success, are scattered throughout the school population. The overarching name for the behavioral condition they exhibit is neurological-based behavior (NBB). A number of different diagnoses, considered mental health issues, are included in NBB. Eight of the major diagnoses are discussed in this chapter, along with symptoms, typical behaviors, and suggestions for teachers.

WHAT TO LOOK FOR IN THIS CHAPTER

- The general nature of neurological-based behavior (NBB)
- The most common diagnoses within NBB and the percentage of the school population they affect
- Student behavior that might indicate the presence of NBB
- General and specific suggestions for working effectively with students with NBB
- The nature of rage, what to expect, and how to deal with it

OVERVIEW OF NEUROLOGICAL-BASED BEHAVIOR

Go to the IRIS Center Resources section of Topic #13: Managing Special Groups, in the **MyEducationLab** for your course and complete the module entitled "What Do You See? Perceptions of Disability."

Neurological-based behavior is behavior that results from cerebral processes that do not occur in a "normal" manner. Common diagnoses within NBB include attention-deficit hyperactivity disorder (ADHD), learning disabilities, sensory integration dysfunction, bipolar disorder, oppositional defiant disorder, autism spectrum disorder, fetal alcohol spectrum disorder, and brain injuries, all of which receive attention in this chapter. The behavior of students with these diagnoses is often inconsistent and unpredictable (Kranowitz, 1998) and does not respond well to teachers' ordinary discipline techniques. Until recently, knowledge was sparse about working effectively with students with NBB, but important advances have been made in the past two decades.

Scenario 1*

Tyler began the morning by refusing to participate in opening activities. He chose instead to make beeping sounds. After the opening activities, the class was to read quietly on their own for 10 minutes, but Tyler decided to sing loudly. When asked to stop, he began to hoot. He was belligerent and noisy for some time. He poked Jackie with a pencil, chewed the eraser off his pencil and swallowed it, and insisted on writing on his math sheet with a tiny piece of pencil lead moistened with spittle. He refused to comply with academic instructions until almost time for recess. During recess, Tyler pushed, poked, hit, and tried to choke other students. He laughed when they protested. He engaged in violent play fantasies and was extremely argumentative with the teachers on duty, swearing at them and insisting they could not make him do anything he didn't want to do. Finally, Tyler had to be led physically back to the classroom. He screamed that his rights were being violated and that he would sue the school and kill the teachers. Tyler worked the rest of the morning alone in the resource room with the

---

*For this chapter, Dr. Cook has provided seven scenarios describing episodes of behavior of real students with whom she has worked. The students' names have been changed to ensure anonymity.

resource teacher. In the afternoon, Tyler was well-behaved, compliant, and willing to participate and learn.

Application: After you have read this chapter, you will be asked in the Activities section to return to this scenario and, with a fellow teacher or classmate, discuss the situation and reflect on how one might deal with it effectively.

Go to the IRIS Center Resources section of Topic #11: Communication Skills, in the **MyEducationLab** for your course and complete the module entitled "Effective School Practices: Promoting Collaboration and Monitoring Students' Academic Achievement."

Students such as Tyler behave erratically or inconsistently for reasons that are not apparent to the untrained eye. Generally speaking, they behave as they do because they have difficulty processing information correctly due to compromised cerebral functioning occasioned by chemical imbalances, congenital brain differences, brain injuries, or brain diseases. Students with those diagnoses usually show high degrees of inattention, hyperactivity, impulsivity, excess emotionality, anxiety, inconsistent emotional responses, unpredictable intense mood swings, withdrawal, and episodes of rage (Kranowitz, 1998; Greene, 2001; Papolos and Papolos, 2002; Hall and Hall, 2003; Cook, 2004a). The **neurological differences** they experience are often difficult to diagnose, so these students sometimes do not receive the help they need for several years after they experience the onset of symptoms (Papolos and Papolos, 2002).

Please remember that students with NBB are not abstractions, but real people struggling to deal with life. When ordinary discipline procedures do not help them remain productive in the classroom, it is not because the students are "bad" or "too far gone" or come from "horrible families." Rather, they behave as they do because of the way their brains work, and their brains cannot always control their behavior in ways that serve them best.

PRINCIPAL DIAGNOSES RELATED TO NEUROLOGICAL-BASED BEHAVIOR

The various diagnoses associated with neurological-based behavior are considered to be mental health conditions (American Academy of Child and Adolescent Psychiatry, 2004a). Some of these conditions are due to biological factors such as genetics and chemical imbalances in the body, whereas others are due to environmental factors such as violence, extreme stress, and significant losses of persons or home. Sometimes, biological and environmental factors play a joint role.

The following are some of the diagnoses within NBB that appear prominently in the literature and affect students adversely: **attention-deficit hyperactivity disorder,** accompanied by restlessness and short attention span; **affective disorders** that affect mood or feeling, such as **bipolar disorder,** in which individuals cycle between mania and depression; **anxiety disorders** that involve fear and extreme uneasiness; **post-traumatic stress disorder,** which adversely affects students who have witnessed or heard about traumatic events; **conduct disorder,** in which individuals regularly breach society's moral constraints; **oppositional defiant disorder,** in which students oppose and defy teachers and others; **autism spectrum**

disorder, in which the child fails to develop normal speech patterns or personal relationships; and **fetal alcohol spectrum disorder,** in which students show poor impulse control, poor judgment, lack of common sense, and learning difficulties. Most of these disorders are treated with medications, some of which may adversely affect students' attention, concentration, and stamina (National Institute of Mental Health, 2008).

Few educators realize how prevalent these conditions are among school students. Consider the following:

- Childhood mental health conditions are now so common that some psychiatrists are calling them a "plague" (DeAngelis, 2004).
- You can expect, on average, about one in five of your students to have one or more mental health conditions that affect behavior in school (National Institute of Mental Health, 2008).
- As many as one in 10 students may suffer from a serious emotional disturbance (National Institute of Mental Health, 2008).
- Only 20 percent of children with mental health disorders get the kind of treatment they need (DeAngelis, 2004).
- Attention-deficit hyperactivity disorder, ADHD, is the most commonly diagnosed mental health disorder in children, affecting 3 to 5 percent of school-age children (National Institute of Mental Health, 2005).
- Suicide is the third leading cause of death for 15- to 24-year-olds and the sixth leading cause of death for 5- to 14-year-olds (American Academy of Child and Adolescent Psychiatry, 2008).
- An estimated 60 percent of teenagers in juvenile detention have behavioral, cognitive, or emotional problems (National Institute of Mental Health, 2008).
- Twenty-two percent of youths in juvenile justice facilities have a serious emotional disturbance, and most have a diagnosable mental disorder (Jans, Stoddard, and Kraus, 2004).
- Diagnosis of a single individual often reveals a constellation of mental health symptoms that exist simultaneously (Feldman, 2004). Two or more simultaneous diagnoses are called *co-morbid diagnoses.*
- Mental health disorders are biological in nature. They cannot be overcome through willpower and are not related to a person's character or intelligence.
- Serious mental illnesses can now be treated effectively, bringing a 70 to 90 percent reduction in symptoms. Treatment often includes a combination of pharmacological and psychosocial support (National Institute of Mental Health, 2008).

In addition to the diagnoses just mentioned, you may encounter students with explosive behavior disorder, paranoia, obsessive compulsive disorder, substance dependence, phobias, eating disorders, and Tourette's syndrome. Treatment for these disorders varies. If you wish to learn more about any of them, you can find them discussed at length on the Internet. As noted, these disorders are usually treated with medication, which often affects students' attention, memory, abstract thinking, and organizational skills (Davidson, 2002).

A WORD ABOUT BRAIN INJURIES

Go to the Simulations section of Topic #9: Enhancing Student Motivation, in the **MyEducationLab** for your course and complete the simulation entitled "Helping All Students Believe They Can Achieve."

Injuries to the brain often affect its ability to function normally. The incidence of **brain injuries,** both traumatic and nontraumatic, has increased dramatically in recent years (Brain Injury Society, 2006). Traumatic injuries result from blows to the head incurred during events such as accidents, sporting events, or assaults. Nontraumatic injuries result from disrupted blood flow to the brain (as in strokes), or from tumors, infections, drug overdoses, and certain medical conditions (Brain Injury Society, 2006). The effects of severe injuries are readily apparent, but mild injuries may go unrecognized even if they have a significant effect on behavior.

INDICATORS OF NBB

Three indicators can alert you to the possibility that a given student is experiencing NBB. The indicators are behavior difficulties, language difficulties, and academic difficulties. **Behavior difficulties** are frequently the first indication that something unusual is occurring in the student, especially if the behavior is atypical, inconsistent, compulsive, or immune to normal behavior management. Such behavior may result from a neurological event that is promoting confusion, uncertainty, fear, or frustration.

Language difficulties include problems in understanding, processing, and expressing information verbally. Classroom interactions operate on the assumption that language is understood more or less the same by all students and teachers. But this is not so for students with NBB, who often do not interpret, understand, process, respond to, or use language properly (Cook, Kellie, Jones, and Goossen, 2000; Greene, 2001; Hall and Hall, 2003a; Cook, 2004a). Language difficulties can be further exaggerated by environmental stimulation, fatigue, medication, hunger, or stress. To give yourself a feeling of what students with language difficulties may experience, try reading the text in Figure 3.1.

If you notice students who seem to have difficulty understanding, or who are not complying with expectations or requests, try using fewer words and increase the wait time for compliance. Make your directions clear, concrete, and consistent. You may need to show directions physically as well as explain them verbally. Ask students to repeat the directions or show you what they are supposed to do.

Academic difficulties vary among students with NBB. Some of those difficulties are easily recognized and dealt with. Not all, however, are easily remedied. Memory is often compromised in students with NBB, resulting in variable gaps in learning. Difficulties with fine and gross motor skills, comprehension, and language

Figure 3.1   Example of Text as Seen by Students with Language Difficulties

and mathematic skills add to the problem. Comprehensive assessments by school psychologists often reveal difficulties that require special attention. In those cases, students are usually eligible to receive specialized services.

If you have a student with NBB who has been approved for special services, take note of what the special teachers do. You can adapt and use some of their strategies in your normal teaching. Doing so will benefit not only students with NBB, but other students as well. One example of such adaptation is to provide differentiated instruction, using Howard Gardner's theory of multiple intelligences (1999) to teach concepts in as many different ways as possible. That approach provides support for students by helping with comprehension while pinpointing specific student strengths and weaknesses.

SENSORY INTEGRATION DYSFUNCTION (SID)

Sensory integration dysfunction (SID)—also called **sensory processing disorder**—seems to be a core factor in NBB. Sensory integration refers to the process of organizing, interpreting, and responding to information taken in through the senses. The process occurs automatically and usually keeps us informed, ready to act, and better able to protect ourselves. At times and for some people, however, flaws in the process result in incorrect perception and interpretation of information. Impaired processing of information leads in turn to poor learning and inappropriate behavior. Most teachers know little about SID, even though it seems to be a major cause of hyperactivity, inattention, fidgety movements, inability to calm down, impulsivity, lack of self-control, disorganization, language difficulties, and learning difficulties (Kranowitz, 1998; Kranowitz, Szkut, Balzer-Martin, Haber, and Sava, 2003; Cook, 2004b).

Some students' sensory processing systems seem to be easily overwhelmed by excess visual and auditory stimulation. You can help those students by keeping the classroom neat and tidy, removing sources of unpredictable loud noise, enlarging printed questions or directions, and standing in front of a solid white overhead screen when giving instructions and directing lessons, all of which reduce distractions from extraneous sources. It is also wise to give directions more slowly and distinctly, check to ensure students have understood correctly, and maintain a sense of calm in the classroom.

Scenario 2

Jimmy entered kindergarten in September. By January, his behavior was worse than when he began school. Every day he had a series of tantrums, usually beginning when he arrived at school. He sometimes complied with directions, but more often, especially during changes of activity, he might scream, cry, kick, flail his arms, fall to the floor, or run out of the classroom. During his "episodes," he has kicked and hit staff members and assaulted students who were in his way. Jimmy's home life is unremarkable. He has an older sibling, both parents, and lives in a quiet neighborhood. His family environment is loving and stable. His parents are very concerned about his behavior. Jimmy does not have any diagnosed neurological conditions. His mother did not drink or use illicit substances during her pregnancy. The pregnancy and his birth were deemed typical.

Commentary: This child, with no diagnosis other than his behavior to suggest neurological dysfunction, was having a terrible experience in school. His teacher ultimately changed the classroom environment to cut down sensory stimulation. Jimmy's behavior then improved considerably.

The following sections present additional information about a few of the mental health diagnoses teachers can expect to encounter in their students—attention-deficit hyperactivity disorder, bipolar disorder, oppositional defiant behavior, learning disabilities, autism spectrum disorder, and fetal alcohol spectrum disorder.

ATTENTION-DEFICIT HYPERACTIVITY DISORDER (ADHD)

Attention-deficit hyperactivity disorder is a neurodevelopmental disorder characterized by short attention span, weak impulse control, and hyperactivity, all of which inhibit learning and can foster misbehavior. ADHD can begin in infancy and extend into adulthood, with negative effects on the individual's life at home, in school, and in the community. It is estimated that ADHD affects 3 to 9 percent of the school-age population. The cause of ADHD is not known, although altered brain structure and function are suspected. The role of heredity is not as significant as once thought. Males are more likely than females to have the condition. Among students with ADD, males typically have ADD with hyperactivity, whereas females typically have ADD without hyperactivity (Amen, 2001). ADHD often occurs in combination with other diagnoses.

OPPOSITIONAL DEFIANT DISORDER (ODD)

Teachers expect that from time to time some of their students will talk back to them, argue, and disregard directives. Teachers don't enjoy such behavior, but they realize it is a normal occurrence in human development. However, an occasional student behaves in a manner that is so uncooperative and hostile that it damages the student's social, family, and academic life. That sort of behavior is characteristic in a diagnosis called oppositional defiant disorder (ODD). The American Academy of Child and Adolescent Psychiatry (2004b) lists the following as symptoms of ODD:

- Frequent temper tantrums
- Excessive arguing with adults
- Active defiance and refusal to comply with adult requests and rules
- Belligerent and sarcastic remarks, made when directly praised
- Deliberate attempts to annoy or upset people
- Blaming others for one's own mistakes or misbehavior
- Being touchy or easily annoyed by others
- Speaking hatefully when upset
- Seeking revenge

The AACAP (2004b) reports that 5 to 15 percent of all school-age children have ODD. Its cause is not known. If you have a student who displays the characteristics of ODD, you might consider using positive reinforcement when the student shows flexibility or cooperation. Indirect or earshot praise sometimes works well, such as when the student "overhears" two adults talking positively about him or her (intending to be overheard). It is also helpful to reduce the number of words you use when speaking to a student with ODD (Hall and Hall, 2003). A suggested procedure is to say and show what you mean, just once, and then do not explain yourself further. Students will ask for more information if they need it, and then you can provide what they need. Also consider taking personal time-out if you feel your responses are about to make the conflict worse. This allows you to calm down, and it also presents a good model for the student.

BIPOLAR DISORDER

Bipolar is an affective disorder characterized by severe mood swings that occur in cycles of mania and depression, or highs and lows. Individuals with bipolar disorder can change abruptly from irritable, angry, and easily annoyed, to silly, goofy, giddy, and disruptive, after which they return again to low-energy periods of boredom, depression, and social withdrawal (American Academy of Child and Adolescent Psychiatry, 2004c). The abrupt swings of mood and energy, which in some cases occur several times a day, are often accompanied by poor frustration tolerance, outbursts of temper, and oppositional defiant behavior. Students with bipolar disorder are also frequently diagnosed with sensory integration dysfunction (Papolos and Papolos, 2002).

The cause of bipolar disorder is not known. The disorder was once thought to be rare in children, but recent research shows it can begin very early in life and is much more common than previously believed. The condition in children is sometimes misdiagnosed as ADHD, depression, oppositional defiant disorder, obsessive compulsive disorder, or separation anxiety disorder. The misdiagnosis can lead to treatment with stimulants or antidepressants—medications that can make the bipolar disorder worse. Proper drugs can stabilize mood swings, and cognitive therapy and counseling can often help. Indicators of bipolar disorder in school students include the following:

- Hysterical laughing and infectious happiness for no evident reason
- Belligerence and argumentation, followed by self-recrimination
- Jumping from topic to topic in rapid succession when speaking
- Blatant disregard of rules because they think they do not pertain to them
- Arrogant belief that they are exceptionally intelligent
- Belief they can do superhuman deeds without getting seriously hurt

The bipolar condition interferes with the quality of sleep. Students who are affected often wake up tired. At school, they may show irritability and nebulous thinking during morning hours, but become able to function better in the afternoon (Papolos and Papolos, 2002).

LEARNING DISABILITIES (LD)

Learning disabilities (LD) are neurobiological disorders that interfere with learning in specific subjects or topics. They are categorized by the academic areas in which difficulties are identified. They affect students of average to above-average intelligence, making it difficult for them to receive and process information. Some of the common learning disabilities are *dyslexia,* which is difficulty in processing language; *dyscalculia,* difficulty with basic mathematics; *dysgraphia,* difficulty with handwriting and spelling; and *dyspraxia,* difficulty with fine motor skills (National Council for Learning Disabilities, 2005).

Because LD is so often confused with other diagnoses, it is useful to note that learning disabilities are *not* the same as attention disorders, although the two may occur together. Nor are learning disabilities the same as mental retardation, autism, hearing or visual impairment, physical disabilities, or emotional disorders. Learning disabilities are *not* caused by lack of educational opportunities, frequent changes of schools, poor school attendance, or lack of instruction in basic skills.

Learning disabilities *are* difficulties in learning certain topics, especially in reading, writing, and mathematics. They appear to be inherited, and they affect girls as frequently as boys. Students never outgrow their particular LD, but with support and intervention can be successful in learning and life.

Indicators of LD

At various stages, individuals with average or above-average intelligence may display characteristics that indicate learning disabilities. Indicators of LD include the following:

- Inability to discriminate between/among letters, numerals, or sounds
- Difficulty sounding out words; reluctance to read aloud; avoidance of reading and/or writing tasks
- Poor grasp of abstract concepts; poor memory; difficulty telling time
- Confusion between right and left
- Distractibility, restlessness, impulsiveness; trouble following directions
- Saying one thing but meaning another; responding inappropriately
- Slow work pace; short attention span; difficulty listening and remembering
- Eye–hand coordination problems; poor organizational skills (National Council for Learning Disabilities, 2005)

Specialized psychological and academic testing is needed to confirm diagnoses of LD. The law requires that the diagnosis be made by a multidisciplinary group, including the teacher, student, other school staff, family members, and professionals such as psychologists, reading clinicians, and speech and language therapists. Based on their assessment and on the availability of resources, special services may be provided to the student at school.

About Dyslexia

Dyslexia is the most widespread and commonly recognized of all learning disabilities, affecting over 40 million U.S. children and adults (Dolphin Education,

2006). It is characterized by difficulties in word recognition, spelling, word decoding, and occasionally with the phonological (sound) component of language. From a young age, students with dyslexia show deficits in coordination, attention, and reading, which often damage their self-concept and sense of competence. The other cognitive faculties in people with dyslexia are believed to function properly.

The cause and effects of dyslexia are of much interest to doctors and research scientists. Harold Levinson (2000), a psychiatrist and neurologist, concluded in the late 1960s that dyslexia is due to a signal-scrambling disturbance involving the inner ear and the cerebellum. Levinson reports that the inner ear/cerebellum interaction can also promote attention deficits, fears, phobias, and panic. Levinson's examinations of thousands of students with reading disabilities showed that while none of the students showed evidence of a brain or linguistic impairment, over 95 percent had clear-cut balance, coordination, and rhythmic difficulties that are indicators of an inner ear/cerebellar dysfunction. Levinson hypothesized that the inner ear acts as a "fine-tuner" to the brain. The degree of dyslexia is dependent on (1) the number of inner-ear circuits that are not working properly, (2) the degree of signal scrambling, and (3) the ability of normal cerebral processors to descramble or otherwise compensate for scrambled signals. Levinson points out that many people with dyslexia are very high achievers, as exemplified by Albert Einstein, Thomas Edison, and Winston Churchill. Sally Shaywitz and Bennett Shaywitz (2003) also helped establish the neurological basis for the disorder.

Scenario 3

The class had just finished a discussion of a chapter in the book they were reading. Justin actively participated in the discussion, making correct and well-thought-out responses. Mr. Gatta, the teacher, then instructed the class to complete a chapter summary sheet at their desks. Justin needed to be told a second time to get started. Justin put his feet up on his desk and began to belch loudly. The students laughed. Mr. Gatta asked Justin to stop belching and take his feet off his desk, whereupon Justin put his feet down and wrapped his legs around the legs of his desk. He then leaned back and made himself fall backwards, pulling his desk on top of him. When Mr. Gatta came to help disentangle Justin from the furniture, Justin grabbed the desk, wrapped his legs tighter around it, squealed loudly, and laughed uncontrollably.

Commentary: Justin shows great reluctance to write down answers, even though he can say them correctly. His behavior may be linked to a learning disability, and there may also be other intricate neural issues involved. What do you think Mr. Gatta might do to help Justin behave more normally and enjoy greater success in school?

AUTISM SPECTRUM DISORDER (ASD)

Autism spectrum disorder (ASD) includes various diagnoses of abnormal development in verbal and nonverbal communication, along with impaired social development and restricted, repetitive, and stereotyped behaviors and interests (Faraone, 2003). It also includes pervasive developmental disorder (delays in the development of socialization and communication skills) and Asperger syndrome (a pattern of behavior among students of normal intelligence and language development who also exhibit autistic-like behaviors and marked deficiencies in social and communication skills). Approximately one in every 150 children is diagnosed with autism. It occurs in every ethnic and socio-economic group and affects four times as many males as females. Students with ASD may show extreme hyperactivity or extreme passivity in relating to people around them. In its milder form, autism resembles a learning disability. Indicators of ASD include the following:

- Self-stimulation, spinning, rocking, and hand flapping
- Obsessive compulsive behaviors such as lining objects up evenly
- Repetitive odd play for extended periods of time
- Insistence on routine and sameness
- Difficulty dealing with interruption of routine schedule and change
- Monotone voice and difficulty carrying on social conversations
- Inflexibility of thought and language (e.g., one student with autism refused to wear his winter jacket during subzero weather in early December because he had learned winter did not officially begin until December 21)

Manifestations of autism vary enormously in severity. Sensory integration dysfunction is also common in students with ASD, and sensory overload can lead to behavior problems in school. Modifying the physical environment can do much to improve behavior and academic achievement of students with ASD.

Some people with autism never develop language and need full-time care around the clock, whereas others become fully functioning, independent members of society, as exemplified by Temple Grandin, perhaps the world's most accomplished and well-known adult with autism. Dr. Grandin has appeared on major television programs such as the *Today Show, Larry King Live, 48 Hours,* and *20/20,* and has been featured in publications such as *Time, People, Forbes, U.S. News and World Report,* and the *New York Times* (see www.templegrandin.org).

Scenario 4

Tay is extremely noisy. Even during quiet work time, she taps, hums, or makes other noises. When the teacher asks her to stop, she denies doing anything. She talks very loudly. When classmates ask her to be quiet, she ignores them. Tay wears three pairs of socks all the time and adjusts the cuffs on each pair a number of times a day. She cannot settle down and focus until her socks are just right. She will not change shoes for gym class. When the gym teacher tried to make her do so, Tay swore at her and ran out of the gym and away from school, crying hysterically. When dashing across the street, Tay ran into the side of a parked car, then fell to the road and sobbed until a teacher came to get her.

Commentary from Tay's Teacher: Tay is diagnosed with ASD with extreme SID. Outside noise bothers her greatly, so she makes her own noise to drown it out. It is speculated that she wears the three pairs of socks to put extra pressure on her feet, which would be an indicator of SID, as is her continual cuff adjustment. Things that have been done to help her benefit more from school include (a) providing ear covers to block outside noise, (b) using a portable radio/CD player with headphones to drown out other noise, (c) giving her gum or mints to help keep her mouth quiet, (d) over-looking her sock rituals, which are not a major issue, and (e) compromising by allowing Tay to decide whether she will change shoes for gym class or move to an alternate activity arranged for her, which includes instruction in social skills in her individualized education program.

FETAL ALCOHOL SPECTRUM DISORDER (FASD)

FASD is a group of neurobehavioral and developmental abnormalities that includes fetal alcohol syndrome (FAS), alcohol related neurodevelopmental disorder (ARND), and partial fetal alcohol syndrome (pFAS). The spectrum affects about 1 percent of the population in the United States (Clark, Lutke, Minnes, and Ouellette-Kuntz, 2004). The disorder results from the fetus being exposed to alcohol from the mother's blood. Ingestion of even small amounts of alcohol by the mother, as little as one ounce per week, has been linked to ADHD and delinquent and aggressive behavior in the child. The Centers for Disease Control and Prevention contend that no level of alcohol consumption during pregnancy is considered to be safe (CDC, 2004). It is now accepted that women who drink during pregnancy, even in the earliest stages, are at risk of having a child with fetal alcohol spectrum disorder.

The symptoms and characteristics of FASD appear in a variety of combinations, with the overall condition ranging in severity from mild to extreme. Individuals with FASD can exhibit any combination of the behaviors in any degree of severity (American Academy of Pediatrics, 2004). Two people with the same diagnosis can behave differently from each other and can have different levels of skills.

Alcohol is the most toxic and damaging substance to which unborn children are normally exposed, and it is the leading cause of mental retardation in the Western world (Institute of Medicine, 1996). Even so, most individuals with FAS and other diagnoses on the FASD continuum have normal intelligence (Streissguth, Barr, Kogan, and Bookstein, 1997). At the same time, many have compromised adaptive and social skills, including poor impulse control, poor judgment, tendency to miss social cues, lack of common sense, learning difficulties, and difficulty with the tasks of daily living. ADHD is usually co-morbid with FASD, and behavior difficulties are a main issue for students with FASD (Kellerman, 2003).

Scenario 5

Sam, age 10, never sits still in class. He is always talking and calling out answers in class even though they are usually wrong. Yesterday he pushed a classmate when they were coming in from recess. The teacher spoke to him, reminded him of the rules, and told him he could not go out for recess that afternoon. This morning, Sam was reminded to keep his hands to himself or he would lose recess again. Sam repeated word for word what he was told: "I will keep my hands to myself and if I don't I won't be able to go out for recess this afternoon." Fifteen minutes later Sam pushed Jonathan. When the teacher spoke to him, Sam claimed he didn't do anything and it wasn't his fault.

Commentary: Sam has been diagnosed with fetal alcohol spectrum disorder and ADHD. His repeating back the words and consequences indicates language-processing difficulties common to FASD. Like other students with the condition, he reacts automatically to situations without always remembering what he did. Calling out and inability to sit still indicate ADHD.

THE RAGE CYCLE

Rage is not a type of neurological disorder, but rather an extreme kind of behavior sometimes exhibited by students with NBB. It is manifested as an explosion of temper that occurs suddenly, with no real warning, and may turn violent (Packer, 2005). The process is traumatic for everyone and should be understood as a neurological event that leads to behavior over which the student has little control. Rage differs from tantrums, which are goal-directed with the purpose of getting something or getting somebody to do something. Rage is not goal-oriented, but rather a release of built-up tension or frustration. (Tantrums sometimes evolve into rage.) Once a rage episode has begun, there is little one can do to stop it. It may only last for a few minutes, or may continue for hours. While it usually has to run its course, it can be softened and controlled somewhat by teachers and other adults.

The **rage cycle** proceeds through five phases, identified as pre-rage, triggering, escalation, rage, and post-rage. These phases, their characteristics, and how you can help in each of them are described in the paragraphs that follow (Greene, 2001; Echternach and Cook, 2004; Cook, 2005; Hill, 2005; Packer, 2005).

Phase 1. Pre-Rage.   This is the time just before something triggers the rage event and sets it in motion.

Phase 2. Triggering.   Triggers are precipitating events that provoke episodes of rage, apparently by stimulating neurochemical changes in the brain that greatly heighten the fight/flight/freeze reactions (self-protective responses). Triggering conditions seem to be associated frequently with work transitions, sensory overload, being told "No," fatigue, frustration, confusion, hunger, central nervous system executive dysfunction, anxiety, and mood swings. For children with ADHD, triggers tend to be related to sensory and/or emotional overstimulation. For children with bipolar disorder, triggers are often related to having limits set on their behavior (Papolos and Papolos, 2002). In the triggering phase students may appear angry, confused, frustrated, dazed, tense, or flushed, and they may swear and use other rude language.

What You Can Do to Help during This Phase of the Rage Cycle

- Recognize that a rage episode may be forthcoming and you may not be able to prevent it.
- Understand that this is a neurological event. The student's flight/fight/freeze responses are strongly activated.
- Understand that the rage is not intentional or personal toward you.
- Stay calm. Use a quiet tone of voice. Do not become adversarial.
- Use short, direct phrases and non-emotional language.
- Do not question, scold, or become verbose.
- Use nonthreatening body language. Stand on an angle off-center to the student, at least a long stride away. Make sure the student can see your hands.
- Use empathetic verbal support ("It sounds like you're upset." "That would upset me too.").
- Deflect control elsewhere ("The clock says it's time to clean up," "The big rule book in the office says . . .").
- Calmly, quietly, and succinctly use logical persuasion to provide the student an alternative behavior.

Phase 3: Escalation.   Following the triggering, the rage may escalate mildly or rapidly. In *mild escalations,* the student may begin to get angry; call names; swear; exhibit startled verbal or physical responses; talk rapidly; increase the volume and cadence of speech; and show tension in arms, hands, and body. *Rapid escalations* are characterized by violent temper, hostility, aggressive comments ("Leave me alone," "I'm going to kill you"), profanity, flushed face, and clammy body. The student may show fists and throw objects or furniture.

What You Can Do to Help during This Phase of the Rage Cycle

- Stay calm.
- Ensure the safety of others by clearing them from the room or supporting them to ignore the escalation.
- If the student threatens you, walk away.
- Calmly direct the student to a safe place (e.g., Quiet Room or designated area) to allow the energy to dissipate.
- When speaking to the student, use short, direct phrases and non-emotional language.
- Use body language that is nonthreatening and nonconfrontational.
- Use supportive empathy to acknowledge the student's feelings.
- Calmly, quietly, and succinctly use logical persuasion to provide the student an alternative.

- Praise the student as soon as he or she begins to respond to your direction.
- Do not address the student's inappropriate language, threats, or other behavior at this time. The student cannot process the information and may only become further inflamed.

Phase 4: Rage or Meltdown.   Here, the student is caught up in the rage.

What You Can Do to Help during This Phase of the Rage Cycle
- Allow the student space to go through the physical manifestations.
- Do not restrain the student unless there is an immediate threat to physical safety.
- Do not question, make sarcastic comments, or try to talk the student out of the rage.
- Do not try to make the student understand instructions.
- While the student is going through the cycle of reactions, support others in the room and help ensure that their interpretations of the rage event are correct.

Phase 5: Post-Rage or Post-Meltdown.   After a rage event, the student may or may not remember the behavior or the triggering causes. This is a low point for the student because he or she has expended a great amount of energy and is left confused and often embarrassed. The student will now be tired, passive, headachy, and sometimes remorseful and apologetic. He or she may need sleep or may be able to continue the day.

What You Can Do to Help during This Phase of the Rage Cycle
- Reassure the student that he or she is all right now.
- When the student is ready, help him or her put language to the event.
- Help him or her plan what to do the next time a rage occurs—such as finding a sensory-friendly refuge (a safe place or room in which to rage), using words to get what they need, and remaining in a safe place until able to calm down.
- After the rage event and when the student is calm, take care of yourself. Relax, drink water, and remind yourself that it was not personal and that you did the best you could. Meanwhile, document your observations, hold debriefing conversations with a colleague, and listen to reflections made by anyone involved. Note any evident triggers, sensory influences, or other environmental characteristics that may be associated with the rage. It is perfectly acceptable for you *not* to talk during the rage, but just be there with the student, without crowding.

Scenario 6

Calley is noncompliant, argumentative, and loud. He often tries to slap, bite, and scratch teachers and classmates. He makes personal threats and has defaced desks and walls. He often prints f--- on papers, desks, and walls. His profanity distances him from others in the class. At the same time, he is vulnerable because his aggressive profanity sometimes brings reprisals from other students.

Calley is also a danger to himself. When angry, he chews on things such as pencils, paper, erasers, math manipulatives, and his clothing. He usually spits the material out, but sometimes swallows it. One of his disturbing traits is tying himself up when distressed. Once, he tied his wrists together with his shoelaces while in the Quiet Room. The next time he was sent to the Quiet Room, he had to remove his shoes, but Calley used his socks to tie his wrists together. A few days after that, he tore up his t-shirt, knotted it into a rope, and again tied himself up. Then he began to scream for the teacher, "Help me, I'm choking! Untie me, you stupid c---! I'm dying, you wh---. Are you going to let me die, you b----?!!"

Commentary from Calley's Teacher: Teaching Calley was a real experience. Something set him off about three days each week. But he really taught me a lot during the two years I worked with him. He was assessed several times and was diagnosed with ADHD, SID, language processing disorder, and severe academic delay. The poor boy was terribly frustrated, and as you can imagine, his behavior very much got in the way of his academic progress.

MEDICATION FOR STUDENTS WITH BEHAVIORAL ISSUES

The U.S. National Institute of Mental Health (2006) reports that most childhood mental health problems are treatable with medication. However, because medication is controversial, the decision as to whether to use it is ultimately made by the parents. If the parents give approval for medication at school, established policies stipulate where the medicine must be stored, who is responsible for administering it, and what teachers and other educators are allowed to say about it. Teachers should learn about medication policies at their school and their attendant responsibilities.

Monitoring the effects of medication is usually a shared responsibility among parents, school, and the medical practitioner, with school personnel asked to watch for any unusual behavior or symptoms during the school day. If teachers are asked to give reports of how the child behaved, they are to state them in the following manner: "During the math lesson, Jason got up five times without permission. On one occasion he berated another student." Teachers should not make emotionally charged commentary such as, "Jason was badly out of control and seriously disrupted the class with his antics." In other words, teachers should make sure they avoid vocabulary that reflects their own emotional reactions to the student's behavior.

CONCLUDING REMARKS

When working with students with NBB it important to be as proactive as possible in ensuring student success. Strategies for this purpose include the following:

■ Establish a positive and nurturing rapport with the students. Warmly greet them when they arrive at class. Show interest and talk about pop culture or something they are interested in.

- Modify the classroom to make it sensory friendly. Sit in the student's seat and look at the room from the student's perspective. See if there are things that might be distracting or annoying. It is far more productive to change the classroom than try to change the student.
- Add structure to time periods that are ordinarily unstructured, such as recess and free time. Students with NBB often have difficulty with unstructured time.
- Use and teach humor, which is effective with all students.
- Be careful of eye contact. It can stimulate upper-cortex activity, which is good for academic thinking, but can at times trigger episodes of misbehavior because eye contact combined with a stern tone of voice is often interpreted as a threat.
- Be careful how you react to situations. If you raise your voice, students with NBB will often raise their voices in return.
- When giving students a choice, provide two alternatives you can live with and let the students select the one they prefer.

A positive teacher attitude can greatly improve the quality of service provided to students with NBB and their families. Students experiencing difficulties in neurological processing are human beings first and foremost, who badly need help. They are not predestined to fail. They have many qualities and strengths that can be nurtured and built on as they develop life competencies. One of our most valuable strategies is to use a strengths perspective rooted in the here and now that is solution oriented and devoted to practical outcomes. All small improvements by students with NBB should be celebrated as important steps to a better quality of life, now and in the future.

Scenario 7

Abraham, a 10-year-old student with severe behavior issues, was brought back from gym class. An educational assistant had Abraham by his wrist, escorting him to a private area in the back of the classroom as Abraham loudly spewed a tirade of profanities and death threats. To ensure everyone's safety, we used the "separate and supervise" strategy to isolate Abraham from his peers. He was put in a back room off the side of the classroom where he continued to scream profanities and threats. As the other staff members helped the other students carry on the daily classroom routine, I walked towards the back area of the room where a staff member stood in front of the closed door. Abraham had a history of running away. I opened the door just a fraction and saw Abraham standing with a chair over his head in a threatening pose.

I quietly called in, "You sound angry at me, Abraham." I was deliberately trying to deflect and divert his attention to me in an attempt to engage another part of his brain.

Abraham shrieked, "I'm not f---ing angry at you, I'm angry at Billy!"

"Excellent, Abraham! You put other words to this, way to go!" I said this in an encouraging, sincere, but soft tone. "Why are you angry at Billy?"

Abraham was still shouting and still had the chair over his head. "Because Conrad is my friend!" he screamed.

"Oh, I'm glad Conrad is your friend, but what does Billy have to do with this?" I gently put my index finger to my lips in a shh-ing motion.

"Billy told Conrad to f--- off, and that's not nice," Abraham replied indigently, at a lower volume but still with the chair over his head.

"Great, Abraham, you put words to this! Hey, Abraham, let's add other words to this so you can respectfully tell Billy why you're upset. Billy doesn't even know you are mad at him, and he and Conrad are already eating lunch together. Put the chair down so I can come in."

"NOOOOO!" Abraham screamed. "You'll try to put me in the Quiet Room if I put the chair down."

I answered quietly, "Abraham, as long as you are safe, I'm safe, and the class is safe, you don't need to go to the Quiet Room. Put the chair down so we can plan to get out of here."

Abraham put the chair down, but removed the detachable plastic seat, holding it ready to strike anyone who came close.

"Great, Abraham, you put down the chair, good for you! Now let me help you fix the chair where the seat has come off." I slowly approached from his left, walking on an angle and off-center from him, so he could see me coming and not be startled by any sudden movements I made. I positioned myself between the chair and Abraham, with him on the inside of the room, and myself near the door. Although the screaming had subsided, I was still concerned about my safety. Together, we snapped the seat back on the chair and Abraham quickly sat down. "Thanks, Abraham," I said. "I always have trouble getting those blasted seats back on those chairs."

Abraham was now calm. He had been able to articulate why he was upset without using profanity, and he found a way to let Billy know he was upset and tell Conrad that he was his friend. Within four minutes, Abraham had "fixed things up," made amends, and was with his peers having lunch. Success! It does happen.

Terms and Concepts

affective disorders
anxiety disorders
attention-deficit hyperactivity disorder
autism spectrum disorder
behavior difficulties
bipolar disorder
brain injuries

conduct disorder
dyslexia
fetal alcohol spectrum disorder
learning disabilities (LD)
neurological-based behavior (NBB)
neurological differences
oppositional defiant disorder
post-traumatic stress disorder

rage
rage cycle
sensory integration dysfunction (SID)
sensory processing disorder

Activities

1. In your journal, make entries from this chapter that you might wish to incorporate into the system of discipline you will create.
2. With one or more classmates or fellow teachers, go back to Scenario 1 at the beginning of the chapter. Discuss how you might help Tyler move past his inappropriate behavior. The commentary from Tay's teacher in Scenario 4 might help you organize your thoughts. Share your conclusions with peers.
3. Individually or in collaboration with others, select Scenario 4, 5, or 6. With a partner, discuss what you might do to minimize the disruptive behavior of the student involved and otherwise improve the overall situation.

References

Amen, D. 2001. *Healing ADD: The breakthrough program that allows you to see and heal the six types of attention deficit disorder.* New York: G.P. Putnam's Sons.

American Academy of Child and Adolescent Psychiatry. 2004a. Child psychiatry facts for families: recommendations, help and guidance from the AACAP. http://pediatrics.about.com/library/bl_psych_policy_statements.htm

American Academy of Child and Adolescent Psychiatry. 2004b. Children with oppositional defiant disorder. www.aacap.org/publications/factsfam/72.htm

American Academy of Child and Adolescent Psychiatry. 2004c. Bipolar disorder in children and teens. www.aacap.org/publications/factsfam/72.htm

American Academy of Child and Adolescent Psychiatry. 2008. Teen suicide. www.aacap.org/publications/factsfam/suicide.htm

American Academy of Pediatrics. 2004. Fetal alcohol syndrome. www.aap.org/advocacy/chm98fet.htm

Brain Injury Society. 2006. *1998 newsletter.* Fall Issue. http://biac-aclc.ca/en

CDC. 2004. Alcohol consumption among women who are pregnant or who might become pregnant—United States, 2002. Centers for Disease Control and Prevention. www.acbr.com/fas

Clark, E., Lutke, J., Minnes, P., and Ouellette-Kuntz. 2004. Secondary disabilities among adults with fetal alcohol spectrum disorder in British Columbia. *Journal of FAS International, 2,* 1–12.

Cook, P. 2004a. *Behaviour, learning and teaching: Applied studies in FAS/FAE.* (Distance Education Curricula). Winnipeg, Canada: Red River College.

Cook, P. 2004b. *Sensory integration dysfunction: A layperson's guide.* Booklet available from Paula Cook. Internet contact: pcook59@shaw.ca

Cook, P. 2005. *Rage: A layperson's guide to what to do when someone begins to rage.* Booklet available from Paula Cook. Internet contact: pcook59@shaw.ca

Cook, P., Kellie, R., Jones, K., and Goossen, L. 2000. *Tough kids and substance abuse.* Winnipeg, Canada: Addictions Foundation of Manitoba.

Davidson, H. 2002. *Just ask! A handbook for instructors of students being treated for mental disorders.* (2nd ed.). Calgary, Canada: Detselig Enterprises.

DeAngelis, T. 2004. Children's mental health problems seen as "epidemic." *APA Monitor on Psychology, 35* (11), 38.

Dolphin Education. 2006. Dyslexia research: 4. The incidence of dyslexia. www.dolphinuk.co.uk/education/case_studies/dyslexia_research.htm

Echternach, C., and Cook, P. 2004. *The rage cycle.* Paper available from Paula Cook. Email pcook59@shaw.ca

Faraone, S. 2003. *Straight talk about your child's mental health.* New York: Guilford Press.

Feldman, E. 2004. *Impact of mental illness on learning.* Keynote address at the 9th Midwest Conference on Child and Adolescent Mental Health, Grand Forks, ND.

Gardner, H. 1999. *Intelligence reframed: Multiple intelligences for the 21st century.* New York: Basic Books.

Greene, R. 2001. *The explosive child.* New York: HarperCollins.

Hall, P., and Hall, N. 2003. *Educating oppositional and defiant children.* Alexandria, VA: Association for Supervision and Curriculum Development.

Hill, P. 2005. Pharmacological treatment of rage. www.focusproject.org.uk/SITE/UPLOAD/DOCUMENT/Hill

Institute of Medicine. 1996. Fetal alcohol syndrome: Diagnosis, epidemiology, prevention, and treatment. www.come-over.to/FAS/IOMsummary.htm

Jans, L., Stoddard, S., and Kraus, L. 2004. *Chatbook on mental health and disability in the United States.* An InfoUse report. Washington, DC: U.S. Department of Education, National Institute on Disability and Rehabilitation Research.

Kellerman, T. 2003. The FAS community resource center. www.come-over.to/FASCRC

Kranowitz, C. 1998. *The out-of-sync child.* New York: Skylight Press.

Kranowitz, C., Szkut, S., Balzer-Martin, L., Haber, E., and Sava, D. 2003. *Answers to questions teachers ask about sensory integration.* Las Vegas, NV: Sensory Resources LLC.

Learning Disabilities Association of America. 2005. Accommodations, techniques, and aids for teaching. www.ldanatl.org/aboutld/teachers/understanding/accommodations.asp

Levinson, H. 2000. *The discovery of cerebellar-vestibular syndromes and therapies: A solution to the riddle—dyslexia* (2nd ed.). Lake Success, NY: Stonebridge Publishing.

National Council for Learning Disabilities. 2005. The ABCs of learning disabilities. www.ncld.org

National Institute of Mental Health. 2005. Health information quick links. www.nimh.nih.gov

National Institute of Mental Health. 2006. Medications. www.nimh.nih.gov/publicat/medicate.cfm#ptdep1

National Institute of Mental Health. 2008. Health information quick links. www.nimh.nih.gov

Packer, L. 2005. Overview of rage attacks. www.tourettesyndrome.net/rage_overview.htm

Papolos, D., and Papolos, J. 2002. *The bipolar child.* New York: Broadway Books.

Shaywitz, S., and Shaywitz, B. 2003. Drs. Sally and Bennett Shaywitz on brain research and reading. www.schwablearning.org/Articles.asp?r=35

Streissguth, A., Barr, H., Kogan, J., and Bookstein, F. 1997. Primary and secondary disabilities in fetal alcohol syndrome. In A. Streissguth and J. Kanter (Eds.), *The challenge of fetal alcohol syndrome: Overcoming secondary disabilities* (pp. 23–39). Seattle: University of Washington Press.

4

What Are the Foundations That Underlie Today's Best Systems of Discipline?

Prior to the 1950s, discipline was thought of as punitive actions teachers took to stifle student misbehavior. It was taken for granted that students knew how to behave properly, and to ensure they did, teachers applied unpleasant consequences to get students back on track when they misbehaved. The community expected teachers to do so, and students were well aware of it. Detention and the paddle were much in evidence into the 1940s.

However, that picture began to change around the middle of the twentieth century. By the end of World War II, newer attitudes toward student behavior and discipline were gaining ground. Society was growing more tolerant of behavior a bit outside the norm, and with that tolerance came an inclination to treat school-aged children more considerately and humanely. Bit by bit corporal punishment and other forceful means of controlling misbehavior fell out of favor.

At the same time, society began asking schools to assume a stronger role in teaching students to be civil, responsible, and self-controlled. The schools took on that challenge, more or less by default, and by the end of the twentieth century, the sternly coercive teacher was gone, replaced by gentler teachers who used "friendly persuasion" to encourage students to behave properly. New skills were needed for this approach, to say the least. This chapter reviews the progressive development of the new management skills that took discipline from where it was in the middle of the twentieth century to where it is today. Within that progression there shine a number of landmark contributions from great thinkers in education, psychology, and psychiatry, each of whom provided one or more powerful ideas that changed the nature of discipline. Nine of those important contributions are described in this chapter. Most of them are still seen in today's most up-to-date systems.

A PREVIEW OF THIS CHAPTER

Since 1950, school discipline has undergone a significant change. Once forceful and authoritarian, it has evolved progressively toward using noncoercive influence techniques that help students develop self-control and accept responsibility. Beginning in 1950 and carrying up to the present, a number of great educational thinkers

61

moved the process forward with new concepts and skills, particularly in the areas of understanding group behavior, shaping behavior, increasing student choice, managing lessons to forestall misbehavior, communicating positively and helpfully, establishing democratic teaching, ensuring the right to teach and the right to learn without disruptions, promoting student self-discipline, and organizing classrooms into democratic communities of learners.

WHAT TO LOOK FOR IN THIS CHAPTER

- Fritz Redl and William Wattenberg's findings concerning group behavior and how it affects individual behavior
- B. F. Skinner's discoveries on how human behavior can be shaped through reinforcement
- William Glasser's conclusions about behavior choices and how we can help students make better choices
- Jacob Kounin's discoveries about the effects of lesson organization on student behavior
- Haim Ginott's conclusions about the most effective ways of communicating with students
- Rudolf Dreikurs's conclusions about democratic teaching and learning
- Lee and Marlene Canter's advice to help teachers take charge in the classroom
- Barbara Coloroso's advice on helping students develop self-control and a sense of responsibility
- Alfie Kohn's contentions about the value of forming classes into communities of learners

UNDERSTANDING GROUP DYNAMICS: FRITZ REDL AND WILLIAM WATTENBERG

In 1951 Fritz Redl and William Wattenberg disseminated the first theory-based approach to humane classroom discipline. It focused on helping teachers understand how **group behavior** affects individual behavior. They contended that much student misbehavior is caused by forces detectable in larger groups. Their ideas opened educators' minds to new ways of dealing with misbehavior and set in motion the progressive changes that have resulted in what we now call "modern discipline."

Redl, a psychiatrist, and Wattenberg, an educational psychologist, believed that if teachers are to understand and deal effectively with individual behavior, they must first understand forces that are generated within groups. They called these forces **group dynamics.** Their work introduced many concepts that were new to educators, such as that people in groups behave differently than when by themselves and that we can learn to predict what students in classrooms *are likely* to do—and *not* do—when in groups and when by themselves. They explained

that group dynamics account for phenomena such as group spirit, group norms and expectations, imitative behavior, desire to excel, scapegoating of certain students, and hiding places for nonachievers.

In any class, they said, students take on various **student roles** such as leader, follower, clown (who shows off), instigator (who provokes misbehavior), and scapegoat (on whom blame is placed even when not deserved). They urged teachers to be watchful for these roles, bring them to the class's attention, be prepared to encourage or discourage them as appropriate, and, when necessary, limit the roles' detrimental effects.

Students also expect and exert pressure on teachers to fill certain **teacher roles,** such as role models, sources of knowledge, referees, judges, and surrogate parents. Teachers need to be aware that students hold these expectations and should discuss their implications with students.

Redl and Wattenberg further urged teachers to behave toward students in a helpful manner, remain as objective as possible, show tolerance, keep a sense of humor, and help students maintain positive attitudes toward school and the class. All these things, they said, can be thought of as **influence techniques,** to be used instead of **punishment** to control student behavior. Positive influence techniques include **supporting self-control,** offering **situational assistance,** and **appraising reality** (where teachers help students become aware of underlying causes of desirable and undesirable behavior). One of Redl and Wattenberg's suggestions that did not appear widely in practice until many years later was to involve students in setting class standards and deciding how transgressions should be handled, a participatory approach that is featured in most of today's systems of discipline.

Finally, Redl and Wattenberg advised teachers to identify the causes of student misbehavior, believing that by attending to causes teachers could eliminate most misbehavior. They pointed out the detrimental effects of punishment and explained why it should not be used in class discipline.

Despite Redl and Wattenberg's remarkable contributions, teachers never adopted their approach enthusiastically. Teachers found the new ideas interesting, persuasive, and in many ways helpful, but all in all they found the approach overly complicated and cumbersome—or perhaps just too new and different.

PRINCIPLES OF BEHAVIOR SHAPING: B. F. SKINNER

Even before Redl and Wattenberg published their conclusions about group dynamics, Harvard behavioral psychologist Burrhus Frederic Skinner (1904–1990) was investigating how our voluntary actions are influenced by what happens to us immediately after we perform a given act. Skinner never concerned himself directly with classroom discipline, but in the early 1960s his followers used his ideas to develop **behavior modification,** which was widely used to speed and strengthen learning and help students change their behavior for the better. Principles of behavior modification are still widely used in teaching, child rearing, and improving human relations.

Skinner's conclusions were reported in a number of publications, two of which were his book *Science and Human Behavior* (1953) and his article "The Science of Learning and the Art of Teaching" (1954). His findings convinced him that much if

not most of our voluntary behavior is shaped by reinforcement (or lack thereof), which we receive immediately after performing an act. For purposes here, reinforcement can be thought of as reward, although *reward* is a term Skinner never used. Simply put, when we perform an act and are rewarded (reinforced) for doing so, we become more likely to repeat that act and even try harder in the future.

Instead of *reward*, Skinner used the term **reinforcing stimulus.** He learned that a stimulus (something the individual receives) affects a particular behavior only if it is received very soon after that behavior occurs. Reinforcing stimuli that are now commonly used in the classroom include knowledge of results; peer approval; awards; free time; and smiles, nods, and praise from the teacher. In years past, teachers used rewards such as candy, popcorn, and tangible objects, but that practice died out quickly once teachers learned that students worked mainly to get the reward, with unsatisfactory residual learning once the rewards were removed.

Behavior modification (also a term Skinner never used) is widely used today to shape student behavior in desirable directions through systematic **reinforcement.** The way in which reinforcement is provided affects subsequent behavior. *Constant reinforcement*, given every time a student behaves as desired, helps new learning become established. The teacher might praise Juan every time he raises his hand, or privately compliment Marieta every time she turns in required homework. *Intermittent reinforcement*, given occasionally, is sufficient to maintain desired behavior once it has become established. After students have learned to come into the room and immediately begin work, the teacher will only occasionally need to express appreciation. Behaviors that are not reinforced eventually disappear. If Robert raises his hand in class but is never called on, he will eventually stop raising his hand. **Shaping behavior** is done through **successive approximation,** in which behavior comes closer and closer to a pre-set goal. This process is helpful in building skills incrementally. Skinner did not advocate using punishment in shaping behavior, as he considered its effects unreliable.

Although Skinner did not concern himself with classroom discipline per se, his discoveries affected it strongly. In the 1960s, many primary grade teachers used behavior modification as their entire discipline system, rewarding students who behaved properly and ignoring those who misbehaved. But before many years had passed, teachers had abandoned behavior modification as a primary approach to discipline. Some felt it was little more than bribing students to behave acceptably. Others found it overly cumbersome and inefficient in teaching students what *not* to do—it quickly became evident that it was far easier just to teach students how they *should* and *shouldn't* behave. Unlike laboratory animals, humans do not have to learn those things through lengthy processes involving the application and withholding of reinforcing stimuli.

That said, it is nevertheless true that although teachers do not use reinforcement as an overarching approach to discipline, they still make extensive use of rewards such as praise and approval to motivate and support students. All in all, Skinner's great contribution to discipline was to establish scientifically that people will engage in and learn from activities that bring them pleasure.

BEHAVIOR AS CHOICE: WILLIAM GLASSER

 William Glasser is unique among authorities featured in this book in that he was both a pioneer in the earlier movement toward modern discipline and, later, the contributor of an exemplary approach to modern classroom discipline. Here we note only his early contributions. Later, in Chapter 8, his modern approach to discipline is discussed in detail. Glasser gained instant notoriety in discipline in 1969, with the publication of his extremely influential book, *Schools without Failure*. That was his second major book in only four years and was later acclaimed as one of most influential education books of the twentieth century. Glasser's name was already widely known because of his 1965 book, *Reality Therapy: A New Approach to Psychiatry*, in which he urged psychotherapists to move their main focus *away* from probing into what happened to troubled individuals in the past (the classical approach) and *toward* helping individuals learn to resolve their problems within the context of present reality. Glasser had been counseling delinquent adolescents and found that reality therapy worked especially well with them. That experience launched a long career of writing about education, speaking with educators, and working to apply his ideas in schools.

Before it influenced classroom practice, reality therapy gained acceptance in the field of psychiatry and became widely used. In Glasser's mind, a great number of our personal problems can be traced to unsatisfactory or nonexistent connections with people on whom we depend. Reality therapy provided a means for troubled people to connect or reconnect with others important in their lives. Very briefly, the guidelines for using the principles of reality therapy are as follows:

- *Focus on the present.* Avoid discussing the past. Don't discuss symptoms or complain. Talk about possible thoughts and actions within present-time reality—that is, what one might do here and now to resolve the problem.
- *Stay away from criticizing and blaming.* These are harmful external control behaviors that destroy relationships.
- *Remain nonjudgmental and noncoercive.* Emphasize the value of appraising everything one does in terms of the results. If actions are not providing desirable results, the old behaviors are not working. New ones are needed.
- *Don't get bogged down in excuses.* Whether legitimate or not, excuses stand directly in the way of making the needed connections with others.
- *Work toward specific workable plans for reconnecting with people as needed.* Follow through on plans and evaluate results and efforts. Plans are always open to rejection or revision.
- *Show patience and support for the troubled individual, but keep focusing on addressing the source of the problem—the disconnectedness.* Whatever the difficulty might be, reconnecting is the best possible solution to the problem (The William Glasser Institute, 2009).

Although reality therapy was quickly embraced in the counseling community, classroom teachers took relatively little notice of it until Glasser's book, *Schools without Failure*, appeared in 1969 and showed how the principles of reality therapy could be used to advantage in everyday interactions with students. In addition, he introduced three new ideas that gained educators' immediate attention:

· **1.** *Failure* is one of the most disheartening things that can happen to students in school. Because it so badly damages students' motivation to persevere, it should be abolished, and curriculum changes and teacher support should be put into effect that enable all students to experience a degree of success in school.

· **2.** Students *choose* to behave as they do. No one makes them misbehave and no one can force them to learn. Teachers should view **behavior as choice** and influence students to make better choices in how they behave, thus leading to success in school.

· **3.** Behavior tends to improve when students are asked to participate in reflecting on difficulties in the classroom and taking steps to resolve them. Glasser proposed *classroom meetings* as the vehicle for involving students meaningfully. He described in detail how to organize and conduct classroom meetings and urged teachers to make them a regular part of the curriculum.

These three contributions had a major impact on teaching and discipline. They came at a time when people were beginning to question the overall value of Skinnerian reinforcement theory. Advocates of behavior modification through reinforcement were insisting that teachers worth their salt could use the procedure to control student behavior, and if they failed to do so, the misbehavior was their fault, not the students'. This view was seriously off-putting to teachers whose experience taught them that behavior modification was of little value in stopping misbehavior.

Glasser's approach to discipline emphasized rules students were to follow, combined with consequences for breaking them. Students, not teachers or administrators, were to assume responsibility for proper behavior. When students misbehaved, they were asked in a friendly tone to state what they had done and to evaluate the effect their actions had on the student, classmates, and teacher. Students were further asked to identify and commit themselves to subsequent behavior that would be more appropriate.

Glasser acknowledged that the process he advocated was somewhat tedious. But he insisted that students who saw themselves as failures would only improve if they had ongoing supportive involvement with successful people, such as teachers, who provided positive influence and accepted no excuses for improper behavior.

Teachers were enthusiastic about many of Glasser's earlier teachings. However, they found putting them into practice was overly labor intensive. Most teachers wove bits and pieces of Glasser's approach into their teaching, but few managed successfully to implement his approach fully. Later in Chapter 8 we will see Glasser's subsequent contributions that continue to have profound influence on teaching and discipline today.

LESSON MANAGEMENT: JACOB KOUNIN

In the late 1960s, Jacob Kounin, an educational psychologist at Wayne State University, conducted studies attempting to pinpoint what outstanding teachers said or did when students misbehaved that led to good classroom discipline. As reported

in his 1971 book, *Discipline and Group Management in Classrooms,* he had tried to identify the effects of specific things teachers did *in response* to student misbehavior, but his data revealed nothing along those lines. Still, it was evident that some teachers were able to maintain excellent class behavior while others were not. Kounin analyzed his data again and made a surprising finding—that good discipline was not so much dependent on what teachers did when misbehavior occurred, but on how they presented lessons and dealt with various groups in the class.

Specifically, Kounin found that teachers of well-behaved classes displayed a constant awareness of what all students were doing in the classroom. He used the term **withitness** in referring to their degree of awareness. He found that teachers with higher levels of withitness were able to monitor and interact with groups of students doing independent work even while teaching lessons to smaller groups. He called the act of attending to two or more classroom events simultaneously **overlapping** and considered it one of the most important teacher capabilities.

Kounin also saw that the more effective teachers managed their lessons in ways that kept students alert, on task, and involved. He found that good teachers used identifiable procedures for gaining student attention and clarifying expectations. Of particular interest was what he called **group alerting,** in which teachers gain students' full attention before giving directions or making explanations. They then use tactics that keep students actively involved in lessons, maintaining student **accountability** by regularly calling on students to respond, demonstrate, or explain. Yet another important aspect of teaching was maintaining lesson **momentum**—a forward movement, with no confusion or dead spots, that kept students alert and involved. He determined that teachers can maintain momentum by starting lessons with dispatch, keeping a steady pace, making efficient transitions among activities, and bringing lessons to a satisfactory close. In using all these procedures, good teachers demonstrated **smoothness** in their lessons, meaning a steady progression without abrupt changes. In the process, teachers did not overexpose students to a given topic, thus avoiding **satiation,** which was manifested in student boredom, frustration, misbehavior, and disengagement from lessons. Kounin found that satiation can be held at bay for a long time if teachers use activities that students find enjoyable and challenging.

These findings led Kounin to conclude that the most important factors in managing behavior are (1) presenting lessons that students find engaging, (2) managing those lessons to keep students involved and accountable, and (3) keeping track of what is going on in all parts of the classroom at all times and making that fact evident to students. Kounin wrote:

> [These findings] required unlearning on my part, in the sense of having to replace the original question by other questions. Questions about disciplinary techniques were eliminated and replaced by questions about classroom management in general, [and] *preventing* misbehavior was given higher investigative priority than *handling* misbehavior. (p. 143, italics added)

He went on to say:

> The business of running a classroom is a complicated technology having to do with developing a non-satiating learning program; programming for progress, challenge,

and variety in learning activities; initiating and maintaining movement in classroom tasks with smoothness and momentum; coping with more than one event simultaneously; observing and emitting feedback for many different events; directing actions at appropriate targets; maintaining a focus upon a group; and doubtless other techniques not measured in these researches. (1971, pp. 144–145)

The connection Kounin identified between teaching and student behavior led to a new line of thought concerning how teaching style affects student behavior. Although his findings were and still are highly acclaimed, teachers wanted effective tactics for stopping misbehavior quickly. They did not find them in Kounin's work.

? How would you apply Kounin's ideas to the following?

1. Major factors to keep in mind when planning your lessons
2. Your ability to carefully oversee what is occurring in your classroom
3. How, specifically, you will attend to alerting, student accountability, momentum, smoothness, and the threat of satiation

---

CONGRUENT COMMUNICATION: HAIM GINOTT

In the same year that Kounin published his work, another small book appeared that had immediate and lasting influence on teaching. The book was Haim Ginott's *Teacher and Child* (1971), in which Ginott explained the critical role of communication in teaching and discipline, contending that student learning and behavior are greatly influenced by the way teachers talk with students. His explanations of that phenomenon had a powerful effect in establishing the personal, caring tone that prevails in discipline today.

Ginott, a classroom teacher early in his career, later held professorships in psychology at Adelphi University and New York University Graduate School. He also served as UNESCO consultant in Israel, was resident psychologist on the *Today* show, and wrote a weekly syndicated column entitled "Between Us" that dealt with interpersonal communication. In his book *Teacher and Child*, Ginott reminds us that learning always takes place in the "present tense" and is intensely personal to students. Teachers must remain free from prejudgments about students and remember that each learner is an individual who requires much personal attention.

Ginott coined several terms to help convey his messages about the power of communication. He strongly emphasized **congruent communication,** meaning communication that is harmonious with students' feelings about situations and themselves. He used the term *sane messages* to refer to communication that addresses *situations,* rather than the students' character or past behavior. He emphasized that **teachers at their best,** using congruent communication, do not preach, moralize, impose guilt, or demand promises. Instead, they **confer dignity** on their students by treating them as social equals capable of making good decisions. In contrast, **teachers at their worst** label students, belittle them, and denigrate their character.

Effective teachers also **invite cooperation** from their students by describing the situation when a problem occurs and indicating what needs to be done. They

do not dictate to students or boss them around—acts that demean students and provoke resistance. Above all, teachers can rely on a **hidden asset,** which is to ask themselves, "How can I be most helpful to my students right now?" Innumerable classroom difficulties are avoided when teachers make use of that asset.

Ginott said teachers should feel free to express their anger and other feelings, but when doing so should use **I-messages** rather than **you-messages.** Using an I-message, the teacher might say "I am very upset." Using a you-message (usually counterproductive), the teacher might say "You are being very rude." Ginott also suggested using **laconic language**—short and to the point—when responding to or redirecting student misbehavior.

Ginott had a great deal to say about praise as well, and his contentions came as a surprise to most teachers. For example, he insisted that **evaluative praise** is worse than no praise at all and should never be used. An example of evaluative praise is "Good boy for raising your hand." Instead of evaluative praise, which comments on student character, teachers should use **appreciative praise,** which responds to effort or improvement (e.g., "I can almost smell those pine trees in your drawing").

Ginott asked teachers to always respect students' privacy. They should never pry when students do not wish to discuss personal matters, but should show they are available if students want to talk.

With regard to correcting inappropriate behavior, Ginott advised simply teaching students how to behave properly, instead of reprimanding them when they misbehave, and he urged teachers assiduously to avoid asking **why questions** when discussing behavior—for example, "Why did you speak to Susan that way?" or "Why didn't you get your homework done?" Why questions make students feel guilty and defensive.

Ginott also placed sanctions on sarcasm and punishment. Sarcasm is almost always dangerous and should not be used when communicating with students. Punishment should never be used; it only produces rancor and vengefulness, while never making students really want to improve. Teachers should simply send a message that focuses calmly on the *behavior*—not the character—that needs to be corrected.

Finally, Ginott urged teachers to continually strive for **self-discipline** in their work with students. They must be careful not to display the behaviors they are trying to eradicate, such as raising their voice to end noise, acting rude toward students who are impolite, and berating students who use inappropriate language.

Ginott admitted that his suggestions would not produce instantaneous results. They had to be used repeatedly over time for their power to take effect. Ginott said that although misbehavior can be squelched, **genuine discipline** (by which he meant self-discipline) never occurs instantaneously, but rather in a series of small steps that result in genuine changes in student attitude. He summed up his ideas as follows:

As a teacher I have come to the frightening conclusion that I am the decisive element in the classroom. It is my personal approach that creates the climate. It is my daily mood that makes the weather. As a teacher I possess tremendous power to make a child's life miserable or joyous. I can be a tool of torture or an instrument of inspiration. I can humiliate or humor, hurt or heal. In all situations it is my response that decides whether a crisis will be escalated or de-escalated, and a child humanized or dehumanized. (p. 13)

It would be difficult to find a teacher who disagrees with Ginott's views. Indeed, his ideas are reiterated in most of today's popular systems of discipline. True, they will not serve to halt misbehavior abruptly, but over time their effects will be strong and lasting.

> **?** Suppose someone in your class has spilled paint on the classroom carpet or floor. Describe Ginott's responses to the following:
>
> 1. The situation and what needs to be done
> 2. Identifying and correcting the student at fault
> 3. Asking why the spill happened
> 4. Communicating with sane messages and conferring dignity

HUMAN NEEDS AND DEMOCRATIC TEACHING: RUDOLF DREIKURS

In 1972 psychiatrist Rudolf Dreikurs put forth two new ideas in classroom discipline. The first was that all students (indeed, all humans) have an inborn need for **belonging** that functions as a driving force in their lives. He believed that when students are unable to satisfy this prime need—their genuine goal—they turn by default to certain **mistaken goals** they think might help satisfy this need. Those mistaken goals lead students to misbehave by seeking attention, seeking power, seeking revenge, or withdrawing from class activities. Dreikurs's second major contention was that learning occurs best in **democratic classrooms** that promote a sense of belonging and help students acquire self-discipline. He characterized democratic classrooms as those where students participate actively in class decision making and are treated as social equals by their teachers.

Dreikurs (1897–1972) was born in Vienna, Austria. After receiving his medical degree, he entered into a long association with renowned Austrian psychiatrist Alfred Adler. Dreikurs immigrated to the United States in 1937 and became director of the Alfred Adler Institute in Chicago and professor of psychiatry at the Chicago Medical School. His interest in child and family counseling prompted his concern about discipline in families and schools.

As noted, Dreikurs concluded that the **genuine goal of student behavior** is a sense of belonging. Students sense belonging when the teacher and others give them attention and respect, involve them in activities, and do not mistreat them. When students are unable to gain a sense of belonging, they often turn to the mistaken goals he called **attention seeking, power seeking, revenge seeking,** and **displaying inadequacy.** The pursuit of those mistaken goals often involves misbehavior. When seeking attention, students talk out, show off, interrupt others, and demand teacher attention. When seeking power, they drag their heels, make comments under their breath, and sometimes try to show that the teacher can't make them do anything.

When seeking revenge, they try to get back at the teacher and other students by lying, subverting class activities, and maliciously disrupting the class. When displaying inadequacy, they withdraw from class activities and make no effort to learn.

Dreikurs said the best way for teachers to deal with misbehavior is to identify and address the mistaken goal it reflects and discuss with students, in a friendly and nonthreatening manner, the faulty logic those goals involve. Dreikurs suggests calmly asking, "Do you need me to pay more attention to you?" or "Could it be that you want to show that I can't make you do the assignment?"

> **?** Dreikurs's advice concerning addressing mistaken goals never found widespread favor among teachers. Consider the apparent contradictions between Dreikurs's suggestions and those from other authorities:
>
> 1. Is the source of motivation best explained by a "desire to belong," as Dreikurs maintained, or by a cluster of needs and wants, as reviewed in Chapter 2?
> 2. Do you agree with Dreikurs's contention that almost all classroom misbehavior can be thought of as four "mistaken goals" that students pursue when unable to gain a feeling of belonging, or could misbehavior be better understood in terms of a variety of actions students exhibit for many different reasons, as listed in the second half of Chapter 2?

Dreikurs's second main contention had to do with the nature and importance of democratic classrooms and has garnered more enthusiastic support. He stressed that a fundamentally important goal of education is to help students develop self-control, based on **social interest** (the well-being of all students in the class, including oneself). Students gain self-control as they become able to show initiative, make reasonable decisions, and assume responsibility in ways that benefit themselves and others. Social interest is fostered by conditions that improve the school experience for everyone; hence every student has a stake in responsible classroom conduct. Dreikurs said that discipline based on social interest is likely to occur only in democratic classrooms, in which teacher and students work together to make decisions about how the class is to function. Dreikurs contrasted democratic classrooms with autocratic classrooms and permissive classrooms, as follows: In **autocratic classrooms,** the teacher makes all decisions and imposes them on students, doing nothing to help students show personal initiative and accept responsibility. In **permissive classrooms,** the teacher fails to require that students comply with rules, conduct themselves humanely, or deal with the consequences of their misbehavior.

Here are some of the many suggestions Dreikurs offers teachers for promoting democratic classrooms:

- Always speak in positive terms; never be negative.
- Encourage students to strive for improvement, not perfection.
- Emphasize students' strengths while minimizing their weaknesses.
- Help students learn from mistakes, which are valuable elements in the learning process.

- Encourage independence and responsibility.
- Show faith in students; offer them help in overcoming obstacles.
- Encourage students to help each other.
- Show pride in student work; display and share it with others.
- Be optimistic and enthusiastic—a positive outlook is contagious.
- Use encouraging remarks such as, "You have improved." "Can I help you?" "What did you learn from that mistake?" (Dreikurs and Cassel, 1972, pp. 51–54).

This list of suggestions corresponds closely to suggestions made in today's most effective systems of discipline. Dreikurs's lasting contribution has been his championing of democratic classrooms that reflect the qualities of the foregoing list.

ASSERTIVE DISCIPLINE: LEE AND MARLENE CANTER

In 1976, Lee and Marlene Canter, both classroom teachers, published a book entitled *Assertive Discipline: A Take-Charge Approach for Today's Educator*. In that book they introduced a discipline approach called Assertive Discipline, which took the educational world by storm and for the next 20 years was far and away the most popular discipline system in U.S. schools.

The Canters' approach urged teachers to "take charge" in the classroom and showed them how to do so—just what teachers were looking for at a time when a prevailing permissiveness was making teaching ever more difficult. The Canters provided a simple but well-structured plan that enabled teachers to interact with students in a calm, insistent, and consistent manner. The rationale for their plan was that students had a **right to learn** in a calm, orderly classroom, and teachers had a **right to teach** without being interrupted by misbehavior.

Assertive Discipline prompted students to choose to conduct themselves properly, rather than improperly, in school. To ensure they did so, the following were needed:

- A clear set of rules for class behavior.
- Positive consequences such as recognition and praise that were applied when students complied with the rules.
- Negative consequences that were applied when students broke the rules. The negative consequences were organized into a hierarchy that became progressively more unpleasant if students continued to break rules. Misbehavior ended when teachers applied a consequence that was distasteful enough that students would choose to comply with class rules rather than endure the consequence.

While Assertive Discipline was enthusiastically accepted at first, it was criticized as being too controlling. To correct that shortcoming, the Canters added provisions to give misbehaving students positive attention by talking helpfully with them and working to establish mutual trust and respect.

In helping get across their views, the Canters depicted three types of teachers and what their classes were like: Hostile teachers behave in a manner that suggests they see students as adversaries. They feel that to maintain order and teach properly, they must keep the upper hand. They attempt to do by laying down the law, accepting no nonsense, and using commands and stern facial expressions. They sometimes give needlessly strong admonishments such as: "Sit down, shut up, and listen!" Such messages communicate a dislike for students and make students feel they are being treated unjustly.

Nonassertive teachers are overly passive. They fail to specify clear and reasonable expectations for class behavior and are inconsistent in responding to misbehavior, allowing certain acts one day and disapproving of them the next. They often make statements such as, "For heaven's sake, please try to behave like ladies and gentlemen" or "How many times do I have to tell you no talking?" They come across as wishy-washy, and after a time students stop taking them seriously. Yet, when those teachers become overly frustrated, they sometimes come down very hard on students. This inconsistency leaves students confused about expectations and enforcement.

Assertive teachers clearly, confidently, and consistently model and express class expectations. They work to build trust with the class. They teach students how to behave so they can learn and relate to others more productively. Such teachers help students understand which behaviors promote success and which lead to failure. Assertive teachers recognize students' needs for consistent limits on behavior, but at the same time are mindful of students' needs for warmth and encouragement. Because they realize students may require direct instruction in how to behave acceptably in the classroom, they might be heard to say, "Our rule is no talking without raising your hand. Please raise your hand and wait for me to call on you."

The Canters provided a number of examples of how the plan can be put into effect at different grade levels. The plans followed this sequence:

1. Explain why rules are needed.
2. Teach the specific rules.
3. Check for understanding.
4. Explain how you will reward students who follow rules.
5. Explain why there are corrective actions for breaking the rules.
6. Teach the corrective actions and how they are applied.
7. Check again for understanding.

> **?** Once again, read the Canters' depiction of assertive teachers. Does it seem to describe the qualities you'd want in a teacher? In any case, the widespread use of Assertive Discipline faded away rather abruptly and by the turn of the century it had largely disappeared from the educational scene. Can you see anything inherent in the approach that would have resulted in such an abrupt disaffection?

RESPONSIBILITY AND INNER DISCIPLINE: BARBARA COLOROSO

 Barbara Coloroso believes that a major goal of education is to teach students to conduct themselves in an acceptable manner, and that if they are to become able to do so they must acquire an inner sense of responsibility and self-control. This self-control enables students to take positive charge of their lives while respecting the rights of those around them. This process can best be made to occur when students are given responsibility for making decisions and managing the outcomes of those decisions. Classrooms are ideal places to learn this process, and teachers are in an ideal position to help. The paragraphs that follow present Coloroso's suggestions for helping students in this manner. Most of the material presented here comes from her book, *Kids Are Worth It: Giving Your Child the Gift of Inner Discipline* (1994, 2002). To see more of Coloroso's contributions, consult her website: www.kidsareworthit.com.

Teachers help students learn self-control by taking the following steps when students misbehave:

- Show students what they have done wrong.
- Give students ownership of the problems involved.
- Suggest strategies for solving the problems.
- Make sure students' dignity remains intact.

Go to the Building Classroom Discipline Video Showcase section of Topic #3: Models of Classroom Management, in the **MyEducationLab** for your course and watch the video entitled "Barbara Coloroso—Inner Discipline."

These steps help students acquire integrity, wisdom, compassion, and mercy, all of which promote inner discipline. Teachers must make sure their responses are never hurtful or likely to provoke anger, resentment, or additional conflict.

When misbehavior is serious, Coloroso would also have teachers quickly guide students through a process of *restitution, resolution,* and *reconciliation.* **Restitution** means doing what is necessary to repair damage that was done. **Resolution** means identifying and correcting whatever caused the misbehavior so it won't happen again. **Reconciliation** establishes healing relationships with people who were hurt or offended by the misbehavior. The offending student is asked to make decisions concerning future behavior, follow up accordingly, and then learn from the results of those decisions, even if they bring discomfort. The teacher intervenes only when students' decisions lead to situations that are physically dangerous, morally threatening, or unhealthy. Otherwise, students deal with matters on their own.

When given this freedom of choice, students will not always make the best decisions, but even when the results are unpleasant for them, they can see what has gone wrong and will learn that they can take control over their lives through the decisions they make. When teachers understand this process, they realize it is counterproductive to nag and warn students about how to behave. Moreover, they do not rescue students by solving thorny problems for them, because doing so would send the message that students lack the ability to make decisions and the power to follow through—in other words, they require another person to take care of them. When students are given ownership of problems and situations, they know it is up to them to make matters better. Teachers are there to offer advice and support, but not to provide solutions. Inner discipline is acquired through learning how to think, not just what to think. The following are additional points that Coloroso emphasizes:

- Students have the right to be in school, but they also have the responsibility to respect the rights of those around them. Rights and responsibility go hand in hand.
- School should be neither adult dominated nor student controlled. Rather, it should be a place where joint efforts are made to create a sense of community in which everyone can relate, grow, and create.
- Teachers should never treat students in ways they, the teachers, would not want to be treated. Students have dignity and innate worth, and deserve to be treated accordingly.
- Rather than rescuing students or lecturing them when they misbehave, teachers should give students opportunities to solve their problems in ways that everyone finds acceptable.
- If a discipline tactic works, and leaves student and teacher dignity intact, use it.
- Self-worth and dignity are to be maintained; anything that damages them is to be avoided.
- Students who consistently experience realistic consequences for misbehavior learn that they themselves have positive control over their lives. In contrast, students who are bribed, rewarded, and punished become dependent on others for approval. They work to please the teacher and try to figure out how to avoid getting caught when they misbehave.
- When reasonable consequences are invoked, students may cry, beg, argue, and sulk. They should not get their way by doing so.

> **?** It is often said that some of the very best teaching is done by athletic coaches. And yet few if any of them conduct their programs in a democratic manner that calls on student athletes to give input on how they would like to practice or help make major decisions about the program. The language that teacher coaches often use is hardly of the type advocated by Haim Ginott. Why does this discrepancy between good coaching and good teaching seem so evident and significant? Much the same can be said with regard to drama and music teachers and their programs (but their language is usually a bit more genteel).

CLASSROOM LEARNING COMMUNITIES: ALFIE KOHN

Alfie Kohn is deeply troubled by teaching that tries to force students to behave compliantly. He often begins his workshops by asking teachers, "What are your long-term goals for the students you work with? What would you like them to be—to be like—long after they've left you?" (2001, p. 60). Teachers say they want their students to be caring, happy, responsible, curious, and creative, a conclusion that Kohn finds

unsettling because it exposes a yawning chasm between what we want and what we are doing, between how we would like students to turn out and how our classrooms and schools actually work. We want children to continue reading and thinking after school has ended, yet we focus their attention on grades, which have been shown to reduce interest in learning. We want them to be critical thinkers, yet we feed them predigested facts and discrete skills—partly because of pressure from various constituencies to pump up standardized test scores. We act as though our goal is short-term retention of right answers rather than genuine understanding. (Kohn, 2001, p. 61)

Kohn, a former teacher, is now a full-time writer and lecturer with a number of influential books to his credit. He is critical of many educational practices and is the foremost proponent of converting ordinary classrooms into caring, supportive communities of learners, where students work together as they delve into topics they find interesting. He stresses these points in his addresses, appearances on radio and television programs, and books such as *Punished by Rewards: The Trouble with Gold Stars, Incentive Plans, A's, Praise, and Other Bribes* (1993, 1999) and *Beyond Discipline: From Compliance to Community* (1996, 2001, 2006). He has appeared on well over 200 radio and television programs, including *Oprah* and *The Today Show*, and speaks at major conferences. His website is www.alfiekohn.org.

Kohn thinks traditional instruction—the type in which the teacher selects the curriculum; does the planning; delivers the lessons through lecture, demonstration, guided discussion, reading assignments, worksheets, and homework; and uses tests to evaluate progress—is falling disastrously short of the expectations we hold for it. That kind of instruction is aimed at getting students to behaviorally demonstrate certain specific objectives, usually on tests. But it gives little attention to exploring ideas, seeking new solutions, looking for meaning or connections, or attempting to gain deeper understanding of the phenomena involved. In the instruction commonly used today, students remain relatively passive. They listen, read assignments, answer questions when called on, and complete worksheets, all with little give and take. Instruction and learning are deemed successful in the extent to which students show on tests they have reached the stated objectives. But this approach, says Kohn, makes students focus on outcomes that are shallow, relatively insignificant, and of little interest or relevance to them (1999). Students come to think of correct answers and good grades as the major goals of learning. They rarely experience the satisfaction of exploring interesting topics in depth and exchanging views and insights with others.

Kohn goes on to say that students taught in this way develop a poor attitude toward learning. To them, learning is not an exciting exploration, but just a way of getting the work done. Once they have done the "stuff," they quickly forget much of it as they move on to learn more new stuff. They strive to get the right answers, and when they do not, or if they don't make top scores on the test, they experience a sense of failure that is out of place in genuine learning where making mistakes is the rule. While students may seem to be learning well, they are actually doing poorly because they are not thinking widely and exploring ideas thoughtfully.

Kohn argues for instruction that is very different from the traditional. He says, first, that students must be taken seriously, meaning teachers must honor them as individuals and seek to determine what they need and enjoy. Further, teachers must recognize that students construct their knowledge and skills out of experiences. When students explore, grapple with ideas, and try to make sense of them, they make many mistakes, but that is always part of learning. Teachers facilitate the process by seeking out students' interests and finding what lies behind their questions and mistakes.

Kohn believes students learn most avidly and have their best ideas when they get to choose which questions they want to explore. Conversely, their achievement declines when they have no choice or control over learning. Kohn finds it astonishing that present-day instruction ignores these facts, given the difference they make.

Kohn believes his concerns can best be addressed by transforming schools and classrooms into **learning communities,** meaning

> place[s] in which students feel cared about and are encouraged to care about each other. They experience a sense of being valued and respected; the children matter to one another and to the teacher. They have come to think in the plural: they feel connected to each other; they are part of an "us." And, as a result of all this, they feel safe in their classes, not only physically but emotionally. (2001, pp. 101–102)

Kohn suggests the following as ways to develop a greater sense of community in schools and classrooms:

■ *Show respect for students.* Students behave more respectfully when important adults in their lives behave respectfully toward them. They are more likely to care about others if they know they are cared about. If their emotional needs are met, they show a tendency to help meet other people's needs rather than remaining preoccupied with themselves.

■ *Help students connect.* Connections among students are established and enhanced through activities that involve interdependence. Familiar activities for enhancing connections include cooperative learning, getting-to-know-you activities such as interviewing fellow students and introducing them to the class, and finding a partner to check opinions with on whatever is being discussed at the moment. Kohn also suggests using activities that promote **perspective taking,** in which students try to see situations from another person's point of view.

■ *Use classroom meetings.* Kohn says the overall best activity for involving the entire group is a class meeting. He suggests holding class meetings at the beginning of the year to discuss matters such as, "What makes school awful sometimes? Try to remember an experience during a previous year when you hated school, when you felt bad about yourself, or about everyone else, and you couldn't wait for it to be over. What was going on when you were feeling that way? How was the class set up?" Kohn says not enough teachers use this practice, particularly in elementary schools where an aggressively sunny outlook prevails.

■ *Provide classwide and schoolwide activities.* To develop a sense of community, students need many opportunities for the whole class or the whole school to collaborate on group endeavors. This might involve producing a class mural, producing a class newsletter or magazine, staging a performance, taking care of the school grounds, or doing some community service.

■ *Reflect on academic instruction.* In class meetings talk about how the next unit in history might be approached, or what the students thought was best and worst about the math test. Academic study pursued in cooperative groups enables students to make connections while learning from each other, and units of study in language arts and literature can be organized to promote reflection on helpfulness, fairness, and compassion.

Terms and Concepts

From Redl and Wattenberg
appraising reality
group behavior
group dynamics
influence techniques
punishment
situational assistance
student roles
supporting self-control
teacher roles

From Skinner
behavior modification
reinforcement
reinforcing stimuli
shaping behavior
successive approximations

From Glasser
behavior as choice

From Kounin
accountability
group alerting
momentum

overlapping
satiation
smoothness
withitness

From Ginott
appreciative praise
conferring dignity
congruent communication
evaluative praise
genuine discipline
hidden asset
I-messages
inviting cooperation
laconic language
self-discipline
teachers at their best
teachers at their worst
why questions
you-messages

From Dreikurs
attention seeking
autocratic classroom
belonging

democratic classroom
displaying inadequacy
genuine goal of student behavior
mistaken goals
permissive classroom
power seeking
revenge seeking
social interest

From the Canters
assertive teachers
nonassertive teachers
right to learn
right to teach

From Coloroso
reconciliation
resolution
restitution

From Kohn
learning communities
perspective taking

Activities

1. In your journal, enter items of information from this chapter that you consider pertinent to the components of a personal system of discipline.

2. In small groups, discuss your appraisal of the relative merits of the nine important milestones presented in this chapter and rank them in terms of their applicability in classrooms today.

References

Canter, L., and Canter, M. 1976. *Assertive Discipline: A take-charge approach for today's educator.* Seal Beach, CA: Lee Canter & Associates. The second and third editions of the book, published in 1992 and 2001, are entitled *Assertive Discipline: Positive behavior management for today's classroom.*

Coloroso, B. 2002. *Kids are worth it: Giving your child the gift of inner discipline.* Littleton, CO: Kids Are Worth It!

Dreikurs, R., and Cassel, P. 1995. *Discipline without tears.* New York: Penguin-NAL. (Original work published 1972.)

Ginott, H. 1971. *Teacher and child.* New York: Macmillan.

Glasser, W. 1965. *Reality therapy.* New York: Harper & Row.

Glasser, W. 1969. *Schools without failure.* New York: Harper & Row.

Kohn, A. 1993, 1999. *Punished by rewards: The trouble with gold stars, incentive plans, A's, praise, and other bribes.* Boston: Houghton Mifflin.

Kohn, A. 1999. *The schools our children deserve: Moving beyond traditional classrooms and "tougher standards."* Boston: Houghton Mifflin.

Kohn, A. 2001. *Beyond discipline: From compliance to community.* Upper Saddle River, NJ: Merrill/Prentice Hall. 1996 edition published Alexandria, VA: Association for Supervision and Curriculum Development.

Kounin, J. 1971. *Discipline and group management in classrooms.* New York: Holt, Rinehart, and Winston.

Redl, F., and Wattenberg. W. 1951. *Mental hygiene in teaching.* New York: Harcourt, Brace & World.

Skinner, B. 1953. *Science and human behavior.* New York: Macmillan.

Skinner, B. 1954. The science of learning and the art of teaching. *Harvard Educational Review, 24,* 86–97.

The William Glasser Institute. 2009. Reality therapy. http://wglasser.com/index

PART TWO

What Are Some of Today's Most Outstanding Approaches to Classroom Discipline?

This section contains seven chapters, each of which describes an excellent, commercially available approach to classroom discipline. The approaches are complete in that they (1) give ample attention to softening the factors that promote misbehavior, (2) provide ongoing support to help students remain engaged in lessons, (3) contain mechanisms for addressing misbehavior in a positive manner that benefits students over the long run, and (4) clarify ways of communicating effectively with students. These approaches, sometimes called *models,* are available in book form, with associated websites that provide commentary and updates from the program creators. Those authorities, except for William Glasser, who is now retired, make themselves available for conference presentations and staff development programs nationally and internationally. The seven chapters and their authors are as follows:

CHAPTER 5 How Does Ronald Morrish Use Purposeful Teacher Guidance to Establish Class Discipline?

Morrish, a former teacher, calls his approach *Real Discipline,* which he describes as an organized set of tactics that good teachers have used for generations to help students become well-mannered and self-directing.

CHAPTER 6 How Do Harry and Rosemary Wong Use Responsibilities and Procedures to Establish Class Discipline?

Harry and Rosemary Wong, authors of the all-time best-selling book in education, explain why and how students should be helped to understand their roles in the class and trained to follow procedures quickly and correctly. This greatly enhances learning and efficiency in all class activities and significantly reduces the incidence of misbehavior.

CHAPTER 7   How does Fred Jones Establish Class Discipline by Keeping Students Responsibly Involved?

Jones, a psychologist, shows how to organize the classroom to keep students actively involved in lessons through Say, See, Do Teaching, "working the crowd," effective body language, and incentives that help students develop self-control.

CHAPTER 8   How Does William Glasser Use Choice Theory and Quality Education to Establish Class Discipline?

Glasser, a psychiatrist, emphasizes that we cannot successfully make students do anything, and therefore must use legitimate influence that prompts students to choose to do the right thing. He explains how to exert such influence through quality communication, choice management, and quality teaching.

CHAPTER 9   How Does Spencer Kagan Use Structures and Teacher–Student Same-Side Collaboration to Establish Class Discipline?

Kagan, a psychologist, shows teachers how to involve students in making collaborative decisions about behavior and other matters that help keep classrooms calm and purposeful. He provides a number of *structures*, or sets of procedures for teachers to use when students disrupt. The structures halt the disruption, provide acceptable ways for students to meet their needs in the classroom, and lead to long-term improvements in behavior.

CHAPTER 10   How Does Marvin Marshall Establish Discipline by Activating Internal Motivation and Raising Student Responsibility?

Marshall, a former teacher and administrator, calls his approach *Discipline without Stress*. The approach emphasizes increasing the level of responsibility among students. It uses four levels of social development to influence students to conduct themselves properly. At the highest level, students conduct themselves in accordance with what they believe to be the right thing to do.

CHAPTER 11   How Does Craig Seganti Use Positive Teacher Leverage and Realistic Student Accountability to Establish Class Discipline?

Seganti, a classroom teacher in inner-city Los Angeles, explains how to keep students actively engaged in lessons while conducting themselves in a courteous manner. He describes the teaching style he has found effective and his system of benign leverage that keeps students well-mannered and on track.

5

How Does Ronald Morrish Use Purposeful Teacher Guidance to Establish Class Discipline?

Ronald Morrish believes that discipline is best established through purposeful teacher guidance, in which the teacher sets standards and helps students understand exactly how they are expected to behave. Morrish cautions us against assuming that all students come to school knowing how to behave responsibly. Many do not, he says, and they must be taught the necessary social skills and self-control. He adds that self-control develops over time, and the process rarely occurs without the help of supportive adults—help that is often absent from students' lives today. Teachers are in an ideal position to provide the support, but many are not sure how to do so.

To make matters more difficult, says Morrish, the advice teachers get from today's popular systems of discipline is counterproductive, because most of today's discipline systems urge teachers to involve students in decision making even when students are not mature enough to make decisions responsibly. As a consequence, teachers waste large amounts of time negotiating and haggling with students about behavior in school. Morrish provides a remedy for this situation. He asks teachers to begin by helping students do two things: (1) differentiate between right and wrong and (2) comply with adult authority. Later, when they became mature enough, students are invited to participate in class decision making.

Ronald Morrish was a teacher and behavior specialist in Canada for 26 years before becoming an independent consultant in 1997. Now he writes, makes conference presentations, conducts professional development programs, presents courses for teachers, and works with parent groups and child care providers around the world. He has authored three books. The first, *Secrets of Discipline* (1997), was also produced as a video. In that work, Mr. Morrish discusses 12 keys for raising responsible children without engaging in deal making, arguments, and confrontations. His second book, *With All Due Respect* (2000), focuses on improving teachers' discipline skills and building effective schoolwide discipline programs through a team approach. In 2003, he published *FlipTips*, a mini-book of discipline tips and maxims excerpted from his books and presentations. Morrish's website is www.realdiscipline.com.

A PREVIEW OF THIS CHAPTER

The best approach to discipline emphasizes rules, teacher influence, and student compliance. Teachers make the rules; it is a major mistake to involve students in making decisions about discipline until they are mature enough to do so. Then teachers provide a balance of compliance training, teaching proper behavior, and helping students learn to manage choice. The way to plan for discipline is to clarify expectations, provide a structure for achieving them, and teach students what they are supposed to do. When students fail to comply with expectations, have them repeat the behavior in an acceptable manner. In short, establish rules, teach the behavior, require compliance, and redo misbehavior properly—and the result will be acceptable behavior.

WHAT TO LOOK FOR IN THIS CHAPTER

- What Morrish thinks has gone wrong with discipline
- What Morrish means by *Real Discipline*
- The three major phases in Real Discipline
- The value of training for compliance
- Morrish's suggestions for planning discipline in your classroom
- Morrish's cautions about promoting self-indulgence in students.
- What to do when students fail to comply with expectations or teacher directions

HOW AND WHY MODERN DISCIPLINE HAS GONE WRONG

Morrish (2005) agrees with other authorities that school discipline is an ever-growing problem, as students become increasingly defiant and manipulative. He places some of the blame on undesirable trends in society but he also assigns much of it to discipline approaches that call on students to decide how they will behave in school. He points out that for over three decades discipline experts have erroneously claimed that plentiful student choice leads to self-esteem, responsibility, and motivation to achieve. As those experts see it, the teacher's role is to encourage good choices and discourage poor ones.

That approach has failed, Morrish contends, for three reasons. First, it does not demand proper behavior from students, but instead allows them, if they don't mind the consequences, to choose to behave discourteously and irresponsibly. Systems based on fear of consequences, he explains, cannot be effective unless students truly find the consequences unacceptable—and many do not. Second, the approach doesn't adequately teach students how they are expected to behave in school. And third, it leaves teachers to bargain and negotiate endlessly, and often fruitlessly, to get students to cooperate.

Morrish believes effective school discipline requires a different approach—students must be taught what is acceptable and what is unacceptable before they are given latitude to make choices. Otherwise, they are likely to choose whatever appeals to them at the time, and teachers will have a difficult time living with many of those choices. All of us want students to be successful in school, but today's discipline too often allows them to underachieve, behave discourteously, engage in high-risk behaviors, contribute little or nothing to the school environment, and use intimidation and violence in dealing with others. Clearly, says Morrish, discipline based on student choice is not producing the results we want.

Morrish also feels teachers have been sidetracked into focusing on what he calls behavior management rather than *Real Discipline*. Both are needed, he says, but there is an important distinction between the two. **Behavior management** is about making the learning environment functional, keeping students on task, and minimizing disruptions. It attempts to deal with whatever behavior students bring to school. Although it is important in teaching, management does little to help students develop responsible behavior.

Real Discipline, on the other hand, teaches students how to behave properly. It requires them to show courtesy and consideration. It teaches needed social skills and trains students to work within a structure of rules and limits. It does these things while protecting students from self-defeating mistakes they are otherwise likely to make.

MORRISH'S SOLUTION—REAL DISCIPLINE

Morrish calls his approach *Real Discipline*. He explains that it is not a new theory, but an organized set of techniques that great teachers and parents have used for generations in teaching children to be respectful, responsible, and cooperative. It emphasizes careful teacher guidance to ensure that children learn how conduct themselves in an acceptable manner. As Morrish puts it:

> Real Discipline is a lot more than simply giving choices to children and then dealing with the aftermath. We have to teach them right and wrong. We have to teach them to respect legitimate authority. We have to teach them the lessons that have been learned by others and by ourselves. Then, and only then, will we enjoy watching them develop into adults. (1997, p. 33)

Morrish says these provisions are necessary because children, in their early years, are impulsive and self-centered. If they are to develop into contributing members of society, they must learn to cooperate, behave responsibly, and show consideration for others. Some young students have parents and role models who teach them these things. But many children are overly indulged and never called to account for their behavior. They remain self-centered and grow up concerned only with their own needs, without regard for those of others. They want things their way, cooperate in school only when they feel like it, and show little consideration for teachers and fellow students. For many, abusive language and bullying are the rule of the day.

In part, this condition has occurred because we live in a society that stresses individual rights and freedom but has lost sight of personal responsibility, without which rights and freedom mean little. Personal responsibility is too important to leave to chance. We must live with certain requirements that put constraints on individual freedom. We do so in exchange for life that is safer, more secure, and more orderly. Morrish does believe students should be allowed to make choices, but only when they are sufficiently mature to make them intelligently. Students do not innately know how to do so. Before they can, they must develop respect for, and a degree of compliance with, authority.

MAXIMS REGARDING THE MINDSET FOR REAL DISCIPLINE

In 2003, Morrish published a small spiral-bound book called *FlipTips*, containing comments and maxims from his various publications and presentations. They reflect the mindset that Morrish would like teachers to acquire. Here are a few of the tips that illustrate Morrish's ideas on discipline:

- Discipline is a process, not an event.
- Discipline is about giving students the structure they need for proper behavior, not the consequences they seem to deserve for misbehavior.
- Discipline comes from the word *disciple*. It's about teaching and learning, not scolding and punishing.
- Discipline isn't what you do when students misbehave. It's what you do so they won't.
- Discipline isn't about letting students make their own choices. It's about preparing them properly for the choices they will be making later.
- Don't let students make choices that are not theirs to make.
- Train students to comply with your directions. Compliance precedes cooperation. If you bargain for compliance now, you'll have to beg for it later.
- Always work from more structure to less structure, not the other way around.
- To prevent major behavior problems, deal with all minor behavior problems when they occur.
- Students learn far more from being shown how to behave appropriately than from being punished.
- The best time to teach a behavior is when it isn't needed, so it will be there when it is needed. Today's practice is tomorrow's performance.
- If you teach students to be part of the solution, they're less likely to be part of the problem.
- When dealing with adolescents, act more like a coach and less like a boss.
- A single minute spent practicing courtesy has more impact than a one-hour lecture on the importance of it.
- To stop fights, stop put-downs. Verbal hits usually precede physical hits.
- Discipline should end with the correct behavior, not with a punishment.
- Rapport is the magical ingredient that changes a student's reluctance to be controlled into a willingness to be guided.

THE THREE-PHASE APPROACH TO REAL DISCIPLINE

Rather than approach discipline from the perspective of choice, Real Discipline asks teachers to guide students through three progressive phases called *training for compliance, teaching students how to behave,* and *managing student choice.* Each of these **three phases of Real Discipline** is aimed at a particular goal and involves a certain set of strategies, as explained in the following paragraphs.

Go to the Building Classroom Discipline Video Showcase section of Topic #3: Models of Classroom Management, in the **MyEducationLab** for your course and watch the video entitled "Ronald Morrish— Real Discipline."

Phase 1: Training for Compliance

This first phase in teaching students Real Discipline involves training students to accept adult authority and comply with it automatically. Basic compliance should initially be taught as a *nonthinking activity*. Nonthinking activities are habits you don't have to reflect on or make choices about, such as stopping at red lights or saying "thank you" when a person does something nice for you. Students should be carefully trained in how to pay attention, follow directions, and speak respectfully, to the point they do these things automatically.

Compliant classroom behavior is taught through direct instruction and close supervision. If you want students to raise their hands before speaking, tell them what you expect and show them how to do it. Then have them practice it until it becomes habitual. When students make mistakes, show them again how to do the act properly and, again, practice it. Morrish says to start small, and you will see a general attitude of compliance grow out of many small compliances.

Morrish observes that compliance receives virtually no attention in most approaches to discipline. He finds this strange, given that compliance helps students conduct themselves properly and provides the basis for later decision making.

Compliance is based on the fundamental recognition that there are effective ways of behaving in civilized societies, with limits to what people do. Therefore, in compliance training, teachers address all misbehavior. They do not overlook small misbehaviors, as they are advised in many discipline programs. When teachers overlook small misbehaviors, they are soon overwhelmed with explaining, negotiating, and tending to consequences. This overload causes them to "pick their battles" and not "sweat the small stuff." Thus, they may allow students to lie on their desks during opening routines, talk during announcements, throw their jackets in the corner instead of hanging them up, and wander around the room instead of getting ready to work.

Such minor misbehavior might seem unimportant, but it should never be overlooked. Poor habits easily expand to poor behavior overall. If you walk by students who are doing something wrong and you say nothing, they interpret that as meaning you don't care, and the next thing you know they are engaged in disruptive misbehavior. Don't get the idea you can't manage such behavior, but do understand that you can't manage it by scolding and doling out consequences.

> Morrish says the best approach is to tell students what you want them to do and then insist they do it properly. When they do something wrong, have them do it right. That is how you establish good practices and habits in your classes. Students get the picture quickly. ■

Morrish asks teachers to train their students to comply with rules, limits, and authority. *Rules* indicate how students are to behave. An example might be "Show courtesy and respect for others at all times." *Limits* specify behavior that will *not* be allowed. An example would be, "No name-calling in this room." *Authority* refers to power that has been assigned to certain individuals. By custom and law, teachers are given legitimate authority to control and direct students in school, and they should use it to set and maintain standards of conduct.

Rules in Training for Compliance

Just as we need rules for structure and predictability in everyday living, so do we need rules for classroom behavior. Teachers should make the rules. There is no need to ask students if they agree with them. Students are supposed to learn rules, not determine them. Therefore, teach students why we have rules and why they are made by people in positions of authority. Explain your rules to students and take their opinions into account, but don't pretend they are helping decide what the class rules are to be.

When you establish rules, you must commit to ensuring they are obeyed. As Morrish points out, you really don't have rules unless you can enforce them. Your enforcement should be consistent, even for misbehavior that seems incidental, such as carelessly dropping rubbish on the floor or talking during quiet study time. As noted earlier, small infractions have a way of growing into large infractions.

Morrish says *insistence* is the best strategy for enforcing rules. Punishment is rarely needed. You must be absolutely determined that students will do what you want them to, and you must be willing to persist until they do. You should develop the mindset that once you give an instruction, there is no question about students' doing what you say. Morrish does not suggest that punishment never be used, but he does point out that punishment does not teach cooperation or responsibility and that it sometimes produces unwanted side effects. However, punishment can do two things well. First, it can teach that "no means no," a message that students need to learn quickly. Second, punishment can bring misbehavior to a stop when other methods can't.

> **?** Students usually enter Mrs. James's class casually, talking and joking among themselves. Mrs. James doesn't mind because she likes to use the first few minutes of class time to review her lesson plans and chat with individual students whose assignments have not been completed correctly. What would Ron Morrish say about her approach? What do you think he would have her do differently?

Limits in Training for Compliance

As with rules, limits on behavior are set and enforced by teachers, in accordance with established standards. Teachers do not negotiate those limits with students. Morrish says the first secret of good discipline is: *Never give students a choice when it comes to limits.* You set limits in many ways, formally and informally. For example, you may work with students so they know that when they arrive in the classroom, they are to hang up their jackets and get ready for work immediately (rules). They also know they are not allowed to scuffle or swear (limits). You have taught them these requirements and have had them practice the behaviors. Students do not have any say in them. If they have questions about the limits, you should select a time to explain the reasons behind them, but in no case are students allowed to ignore your directions. Your word is final.

Morrish laments that limits in today's classrooms are so often compromised by bargaining between teacher and students. He says that the more teachers give special privileges in exchange for behaving properly, the more students are likely to misbehave. Bargaining simply does not produce the results teachers intend. Teachers expect that once the bargaining is done, students will assess the possible outcomes of their behavior choices and thus make good choices accordingly. However, the main effect on students is not better choice making, but feeling that everything in the class is decided through bargaining. All that does is give students power in decisions they are not well-prepared to make.

Authority in Training for Compliance

Morrish insists we need to reestablish teacher authority in the classroom, and he reminds teachers where their authority comes from—law, custom, and professionalism. The power of teacher authority comes from teachers' knowing their responsibilities, knowing why they are setting limits, and knowing what they expect their students to learn. It is conveyed by tone of voice, choice of words, and the way teachers present themselves. Teachers should clearly communicate what they expect of students and then accept nothing less. They should make clear that no negotiation is involved. They do this without threatening or raising their voices. They simply say, with authority in their voice, "This is what you must do. This is the job you are here for. Now let's get on with it" (1997, p. 65).

If, in this process, students question your authority, tell them, "It is my job." If they challenge your right to make demands, tell them, "It is my job." Morrish says not to worry if your students don't like some of the things you expect them to do. It is respect you need at this point, not appreciation. Appreciation will come later, provided respect comes first.

Morrish acknowledges that many teachers become uneasy when asked to train their students for compliance. They fear automatic compliance will make their students passive, submissive, and unable to think for themselves. But Morrish insists that today's discipline gives students too much freedom of choice, not too little. What we need, he says, is a balance, which is achieved through the three phases of Real Discipline.

Phase 2: Teaching Students How to Behave

The second phase in Real Discipline focuses on teaching students the skills, attitudes, and knowledge needed for cooperation, proper behavior, and increased responsibility. In preparation for this phase, you have already established the class rules and have taught them to students through explanation, demonstration, practice, corrective feedback, and repetition. Students understand the need for rules, and they will comply with them if they accept your authority. This process teaches students to be courteous, work and play harmoniously together, resolve conflicts, set personal goals, organize tasks, and manage time. Most teachers erroneously assume students will somehow learn those skills from experience. You can't wait for experience to teach them these things, even if experience were capable of it.

Today's students must be taught what to do, if you are to have order and acceptable behavior in your classes. The best way to teach behavior skills is through direct instruction and carefully supervised practice.

When students fail to comply with expectations, don't scold or punish them. Simply have them redo the behavior in an acceptable manner and continue to practice it. ■

Phase 3: Managing Student Choice

The third phase of Real Discipline is called *choice management*. It helps students move toward greater independence by offering them more and more choices as they show capability for handling them. One basic requirement in choice making is that students must take into account the needs and rights of other students and school personnel. You must ensure they do so.

Morrish explains that choice management also requires specification of who has the right, or duty, to make a particular choice. Teachers have to make certain choices. Students can be allowed to make others. As a rule of thumb, if students don't care about the outcome of a particular goal, they should not be allowed to make choices about it. To illustrate, most people assume that students who do poor class work should receive low marks that will motivate them to do better in the future. This may work for some highly motivated students, but it does nothing for those who don't care and are perfectly willing to accept the low grades. If Alana indicates she doesn't care about her performance in important class matters, you should say to her, "That's okay, Alana, because I do care and that's why this is my choice. Someday, when you care about it as much as I do, it will become your choice" (Morrish, 1997, p. 101). Suppose Alana hands in poor work. You say to her: "Alana, your work is disorganized and incomplete. I'm not accepting it. Take it back, please, and fix it up. I'll mark it when it is done properly" (Morrish, 1997, p. 105).

Teachers must make decisions for students like Alana until those students begin to care about quality and completeness. The teacher should never suggest that Alana can choose to do poor work if she wants to. Morrish says this is one area where we truly need to get back to basics, meaning we should expect students to do quality work and accept nothing less. Morrish reiterates: Schools are not democracies. Teachers must be willing to make the decisions that are theirs to make (1997).

When you encounter a student such as Alana, continue to work toward the major goal of Real Discipline, which is to help students become self-disciplined and conduct themselves properly even when you are not present. This is not likely to occur in discipline systems where students learn to do what is advantageous rather than what is right.

In *Secrets of Discipline: 12 Keys for Raising Responsible Children*, Morrish (1997, pp. 93–94) relates a classroom incident that epitomizes self-discipline. Morrish was visiting a combination grade 2/3 class when the teacher told her students she would be leaving the classroom for a few minutes. The students were to continue working quietly. She asked them, "What does this mean you need?" Hands were raised. A student answered, "Self-discipline." The teacher continued, "What does self-discipline mean?" Another student answered, "It means we behave when you're not with us, exactly the same way we behave when you are standing right next to us." The teacher and Morrish both left the room but Morrish stopped in the hallway to watch the students from a distance. He observed that the students continued to work as if the teacher were in the room with them. Later he asked the teacher how she had accomplished that result. She said she had the class practice the skill from the first day. She would stand next to them and ask them to show their best behavior. Then she challenged them to continue behaving that way as she moved farther and farther away. Before long the students had learned how to maintain their behavior when the teacher left the room.

But if students misbehaved when the teacher was out of the room, what should she do? Morrish says she should first ask the students, "What happened?" When they told her, she would follow with, "Would you have made the same decision if I had been standing right next to you?" Usually the students will say "No." Then the teacher asks, "Why do you need me standing next to you to make a good decision?"

As students become older and move toward independence, Real Discipline has already taught them three things about making independent choices: First, that independence requires balancing personal rights with personal responsibility; second, that the rights and needs of others must be taken into account; and third, that students should look at every unsupervised situation as an opportunity to demonstrate personal responsibility. Morrish points out that independence isn't "doing your own thing": It's doing what's right when you are on your own.

PLANNING AND IMPLEMENTING THE DISCIPLINE PROGRAM

Real Discipline calls on teachers to be proactive, meaning they anticipate problems, keep them from occurring if possible, and prepare carefully for attending to problems that might occur. Morrish (2000) guides teachers through eleven steps in organizing their discipline system:

- *Decide in advance how you want your students to behave.* Think through matters such as the following: How students will demonstrate courtesy, the words and tone of voice they will use, how they will speak to you, what other signs of courtesy they will show, how they will treat visitors, how they will welcome new students to the class, how they will listen to you and other students, how they will contribute to class discussions, how they will help substitute teachers, what they will do when upset or when they disagree with you or others, how they will respond to other students who need assistance, how they will deal with losing, how they will comply when you tell them what to do, how they will respond when you correct them, and how they will behave when you step out of the room.

- *Design the supporting structure.* When you have in mind how you want students to behave, design a structure that will support your goals. This structure will consist mostly of procedures, such as how students will enter and exit the room, what they will do if they arrive late, how they will handle completed work, how they will request assistance, what they should do about missed assignments, what they should do if they finish work early, what they should do if the teacher does not appear on time, how they will learn the class rules and enforcement procedures, and what the specific limits on behavior are.

- *Establish a threshold for behavior at school.* You must not allow students to bring negative behaviors to the class from home and community. You must create a clear separation between school and outside school. Say to students, "You're now at school. Remember how you behave when you are here." Then enforce the courtesy, rules, and work habits required in your class.

- *Run a two-week training camp.* Effective teachers work hard on discipline expectations and procedures during the first two weeks of the year or term. They use this time to establish clear limits, expectations, routines, appropriate behavior, and compliance. Morrish maintains that the investment you make in discipline during these first two weeks determines how the rest of the school year unfolds. This does not suggest you overlook academic work. In the early stages, academic work is a lower priority than proper behavior, but as students acclimate to Real Discipline, academic work moves to highest priority.

■ *Teach students how to behave appropriately.* Morrish believes that students should be taught any skills required for school success, including how to behave in school assemblies, on school buses, and in the school cafeteria. They need to learn how, and why, to dress appropriately for school. They should be taught how to treat new students and be good role models for younger students. In addition, Morrish (2000, pp. 94–103) has articulated "Ten Great Skills" you should teach your students. The skills are presented here in abbreviated form.

1. *Courtesy.* Teach students how to greet others, say "please" and "thank you," listen when others speak, and acknowledge good effort by others.

2. *How to treat substitute teachers.* Teach students to behave for others just as they would for you. Show them how to welcome visitors and help them.

3. *Conflict prevention.* Help students recognize events that lead up to various troublesome incidents and then problem solve alternative ways of avoiding the conflict. Teach them how to respond to teasing and avoid people and situations that provoke trouble.

4. *Self-discipline.* Work to help your students understand they should make the same behavior decisions when you are not there as when you are present. Talk about various hypothetical behavior situations. Ask how your students would behave if you were there and if they can commit to that same behavior when you are not beside them.

5. *Concentration.* Help students learn to ignore distractions. Give them practice by having them maintain concentration when a student you have selected to help you makes noise or speaks to you.

6. *Being part of the solution rather than part of the problem.* Teach students how to do such things as help classmates with learning, stop someone from teasing, keep students from fighting, and keep the classroom and school grounds neat. Congratulate them when they do those things. When you see them fail to do so, ask them why they didn't help.

7. *Thinking about others.* Children are self-centered and therefore have to be taught to take others into account. Ask students to try to help someone every day. Periodically call on them to identify others who helped them.

8. *Perseverance.* Students won't ordinarily persevere at tasks they find difficult or boring, unless strongly influenced to do so. Speak with them about the importance of completing tasks. Have them complete something you assign every day and do not allow them to quit or change tasks.

9. *Being a good role model for younger students.* Students learn many of their behaviors by watching siblings, friends, parents, and teachers. Urge your students to try to make a positive impression on younger students. Ask them to consider the effects of their words, jokes, body language, and conversational topics. Ask them to model compliance with school routines.

10. *Being a good ambassador for your class and school.* Help students understand they are ambassadors for their school and class. When they behave well

in public, people notice and conclude the students come from a good school and good family. Ask students to conduct themselves in that manner to bring credit to themselves, the school, and their parents.

- *Set the stage for quality instruction.* Discipline cannot succeed in an environment where students are coerced to endure boring, tedious lessons and activities. You must make your classes interesting and worthwhile. Ask questions that force students to expand their thinking. Increase the amount of hands-on activities. Make use of group learning activities. Include activities based on sports, music, drama, and crafts. Ask students to make presentations to the class and to younger students. These approaches keep students interested, making it less likely they will behave disruptively.

- *Provide active, assertive supervision.* Good discipline requires that you take certain steps to forestall misbehavior. Remind students of rules and expectations ahead of time. Remind them of limits that might apply. Be specific and don't oververbalize. Govern and correct small misbehaviors. Reinforce good social skills when you see them. Move briskly around the classroom. Talk briefly with various students if it does not interrupt their work. Let everyone see your presence. Move with a sense of purpose. Make eye contact with students.

- *Enforce rules and expectations.* Most teachers believe they should make students aware of unpleasant consequences that accompany misbehavior and use them for warnings and rule enforcement. But neither the warnings nor the consequences themselves are very effective in getting students to conduct themselves properly. Success depends on the teacher's ability to *require* good behavior. You must be willing to establish your natural authority and take charge of students. There is no game playing involved. Don't allow them to decide whether or not to comply with rules. Don't allow them to call you by your first name, talk back, run around the room, or throw things at each other.

  Teachers worry that some students will confront them over expectations and rule enforcement they don't like. You can limit that concern by addressing all small infractions such as discourteous language or failure to clean up. When they learn to comply on small matters, they will continue to do so on large matters. Meanwhile, connect with your students on a personal basis. Listen to them and take their concerns into account. Capitalize on their interests. Be understanding and supportive when a student is going through a hard time. Establish rapport, but combine it with insistence.

- *Focus on prevention.* Real Discipline goes to lengths to prevent misbehavior. Discipline isn't as much what you do when students misbehave as it is what you do in advance so they won't misbehave. Use the suggestions presented earlier for making classes interesting and engaging. Do not allow verbal put-downs in your classes. Discuss potential behavior situations with students and devise ways of avoiding the problems.

- *Set high standards.* In Real Discipline, underachievement is not a student choice. You must make it clear you will not accept underachievement in any form, whether academic or social. When students do something inadequately or improperly, have them do it over again. Challenge your students and get them excited about improving everything they do in school.

■ *Treat parents as partners.* Keep parents informed about serious incidents and repetitive misbehavior involving their child, but don't worry them with minor matters—take care of those yourself. When you need to communicate with parents, do so personally if possible. Don't send notes. Suggest ways they might help the student do better in school, but never suggest punishment. Talk with parents, not down to them. Reassure them that you and they both want success for their child and that you want to work together with them to make that happen.

DEVELOPING TEACHER–STUDENT RELATIONSHIPS

Two very important considerations in classroom discipline are (1) relations between teacher and students and (2) students' understanding that discipline benefits everyone in the class. If students like you, they will want to please and not disappoint you. Further, they will more likely understand and accept that your rules increase safety, security, and proper treatment for everyone. People often wonder why different teachers, when using the same set of discipline tactics, get vastly different results. That happens because students react differently to those teachers on a personal basis. When students like their teacher and believe he or she likes and wants to help them, they will abide by most requests. If they do not like the teacher, they will be less enthusiastic about cooperating. Morrish provides the following suggestions for strengthening relationships with your students:

■ *Consistently focus on the positive.* Look for things students do right, rather than things they do wrong. Show a genuine sense of understanding when they make mistakes and, in a positive manner, help them improve. It is much better to help than criticize.

■ *Wipe the slate clean after students make mistakes.* Deal with the mistake in a positive manner and move on. Don't hold grudges; they don't help in any way. The important thing is what the student does now.

■ *Don't back away from discipline.* Students don't often say they appreciate discipline. They don't like having to obey rules, and they don't enjoy practicing appropriate behavior. Nevertheless, they understand discipline is a teacher role and they expect it. They interpret the time and effort you expend as signs of concern for them, and later they will remember you with appreciation.

■ *Lead the way.* Students learn more from watching you than from hearing what you say. Model civilized behaviors and attitudes. Listen to students. Speak kindly to them. Be helpful and give credit when it is due.

■ *Never humiliate students when correcting their misbehavior.* Morrish says teachers unintentionally use humiliation more than they imagine, as when they scold students in front of their friends or display work to show how it could have been done better. Whenever students need to be corrected, show them how to behave properly and have them practice until the behavior become habitual.

■ *Don't accept mediocrity.* Some teachers fail to set sustainable standards of learning and behavior, believing they need only to befriend students in order to obtain their cooperation. Standards are essential if students are to recognize success and maintain their determination to improve. If you willingly accept mediocrity, that is what you will get. Reasonable standards tell students you believe they are bright and sensitive enough to learn and behave properly.

CONSEQUENCES IN REAL DISCIPLINE

Morrish believes that consequences, when structured and applied correctly, are very helpful in teaching students how to conduct themselves properly. But the consequences he advocates are not punishments. Instead, they involve teaching proper behavior and having students practice that behavior. When students speak discourteously, the consequence is for them to stop and speak again in a proper manner. Consequences are also applied when a student continues to push the boundary of acceptable behavior. In that event, apply a consequence that stops the behavior. You need to get across the idea that "no means no."

Morrish says you should explain to your students why consequences are applied when they misbehave and that those consequences are designed to help them learn. He provides examples of types of consequences:

- *Compensation.* Have the student do something positive to make up for negative behavior. This might include making the victim of bad behavior feel better or the school look better.
- *Letter writing.* Have the offending student write a letter to the person who was offended, including a statement of commitment for better behavior in the future.
- *Improvement plan.* Have the student make a plan for handling the situation better in the future. Keep track to ensure the student follows through.
- *Teaching younger children.* Have the offending student write and illustrate a story about the incident to read to younger children, emphasizing what was done wrong and what was learned from the experience (Morrish, 2000, p. 66).

ABOUT MOTIVATION AND REWARDS

Many experts in school discipline assert that we can't *make* students do anything—that the best we can do is provide an environment so appealing that students will naturally work and conduct themselves in approved ways. Morrish doesn't agree. He says we should certainly make learning as enticing as possible, but it is ridiculous to believe we cannot make students do anything. The very purpose of discipline, he says, is to make students do what they don't want to do. He points out that students ordinarily do not want to obey rules, don't want to stay quiet, don't want to do homework, don't want to study for tests, and so forth. We use discipline to ensure that they set aside their natural desires and accept education's plans for helping them succeed in life.

He goes on to say that Real Discipline does not rely on high natural motivation. Instead, it teaches students how to persevere and work through activities that are not especially appealing. To the extent you can make instructional activities interesting, do so, and everyone will enjoy school more, including you. But when that is not possible, don't shy away from teaching students what they need to know, even when lessons are tedious.

Morrish also advises teachers to forego praise and reward when students merely do what is expected of them. He says occasional rewards are fine, because they give special recognition when it is needed. But overall, rewards are vastly overused and students often see them as ends in themselves. Teachers have two powerful natural rewards at their disposal, but they are not stickers, points, or special privileges. Rather, they are what you always have with you—your personal attention and approval.

Teachers these days also dispense copious quantities of praise. Morrish says some of them really spread it on thick. But we must be cautious about that, too. Beyond a certain point, praise actually reduces motivation while increasing dependency. Students develop healthier attitudes when teachers praise work and behavior only when they deserve recognition.

> **?** Suppose Carmelo has defaced a bulletin board in the room. What sort of consequence would Morrish suggest for that behavior? Suppose Carmelo has helped Anthony resolve a personal problem with another student. What sort of reward would Morrish suggest for that behavior?

DON'T PROMOTE SELF-INDULGENCE

Many educators believe low self-esteem is the root cause of antisocial behavior. Morrish sees the picture differently. He acknowledges that students who do poorly in school and get into trouble sometimes (but not always) have low self-esteem, while those who do well tend to have high self-esteem. But self-esteem does not determine success or failure. It is the other way around, he says—success in school or lack thereof influences self-esteem. If you are competent and successful, you usually think better about yourself than if you are incompetent and unsuccessful.

Morrish goes on to say that teachers who try to build student self-esteem directly may actually do more harm than good, especially if they never allow failure, never put pressure on students to excel, and permit students to express themselves freely without fear of rebuke. These things remove students from the helpful criticism that normally follows serious misbehavior, and as a result, students become more self-indulgent. They gradually lose their sense of shame and begin to rationalize their misdeeds with explanations such as "I just felt like it. It made me feel good." As Morrish puts it,

> In the real world, the most likely result of attempting to raise self-esteem directly is that children will feel much better about themselves while they continue to misbehave.
>
> Genuine self-esteem does not grow in students who are allowed to do as they please. Rather, it comes from increased competence in academic and social matters and the ability to overcome obstacles. If we teach students academic and social skills, if we hold high expectations for them, we will see them come to think well of themselves, based on the reality of positive competence. The real hallmark of self-esteem is one's balanced view of personal competence in relation to the surrounding world. (1997, p. 121)

WHEN STUDENTS FAIL TO COMPLY

Go to the Simulations section of Topic #13: Managing Special Groups, in the **MyEducationLab** for your course and complete the simulation entitled "Developing Behavior Change Plans for Students Who Demonstrate Serious and/or Persistent Disruptive Behaviors."

Occasionally a student may fail to comply with your directions or may, in the heat of the moment, display other inappropriate behavior. Suppose one of your students has behaved discourteously toward you in class. Many teachers, if the infraction is serious enough, will send the offending student to time-out for an indefinite period before allowing the student to rejoin the class. That does nothing positive for the student. Instead of time-out or some other consequence, you should insist on a *do-over*. Have the student repeat the behavior in an acceptable manner. If a student speaks to you disrespectfully, tell him or her to start over and do it courteously this time. The same procedure applies any time a student fails to follow directions or comply with class standards.

Many teachers make the mistake of using *if–then statements*, such as, "If you speak to me in that manner again, then you will be going to the principal's office." Teachers should not use such statements with misbehaving students. They should give students no choice in the matter. They should say, "We don't speak that way in this class. Start over." Most of the time, that is all you need to do. Remember, your most important and powerful tool is *insistence.* You must convey to students they have no choice in the matter, other than to do as you instruct. Morrish says that students who are never required to act appropriately seldom will.

If a student still refuses to do as you direct, repeat your instruction in a serious tone of voice. If that doesn't work, use a mild punishment such as time-out to get across the message that you mean what you say. Then after a short time, bring the student back to the task correctly. The discipline procedure does not end with the time-out. The student is still expected to show proper behavior. Only positive practice ensures that. Morrish says that most of the time punishment is unnecessary—we only need to have students redo their behavior correctly.

Summary Rubric

APPLYING REAL DISCIPLINE IN THE CLASSROOM

- Real Discipline is a process that leads to cooperative and responsible behavior. It takes time. There are no shortcuts.
- From the beginning, communicate to your students that you are committed to providing a classroom in which they can learn easily, without threat or put-downs, and where teacher and students alike courteously and willingly do the jobs expected of them.
- Tell students about duties in the class—what your job is and what their job is. You might wish to explain that your job is to provide a quality learning environment, teach students the best you can, and treat everyone with respect and courtesy, while their job

is to follow your directions, do the best they can to learn, and treat everyone with respect and courtesy.

- Make it plain that you will steadfastly help students make the most of their opportunities to learn. Inform them, using examples, why it is necessary they follow your directions, every time. Show them how you will teach directions for simple activities such as beginning work when entering the classroom and handing in homework or class assignments.
- Project an image of friendly authority as you introduce the rules of behavior for the class. Discuss the rules thoroughly and make sure students understand how rules help everyone learn things they need to

know in life. Tell the students you will insist they follow the rules, but you will teach them how to do so and always help them. Follow through and have students practice proper behavior.

■ During the first days of school, ask in advance if students remember the rules for beginning work, having only school materials on their desks, and so forth.

Terms and Concepts

behavior management
Real Discipline
three phases of Real Discipline

Concept Cases

CASE 1: KRISTINA WILL NOT WORK

Kristina, a student in Mr. Jake's class, is quite docile. She socializes little with other students and never disrupts lessons. However, despite Mr. Jake's best efforts, Kristina will not do her work. She rarely completes an assignment. She is simply there, putting forth no effort at all. *What would Ronald Morrish suggest to help Kristina and Mr. Jake?*

Morrish would have Mr. Jake remind Kristina of the class rule about everyone doing their best to learn. He would insist that Kristina begin her work and follow through. Mr. Jake might need to stand beside her to help her get started. He would not punish her, but would continue to press her to comply with the assignment. He might ask questions such as, "Do you know what you are supposed to do in this activity?" "Do you understand why it needs to be done?" "Can I count on you to do your part?" As Kristina improves, Mr. Jake might make comments to her such as, "You made a good effort today. I can see you are trying. Thank you for that." If more intervention was required, Morrish would consider assigning Kristina to the school's study hall or keeping her in the classroom for additional time (a productive extension of her day, rather than a punitive detention). He might also have her create a daily plan for accomplishing her schoolwork, involve her parents in the process, or assign an older student to mentor her.

CASE 2: SARA WILL NOT STOP TALKING

Sara is a pleasant girl who participates in class activities and does most, though not all, of her assigned work. She cannot seem to refrain from talking to classmates, however. Her teacher, Mr. Gonzales, has to speak to her repeatedly during lessons, to the point that he often becomes exasperated and loses his temper. *What suggestions would Ronald Morrish give Mr. Gonzales for dealing with Sara?*

CASE 3: JOSHUA CLOWNS AND INTIMIDATES

Joshua, larger and louder than his classmates, always wants to be the center of attention, which he accomplishes through a combination of clowning and intimidation. He makes wise remarks, talks back (smilingly) to the teacher, utters a variety of sound-effect noises such as automobile crashes and gunshots, and makes limitless sarcastic comments and put-downs of his classmates. Other students will not stand up to him, apparently fearing his size and verbal aggression. His teacher, Miss Pearl, has come to her wit's end. *Would Joshua's behavior be likely to improve if Ronald Morrish's techniques were used in Miss Pearl's classroom? Explain.*

CASE 4: TOM IS HOSTILE AND DEFIANT

Tom has appeared to be in his usual foul mood ever since arriving in class. On his way to sharpen his pencil, he bumps into Frank, who complains. Tom tells him loudly to shut up. Miss Baines, the teacher, says, "Tom, go back to your seat." Tom wheels around, swears loudly, and says heatedly, "I'll go when I'm damned good and ready!" *How would Ronald Morrish have Miss Baines deal with Tom?*

You Are the Teacher

HIGH SCHOOL BIOLOGY

You teach an advanced placement class in biology to students from middle- to upper-income families. Most of the students have already made plans for attending college. When the students enter the classroom, they know they are to go to their assigned seats and write out answers to the questions of the day that you have written on the board. After that, you conduct discussions on text material that you assigned students to read before coming to class. During the discussion, you call randomly on students to answer questions and require that they support their answers with reference to the assigned reading. Following that, students engage in lab activity for the remainder of the period.

A TYPICAL OCCURRENCE

You have just begun a discussion about the process of photosynthesis. You ask Sarolyn what the word *photosynthesis* means. She pushes her long hair aside and replies, "I don't get it." This is a comment you hear frequently from Sarolyn, even though she is an intelligent girl. "What is it you don't understand?" "None of it," she says. You say, "Be more specific! I've only asked for the definition!" Sarolyn is not intimidated. "I mean, I don't get any of it. I don't understand why plants are green. Why aren't they blue or some other color? Why don't they grow on Mercury? The book says plants make food. How? Do they make bread? That's ridiculous." You gaze at Sarolyn for a while, and she back at you. You ask, "Are you finished?" Sarolyn shrugs. "I guess so." She hears some of the boys whistle under their breath; she obviously enjoys their attention. You say to her, "Sarolyn, I hope someday you will understand that this is not a place for you to show off." "I hope so, too," Sarolyn says. "I know I should be more serious." She stares out the window. For the remainder of the discussion, which you don't handle as well as usual, you call only on students you know will give proper answers. The discussion completed, you begin to give instructions for lab activity. You notice that Nick is turning the valve of the gas jet on and off. You say to Nick, "Mr. Contreras, would you please repeat our rule about the use of lab equipment?" Nick drops his head and mumbles something about waiting for directions. Sarolyn says calmly, "Knock it off, Nick. This is serious business." She smiles at you. After a moment, you complete your directions and tell the students to begin. You walk around the room, monitoring their work. You stand behind lab partners Mei and Teresa, who are having a difficult time. You do not offer them help, believing that advanced placement students should be able to work things out for themselves. But as they blunder through the activity, you find yourself shaking your head in disbelief.

CONCEPTUALIZING A STRATEGY

If you followed the suggestions of Ronald Morrish, what would you conclude or do with regard to the following?

- Pinpointing the problems in your class
- Preventing the problems from occurring in the first place
- Putting an immediate end to the misbehavior
- Maintaining student dignity and good personal relations
- Using the situation to help the students develop a sense of greater responsibility and self-control

Activities

1. Make entries in your journal concerning ideas from Morrish's Real Discipline that you might wish to include in your personal system of discipline.
2. Refer back to "What to Look for in This Chapter." For each item listed there, test yourself to see if you understand what Morrish was advising or teaching.

3. Ronald Morrish makes some interesting contentions about the role of student choice in discipline. Outline your understanding of his points and indicate whether you agree with them, and why. Discuss your conclusions in class, if possible.

References

Morrish, R. 1997. *Secrets of discipline: 12 keys for raising responsible children.* Fonthill, Canada: Woodstream Publishing.

Morrish, R. 2000. *With all due respect: Keys for building effective school discipline.* Fonthill, Canada: Woodstream Publishing.

Morrish, R. 2003. *FlipTips.* Fonthill, Canada: Woodstream Publishing.

Morrish, R. 2005. What is Real Discipline? www.realdiscipline.com

6

How Do Harry and Rosemary Wong Use Responsibilities and Procedures to Establish Class Discipline?

Harry and Rosemary Wong are today's most widely followed authorities in classroom management. They believe the key to desirable classroom behavior and learning lies in (1) clarifying the *responsibilities* of teachers and students and (2) teaching the *procedures* students are expected to follow in class. The Wongs urge teachers to address these matters and have students practice the procedures. They have found that once students are habituated to responsibilities and procedures, misbehavior fades away, allowing teaching and learning to occur as intended. The Wongs get their points across through pithy aphorisms, such as the following:

■ The main problem in teaching is not poor discipline, but poor classroom management.
■ Responsibilities clarify what everyone is supposed to do.
■ Effective teachers spend most of the first two weeks teaching students to follow classroom procedures.
■ What you do on the first day of school determines your success for the rest of the year.

Harry Wong, now an educational speaker and consultant, previously taught science at the middle school and high school levels. He received numerous awards, including the Outstanding Secondary Teacher Award, the Science Teacher Achievement Recognition Award, the Outstanding Biology Teacher Award, and the Valley Forge Teacher's Medal. Rosemary Wong taught grades K–8 and served as media coordinator and student activity director. She was chosen as one of California's first mentor teachers and has received the Silicon Valley Distinguished Woman of the Year Award. She works with her husband and is CEO of their publishing company. At the time of this writing, their book *The First Days of School* had sold almost four million copies, making it the best selling education book of all time. They have also produced a video series entitled *The Effective Teacher*, which won the Gold Award in the International Film and Video Festival and the Telly Award as the best educational staff development video. Because Harry is scheduled for speaking for

101

years in advance, he and Rosemary write a monthly column at www.teachers.net that permits more people to access their ideas. You might also wish to look at the Wongs' website at www.effectiveteaching.com.

A PREVIEW OF THIS CHAPTER

The main trouble in teaching is not discipline—it is a failure to teach fully the roles, responsibilities, and procedures that make the classroom run like clockwork. Everything we ask students to do involves a procedure, and when students follow procedures automatically, they learn better, behave better, and are easier to teach. The way to begin classes successfully is to spend the first days of school carefully teaching students (a) the proper roles and responsibilities of students and teacher, and (b) to follow the procedures exactly as expected of them. In short, clarify roles, clarify responsibilities, and explain and practice procedures until they become automatic. The result will be good learning and good behavior.

WHAT TO LOOK FOR IN THIS CHAPTER

■ An overview of Harry and Rosemary Wong's suggestions for establishing classes that run smoothly with little misbehavior

■ What is meant by *procedures* and why they are crucial to well-functioning classrooms

■ An extensive list (although not a complete one) of important procedures students should learn to follow automatically

■ The Wongs' advice on how to begin a class successfully, with attention to the first five minutes, the first day, and the first 10 days of school

■ The Wongs' commentary about cooperative group work

A QUICK READ OF THE WONGS' PRINCIPAL SUGGESTIONS

Go to the Building Teaching Skills and Dispositions section of Topic #5: Creating Positive Student–Teacher Relationships, in the **MyEducationLab** for your course and complete the activity entitled "Establishing Caring and Respectful Relationships."

The Wongs' ideas presented here are gleaned from the following sources: Starr (1999), Glavac (2005), and Wong and Wong (2000a,b, 2004a,b, 2005).

About Roles and Responsibilities

Help students understand *your* responsibilities and *their* responsibilities in the classroom. The following example, appropriate for secondary classes, appears on the cover of *The First Days of School* (2004b):

My Responsibilities as Your Teacher

1. To treat you with respect and care as an individual.
2. To provide you an orderly classroom environment.
3. To provide the necessary discipline.
4. To provide the appropriate motivation.
5. To teach you the required content.

Go to the Building Teaching Skills and Dispositions section of Topic #4: Establishing Classroom Norms and Expectations, in the **MyEducationLab** for your course and complete the activity entitled "Creating A Supportive Classroom Environment."

Your Responsibilities as My Students

1. To treat me with respect and care as an individual.
2. To attend classes regularly.
3. To be cooperative and not disruptive.
4. To study and do your work well.
5. To learn and master the required content.

About Classrooms and Procedures

- The single most important factor governing student learning is not discipline; it is how a teacher manages a classroom.
- Your classroom need not be chaos; it can be a smoothly functioning learning environment.
- A well-managed classroom is task oriented and predictable.
- *Ineffective teachers* begin the first day of school attempting to teach a subject. They then spend the rest of the school year running after students.
- *Effective teachers* spend most of the first two weeks of the school year teaching students to follow classroom **procedures** so that students are better able to learn.
- What is done on the first day of school or a class—even the first few minutes—can make or break a teacher.
- The very first day, the very first minute, the very first second of school, teachers should begin to establish a structure of procedures and routines for the class.

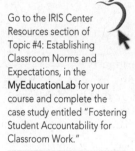

Go to the IRIS Center Resources section of Topic #4: Establishing Classroom Norms and Expectations, in the **MyEducationLab** for your course and complete the case study entitled "Fostering Student Accountability for Classroom Work."

About School

- School is where students go to learn how to be productive citizens and reach their potential as human beings.
- School should be challenging, exciting, engrossing, and thought provoking, but it must have structure to ensure success.
- You cannot give students self-esteem, but you can ensure they find success in school.

Go to the IRIS Center Resources section of Topic #4: Establishing Classroom Norms and Expectations, in the **MyEducationLab** for your course and complete the case study entitled "Norms and Expectations."

About Teaching

- Teaching is a craft—a highly skilled craft that can be learned.
- By far the most important factor in school learning is the ability of the teacher. The more capable the teacher, the more successful the student.
- Good teachers enhance the life and spirit of the students they teach.
- Stop asking, "What am I supposed to do?" Start asking, "What must I know that will help me accomplish what I need to do?"
- What you do on the first day of school determines your success for the rest of the year.
- Start class immediately. Do not take roll until later.
- Learning is often most effective when it takes place in a supportive community of learners.

- The more students work together responsibly, the more they learn.
- Short assignments produce higher student achievement.
- Intersperse questions throughout a lesson. Ask a question after you have spoken a few sentences rather than many. By doing so, you significantly increase student learning and retention.
- Students usually learn more from an activity-question approach than from a textbook-lecture approach.
- Teachers go through four stages of development—fantasy, survival, mastery, and impact. Good management moves you quickly from fantasy to mastery.
- You can have your achievements or you can have your excuses.
- Those who teach well never cease to learn.

About Testing and Evaluation

- If a student cannot demonstrate learning or achievement, it is the teacher's fault, not the student's.
- Use criterion-referenced tests to evaluate student performance.
- The more frequent the tests, the higher the achievement.
- Grade on what is learned, not on the curve—a procedure that has done great harm.

About Discipline

- Classroom rules indicate the behavior you expect from students. In order to provide a safe and effective learning environment, establish and enforce appropriate rules.
- Rules of behavior set limits, just as do rules in games. They create a work-oriented atmosphere in the classroom.
- Behavior associated with rules must be taught through discussion, demonstration, and practice.
- Consequences should be attached to rules—positive consequences for compliance and negative consequences (not punishment) for noncompliance.
- Explain your discipline plan (rules and consequences) to students on the first day of school.

About the First Day of Class

- Have your classroom ready for instruction and make it inviting.
- Organize your classroom with a script.
- Stand at the door and greet students as they enter.
- Give each student a seating assignment and a seating chart.
- Position yourself in the room near the students. Problems are proportional to distance.
- Post an assignment in a consistent location for students to begin when they enter the room.
- Display your diploma and credentials with pride. Dress in a professional manner that models success and shows you expect achievement.

About the First Week of Teaching

- The two most important things you must teach the first week of school are discipline and procedures.
- Explain your discipline plan to students and put it in effect immediately.
- State your procedures and begin rehearsing them until they become automatic.

A DISCIPLINE PLAN

Although this chapter focuses on the management of procedures, the Wongs remind us that even with good management teachers need a discipline approach that contains rules and consequences. They suggest you clarify that approach with students on the first day of school. They have found that most teachers want to begin teaching lessons before discipline and routines are addressed. When misbehavior occurs, those teachers apply punitive measures that are counterproductive. Without a discipline plan that begins the first day of school, you are setting yourself up for failure.

The Wongs are not particular about the discipline plan you use, other than to say that you should (1) develop one that is suited to your requirements and your students' needs, and (2) make sure it includes rules of behavior, procedures for teaching those rules, and consequences that are applied when students comply with or break rules. As for the rules themselves, the Wongs (2004b) suggest you think through carefully the kind of behavior you expect from students, write your expectations as rules, post them in the class, and go over them with students on the first day. You will have firm confidence in your ability to manage the class if you and your students understand clearly what is expected.

The Wongs suggest you limit the number of rules to a maximum of five, stated in a positive manner when possible (although in some cases it is more effective to state them in a negative manner, such as "No fighting"). Here are five universal rules the Wongs provide as examples:

- Follow directions the first time they are given.
- Raise your hand and wait for permission to speak.
- Stay in your seat unless you have permission to do otherwise.
- Keep hands, feet, and objects to yourself.
- No cursing or teasing (2004b, p. 146).

Introduce the rules on the first day of class and post them in a prominent place. The Wongs suggest introducing them as follows, using your own language and explanations:

"The rules for our class are to help you learn in a classroom that is safe and effective. They help make sure that nothing will keep you from being successful in this class.

We will be working together closely. We need to keep this classroom a place where you will never have fear of being ridiculed or threatened. Because I care about all of you and want you to succeed, I will not allow anyone to do anything that will interfere with someone who is trying to learn.

In the same way, my job is to teach you and help you be successful, so I will not allow you to do anything that will interfere with my teaching and our group success and enjoyment.

So that I can teach and all of us can learn in the best possible conditions, I have a set of rules that help make this classroom safe, orderly, and productive. I'd like to explain these rules to you so you understand clearly what they mean and how I will enforce them."

PLANNING AND ORGANIZING

Organization enables you to keep on schedule, know where things are, and make your time and space work for you. It eliminates chaos, lets you get things done, and allows you some time to enjoy life. Good ideas for organization are found in the best practices of outstanding teachers, who "beg, borrow, and steal" ideas from any sources available.

PROCEDURES AND WHAT THEY ENTAIL

Go to the Simulations section of Topic #8: Planning, Conducting, and Managing Instruction, in the **MyEducationLab** for your course and complete the simulation entitled "Effectively Handling Transitions."

Student behavior and student achievement are directly related to how well teachers establish good, workable classroom procedures, beginning the very first day. Students accept and appreciate uniform procedures that provide security while minimizing confusion. Lacking those procedures, students are likely to behave undesirably and develop poor work habits that are difficult to correct.

To establish good procedures, do two things: First, decide what **routines** are necessary for the activities you will provide, and second, make lists of the procedural steps students must follow in order to participate in and benefit from the activities. If you do these two things, you will end up with a very large number of procedures. But remember that every time you want students to do something, they need a procedure to follow—for example, how to enter and exit the classroom; how dismissal occurs at the end of the period or day; how to begin and finish work; how to come to attention; what to do on returning after being absent; what to do when arriving tardy; how the class is to get quiet when necessary; how the period or day is to begin; how to ask for help from the teacher or others; how to indicate when you don't understand or need help; how to move about the classroom; how papers, materials, and supplies are to be distributed and collected; how everyone is to listen to and respond to questions; how to work cooperatively with others; how groups are changed; how to keep your student notebook; how directions are given for each assignment and how to find the directions; and how to walk in the corridors. The Wongs give specific attention to these matters and many more.

Good procedures allow a great variety of activities to occur, often several at the same time, with little confusion. But you have to teach students the procedures, not just talk about them. The Wongs suggest a three-step method for teaching procedures:

- *Explain.* The teacher states, explains, and demonstrates the procedure.
- *Rehearse.* The students practice the procedure under teacher supervision.

- *Reinforce.* The teacher provides re-teaching, rehearsal, and reinforcement until the procedures become habituated.

Examples of Procedures in a Fourth-Grade Classroom

Go to the Building Teaching Skills and Dispositions section of Topic #4: Establishing Classroom Norms and Expectations, in the **MyEducationLab** for your course and complete the activity entitled "Establishing Rules and Routines."

The following procedures, which the Wongs credit to teacher Nathan Gibbs, show how one teacher has structured his fourth-grade class for success. You may teach kindergarten or high school physical education and feel these procedures do not apply to you. The Wongs remind us repeatedly that while this scheme is what works for one particular teacher, it reflects realities that exist in all classrooms. (These procedures may be tedious to read, but please consider them carefully, as they touch on many things that are important in all classrooms.)

Nathan makes his classroom a place where students feel genuinely cared for. He provides personalized instruction within a warm, relaxed, refined learning environment. On the first day of school he gives his students a written list of all the classroom procedures, with a cover page that says, "Follow these procedures to reward yourself with complete success."

Nathan spends the first two weeks of class teaching the procedures, and he expects students to follow them to the letter. The number of procedures may seem overwhelming, but Nathan says his students appreciate them. Here is what Nathan emphasizes (Wong and Wong, 2004a):

> "You will be safe in this class. I will do my best for you, and I want you to do your best for yourself. Be ready to learn and do the best you can."

Morning Entry Procedures

- Empty your backpack, place it neatly outside, and bring in homework and needed supplies.
- Enter the classroom in a quiet and orderly manner.
- Greet your teacher as you enter and say "hi" to all your classmates.
- Turn in homework or keep at desk if it is to be graded in class.
- Begin on your seat work.

Desk Procedures

- Only your notebook, assignment book, textbooks, reading book, and supply box belong in your desk.
- Toys, food, and loose paper do not belong in your desk.
- Keep hands, feet, paper, books, and pencils off your neighbors' desks.
- Push in your chair every time you get up.
- Clean your desk and the area around it before you leave.

Line-Up Procedures

- When dismissed, stand in two equal lines and wait quietly.
- First excused line goes out of room, and then the second line follows.
- No talking while still in the hallway.

Lunch Procedures

- When excused for lunch, get your lunch if you brought it.
- Lunch Leaders stand in front with lunch buckets.
- Follow the line-up procedures.
- When dismissed by teacher, walk to the cafeteria.
- If you have brought your lunch, go and sit at the correct table.
- Say "hello" to any adult in the cafeteria.
- If you are buying lunch, get your card from the slot and wait quietly in line.
- Eat nicely and neatly.
- Talk with a low voice.
- Clean up your mess and encourage others to do so.
- Raise your hand when you would like to be dismissed.
- Put all leftover food and trash in the trashcans.
- Place your lunchbox in the bucket when you leave.
- Walk to the play area.

Lunch Leader Procedures

- Line up first in line.
- Bring lunch bucket to the multipurpose room and back from the multipurpose room.
- Clean out lunch bucket when needed.
- Remind classmates at the end of day to retrieve their lunchboxes from buckets.
- Make sure our class is cleanest of all in the multipurpose room.

Bus Pick-Up Procedures

- Walk quickly to bus area.
- Quietly wait behind the line for the bus.
- Show respect for the teacher on duty.
- Show respect for the bus driver.
- On the bus, stay in your seat and talk quietly.
- Follow the bus rules or you will lose your bus pass.
- Be a good role model and a helper for the younger students on early-out Wednesday.

Car Pick-Up Procedures

- Walk to car pick-up area near the primary wing.
- Don't walk onto the blacktop where cars park or drive.
- Show respect for the teacher on duty.
- Quietly wait for your ride.
- If your ride is more than 10 minutes late, go sit quietly in the office and wait.
- When your ride arrives, the driver must get out of the car and sign you out in the Late Log.
- Be a good role model and a helper for the younger students on early-out Wednesday.

Bicycle Rider Procedures

- Walk your bike on campus before and after school.
- Lock your bike to the bike rack.
- Leave other bikes alone.
- Wear your helmet while riding your bike.
- Obey all traffic laws.
- Come straight to school and go straight home.

Walker Procedures

- Walk straight to school.
- Walk straight home.
- Obey all traffic laws.

Going to Other Parts of School

- Line up quietly when asked.
- Walk single file, on the right side of the walkway.
- Enter the other classroom or library silently with good manners.
- Greet the teacher as you enter.
- Remember you are representing yourselves and our class.

Basic Assembly Procedures

- Line up inside or outside our classroom first.
- Follow the student council representatives to the correct area.
- Pay attention and sit where you are instructed to.
- Quietly sit on chairs or benches or with legs crossed on floor.
- Remember to conduct yourself responsibly while waiting, watching, and after the assembly.
- Show respect for the presentation.
- Be patient if you have a question for the presenter.
- Return to the classroom in a quiet, orderly manner.

End of the Day Procedures

- Copy down the homework assignment in your notebook.
- Clean around your desk.
- Pack your assignment book and what you need for homework.
- Wait for the teacher to call your number to get your backpack.
- Leave only when dismissed by the teacher.
- On leaving, say "goodbye" to your classmates and teacher.
- Make sure to be to the bus on time.
- Remember to tell your family about your day at school.

Restroom Procedures

- Only one person at a time may go.
- Quietly hold up three fingers and shake your fingers if it is an emergency.
- Wash your hands afterwards.
- Come right back and enter quietly.

Drinking Fountain Procedures

- Drink water at recess, lunch, or when your work is finished.
- Do not line up at the drinking fountain outside or inside the classroom after the recess bell has rung.
- No more than three people at the sink area at any time.
- Wipe the sink after you drink.

Computer Procedures

- Wash your hands before using the computer.
- No more than two people at a computer.
- Refer your questions to the technology assistant.
- Clean up the area around you before you leave.
- Log out of all programs you have been using.
- Shut off the computer at the end of the day if you are the last to use it.

Goals, Yellow Cards, and Red Cards

- When you receive a goal, put it in your "safe place."
- At the end of the week, have all goals totaled for recording.
- If you receive your first yellow card of the week, put it in your slot.
- You must then see the peer counselor and put your entry into the logbook.
- Then check in with the recess aide and sit out for that day.
- If you receive your second yellow card, put your entry in the logbook. Report to Mr. Gibbs to receive counseling.
- For the remainder of the week, sit out at recess after checking in with the duty aide.
- If you ever receive the nasty red card, see Mr. Gibbs when instruction is finished. Choose between the call home and discipline essay. For two full weeks, sit out at recess after checking in with the duty aide.

Peer Council

- Ensure you are talking to all yellow card recipients.
- Check logbook to see that they signed it.
- Report any problems to the teacher.
- Settle as many disputes as possible at recess.

When You Have a Substitute Teacher

- Respect and follow the substitute's directions and rules, even if they are not exactly the same as ours.
- Remember the substitute is taking my place and is an equal of mine.
- Be as helpful as possible. The substitute has a copy of all our class procedures.
- Assist the substitute in finding supplies.

Group Work

- Greet all group members.
- Be prepared with the necessary tools and resources to be successful.

- Collaboration is the key to being a successful learning club.
- All members participate, share, learn from, and help one another.
- Use the same procedures for speaking as you do during class.
- No one group member is to do all the work.
- Practice active listening.
- Cooperate.
- Do your personal best.

Nathan Gibbs's lists of procedures continue for a number of other matters, such as Job Procedures, Technology Assistant, Messengers, Pet and Garden Caretakers, Work Organization, Cleanup, Homework, Turning in Completed Work, Correcting Assignments, Filling out the Student Planner, and Procedures Related to Missing a School Day. If you are interested in Mr. Gibbs's lists for those matters, you can find them on the Internet at http://teachers.net/wong/MAR04.

HOW TO BEGIN A CLASS SUCCESSFULLY

As we have seen, the Wongs place great emphasis on what teachers should do to begin the term or year (see Wong and Wong, 2005). New teachers, the Wongs say with a note of irony, often have bags brimming with lesson plans, boxes of activities, the state performance appraisal instrument, five interpretations of educational foundations, nine theories of child development, conflicting advice from a plethora of educational specialists, and a collection of buzzwords and current educational fads. But they have little idea about what to do in the first days and weeks of school. To help new teachers overcome this problem, the Wongs present a First Day of School Action Plan, which they credit to teacher Sarah Jondahl, who developed a plan of step-by-step procedures associated with preparing the classroom before students arrive, academic expectations, time frames, lesson plans and activities for first days of school, steps in establishing working relations with students and parents, class schedules, maintaining a good learning environment, and procedures in documentation and evaluation of student progress. To illustrate, in preparing the classroom before the first day of school, Sarah lists the following matters that require her attention:

- "Be Prepared" sheet
- Preparation checklist
- Getting organized
- "Cooperative Classroom" dry-erase board
- Student contract for classroom materials
- "Our Class Fits Like A Puzzle" bulletin board
- Classroom door decoration
- "Brag about Me" bulletin board
- "All about Me" bulletin board
- Room arrangement

In the section on establishing relationships with students and parents, she includes the following matters:

- Letter to students
- Open house activities
- Substitute teacher handbook
- New student folder
- Parent letter
- Homework policy
- Homework tip list
- Transportation checklist
- Rules, consequences, and rewards
- Volunteer sheet
- "Welcoming Phone Call" planning sheet
- "Welcoming Phone Call" planning sheet for parents of potential problem students
- "Positive Phone Call" form
- Parent conferences outline

For the section on maintaining a good learning climate, she details what she would do concerning the following:

- Reasons for the behavior management plan
- Rules, consequences, and rewards
- Procedures in behavior management
- First morning greeting and seating arrangement
- Housekeeping ideas
- "Duty Wheel" for student jobs
- Intervention plan packet
- Socio-gram
- Form used to create a socio-gram
- Notes of encouragement
- Student postcard
- "Special News about a Very Special Student" certificate
- "Super Job/Way To Go/Great Day" letter form

The Wongs emphasize that teachers should set high expectations on the first day, plan the entire day right down to the minute, and make sure to give attention to an opening assignment for students, establishing routines, and learning students' names. They stress that during the first week, the most important thing you can do is provide the security of consistency (Wong and Wong, 2004b). If the furniture is movable, align all the desks on the first day facing the teacher and keep them that way until you have a good reason to change. Provide a well-organized, uncluttered, attractive classroom. Have the room ready and inviting when students arrive on the first day. On a bulletin board or elsewhere, post schedules, rules, procedures, and a preview of what is to come. Also post information about yourself, including a picture and a sign that welcomes students to the class. Wear neat clothing, as first perceptions affect how students relate to you. Stand when you speak and use short, clear sentences or phrases. Use a firm but soft voice. When emphasizing, do not point your finger, as it presents an accusatory image.

Your major mission during the first few days is to establish student routines and classroom procedures. If you have very young students, place their name on their coat hooks, desks, and cubbyholes and tell them to use the coat hook, desk, or cubbyhole every day. Set up a seating plan beforehand, as this helps you to get to know your students quickly. Address your students by name as soon as possible.

On the first day, go to school early and take time to double-check everything. Have your first bell-work assignment ready (a short assignment that students begin working on when they first arrive in the room). Make it interesting but fairly easy so students will have an initial sense of accomplishment. Students who fail early tend to create problems in the classroom. Before class begins, tell yourself the following:

- I will establish classroom management procedures from the beginning.
- I will convey that this class will be businesslike, with a firm, competent, and warm teacher.
- I will establish work habits in my students first and worry about content later.

As the students arrive, position yourself outside the door to greet them. This establishes authority and shows you consider them important. If young children are to line up before entering, insist on a straight line. If you pick up your class from another area, don't say: "Follow me" or "Come on." Rather, introduce yourself and then teach the procedure you want students to follow as they walk to your room.

THE FIRST FIVE MINUTES ARE CRITICAL

The Wongs repeat that you should have an assignment for the students to begin working on the second they walk into the room (Wong and Wong, 2000a). This eliminates 90 percent of discipline problems that otherwise arise. There should be no student free time planned into the routines at first. It is better to have too much planned for the class period rather than too little. The first few minutes are crucial to setting the tone in your class. Students must know what they are expected to do. When they come in, remind them of the materials they need that day, and to have pencils sharpened and paper ready. When the bell rings, turn on the overhead projector that displays a warm-up activity, perhaps important information or a brief review of something learned the previous year or term. As students work, take roll while you walk around and observe them. For the next activity, students might be asked to write a reaction to a quote or newspaper article, copy a timeline, brainstorm emotions felt in response to a piece of music, or, later, a quiz on the previous night's reading assignment.

THE FIRST DAY OF SCHOOL

The Wongs suggest you carefully plan your first day of class or school in detail. They describe how art teacher Melissa Pantoja attends to this task (see Wong and Wong, 2000c). They liken Mrs. Pantoja to a coach who scripts the first 25 plays of a game. They say a teacher should not "wing it" in a classroom any more than a coach would wing it on a football field or a pilot would wing it on a flight from Baltimore to Kansas City. The effective teacher goes in with a plan and modifies that plan if conditions change. Here is Mrs. Pantoja's plan for the first day.

Greet Each Student at the Door

- Hand each student a classroom rules sheet (goes in notebook)
- Direct the student to his or her assigned seat (alphabetical)
- Tell the student to read and follow the instructions that are written on the board

Welcome Students to Class and Introduce Myself

- My name
- My family (spouse, kids)
- Education
- Where I'm from and where I live
- Why I wanted to teach

Arriving and Leaving Class

- Teach procedure for arriving in class
- Teach procedure for dismissal from class

Explain Rules and Daily Procedures

- Refer to the rules that are posted at front
- Explain discipline plan and refer to poster
- Go over procedures and refer to poster
- Talk about "We missed you" chart

Number Assignments

- Each person will have a number that represents them
- The number will be on all of their art papers and on their art folder
- This will help all of us to keep our papers straight

Respecting the Classroom and the Art Supplies

- Refer to classroom rules and procedures
- Teach students to be responsible for the art supplies and room

Teacher's Things and Students' Things

- Some things are only for me
- Other things are for you to use as you need them

Art Centers

- Everyone will get a chance to go to all the centers
- Art center board will have names (numbers) that tell us who does what that day

Portfolios
- Each student will be taking a portfolio home
- Papers will be filed in a container until end of semester

Notebooks
- Used for individual students to record their grades and keep track of them
- To store vocabulary words for future use
- To write a weekly journal entry about what they liked most about the week's lesson

THE FIRST 10 DAYS OF SCHOOL

The Wongs (2005) further provide detailed suggestions for procedures during the first 10 days of school. They present a guide they credit to Jane Slovenske, a National Board Certified Teacher. Ms. Slovenske's class uses a *self-manager plan* in which students are taught to manage their own behavior in a responsible manner. Behavior standards are established through class discussions about responsible behavior, treatment of others, and working promptly to the best of one's ability. Once a list of behaviors is agreed on, the students are presented with a *self-manager application* to use as a self-evaluation of their behaviors and standards.

When students are able to manage all of the items on the application, they fill in the form and take it home for parental review. When parents are in agreement with their child's self-evaluation, they sign the form and have the student return it to school. Ms. Slovenske must then agree with the student's self-evaluation. She discusses with students any differences of opinion. Most students, with input from their parents, are honest about self-evaluating their performance. Space here does not permit inclusion of Ms. Slovenske's plan in detail, but you might wish to examine it online at http://teachers.net/wong/JAN05.

PROCEDURES FOR COOPERATIVE WORK GROUPS

Generally speaking, most students do better in school when allowed to work in cooperative learning groups. The Wongs suggest that you call your cooperative groups **support groups,** with each member of the group known as a **support buddy.**

Children need lots of support. Instead of isolating them with seat work, surround them with support buddies and teach them how to support each other. It is important that each student in the group have a specific job to do. Group procedures must be taught clearly. *Ineffective* teachers divide students into groups and simply expect the students to work together. *Effective* teachers teach the group procedures and social skills needed for functioning in a group. Before you begin your first group activity, teach students how to do the following:

- Be responsible for your own work and behavior.
- Ask a support buddy for help if you have a question.
- Help any support buddy who asks for help.
- Ask for help from the teacher only when support buddies cannot supply it.

For further detailed information on how to work with groups, consult Chapter 24 in *The First Days of School* (Wong and Wong, 2004b).

A WORD TO SECONDARY TEACHERS

Secondary teachers sometimes comment that the Wongs' suggestions appear to be too elementary for use in high school, but the Wongs emphasize that their approach works quite well at the high school level. Their website includes testimonials from secondary teachers, many of whom assert that the Wongs' suggestions actually saved their professional careers.

For example, Chelonnda Seroyer (see http://teachers.net/wong/FEB05), a first-year teacher, used the Wongs' ideas as the basis for managing her class and had a very successful year academically. In addition, she was senior class sponsor, homecoming parade assistant, and a member of the support team for the school's efforts related to the No Child Left Behind Act. For her efforts she received the Bob Jones High School "First Year Patriot Award," which is given to the first-year teacher who is recognized for outstanding accomplishments and achievements in academics, athletics, or co-curricular pursuits.

Jeff Smith (see http://teachers.net/wong/APR04) teaches welding at a Career Tech Center in Pryor, Oklahoma. He was almost fired during his first year because of his poor classroom management skills, but happened to hear one of the Wongs' tapes and wrote to say, "You saved my job, and someday I want to help other beginning teachers just like you helped me." Jeff now holds the state record for the most Career Tech students certified under the industry standard welding certification. His former students have the highest pay average for high school graduates in the state. He reports that he always knew his subject matter, but had no clue about classroom management until he encountered the Wongs' ideas.

Ed Lucero (see http://teachers.net/wong/MAR05) teaches high school business, marketing, and finance in Albuquerque, New Mexico. He writes, "Last year was my eleventh year of teaching. I was miserable! Students weren't paying attention. I constantly repeated myself. Students would ignore my instructions and at times talk back. Some students would attempt to call me 'bro' instead of Mr. Lucero." Ed decided if things did not improve, he would leave teaching and return to public accounting. His wife suggested he read the Wongs' *The First Days of School: How to Become an Effective Teacher*. He spent the summer studying their suggestions and when the next school year began he was able to implement them and as a result enjoy the pleasures of teaching.

Summary Rubric

APPLYING THE WONGS' SUGGESTIONS IN THE CLASSROOM

■ Take to heart the Wongs' suggestions for organizing a classroom that promotes learning and proper behavior.

■ Go through the Wongs' suggestions for the multitude of procedures that come into play every day in the classroom. Decide how you will teach those procedures to your students and what you will do when students fail to follow the required procedures.

■ Per the Wongs' suggestions, script in detail the first five minutes, the first day, and the first 10 days of your new semester or year.

■ Beginning on the first day of school, take pains to help students clearly understand your responsibili-

ties, their responsibilities, the discipline plan, and how the class is to function.

■ Through the term or year, continue to practice procedures until they become habituated routines that students are able to follow automatically.

Terms and Concepts

procedures
routines

support buddies
support groups

Concept Cases

CASE 1: KRISTINA WILL NOT WORK

Kristina, a student in Mr. Jake's class, is quite docile. She socializes little with other students and never disrupts lessons. However, despite Mr. Jake's best efforts, Kristina will not do her work. She rarely completes an assignment. She is simply there, putting forth no effort at all. *What would Harry and Rosemary Wong suggest to help Kristina and Mr. Jake?*

The Wongs would advise Mr. Jake to carefully teach Kristina the procedures associated with completing assignments and other work activities. He should ask her to show him that she understands the procedures. He might consider having Kristina work with a support buddy with whom she feels comfortable. He would supply positive consequences for all improvements Kristina shows. If Kristina does not improve, Mr. Jake should talk further with her privately, and in a positive, supportive tone reiterate that he cares about her, wants her to succeed, will let nothing interfere with her progress if he can help it, and will help correct anything that might be standing in the way of her completing her work. If Kristina still doesn't improve, Mr. Jake should seek help from school personnel who are trained to assess Kristina and help provide conditions that improve her likelihood of success.

CASE 2: SARA WILL NOT STOP TALKING

Sara is a pleasant girl who participates in class activities and does most, though not all, of her assigned work. She cannot seem to refrain from talking to classmates, however. Her teacher, Mr. Gonzales, has to speak to her repeatedly during lessons, to the point that he often becomes exasperated and loses his temper. *What suggestions would Harry and Rosemary Wong give Mr. Gonzales for dealing with Sara?*

CASE 3: JOSHUA CLOWNS AND INTIMIDATES

Joshua, larger and louder than his classmates, always wants to be the center of attention, which he accomplishes through a combination of clowning and intimidation. He makes wise remarks, talks back (smilingly) to the teacher, utters a variety of sound-effect noises such as automobile crashes and gunshots, and makes limitless sarcastic comments and put-downs of his classmates. Other students will not stand up to him, apparently fearing his size and verbal aggression. His teacher, Miss Pearl, has come to her wit's end. *Do Harry and Rosemary Wong provide suggestions that might improve Joshua's behavior? Explain.*

CASE 4: TOM IS HOSTILE AND DEFIANT

Tom has appeared to be in his usual foul mood ever since arriving in class. On his way to sharpen his pencil, he bumps into Frank, who complains. Tom tells him loudly to shut up. Miss Baines, the teacher, says, "Tom, go back to your seat." Tom wheels around, swears loudly, and says heatedly, "I'll go when I'm damned good and ready!" *What suggestions might Harry and Rosemary Wong have for helping improve Tom's behavior?*

You Are the Teacher

MIDDLE SCHOOL LIBRARY

You are a media specialist in charge of the middle school library. You see your job as serving as a resource person to students who are seeking information, and you are always eager to give help to those who request it. Each period of the day brings different students to your center. Usually, small groups have been sent to the library to do cooperative research. Always some unexpected students appear who have been excused from physical education for medical reasons but don't like coming to your center, or else they bear special passes from their teachers for a variety of reasons.

A TYPICAL OCCURRENCE

You have succeeded in getting students settled and working when Tara appears at your side, needing a book to read as makeup work for missing class. You ask Tara what kinds of books interest her. She resignedly shrugs her shoulders. You take her to a shelf of newly published books. "I read this one last night," you tell her. "I think you might like it. It's a good story and

fast reading." Tara only glances at it. "That looks stupid," she says. "Don't you have any good books?" She glances down the shelf. "These are all stupid!" Another student, Jaime, is tugging at your elbow. He has a note from his history teacher who wants the source of a particular quotation. You ask Tara to look at the books for a moment while you take Jaime to the reference books. As you pass by a table of students supposedly doing research, you see that the group is watching Walter and Teo have a friendly pencil fight, hitting pencils together until one of them breaks. You address your comments to Walter, who appears to be the more willing participant. Walter answers hotly, "Teo started it! It wasn't me!" "Well," you say, "if you boys can't behave yourself, just go back to your class." The other student smiles and Walter feels he is being treated unjustly. He sits down and pouts. Meanwhile, Tara has gone to the large globe and is twirling it. You start to speak to her but realize that Jaime is still waiting at your side with the request for his teacher. Somehow, before the period ends, Tara leaves with a book she doesn't want and Jaime takes a citation back to his teacher. The research groups have been too noisy. You know they have done little work and wonder if you should speak to their teacher about their manners and courtesy. After the period is over, you notice that profane remarks have been written on the table where Walter was sitting.

What suggestions might the Wongs make that would improve things for you in the Media Center?

Activities

1. In your journal, list concepts and procedures from this chapter that you would like to incorporate into your personal system of discipline.
2. Working alone or with peers, compile a comprehensive list of procedures you would want to teach students in a grade or subject of your choice.
3. Working alone or with peers, select five of the procedures you have identified and specify what and how you would teach your students about them. Share your efforts with the class.

References

Glavac, M., 2005. Summary of major concepts covered by Harry K. Wong. *The Busy Educator's Newsletter.* www.glavac.com

Starr, L. 1999. Speaking of classroom management—An interview with Harry K. Wong. *Education World.* www.education-world.com/a_curr/curr161.shtml

Wong, H., and Wong, R. 2000a. The first five minutes are critical. *Teachers.net Gazette.* http://teachers.net/gazette/NOV00/wong.html

Wong, H., and Wong, R. 2000b. The problem is not discipline. *Teachers.net Gazette.* http://teachers.net/gazette/SEP00/wong.html

Wong, H., and Wong, R. 2000c. Your first day. *Teachers.net Gazette.* http://teachers.net/gazette/JUN00/covera.html

Wong, H., and Wong, R. 2004a. A well-oiled learning machine. *Teachers.net Gazette.* http://teachers.net/wong/MAR04

Wong, H., and Wong, R. 2004b. *The first days of school: How to be an effective teacher.* Mountain View, CA: Harry K. Wong Publications.

Wong, H., and Wong, R. 2005. The first ten days of school. *Teachers.net Gazette.* http://teachers.net/wong/JAN05

7

How Does Fred Jones Establish Class Discipline by Keeping Students Responsibly Involved?

Some years ago, psychologist Fred Jones conducted large-scale studies of outstanding teachers who were considered to be "naturals." He hoped to pinpoint what they did to make teaching and discipline seem so effortless. What he found was that the most successful teachers not only helped students learn, but simultaneously taught them how to manage their behavior responsibly. Jones determined that many desirable results accrued from that combination of learning and responsibility—better self-control, less misbehavior, more positive attitudes, and reduction in teacher workload and stress.

Dr. Jones, an independent consultant in teaching and classroom management, is the developer and disseminator of Fred Jones's *Tools for Teaching*, a book in which he explains the tactics he judges best for motivating students, instructing them effectively, and helping them develop self-discipline. He first became interested in those matters while on the faculties of the UCLA Medical Center and the University of Rochester School of Medicine and Dentistry. He now devotes himself to making presentations and developing materials for educators. Among his popular books are *Tools for Teaching* (2007), *Positive Classroom Discipline* (1987a), and *Positive Classroom Instruction* (1987b). Jones has also developed a video course of study called *The Video Toolbox* (2007) and has published a number of articles in *Education World*. The manual for the videos is authored by Patrick T. Jones. These materials, his program, and his presentations are described on his website at www.fredjones.com. Links to a number of Jones's highly informative articles are also presented in the Linbar Consulting website at www.linbarconsulting.com.

Go to the Building Classroom Discipline Video Showcase section of Topic #3: Models of Classroom Management, in the **MyEducationLab** for your course and watch the video entitled "Fred Jones—Positive Classroom Discipline."

A PREVIEW OF THIS CHAPTER

Misbehavior in most classrooms consists mainly of student passivity, general aimlessness, and massive time wasting. These discipline problems are best resolved by teaching in ways that keep students attentive and responsibly involved in the classroom. Jones advises teachers to use four major teaching strategies: Say, See, Do teaching; working the crowd; using body language effectively; and promoting responsibility through incentive systems. He also emphasizes the value of visual instructional plans, preferred activity time, and providing help efficiently. In short, set limits; enforce them through rules and body language; use Say, See, Do teaching; work the crowd; and provide help and incentives efficiently.

WHAT TO LOOK FOR IN THIS CHAPTER

■ Major problem areas that Jones identified in classrooms

■ Six things that successful teachers do

■ How teachers can use body language to show they mean business

■ How to cut down on wasted time in the classroom

■ How teachers provide individual help to students who need it

■ Suggestions for organizing seating and "working the crowd"

PROBLEMS THAT JONES BROUGHT TO LIGHT

Jones and his associates spent thousands of hours observing and recording in hundreds of elementary and secondary classrooms. From the resultant data, Jones was able to identify misbehaviors that occurred most frequently in classrooms and pinpoint the portions of classes or lessons in which they were most likely to occur. He was also able to identify tactics that highly effective teachers used to prevent or deal with misbehavior, usually rather easily. The five major problem areas Jones found in the less-productive classrooms were massive time wasting, student passivity in learning, student aimlessness, "helpless handraising," and ineffective teacher nagging. Here is what he said about those problems and how to address them.

Massive Time Wasting

The main characteristic of less-productive classes was simply **massive time wasting.** Even though many of the classrooms he studied were in inner-city schools and alternative schools for students with behavior problems, Jones found relatively little student hostility and defiance—the behavior teachers fear and many people believe predominates in schools. Instead, the major problem was the huge amount of time students wasted in school simply talking, goofing off, daydreaming, and moving about the room.

Jones found that one or more of those four behaviors were present during about 95 percent of the classroom disruptions that hindered teaching and learning. Jones found that in well-managed classrooms, one of those disruptions occurred about every two minutes. In loud, unruly classes the disruptions averaged about 2.5 per minute. In attempting to deal with the disruptive misbehaviors, teachers lost an average of almost 50 percent of the time otherwise available for teaching and learning (Jones, 1987a). Jones found that typical classes, on average, did not get down to business until five to seven minutes after the bell rang, while typical in-class transitions from one activity to another took five minutes. In both cases, students, whom Jones describes as expert time wasters, took advantage of the opportunity to dawdle. As Jones put it, they had no vested interest in hustle. They knew that as soon as the transition was over they would have to go back to work, and they were in no hurry for that.

Jones consequently set out to determine how time wasting could be reduced to a minimum. He concluded it could best be reduced by clearly communicating class requirements to students and following through with class rules, establishing and practicing routines, increasing student motivation to engage in activities, and using effective ways of providing help to students who needed it. Jones's suggestions related to these solutions are described later in this chapter.

Student Passivity

Jones also found that students in typical classes were passive rather than active most of the time. They often disengaged from lessons and found more interesting things to do. Their passivity was brought on in large measure by the teaching method being used in most classes, which did not require students to participate actively or show accountability in the early phases of lessons. They merely sat and listened, more or less, while teachers explained and demonstrated. Jones called the teachers' act "bop 'til you drop." He commented that their efforts were similar to actors performing "five matinees a day." But after all that effort, when the lesson transitioned from teacher input to independent student seat work, waving hands would shoot into the air because students didn't know what to do. The hands, he saw, belonged to the same **helpless handraisers** every day. When hands went up, the teachers would begin chasing from student to student, repeating the same information they had tried so hard to provide earlier in the lesson.

Aimlessness

Jones found another cause of wasted time was that students either had scant knowledge of the procedures they needed to follow or chose not to follow them. This lack of knowledge, or disregard of it, resulted in apathy and inaction. Jones believes students usually know, generally if not specifically, what is expected of them, yet many simply disregard those expectations. This is hardly a surprise—we all know from experience that students adjust their behavior to match the standards that a given teacher is able to uphold. As Jones puts it, if your second-period teacher lets you talk and fool around while your third-period teacher does not, you will talk in second period and cool it in third period. The standards in any classroom, he says, are defined by whatever the students can get away with. If teachers do not take the time to teach expectations and procedures carefully—and if they fail to ensure compliance with those expectations—they will invariably get whatever the students feel like giving them. Jones concluded that teaching and enforcing classroom procedures is one of the most important, yet most neglected, areas of classroom management.

Helpless Handraising

Jones found that when teachers were working hard in the first parts of lessons, students seemed to pay attention and understand well enough. But when students were directed to continue work on their own, hands went up, talking began, students rummaged around or stared out the window, and some got out of their seats. That was the point, Jones said, when "the chickens come home to roost" (1987b, p. 14). Often, teachers did not know what to do at that time other than admonish, nag, or re-teach the lesson to the helpless handraisers. That scene, said Jones, merely reflects "another day in the life of a typical classroom" (p. 14). Teachers everywhere can relate to that scenario and the frustration it brings, but few understand how to address it. Later we will explore Jones's solution to the problem.

Ineffective Nagging

Jones's observations revealed that many teachers spend a great deal of time nagging students—telling them over and over what they ought to be doing and to stop doing what they shouldn't be doing. Jones calls their behavior the *nag-nag-nag syndrome*, which many teachers use even though experience has repeatedly shown them it doesn't work. Jones's alternative to nagging is for teachers to calmly show they mean business. As we will see later, they can do this more effectively through body language than through verbal language.

JONES'S CONCLUSIONS ABOUT WHAT EFFECTIVE TEACHERS DO

Jones says that all the highly touted efforts to improve education—all those policies, mandates, and well-intentioned "solutions"—don't mean a thing until they are translated into workable practices in the classroom. Most teachers try their best, not only to maintain reasonable behavior in the room but to implement the latest and best teaching practices. Unfortunately, they usually end up with an increased workload that eventually becomes insupportable.

Jones insists there are easier ways to get things done. Given the proper tools, teachers can in fact teach very well without working themselves to exhaustion—thus escaping the fatigue and disillusionment that are so common in teaching today. He shows how to establish a class structure that promotes active student involvement, purposeful behavior, responsibility, and efficiency. Later in this chapter we will explore in some detail Jones's prescriptions for quality teaching done the easy way. But first, take note of the following five things Jones discovered about effective teachers.

Conserve Time and Don't Allow Students to Waste It

To help teachers make maximum use of time available for instruction, Jones recommends establishing a classroom structure that gives close attention to rules, routines, and responsibility training. These features quickly teach students what they are expected to do and not do in school. Jones includes **incentives** to help with responsibility training, which teaches the class to save time rather than waste it. It puts students on task when the bell rings and promotes 30-second transitions from one activity to another. These two results alone can save 10 minutes of learning time that is so often wasted in every 50-minute class period.

Jones makes it plain to teachers—and wants teachers to make it plain to students—that the purpose of discipline is to help students engage enjoyably in learning. He provides a number of positive and unobtrusive tactics that foster this sort of discipline. He stresses that the best way to manage behavior problems is to prevent their occurrence, and that the best preventive strategy involves attention to room arrangement, class rules, classroom chores, and routines for beginning the class. Following are some of Jones's specific suggestions.

Room Arrangement.   Jones urges teachers to maintain close contact with students and move among them while they are engaged in seat work and cooperative learning. If teachers are to move easily and quickly, classroom seating must be arranged to provide generous walkways. For this purpose, Jones advocates an **interior loop** arrangement, where desks or tables are set with two wide aisles from front to back, with enough distance between side-to-side rows for teachers to walk comfortably among the students, as shown in Figure 7.1.

This arrangement makes it easier for teachers to maintain physical proximity with all students. Jones says proximity is essential for teachers to practice **working the crowd,** by which he means moving about; interacting with students; and using occasional pauses, looks, or slow turns when necessary. These tactics help keep students attentive and actively involved.

Classroom Rules.   Classroom rules are used to formalize expectations about behavior. They are of two types—general and specific. **General rules,** fairly few in number, define the teacher's broad guidelines, standards, and expectations for work and behavior. They should be posted and reviewed periodically. **Specific rules** relate to procedures and routines. They detail exactly what students are to do in various learning activities and how they are to do it. These specific rules must be taught and rehearsed until they are learned like any academic skill. Jones advocates spending the first two weeks making sure students understand them thoroughly.

Classroom Chores.   Jones believes in assigning a classroom chore to every student, if possible. This helps students develop a sense of personal responsibility and ownership in the class program.

Figure 7.1   Jones's Interior Loop Seating Arrangement

Source: Adapted from Jones, F. 2007. *Tools for Teaching.* Santa Cruz, CA: Fredric H. Jones & Associates. Reprinted by permission.

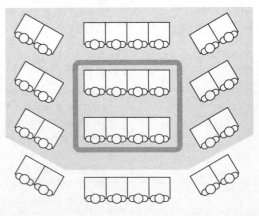

Opening Routines.   Class sessions in most schools begin in a fragmented way, with announcements, taking attendance, handling tardies, and the like. This fragmentation leads to the five to eight minutes of wasted time at the beginning of most classes. You can avoid losing this time simply by beginning lessons promptly. Jones would have students sit down and begin doing **bell work** immediately on entering the room. Bell work engages students and focuses attention on an important lesson to follow. No active instruction is required. Examples of bell work are answering review questions, doing warm-up problems, solving brain teasers, doing silent reading, and writing in journals.

Clearly Communicate They Mean Business

Earlier we saw Jones's contention that many teachers do not know how to show they mean business. They have no specific tactic for doing so other than nagging, which is notably ineffective. Jones suggests a strategy he calls *meaning business*, which is conveyed nonverbally as **body language** involving bodily carriage, eye contact, and tone of voice. Meaning business does away with most of the student back talk and argumentation. It is not only effective, but also low key and nonadversarial, and it increases learning opportunities for those who need it most—the low achievers who spend so much class time goofing off. Jones claims that with a little training in how to mean business, teachers can increase achievement for the bottom half of a class by as much as 50 percent and eliminate the majority of classroom disruptions.

Place Clearly Defined Limits on Behavior

Go to the Simulations section of Topic #4: Establishing Classroom Norms and Expectations, in the **MyEducationLab** for your course and complete the simulation entitled "Responding to Students' Failure to Follow Classroom Expectations."

Setting limits clarifies the line that separates acceptable behavior from unacceptable behavior. It is typically established through class rules and how teachers enforce them. Jones urges teachers to use the first class session to discuss the class rules that set limits on behavior and allow teaching and learning to occur as intended. In those discussions, teachers should ask students to identify examples of desirable and undesirable classroom behavior. This process leads to agreements that become the behavior rules for the class. When the agreements are finalized, they should be posted in the room. Jones would have teachers clearly explain the rules and their rationale, demonstrate the behavior they require, and then have students practice behavior that complies with the rules.

In discussions with your students, you should specify what you will do to help students abide by the rules. Indicate how you will teach behavior associated with the rules, if necessary. Explain how you will show your approval and appreciation when students follow rules properly, along with what you will do when students misbehave. Demonstrate body language, such as eye contact, stares, or **physical proximity,** you will use to remind students what they should be doing. As noted, Jones places great emphasis on body language in managing behavior. He says teachers are most effective in setting limits when they use their bodies correctly but say nothing and take no other action. He emphatically reminds teachers they cannot discipline with their mouths. He says if that were possible, nagging would have fixed every kid a million years ago. When you open your mouth, you often do more harm than good. Here are further recommendations Jones makes concerning body language.

Proper Breathing.   Teachers do well to remain calm in all situations. Calm conveys strength. It is attained and, in part, conveyed through proper breathing. The way teachers breathe when under pressure signals how they feel and what they are likely to do next. You can teach yourself to breathe slowly and deliberately before responding to annoying situations. Jones noted that some teachers take two deep breaths before turning to a misbehaving student. He believes doing so enables them to maintain and project an aura of self-control.

Eye Contact.   Suppose Miss Remy is explaining the process of multiplying fractions. She sees that Jacob has stopped paying attention. She pauses. The sudden quiet causes Jacob to look at Miss Remy and discover that she is looking directly at his eyes. He straightens up and waits attentively. Jones says few physical acts are more effective than eye contact for conveying the impression of being in control. He adds that turning and pointing the eyes and the feet toward students who disengage or disrupt shows teacher commitment to discipline.

Physical Proximity.   Miss Remy has finished her demonstration and has directed students to complete some exercises on their own. After a time she sees from the back of the room that Jacob has stopped working and has begun talking to Jerry. She moves toward him, and Jacob unexpectedly finds her shadow at his side. He immediately gets back to work, without Miss Remy having to say anything. Jones observed that teachers who use physical proximity rarely need to say anything to the offending students to get them to behave.

Body Carriage.   Jones also found that posture and **body carriage** are effective in communicating authority. Good posture and confident carriage suggest strong leadership, while a drooping posture and lethargic movements suggest resignation or fearfulness. Students read body language and are able to tell whether the teacher is feeling in charge or is tired, disinterested, or intimidated. Effective teachers, even when tired or troubled, know to stand tall and move assertively.

Facial Expressions.   Teachers' facial expressions communicate a great deal. They can show enthusiasm, seriousness, enjoyment, and appreciation, all of which encourage good behavior; or they can reveal boredom, annoyance, and resignation, which may prompt lethargy or misbehavior among students. Facial expressions such as winks and smiles demonstrate a sense of humor and personal connection, traits students appreciate in teachers.

Backup Systems.   In addition, you should discuss the **backup systems** you will turn to when students misbehave seriously and refuse to comply with rules or your requests. You must recognize that class rules are meaningless unless you have the power to enforce them. Usually, you can limit misbehavior in a benign manner by using proximity, body language, and personal interest. But there will be times when those tactics fail to cause misbehaving students to comply with the rules. When that happens, you can tell the offending student, "If you are not going to do your work, sit there quietly and don't bother others." And for yet more serious defiance or aggression, you must have a plan for isolating the student or calling for help as needed. These more forceful backup systems should be described plainly to students and also reviewed and approved by your site administrator in advance.

Keep Students Actively Engaged in Learning

Jones found the best teachers keep students actively involved in lessons. To help teachers maintain student involvement, Jones developed a teaching approach he calls **Say, See, Do teaching.** As the name suggests, the teacher says, the students see, and the students do. As we noted earlier, Jones found that many teachers, especially beyond the primary grades, spend major portions of their class periods presenting information while their students remain relatively passive. It is not until the latter part of the lesson that students are asked to do anything with what they are learning. Jones (2001) graphically depicts this old-fashioned approach as follows:

Teacher input, input, input, input, input→Student output

This instructional approach contains built-in factors that promote misbehavior:

1. The large amount of teacher input produces cognitive overload in students, which makes them want to disengage from the lesson.
2. The students sit passively for too long and the urge to do something builds up.
3. The teacher does not adequately work the crowd, that is, interact with individual students, particularly in the back of the classroom.

Effective teachers put students to work from the beginning. They present information and then quickly have students do something with it. This approach is doing oriented, with activities occurring often and at short intervals. It is depicted as follows:

Teacher input→Student output→Teacher input→Student output→Teacher input→Student output

This approach—used during the first part of the lesson—becomes even more effective when augmented with **visual instructional plans (VIPs)** that come into play during the second part of the lesson, when students are asked to work on their own. VIPs are graphic or picture prompts that students use a guides for completing processes or activities. VIPs are displayed in the room, and students are taught to consult them for guidance instead of raising their hands and waiting for the teacher when they get stuck.

To illustrate, Jones (2003) asks you to imagine you are teaching a class to divide 495 by 6. Typically, you would explain and demonstrate the calculation one step at a time, and when finished, your work on the chalkboard might look like Figure 7.2.

Now, Jones says, imagine the helpless handraiser during independent work, stuck on step four. What does the student do? Step four is not evident in this graphic. Our typical technique of laying one step over another produces only a single *summary graphic.* The helpless handraiser will now call for help and do nothing until the teacher arrives to provide yet another tutoring session. Jones's remedy

$$\begin{array}{r} 82 \text{ r } 3 \\ 6\overline{\smash{\big)}\,495} \\ -48 \\ \hline 15 \\ -12 \\ \hline 3 \end{array}$$

Figure 7.2   Summary Graphic

Source: Adapted from Jones, F. 2007. *Tools for Teaching.* Santa Cruz, CA: Fredric H. Jones & Associates.

Figure 7.3   Step-by-Step Graphic

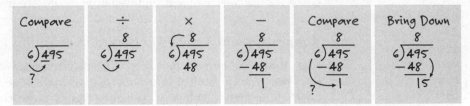

Source: Adapted from Jones, F. 2007. *Tools for Teaching.* Santa Cruz, CA: Fredric H. Jones & Associates.

is to provide a graphic that shows one step at a time and a picture for every step. Such plans are easy for students to consult and follow, allowing them to continue working on their own. See Figure 7.3 for a guide to helping students who forget the steps in long division.

This VIP, with steps shown along the top, offers a set of plans for performance that is simple, clear, and permanent. A student can refer to it at any time to answer the question, "What do I do next?"

Increase Student Motivation and Responsibility through Judicious Use of Incentives

An incentive is a proffered condition that prompts an individual to act. In other words, you promise students something they will enjoy, provided they first do their work and behave properly. The incentive is held in abeyance until the behavior occurs acceptably. Examples of incentives include the opportunity to work with friends or watch a video. Jones features such incentives prominently as a means of motivating students and teaching them to be responsible. He found that some of the most effective teachers use incentives systematically, while less-effective teachers use them improperly or not at all.

Jones says you should discuss with students the nature of the incentives, the kinds you will use, and how you will manage them. Point out that your incentives will all have instructional value. You won't use any that are simply for play or filling in time. Explain also that incentives conserve time by helping students work expeditiously rather than fool around. The saved time is then returned to the students in the form of **preferred activity time (PAT).** In elaborating further on PAT, Jones provides comments and reminders related to (1) Grandma's rule, (2) student responsibility, (3) genuine incentives, (4) preferred activities, (5) educational value, (6) group concern and management, (7) omission training, and (8) backup systems. Let us see what is involved in each.

Grandma's Rule.   **Grandma's rule** states: "First eat your vegetables, and then you can have your dessert." Applied to the classroom, this rule requires that students first do their work, and then they can enjoy a favorite activity. It is a fact of life that children—and we adults, too—prefer to begin with the dessert, promising to eat our vegetables afterward. But as we all know, even the best intentions fade away once the motivation behind them is gone. Incentives fall flat unless they are delivered after, and only after, students have done their work in an acceptable manner. If they don't eat their broccoli, they don't get their ice cream.

Student Responsibility.   Jones contends that properly used incentives help students learn to take responsibility for their decisions and actions. For example, one way students can show responsibility is through cooperating with others. However, because cooperation is voluntary, it is difficult to force it on anyone. When asked to cooperate, students who enjoy goofing off and daydreaming can ask themselves, "Why should I? What's in it for me?" Jones argues that when incentives are provided for cooperation, students see they have something to gain by it. At first they may cooperate primarily to obtain the incentive bonus, but over time, cooperation becomes habituated and enjoyable in itself.

Genuine Incentives.   There is a wide difference between what many teachers might consider to be incentives (e.g., "Let's all work in such a way that we will later be proud of what we do") and what students consider **genuine incentives** (e.g., "If you complete your work on time, you can have five minutes of preferred activity time"). Obviously, students are more motivated by specific outcomes they like than by vague outcomes that mean little to them. Jones comments on the different effects promoted by a promise of "free time" versus a promise of "preferred activity time." He says students won't work for long to earn free time, but they will work hard to gain time for an activity they enjoy. The lesson for teachers is to make sure the incentive is genuine in students' eyes.

To illustrate further, the following statements are not incentives for most students:

"The first person to complete a perfect paper will receive two bonus points."

"If you really work hard, you can be the best class I have ever had."

The first may motivate a few of the most able students, but all the others know they have little chance to win so there's no point in trying. The second statement sounds good to the teacher but means very little to the students and is not sufficient to get them to work.

On the other hand, students respond well to the anticipation of activities such as art, games for learning or review, viewing a video, or having time to pursue personal interests with friends. Such group activities are effective because almost all students desire them sufficiently to make extra effort to obtain them and they are available to all students, not just a few.

Tangible objects, awards, and certificates should not be used as incentives. They do not motivate students highly, nor do they have educational value.

Earning Preferred Activity Time.   PAT may be earned in a number of different ways. Mr. Jorgensen gives his fourth graders three minutes to put away their language arts materials and prepare for math. Any time left over from the three minutes goes later to PAT. In Mrs. Nguyen's English class, if everyone is seated and ready when the bell rings, the class earns two additional minutes of PAT. However, if some or all of the class continues to be noisy, the class loses the amount of PAT they have wasted. Some classes use PAT on the day it is earned, while others accumulate PAT for a future activity. In some instances, PAT may be earned as individual bonuses. When Mickey continues to be unprepared and consequently loses PAT for the class, Mr. Duncan organizes an individual approach for Mickey—if he misbehaves the class is not penalized, but if he conducts himself properly he can earn PAT for the entire class. This arrangement improves Mickey's status with peers and influences him to behave in an appropriate manner.

Educational Value.   It has been emphasized that to the extent feasible, class time, including PAT, should be devoted to activities that have educational value. Work that keeps students occupied but teaches them nothing can seldom be justified. While most educators are comfortable in allowing occasional frivolity in the class, the opposite extreme of holding daily or weekly parties as incentives is difficult to condone. What, then, should one use as PAT?

Jones maintains that when teachers introduce PAT to their students, they must make sure the activity has educational value, that students want to participate in the activity, and that they earn the activity by conducting themselves responsibility. There are many activities with educational value that students enjoy greatly, both individually and in groups. Among the best activities are learning games and enrichment activities that are fun and educational. Examples of such activities are using new vocabulary words to play hangman, completing an art project, or reading a book for pleasure.

In PAT, students are never left to do just anything, nor do they proceed without guidance. The freedom they enjoy lies in being able to choose from a variety of approved activities. Activities can be chosen by vote, with all students engaging in the same activity during the time allotted. Elementary school students often select physical education, art, music, drama, construction activities, or being read to by the teacher. Secondary students often choose to watch a video, hold class discussions on special topics, participate in performances by class members, or work together on projects such as a class magazine. JoLynne Talbott Jones posts on the Jones website (www.fredjones.com) suggestions from teachers for a large number of educationally sound activities that serve very well as preferred activities.

Group Concern and PAT Management.   Jones emphasizes the importance of making sure every student has a stake in earning the PAT incentive for the entire class. This **group concern** motivates all students to keep on task, behave well, and complete assigned work. PAT can be managed thus: The teacher agrees to set aside a period of time in which students might be allowed to engage in a preferred activity. The PAT can be at the end of the school day for self-contained classes—perhaps 15 to 20 minutes. For departmentalized classes, the time can be set aside at the end of the week—perhaps 30 minutes on Friday. The students can decide on the activity for their dessert time, and to earn it they have only to work and behave in accordance with class standards.

The teacher keeps track of the time that students earn. Of course, it is possible that a single student, by misbehaving, can prevent the class from earning full PAT.

Teachers often think it unfair to penalize the entire class when only a few have transgressed. In practice this is rarely a problem, because the class quickly understands that this is a group effort, not an individual one. The group is rewarded together and punished together regardless of who misbehaves. A strength of this approach is that it engenders peer pressure against misbehavior. Ordinarily a misbehaving student obtains reinforcement from the group in the form of attention or laughter. With proper PAT, the opposite is true. The class is likely to discourage individual misbehavior because it takes away something the class members want.

Nevertheless, some students do occasionally misbehave to the detriment of responsible students. When this occurs, the teacher may decide to work with the offending student individually, as was the case with Mickey, mentioned earlier.

Omission Training.   Generally speaking, incentives and PAT bonuses are earned by the entire class. Teachers cannot possibly monitor incentives for all students individually. The exception lies in the occasional student whose misbehavior repeatedly ruins PAT for the rest of the class. The following case explains how **omission training** is useful in earning PAT for the entire class:

> Kevin is a student in Ms. VanEtten's class. He disregards the requirements of PAT and is continually late, loud, and unprepared, thus ruining PAT for the others. Ms. VanEtten privately explains to Kevin that he doesn't have to participate in PAT, since he doesn't care about it, but she does want him to be successful with his own work and behavior. She explains that she will use a timer, and when Kevin behaves in accordance with class rules, he will earn time for himself, and also PAT for the class. When he misbehaves, he loses time for himself but not for the class.

Backup Systems.   As a last option for students who subvert PAT, Jones suggests backup systems, which are hierarchical arrangements of sanctions for putting a stop to unacceptable student behavior. Jones identifies three levels of backup:

1. Small backup responses, conveyed privately or semi-privately to the student: "I expect you to stop talking so we can get on with our work." With such low-keyed messages the student knows the teacher means business. Whispering privately is a constructive way of protecting student dignity.
2. Medium backup responses, delivered publicly in the classroom: "Emily, sit in the thinking chair for three minutes and think about what you have done that caused me to send you there." Or, "Brian, you are late again. You'll have detention with me tomorrow after school." Other medium backup responses include warnings, reprimands, loss of privilege, and parent conferences.
3. Large backup responses are used to deal with repeated disruptions or other intolerable behavior. They require involvement of at least two professionals, usually the teacher and an administrator. They involve trips to the office, in-school or out-of-school suspension, and occasionally placement in special classes or special schools.

Provide Help Efficiently during Independent Work

As we have seen, Jones puts particular emphasis on how teachers should provide help to students who get stuck during seat work. Suppose Mrs. James is teaching a lesson in determining percentages. She illustrates at the board by showing how to calculate 4 percent of three different amounts, asks a couple of questions to verify that students are understanding, and then assigns independent exercises for students to calculate a number of percentages ranging from 5 percent to 120 percent. Almost immediately, Arnell raises his hand for help. If he were the only one, there would be little problem. But Mrs. James sees other hands began to wave, as well. She knows most of those students will sit doing nothing productive while waiting for her.

In his research, Jones asked teachers how much time they thought they spent, on average, when providing help to individuals who raised their hands. The teachers felt that they spent from one to two minutes with each student, but when Jones's researchers timed the episodes, they found that teachers actually spent around four minutes with each student. The amount of time consumed made it impossible for the teacher to attend to more than a few students during the work period. Even if the teacher spent only one minute per contact, several minutes would pass while some students sat and waited.

Jones's research led him to conclude that independent seat work is especially susceptible to four problems: (1) wasted time, (2) insufficient time for teachers to answer all requests for help, (3) high potential for misbehavior, and (4) perpetuation of student dependency on the teacher. Jones determined that all four could be resolved if teachers learned to provide help efficiently, as follows.

First, organize the classroom seating so that all students can be reached quickly. Without that, teachers expend far too much time and energy moving to students who call for help. The interior loop seating arrangement previously described is suggested because it allows easy movement in the room.

Second, use visual instructional plans, which as we noted are graphic reminders displayed in the room that provide clear examples and step-by-step instructions for students to consult. The VIPs show such things as steps in algorithms, the proper form for business letters, directions for independent work, and the like. The reminders are posted where students can see them and thus continue on their own without needing to call for the teacher.

Third, minimize the time used for giving help to students. To see how this can be accomplished, consider that teachers normally give help through an inefficient questioning tutorial, in which the teacher poses questions and makes comments similar to the following:

"What's the problem?"

"All right, what did we say was the first thing to do?" [Waits; repeats question.]

"No, that was the second. You are forgetting the first step. What was it? Think again." [Waits until student finally makes a guess.]

"No, let me help you with another example. Suppose . . ."

In this manner the teacher often re-teaches the concept or process to each student who requests help. Four minutes can be spent very easily in each interaction. In place of these tutorials, Jones trains teachers to give help in 20 seconds or less, with an optimal goal of 10 seconds. If the VIP does not help a student know what to do next, Jones would have teachers do the following when arriving beside the student:

1. (Optional for initial contact) Quickly find anything that the student has done correctly and mention it favorably: "Your work is very neat" or "Good job up to here."
2. Give a straightforward prompt that will get the student going: "Follow step two on the graphic" or "Regroup here." Jones also recommends that, instead of tutoring students through the whole exercise, teachers should prompt students to ask themselves, "What do I do next?"
3. Leave immediately. Don't stay to see if students follow the prompt you have given.

Help provided in this way solves the problems that so often plague teachers during independent work. Students waste little time waiting for the teacher, and students who need help can receive proper attention. Rapid circulation by the teacher also permits better monitoring of work being done by students who do not raise their hands. When errors are noted in those students' work, the teacher should provide help just as for students who have raised their hands.

In summary, Jones provides a number of tactics that enable teachers to work as effectively and efficiently as the "natural teachers" he studied. The tactics can help students learn more easily; develop self-control; and exhibit positive attitudes, responsibility, and consideration for others. Jones has designed his tactics so they can be used easily—they do not tire teachers out.

JONES'S STUDY GROUP ACTIVITY

Jones makes available a free Study Group Activity Guide that can be downloaded from his website. It is associated and aligned with *The Video Toolbox* and is for use by small groups of teachers or student teachers who meet regularly to discuss and practice the skills Jones advocates. The Study Group Activity Guide and *The Video Toolbox* also present class activities that you can use immediately to perfect your management skills. Jones highly recommends meeting and working with colleagues in this manner. He suggests an ideal group contains from three to eight people. The structure he suggests includes focus questions, study group questions, and performance checklists. He provides topics for 12 meetings:

- Working the Crowd and Room Arrangement
- Praise, Prompt, and Leave
- Visual Instructional Plans
- Say, See, Do Teaching
- Rules, Routines, and Standards
- Understanding Brat Behavior
- Calm is Strength
- The Body Language of Meaning Business
- Eliminating Backtalk
- Responsibility Training

- Omission Training and Preferred Activity Time
- Dealing with Typical Classroom Crises

IMPLEMENTING JONES'S APPROACH IN THE CLASSROOM

Jones (1987a, p. 321) suggests that his approach be conceptualized and initiated as a five-tiered system, consisting of: (1) classroom structure, (2) limit setting, (3) Say, See, Do teaching, (4) incentives, and (5) backup systems. The system should be carefully planned in advance and introduced as a whole. As you plan what you will do, you might wish to keep the following in mind:

- Do what you can to preserve and make wise use of instructional time that is so often wasted. A few simple management techniques will conserve this time.
- Structure your classroom and program to encourage attention, active involvement, and responsibility. Use an effective seating arrangement, establish clear routines, and assign individual chores to students.
- Use body language and personal-relations skills more than verbal messages to limit misbehavior and help students stay on track.
- Make use of Say, See, Do Teaching to increase student alertness, involvement, and learning.
- Actively "work the crowd," moving about and interacting frequently with individual students as you teach and monitor their work.

- Learn to give individual help to students in 20 seconds or less, a tactic that eliminates student dependence on your presence and enables you to provide help as needed to all students quickly.
- Use class incentives to foster student involvement and increase responsibility.

If you have progressed into the semester or class year, it would not be absolutely necessary to introduce Jones's suggestions as a full-blown system. You can assess your own behavior and isolate certain discipline tactics you would like to incorporate into your teaching, and then add them incrementally to your teaching repertoire.

> **?** Suppose you have tried hard to implement Jones's discipline system in your classroom. You have established incentives, learned to provide help quickly to students at work, stopped nagging students, used body language to show you mean business, and urged students to work hard and do quality work. And yet, many students disengage from your lessons as you present them. Based only on what is included in this highlighted section, what might you have overlooked that would keep students more actively engaged?

backup systems
bell work
body carriage
body language
general rules
genuine incentives
Grandma's rule

group concern
helpless handraisers
incentives
interior loop
massive time wasting
omission training
physical proximity

preferred activity time (PAT)
Say, See, Do teaching
setting limits
specific rules
visual instructional plan (VIP)
working the crowd

Concept Cases

CASE 1: KRISTINA WILL NOT WORK

Kristina, a student in Mr. Jake's class, is quite docile. She socializes little with other students and never disrupts lessons. However, despite Mr. Jake's best efforts, Kristina will not do her work. She rarely completes an assignment. She is simply there, putting forth no effort at all. *What would Fred Jones suggest to help Kristina and Mr Jake?*

Jones would probably suggest that Mr. Jake take the following steps to improve Kristina's behavior.

1. Make frequent eye contact with her. Even when she looks down, Mr. Jake should make sure to look directly at her. She will be aware of it, and it may be enough to encourage her to begin work.
2. Move close to Kristina. Stand beside her while presenting the lesson.
3. Give Kristina frequent help during seat work. Check on her progress several times during the lesson. Give specific suggestions and then move quickly on.
4. Increase the amount of Say, See, Do teaching with Kristina so she has less information to deal with and is called on to respond frequently.
5. Set up a personal incentive system with Kristina, such as doing a certain amount of work to earn an activity she especially enjoys.
6. Set up a system in which Kristina can earn rewards for the entire class. This brings attention and support from her peers.

CASE 2: SARA WILL NOT STOP TALKING

Sara is a pleasant girl who participates in class activities and does most, though not all, of her assigned work. She cannot seem to refrain from talking to classmates, however. Her teacher, Mr. Gonzales, has to speak to her repeatedly during lessons, to the point that he often becomes exasperated and loses his temper. *What suggestions would Fred Jones give Mr. Gonzales for dealing with Sara?*

CASE 3: JOSHUA CLOWNS AND INTIMIDATES

Joshua, larger and louder than his classmates, always wants to be the center of attention, which he accomplishes through a combination of clowning and intimidation. He makes wise remarks, talks back (smilingly) to the teacher, utters a variety of sound-effect noises such as automobile crashes and gunshots, and makes limitless sarcastic comments and put-downs of his classmates. Other students will not stand up to him, apparently fearing his size and verbal aggression. His teacher, Miss Pearl, has come to her wit's end. *What specifically do you find in Fred Jones's suggestions that would help Miss Pearl with Joshua?*

CASE 4: TOM IS HOSTILE AND DEFIANT

Tom has appeared to be in his usual foul mood ever since arriving in class. On his way to sharpen his pencil, he bumps into Frank, who complains. Tom tells him loudly to shut up. Miss Baines, the teacher, says, "Tom, go back to your seat." Tom wheels around, swears loudly, and says heatedly, "I'll go when I'm damned good and ready!" *How effective do you believe Fred Jones's suggestions would be in dealing with Tom?*

You Are the Teacher

INNER-CITY MAGNET SCHOOL

You are a student teacher in an inner-city magnet school that emphasizes academics. Half of your students are African American. The other half, of various ethnic groups, have been bussed in to take advantage of the instructional program and rich resources. All are academically talented and none has what would be called a bad attitude toward school. Mrs. Warde, the regular teacher of the class, does not seem to rely on any particular scheme of discipline, at least not any that is obvious to you. She simply tells the students what to do and they comply. For the first few lessons you have taught, Mrs. Warde has remained in the room, serving as your aide. The students worked well, and you felt pleased and successful.

WHEN MRS. WARDE LEAVES THE ROOM

Mrs. Warde tells you that she will leave the room during the math lesson so that you can begin getting the feel of directing the class on your own. Mrs. Warde warns you that the class might test you with a bit of naughtiness, though nothing serious is likely to occur. Just be in charge, Mrs. Warde counsels. The math lesson begins well, without incident. The lesson has to do with beginning algebra concepts, which you approach through a discovery mode. You tell the class, "I want you to work independently on this. Think your way through the following equations and decide if they are true for all numbers."

$$a + 0 = a$$
$$a + b = b + a$$
$$a (b + c) = ab + c$$

$$a + 1 = 1$$
$$a \times 0 = a$$

The students begin work, but within two minutes hands are shooting up. You go to help Alicia, who is stuck on the third equation. "What's the matter?" you whisper.

"I don't understand what this means."

"It was like what I showed you on the board. The same."

"Those were numbers. I don't understand it with these letters."

"They are the same as the numbers. They take the place of the numbers. I showed you how they were interchangeable, remember? Go ahead, let me see. Tell me what you are doing, step-by-step."

You do not realize it, but you spend almost five minutes with Alicia. Meanwhile, a few of the students have finished and are waiting, but most are holding tired arms limply in the air. You rush to the next student and repeat your questioning tutorial. Meanwhile, Matt and Alonzo have dropped their hands and are looking at each other's papers. They begin to talk, then laugh. Others follow, and soon all work has stopped and the classroom has become quite noisy. You repeatedly say, "Shhh, shhh!" but with little effect. Finally you sternly tell the class how disappointed you are in their rude behavior.

CONCEPTUALIZING A STRATEGY

If you followed the suggestions of Fred Jones, what would you conclude or do with regard to the following?

- Discussing the misbehavior with the class
- Maintaining student dignity and good personal relations
- Modifying your approach to prevent the recurrence of the misbehavior
- Using the situation to help the students develop a sense of greater responsibility and self-control

Activities

1. Makes notes in your journal concerning elements from Jones's model that you would consider including in your personalized system of discipline.
2. Review the Preview of This Chapter presented on page 120. In as few words as possible, indicate the central meaning and implications of the concepts mentioned there.
3. For each of the following scenarios, first identify the problem that seems to promote the undesired behavior, then describe how Jones would have the teacher deal with it.
   - Mr. Anton tries to help all of his students during independent work time but finds himself unable to get around to all who have their hands raised.

- Ms. Sevier wants to show trust for her class. She accepts their promise to work hard if she will allow them first to listen to a few favorite recordings. After listening, the students talk so much that they fail to get their work done.
- Mr. Gregory wears himself out every day dealing ceaselessly with three class clowns who disrupt his lessons. The other students always laugh at the clowns' antics.
- Mrs. Swanson, who takes pride in her lectures, is becoming frustrated because students begin to gaze out the window and whisper before she has completed what she wants to tell them.

References

Jones, F. 1987a. *Positive classroom discipline.* New York: McGraw-Hill.

Jones, F. 1987b. *Positive classroom instruction.* New York: McGraw-Hill.

Jones, F. 2003. Weaning the helpless handraisers, part 2: Teaching to the visual modality. www.education world.com/a_curr/columnists/jones/jones004 .shtml

Jones, F. 2007. *Tools for teaching.* Santa Cruz, CA: Fredric H. Jones & Associates.

Jones, P. 2007. *The video toolbox.* Santa Cruz, CA: Fredric H. Jones & Associates.

How Does William Glasser Use Choice Theory and Quality Education to Establish Class Discipline?

Psychiatrist William Glasser, one of the greatest educational thinkers of our time, contends that behavior in school will not improve until we change the way we work with students. It has become clear, he says, that trying to force students to learn or behave responsibly is hopeless. Schools would do far better if they emphasized three things that have been shown to produce the results we want: (1) provide a curriculum that is genuinely attractive to students, (2) use **noncoercive discipline** to help students make responsible choices that lead to personal success, and (3) strongly emphasize quality in all aspects of teaching and learning.

Glasser's experience has convinced him that students will not willingly engage in schoolwork unless it offers interesting activities that meet their **basic needs** for security, belonging, power, fun, and freedom—needs, he says, that cannot be suppressed because they are built into the human genetic code. All of us continually make choices to try to meet these needs. Some of the behavior we choose leads to success, other choices lead to trouble or failure. A major role of teachers is to help students make the behavior choices that lead to proper behavior and high-quality learning.

A PREVIEW OF THIS CHAPTER

The main things schools can do to improve student behavior and learning are provide an engaging curriculum, emphasize quality, and influence students noncoercively to make good choices about learning and responsible conduct.

Less-effective teachers use a teaching style Glasser calls *boss teaching*, while more-effective teachers use a style he calls *lead teaching*. Less-effective teachers also display what Glasser calls *seven deadly habits*, whereas more-effective teachers are notable for using *seven connecting habits*. Any program of quality education must meet students' basic needs and will be made better by following the precepts of choice theory. When students break class rules, teachers should use nonpunitive influence tactics to help them direct their attention back to the learning at hand. In short, provide a high-quality, engaging curriculum, and use lead teaching, connecting habits, and positive noncoercive influence to achieve quality learning and appropriate behavior.

WHAT TO LOOK FOR IN THIS CHAPTER

- ■ Glasser's concept of nonpunitive discipline
- ■ The role that choice theory plays in Glasser's approach
- ■ Why today's students do not give their best effort in school
- ■ What Glasser means by *quality teaching*, *quality learning*, and *quality classrooms*
- ■ How Glasser would have you respond when students break class rules

GLASSER'S LONG-LASTING INFLUENCE

Glasser's many contributions to discipline can be assigned to two periods in time. The first spanned the years from 1965 through 1985. In that period, he developed and popularized two major strategies for working more effectively with students in school. His first strategy, as described earlier in Chapter 4, grew out of his new approach to psychotherapy set forth in his critically acclaimed book *Reality Therapy: A New Approach to Psychiatry* (1965). In that approach he moved the focus away from events in the distant past and placed it on helping clients deal with present-day reality. When Glasser worked with juvenile offenders, he found that reality therapy could help them make behavior choices that brought increased success in school. He further developed that line of thinking and in 1969 expressed it in his book *Schools without Failure,* later acclaimed as one of the best education books of the twentieth century. In that book he made the assertion that all students choose to behave as they do. They are not victims of circumstances and are not being forced to do anything against their will. But they can improve the behavioral choices they make and improve their lives accordingly. Certain (better) choices bring success and pleasure, while other (poorer) choices bring frustration and failure. Moreover, teachers can learn how to influence students to make better choices and help them find success in school and life.

In the years since, Glasser's ideas have had a strong impact on thought and practice in school discipline. He wants teachers to understand they have the power and the obligation to help students make better behavior choices, and he provides numerous suggestions for interacting with students in ways that help them succeed.

The second time period in which Glasser made major contributions began in 1986 and has continued to the present day. His contributions during that period are described in this chapter. In 1986 he published *Control Theory in the Classroom,* which provided new insights into effective ways of teaching students. In that book he made two foundational assertions, based on his observations over time. The first was his strong reiteration that we cannot control anyone besides ourselves. We cannot "make" students do anything, but we can influence them to do things that lead to better behavior and increased success. His second assertion was that we simply cannot expect students to work and behave properly in school unless they "believe that if they do some work, they will be able to satisfy their needs enough so that it makes sense to keep working" (1986, p. 15). That means it is up to teachers to make school adequately interesting and otherwise satisfying to students' needs.

Glasser quickly showed teachers how to make school interesting and worthwhile for students. He continued stressing the importance of organizing education so it meets students' needs, holding to his belief that doing so is the best way to ensure student involvement and desirable behavior. In 1996, he changed the name of his approach from *control theory* to **choice theory,** the better to emphasize that student behavior is determined by student choice, not teacher control. In 1998, he published a succession of three books that dealt with choice and quality in school: the second edition of *The Quality School: Managing Students without Coercion* (1998b), *Choice Theory in the Classroom* (1998a), and *The Quality School Teacher* (1998c). In 2001, he published *Every Student Can Succeed*, which he said wrapped up his conclusions about teaching and would be his last book in education.

MAJOR CONCEPTS IN GLASSER'S NONCOERCIVE DISCIPLINE

The major conclusions that Glasser puts forward in his later works include the following:

- *All human behavior is purposeful.* Our behavior is never aimless or accidental. It reflects our attempts to satisfy specific needs.
- *We are responsible for our own behavior.* Because our behavior is purposeful and chosen, we cannot blame our misbehavior on circumstances, fate, or others. Any credit for proper behavior, or blame for improper behavior, goes to us.
- *All of our behavior is our best attempt to meet five basic needs: survival, belonging, power, fun, and freedom.* The school experience should be refined to enable students to meet these five needs more easily.
- *Students feel pleasure when their basic needs are met and frustration when they are not.* Students are usually contented and well-behaved when their needs are being met, but discontented and inclined to misbehave when their needs are not being met.
- *At least half of today's students will not commit themselves to learning if they find their school experience boring, frustrating, or otherwise dissatisfying.* There is no way teachers can make students commit to learning, although they can usually force behavioral compliance temporarily.
- *Few students in today's schools do their best work.* Most students are apathetic about schoolwork. Many students do no schoolwork at all.
- *If today's schools are to be successful, they must create quality conditions that greatly reduce student and teacher frustration.* Students must feel they belong, enjoy a certain amount of power, have some fun in learning, and experience a sense of freedom in the process.
- *What schools require is a new commitment to quality education.* Quality education occurs naturally when the curriculum is attractive and students are encouraged, supported, and helped to learn.
- *The school curriculum should be limited to learnings that are useful or otherwise relevant to students' lives.* Usefulness and relevance are hallmarks of a quality curriculum, which is delivered through activities that attract student interest, involve students actively, provide enjoyment, and lead to meaningful accomplishments.

- *Students should be allowed to acquire in-depth information about topics they consider useful or interesting.* This increases the likelihood of quality learning.
- *Quality learning is evident when students become able to demonstrate or explain how, why, and where their learnings are valuable.* The opportunity for making such explanations should be incorporated into the daily classroom activities.
- *Instead of scolding, coercing, or punishing, teachers should try to befriend their students, provide encouragement and stimulation, and show unending willingness to help.* Their ability to do these things is a mark of quality teaching.
- *Teachers who dictate procedures, order students to work, and berate them when they do not are increasingly ineffective with today's students.* Glasser calls teachers who function in this way **boss teachers.**
- *Teachers who provide a stimulating learning environment, encourage students, and help them as much as possible are most effective with today's learners.* Glasser calls teachers who function in this way **lead teachers.**
- *Motivation is the key ingredient in learning.* Students are motivated by what they find pleasurable at any given time. It is up to teachers to make the curriculum and instruction pleasurable for students. When that is done, most learning difficulties and behavior problems disappear.

We can summarize Glasser's contentions as follows: Human behavior is purposeful. It is motivated internally and chosen by the individual. It represents our best attempt to satisfy one or more of five basic needs built into our genetic structure. We make what we believe to be the best behavior choices we can, given the information we have. We are responsible for our own behavior. All students can do competent work and some quality work in school. Effective discipline and motivation go hand in hand with helping students meet their needs for survival, belonging, freedom, fun, and power.

FURTHER CLARIFICATION OF GLASSER'S NONCOERCIVE DISCIPLINE

Glasser points out the futility of attempting to force students to behave in ways that are contrary to their natural inclinations. For example, when a student is not paying attention because the lesson is boring, it is a losing battle to try to force the student's attention. When lessons are interesting, students pay attention naturally and don't have to be continually cajoled. This fact is fundamental in Glasser's focus on what he calls *quality education,* which depends largely on students engaging willingly in the curriculum.

Glasser had concluded earlier that the majority of today's students are content to do low-quality school work or even none at all. As he put it, "No more than half of our secondary school students are willing to make an effort to learn, and therefore cannot be taught" (1986, p. 3) and "no more than 15 percent of high school students do quality work" (1990, p. 5). His solution is to offer instruction in a form that influences students to do high-quality schoolwork. Nothing less, he says, will suffice.

Glasser says that meeting this goal requires only modest changes in curricula, materials, and physical facilities, but a significant change in the way teachers work with students. Glasser acknowledges that teaching is difficult, and he expresses sympathy for beleaguered secondary teachers who yearn to work with dedicated, high-achieving students but are continually frustrated by the low level of effort their students make. Those teachers have told Glasser that their main discipline problems are not defiance or disruption but, rather, students' overwhelming apathy, resignation, and unwillingness to participate in class activities or assignments. Students, for their part, tell Glasser that the problem with schoolwork is not that it is too difficult, but that it is too boring. For Glasser, this is another way of saying that schoolwork does not meet students' psychological needs. If schooling is to be effective, he says, the curriculum must be organized to meet students' needs; quality schoolwork must replace the fragmented and boring requirements on which students are typically tested and evaluated; teachers must move toward quality teaching; and choice theory, which contributes to success and responsibility, must be given central attention in teaching, learning, and behavior management.

Meeting Students' Needs

Glasser is adamant that education that does not give priority to students' five basic needs is bound to fail. Meeting the needs is not difficult. Glasser says students' **survival** needs are met when the school environment is kept safe and free from personal threat. Students sense **belonging** when they receive attention from the teacher and others and participate actively in class concerns. They sense **power** when the teacher asks them to participate in making decisions about topics to be studied and procedures for working in class, or assigns them responsibility for class duties, such as helping take attendance, caring for class animals, helping distribute and take care of materials, being in charge of media equipment, and so forth. Students experience fun when they are able to work and talk with others, engage in interesting activities, and share their accomplishments. Finally, they sense freedom when the teacher allows them to make responsible choices concerning what they will study, how they will do so, and how they will demonstrate their accomplishments. Glasser frequently mentions the value of cooperative learning teams in helping students meet their basic needs (Glasser, 1998a).

? Which basic need is not being fully met when students indicate or do each of the following?

1. Students look out the window instead of doing their assigned work.
2. Justin is afraid to walk home alone after school.
3. Suzanne sits by herself in the lunch room.
4. Students are not involved in making decisions about how various topics will be studied.
5. Jason feels the teacher does not like him.

Quality Curriculum

Glasser believes that present-day education consists too much of memorizing facts that are irrelevant to students' lives, while quality of teaching is judged by how many fragments of information students can retain long enough to be measured on tests. He says if schools are to be effective, they must be converted into places where students learn useful information and learn it well—that is, they must provide a **quality curriculum**. Any part of the curriculum that doesn't meet this criterion should be discarded as "nonsense" (Glasser, 1992).

Glasser says if students are old enough, you may ask them to identify what they would like to explore in depth. Once the topics have been selected, adequate time should be allocated for them to be learned thoroughly. Learning a smaller number of topics in depth is always preferable to covering many topics superficially. Quality learning requires depth of understanding combined with a good grasp of its value—in fact, students should always expect to be called on to explain why the material they have learned is valuable and, when possible, how and where it can be used. Students should also be asked regularly to assess the quality of their own efforts.

Quality Teaching

Glasser (1993, 1998) stresses the importance of **quality teaching** and says it is rather easy to accomplish, although it requires a change in approach for most teachers. He recognizes it is difficult for teachers to change their teaching style, but nevertheless urges them to work toward the following:

1. *Provide a warm, supportive classroom climate.* This is done by helping students know and like you. Use natural occasions over time to tell students who you are, what you stand for, what you will ask them to do, what you will not ask them to do, what you will do for them, and what you will not do for them. Show that you are always willing to help.

2. *Use lead teaching rather than boss teaching.* This means using methods that encourage students and draw them out, rather than trying to force information into them. (This idea is explained further in the next section.)

3. *Ask students only to do work that is useful.* **Useful work** consists of knowledge and skills that students will make use of in their lives. At times teachers may have to point out the value of the new learnings, but if that value doesn't become quickly evident to students, they will not make a sustained effort to learn. Information to be taught and learned should meet one or more of the following criteria:

- The information is directly related to an important skill.
- The information is something that students express a desire to learn.
- The information is something the teacher believes especially useful.
- The information is required for college entrance exams.

4. *Always ask students to do the best they can.* The process of doing quality work occurs slowly and must be nurtured. Glasser suggests that a focus on quality can be initiated as follows:

- Discuss quality work so that students understand what it means.
- Begin with an assignment that is clearly important enough for students to want do well.
- Ask students to do their best work on the assignment. Do not grade their work, because grades suggest to students that the work is finished.

5. *Ask students to evaluate work they have done and improve it.* Quality usually comes from modifications made through continued effort. Glasser suggests that when students feel they have completed a piece of work on a topic they consider important, the teacher should help them make value judgments about it, as follows:

- Ask students to explain why they feel their work has high quality.
- Ask students how they think they might improve their work further. As students see the value of improving their work, higher quality will result naturally.
- Progressively help students learn to use self-evaluation, improvement, and repetition, or **SIR**, until quality is achieved.

6. *Help students recognize that doing quality work makes them feel good.* This effect will occur naturally as students learn to do quality work.

> There is no better human feeling than that which comes from the satisfaction of doing something useful that you believe is the very best you can do and finding that others agree. As students begin to sense this feeling, they will want more of it. (Glasser, 1993, p. 25)

7. *Help students see that quality work is never destructive to oneself, others, or the environment.* Teachers should help students realize that it is not possible to achieve the good feeling of quality work if their efforts harm people, property, the environment, or other creatures.

? Think back on your own educational experiences. Can you identify a school learning experience that seemed to involve particularly good teaching as well as good effort on your part? What specifically did the teacher do, what did you do, and what, if anything, did those efforts have in common with Glasser's depictions of quality teaching and learning?

More on Lead Teaching

Glasser has much to say about the style of teaching required for quality education. In essence, he says that teachers must replace boss teaching with lead teaching. Teachers must come to realize they cannot force motivation into students and, in the long run, can rarely do high-quality teaching when using the boss approach, where they rarely ask for student input, talk rather than involve students actively, never ask students to evaluate their own work, and use coercion to try to make students comply with expectations.

To illustrate, Mr. Márquez (a boss teacher) introduces his unit of study on South American geography as follows

> Class, today we are going to begin our study of the geography of South America. You will be expected to do the following things:
>
> 1. Learn the names of the South American countries.
> 2. Locate those countries on a blank map.
> 3. Describe the types of terrain typical of each country.

4. Name two products associated with each country.
5. Describe the population of each country in terms of ethnic origin and economic well-being.
6. Name and locate the most important river in each country.

We will learn this information from our textbooks and encyclopedias. You will have two tests, one at . . .

Given these requirements, it is unlikely the students will pursue the work eagerly. Most will do only enough, and only well enough, to get by.

Lead teachers work differently. They realize that genuine motivation to learn resides within students, in the form of needs and interests, and must be activated. Toward that end, lead teachers spend most of their time organizing interesting activities and providing assistance to students. Their manner of teaching might be as follows:

- Discuss many topics of interest with the class.
- Encourage students to identify topics they would like to explore in depth.
- Discuss with students the nature of the schoolwork that might ensue, emphasizing quality and asking for input concerning criteria of quality.
- Explore with students resources that might be needed for quality work and the amount of time such work might require.
- Demonstrate ways in which the work can be done. If possible, illustrate by showing models of student work that reflect quality.
- Emphasize the importance of students continually inspecting and evaluating the quality their own work.
- Make evident to students that everything possible will be done to provide them good tools and a good workplace that is noncoercive and nonadversarial.

To illustrate how lead teaching might proceed, consider the example of Mr. Garcia's introduction to a unit of study on the geography of South America in Figure 8.1.

Choice Theory Applied to the Classroom

Given a high level of motivation, students can learn almost anything taught in school, and when fully engrossed in learning they seldom misbehave. Glasser notes that educators have traditionally assumed that external control (what we do to or for students) determines students' level of motivation. He points out that this assumption is seriously flawed because it is evident that all students will do whatever is most satisfying to them at any given time, if they can. If they choose to work hard and comply with expectations, it is because they get satisfaction from doing so. If they do not experience that natural satisfaction, they may work to please you, but usually not for long. The payoff they receive for their efforts must be sufficient to keep them working.

In explaining choice theory, Glasser emphasized that what we do is not automatically determined by external causes, but rather by what goes on inside us. When we teach someone else, we cannot make them learn. All we can do is open possibilities, provide information, and expose students to good models (such as ourselves).

Figure 8.1   Example of Lead Teaching

"Class, have any of you ever lived in South America? You did, Samuel? Which country? Peru? Fantastic! What an interesting country! I used to live in Brazil. I traveled in the Amazon quite a bit and spent some time with jungle Indians. Supposedly they were head hunters at one time. But not now. At least so they say. Tomorrow I'll show you a bow and arrow I brought from that tribe. Samuel, did you ever eat monkey when you were in Peru? I think Peru and Brazil are very alike in some ways but very different in others. What was Peru like compared to here? Did you get up into the Andes? They have fabulous ruins all over Peru, I hear, and those fantastic Chariots of the Gods lines and drawings on the landscape. Do you have any photographs or slides you could bring for us to see? What a resource you could be for us! You could teach us a lot!

Class, Samuel lived in Peru and traveled in the Andes. If we could get him to teach us about that country, what do you think you would most like to learn? (The class discusses this option and identifies topics.)

We have the opportunity in our class to learn a great deal about South America, its mountains and grasslands, its dense rain forests and huge rivers, and its interesting people and strange animals. Did you know there are groups of people from England, Wales, Italy, and Germany now living in many parts of South America, especially in Argentina? Did you know there are still thought to be tribes of Indians in the jungles that have no contact with the outside world? Did you know that almost half of all the river water in the world is in the Amazon Basin, and that in some places the Amazon River is so wide that from the middle you can't see either shore?

Speaking of the Amazon jungle, I swam in a lake there that contained piranhas, and look, I still have my legs and arms. Surprised about that? If you wanted to learn more about living in the Amazon jungle, what would you be interested in knowing? (Discussion ensues.)

How about people of the high Andes? Those Incas, for example, and their ancestors who in some unknown way cut and placed enormous boulders into gigantic, perfectly fitting fortress walls? Samuel has seen them. The Incas were very civilized and powerful, with an empire that stretched for three thousand miles. Yet they were conquered by a few Spaniards on horseback. How in the world could that have happened? If you could learn more about those amazing Incas and the area in which they lived, what would you like to know?

(Discussion continues in this manner. Students identify topics about which they would be willing to make an effort to learn.) Now let me see what you think of this idea: I have written down the topics you said you were interested in, and I can help you with resources and materials. I have lots of my own, including slides, South American music, and many artifacts I have collected. I know two people who lived in Argentina and Colombia that we could invite to talk with us. We can concentrate on what you have said you would like to learn about. But if we decide to do so, I want to see if we can make this deal: We explore what interests you; I help you all I can. For your part, you will explore some information I think you should know, and all along you agree to do the best work you are capable of. We would need to discuss what you'd like to learn about and some things I want you to learn, and from that we could decide what you might do to show the quality of your learning. In addition, I hope I can persuade each of you to regularly evaluate yourselves as to how well you believe you are doing. Understand, this would not be my evaluation; it would be yours— not for a grade but so you can see what you are doing very well and what you think you might be able to do better. What do you think of that idea? Want to give it a try?"

> **?** Glasser says that one way to improve behavior is through clarifying what a quality existence would be like and then planning the choices that would help bring about that existence. Test yourself in this regard. Jot down two things you feel would contribute to quality in your own teaching, and then identify two choices you could make related to each of them that would probably lead toward the quality you visualize. Exchange your ideas with classmates or fellow professionals.

The Relation of Quality Teaching to Discipline

Teachers who function as leaders of quality classrooms should avoid adversarial relationships with their students, because too often adversity destroys incentives, both for student learning and pleasure in teaching. By staying out of the adversity quagmire, you make it possible to foster quality learning and at the same time reduce discipline problems to a minimum. Glasser acknowledges that no approach can eliminate all behavior problems, but he maintains that misbehavior can be reduced greatly if teachers do the following:

- Work with students to establish standards of conduct in the classroom.
- Begin with a discussion of the importance of quality work (to be given priority in the class) and explain that you will do everything possible to help students learn and enjoy themselves without using force.
- That discussion should lead naturally to asking students about class behavior they believe will help them get their work done and truly help them learn. Glasser says that if teachers can get students to see the importance of courtesy, no other rules may be necessary.
- Also solicit student advice on what should happen when behavior agreements are broken. Glasser says students usually suggest punishment, though they know punishment is not effective. If asked further, they will agree that behavior problems are best solved by looking for ways to remedy whatever is causing the rule to be broken.
- Whenever appropriate, ask students, "What could I do to help?"
- Once agreements and consequences are established, they should be put in writing and all students should sign the document, attesting that they understand the agreements and that, if they break them, they will try—with the teacher's help—to correct the underlying problem.
- Agreements established and dealt with in this way, says Glasser, show that the teacher's main concern lies in quality, not power, and that the teacher recognizes that power struggles are the main enemy of quality education.
- Hold classroom meetings to explore alternatives to inappropriate behavior.

You will note that other authorities—such as Ron Morrish in Chapter 5 and Craig Seganti in Chapter 11—do not agree with Glasser's urgings to involve students in making decisions about class rules of behavior. They consider rule making to be the teacher's job, although they would have you explain to students why the rules exist and what they are intended to accomplish. At this point in time, what would be your preferred approach—making and explaining the rules yourself, or involving students in a total class effort to establish the rules? What is your rationale?

When Rules Are Broken

Go to the Simulations section of Topic #12: Managing Problem Behaviors, in the **MyEducationLab** for your course and complete the simulation entitled "Responding to Mildly Disruptive Behavior."

Teachers must intervene when class agreements or rules are broken. These interventions, which should be nonpunitive, are intended to stop the misbehavior and get the student's mind back on classwork. Suppose that Jonathan has come into the room obviously upset. As the lesson begins, he turns heatedly and throws something at Michael. Glasser would suggest the teacher say the following:

> It looks like you have a problem, Jonathan. How can I help you solve it? [Jonathan frowns, still obviously upset.] If you will calm down, I will discuss it with you in a little while. I think we can work something out.

Glasser says that you, the teacher, should make it clear that you are unable to help Jonathan unless he calms down. You should say this without emotion in your voice, recognizing that anger on your part will only put Jonathan on the defensive. If Jonathan doesn't calm down, there is no good way to deal with the problem. Glasser (1990) says to allow him 20 seconds, and if he isn't calm by then, admit that there is no way to solve the problem at that time. Give Jonathan time-out from the lesson, but don't threaten or warn him. Say something like the following: "Jonathan, I want to help you work this out. I am not interested in punishing you. Whatever the problem is, let's solve it. But for now you must go sit at the table. When you are calm, come back to your seat." Later, at an opportune time, discuss the situation with Jonathan, approximately as follows:

> What were you doing when the problem started? Was it against the rules? Can we work things out so it won't happen again? What could you and I do to keep it from happening?

If the problem involves hostilities between Jonathan and Michael, the discussion should involve both boys and proceed along these lines:

> What were you doing, Jonathan? What were you doing, Michael? How can the three of us work things out so this won't happen anymore?

It is important to note that no time is spent trying to find out whose fault it was, and no blame is assigned to either Jonathan or Michael. You make clear to the boys that all you are looking for is a solution so that the problem won't occur again. Glasser says if you treat Jonathan and Michael with respect and courtesy, if you show you don't want to punish them or throw your weight around, and if you talk to them as a problem solver, both their classroom behavior and the quality of their work will probably improve.

MOVING TOWARD QUALITY CLASSROOMS

Many educators avidly support Glasser's ideas concerning teaching and schooling. Numbers of them have met stringent requirements for being named Glasser Certified Teachers. Several entire schools have done the same. Once they meet the requirements, these schools are officially designated by the William Glasser Institute as Glasser Quality Schools (GQS). Glasser (2001) describes them as schools that meet the following criteria:

- Relationships are based on trust and respect, and all discipline problems (meaning intentional misbehavior) have disappeared.
- Total learning competence is stressed. Student work does not receive credit until it has reached the B level of quality on the traditional ABCDF grading system.
- Students and staff are taught to use choice theory in their lives and in their work at school.
- Students score significantly above average on proficiency tests and college entrance exams, typically at the 80th percentile or better.
- Staff, students, parents, and administrators view the school as a joyful place.

In 2006, Therese Hinder conducted an independent review of seven Glasser Quality Schools in various states with enrollments that reflected a cross-section of the U.S. school population. She found that all of the schools she reviewed adhered closely to Glasser's teachings and that student achievement in all of them ranked in the top category on their statewide student testing program.

Eliminating the Seven Deadly Habits

A fundamental operating principle in Glasser's approach is that teachers and administrators must endeavor to help students be happy at school. Glasser claims that if you are having trouble with a student, you can be absolutely sure the student is unhappy in your class and very likely unhappy in school. Glasser believes most problems between teachers and students are caused by unsatisfactory relationships; he therefore stresses the fundamental importance of maintaining good relationships. Teachers can take a major step toward promoting such relationships simply by consciously avoiding what Glasser calls *the seven deadly habits in teaching* and replacing them with *the seven connecting habits.*

The **seven deadly habits** are teacher acts that prevent the establishment of caring relationships between teachers and students. Glasser identifies the deadly habits as *criticizing, blaming, complaining, nagging, threatening, punishing,* and *rewarding students to control them.* (These same deadly habits are equally detrimental to relationships outside of school.) If teachers are to establish good relationships with students and gain their willing cooperation, they must eliminate these deadly habits from the interactions they have with students.

Emphasizing the Seven Connecting Habits

In place of the seven deadly habits, teachers should make sure they behave in ways that increase a sense of connection between them and their students. These behaviors are epitomized in **seven connecting habits** that Glasser identified as *caring, listening, supporting, contributing, encouraging, trusting,* and *befriending.* Glasser believes—and his quality schools support his contentions—that all students who come to school can do competent work. In order for this to happen, teachers must strongly connect with their students. This connection is accomplished when teachers use the seven connecting habits and give up trying to use external controls to make students behave. Glasser makes his point by describing how we relate to friends (and he does indeed urge teachers to befriend their students); we do not criticize, blame, or speak harshly to our friends. Rather, we use connecting habits when relating with them.

Gaining the Benefits of Quality Classrooms

Here is a brief outline of Glasser's suggestions for teachers who wish to increase the level of quality in their classrooms:

- *Replace deadly habits with connecting habits.* Determine that beginning today, you will assiduously avoid the seven deadly habits when working with your students and replace them with the seven connecting habits.

- *Make plain how you will work with students.* The message you want to get across to students is the following: "We are in this class together. I want to help you to be competent or go beyond. My job is to teach you and help you learn, not to find out what you don't know and punish you for not knowing it. If you have a question, ask me. If you need more time, I'll give it to you. If you have an idea how to do what we are trying to do better, tell me. I'll listen" (Glasser, 2001, p. 113).

- *Befriend your students.* Instead of telling students what they must do and not do, endeavor to befriend all of them. To begin, say something like, "I think an important part of my job is to do all I can to make sure you have a good time learning. You have to come to school and no one's going to pay you for doing schoolwork. So the least I can do is make this class fun for both you and me. I think we can learn a lot and still have a very good time" (Glasser, 2001, p. 54). Then steadfastly make use of the seven connecting habits.

- *Establish reasonable rules of class behavior.* Rely on one fundamental rule of behavior—the Golden Rule. Discuss the Golden Rule with students. A few other rules may occasionally be necessary, but the Golden Rule is fundamental to all.

- *Take the energy out of impending misbehavior.* Replace traditional discipline (external control) with talking and listening to students as soon as you sense that misbehavior is likely to occur. Listen carefully. Inject humor into the situation if you can, but do not make light of students' concerns.

- *Teach things that make a real difference in students' lives.* It is very important that students be able to make good use of what they learn in school. Therefore, make sure your curriculum focuses on skills and knowledge that interest students and make them more knowledgeable and competent. Don't have them memorize anything just for the sake of knowing it. Explain to students that you will not ask them to learn anything that is not useful to them, and when there is doubt, you will explain clearly how the new learning will benefit them.

- *Help students learn to strive for quality.* Tell students you have a new way of teaching in which everyone can do competent work and everyone will make good grades (meaning a grade of B or better). Explain that you will ask students to work at any given assignment until they have achieved an acceptably high level of competence. Nobody will fail or receive a low grade. They can use any resources available to help them, including textbooks, parents, and other students. The primary objective is to do competent work. Beyond that, encourage students to work for even higher quality to help them learn what it feels like to do A-level work.

- *Test students frequently, but productively.* Teach students using your best techniques, then test them regularly. Explain that the tests are for learning only and promise that no one will fail or receive a bad grade. When they have completed the test, have them go back over it and correct any incorrect or incomplete answers. Ask them to explain why the correction is better. Give them the time and help needed to get everything right.

- *Emphasize understanding and making use of new learning.* Ask students to always focus on understanding and using the information and skills being taught. Ask them to share and discuss the learnings with parents or guardians.

- *Provide options for students after competence is achieved.* Students who complete their work competently can then have the option of helping other students or moving ahead to doing something of yet higher quality.

To experience the full sense of Glasser's ideas, consult his book entitled *Every Student Can Succeed.*

> **?** In Glasser's approach, you are encouraged to teach only information and skills that are useful to students or otherwise make a significant difference in their lives. How do you differentiate between instructional topics that have those qualities and those which do not? It would seem, for example, that written and spoken command of the English language would be of enormous benefit to students, and yet great numbers of students find those topics so tedious and boring they gladly avoid them if possible. How do you think you might address this seeming mismatch between value and pleasure in what is being taught?

Summary Rubric

IMPLEMENTING GLASSER'S IDEAS IN THE CLASSROOM

Glasser's ideas for increasing quality in teaching and learning need not be implemented in one fell swoop, but instead can be introduced gradually, allowing teachers to evaluate for themselves what is happening to classroom climate and morale. If you wished to do so, how might you begin? Here are some suggestions:

- Remember that your students' behavior is internally motivated and purposeful, directed at meeting certain needs. Adjust your curriculum as necessary to help students meet those needs.

- Remember also that most of your students will not commit themselves to class activities they find boring, frustrating, or otherwise dissatisfying. Do away with those topics and replace them with something that is both valuable and enjoyable.

- Hold a discussion with your class on how school could be made more interesting and enjoyable. Identify a topic in which they show interest and brainstorm ways to explore it, procedures for reporting or demonstrating accomplishment, personal conduct that would make the class function better, and how disruptions might be handled positively and effectively. The process is mainly for student input, but you might offer some of your opinions as well.

- Following that, indicate that you will try to organize a few activities as students have suggested and that you will do all you can to help them learn and succeed. Meanwhile, give yourself a crash course on functioning as a lead teacher, eliminating the seven deadly habits, and establishing the seven connecting habits in your relations with students.

- As you get underway, hold meetings with your class to discuss new efforts and any results you see in classwork and behavior. The meetings should focus only on improving learning and never be allowed to degenerate into fault finding, blaming, or criticizing.

- Instead of coercing, scolding, and punishing your students to get them to learn and behave properly, befriend them, provide encouragement and stimulation, and show unending willingness to help.

- Ask students what kinds of class behaviors will help them improve class behavior while acquiring quality learning. Ask them to reach class agreements about such behavior. Ask them what should happen when anyone breaks a behavior agreement. Ensure that all their suggestions are positive rather than negative.

- When students misbehave, discuss their behavior and why it was inappropriate for the class. Ask them what they feel they could do to avoid misbehaving in the future. If the misbehavior is serious or chronic, talk with the involved students privately at an appropriate time.

Terms and Concepts

basic needs	noncoercive discipline	seven deadly habits
belonging	power	SIR
boss teachers	quality curriculum	survival
choice theory	quality teaching	useful work
lead teachers	seven connecting habits	

Concept Cases

CASE 1: KRISTINA WILL NOT WORK

Kristina, a student in Mr. Jake's class, is quite docile. She socializes little with other students and never disrupts lessons. However, despite Mr. Jake's best efforts, Kristina will not do her work. She rarely completes an assignment. She is simply there, putting forth no effort at all. *What would William Glasser suggest to help Kristina and Mr. Jake?*

Glasser would first suggest that Mr. Jake think carefully about the classroom and the program to try to determine whether they contain obstacles to Kristina's meeting her basic needs. He would then have Mr. Jake discuss the matter with Kristina, not blaming her but noting the problem of nonproductivity and asking what the problem is and what he might be able to do to help. In that discussion, Mr. Jake might ask Kristina questions such as the following:

- You have a problem with this work, don't you? I believe it is important and will help you in the future. But only you can decide whether or not to do it. Is there anything I can do to help you get started?
- Is there anything I could do to make the work more interesting for you?
- Is there anything in this class that you especially enjoy doing? Do you think that, for a while, you might like to do only those things?
- Is there anything we have discussed in class that you would like to learn very, very well? How could I help you do that?
- What could I do differently that would help you want to learn?

Glasser would not want Mr. Jake to use a disapproving tone of voice with Kristina, but every day make a point of talking with her in a friendly and courteous way about nonschool matters such as trips, pets, and movies. He would do this casually, showing he is interested in her and willing to be her friend. Glasser would remind Mr. Jake that there is no magic formula for success with all students. Mr. Jake can only encourage and support Kristina. Scolding and coercion are likely to make matters worse, but as Mr. Jake befriends Kristina she is likely to begin to do more work of better quality.

CASE 2: SARA WILL NOT STOP TALKING

Sara is a pleasant girl who participates in class activities and does most, though not all, of her assigned work. She cannot seem to refrain from talking to classmates, however. Her teacher, Mr. Gonzales, has to speak to her repeatedly during lessons, to the point that he often becomes exasperated and loses his temper. *What suggestions would Glasser give Mr. Gonzales for dealing with Sara?*

CASE 3: JOSHUA CLOWNS AND INTIMIDATES

Joshua, larger and louder than his classmates, always wants to be the center of attention, which he accomplishes through a combination of clowning and intimidation. He makes wise remarks, talks back (smilingly) to the teacher, utters a variety of sound-effect noises such as automobile crashes and gunshots, and makes limitless sarcastic comments and put-downs of his classmates. Other students will not stand up to him, apparently fearing his size and verbal aggression. His teacher, Miss Pearl, has come to her wit's end. *How do you think Glasser would have Miss Pearl deal with Joshua?*

CASE 4: TOM IS HOSTILE AND DEFIANT

Tom has appeared to be in his usual foul mood ever since arriving in class. On his way to sharpen his pencil, he bumps into Frank, who complains. Tom tells him loudly to shut up. Miss Baines, the teacher, says, "Tom, go back to your seat." Tom wheels around, swears loudly, and says heatedly, "I'll go when I'm damned good and ready!" *How would Glasser have Miss Baines deal with Tom?*

You Are the Teacher

MIDDLE SCHOOL WORLD HISTORY

Your third-period world history class is composed of students whose achievement levels vary from high to well below average. You pace their work accordingly, ask them to work cooperatively, and make sure everyone understands what they are supposed to do. For the most part you enjoy the class, finding the students interesting and refreshing. Your lessons follow a consistent pattern. First, you ask the students to read in groups from the textbook, then you call on students at random to answer selected questions about the material. If a student who is called on is unable to answer a question, the group he or she represents loses a point. If able to answer correctly, the group gains a point. For partially correct answers, the group neither receives nor loses a point. For the second part of the period, the class groups do something productive or creative connected with the material they have read, such as making posters, writing a story, doing a skit, or the like. As appropriate, these efforts are shared with members of the class.

A TYPICAL OCCURRENCE

You call on Hillary to answer a question. Although she has been participating, she shakes her head. This has happened several times before. Not wanting to hurt Hillary's feelings, you simply say, "That costs the group a point," and you call on someone else. Unfortunately, Hillary's group gets upset at her. The other students make comments under their breath. Later, Clarisse also refuses to answer. When you speak with her about it, she says, "You didn't make Hillary do it."

You answer, "Look, we are talking about you, not Hillary." However, you let the matter lie and say no more. Just then, Deonne comes into the class late, appearing very angry. He slams his pack down on his desk and sits without opening his textbook. Although you want to talk with Deonne, you don't know how to approach him at that time. Will is in the opposite mood. Throughout the oral reading portion of the class, he continually giggles at every mispronounced word and at every reply students give to your questions. Will sits at the front of the class and turns around to laugh, seeing if he can get anyone else to laugh with him. He makes some *oooh* and *aaaah* sounds when Hillary and Clarisse decline to respond. Although most students either ignore him or give him disgusted looks, he keeps laughing. You finally ask him what is so funny. He replies, "Nothing in particular," and looks back at the class and laughs. At the end of the period, there is time for sharing three posters students have made. Will makes comments and giggles about each of them. Clarisse, who has not participated, says, "Will, how about shutting up!" As the students leave the room, you take Deonne aside. "Is something wrong, Deonne?" you ask. "No," Deonne replies. His jaw is clenched as he strides past you.

CONCEPTUALIZING A STRATEGY

In accord with Glasser's suggestions, what would you conclude or do with regard to the following?

- Preventing the problems from occurring in the first place

- Putting an immediate end to the misbehavior
- Involving other or all students in addressing the situation
- Maintaining student dignity and good personal relations
- Using follow-up procedures to prevent the recurrence of the misbehavior
- Using the situation to help the students develop a sense of greater responsibility and self-control

Activities

1. Make notes in your journal concerning information from Glasser's teachings that you might like to incorporate into your personal system of discipline.
2. Give your appraisal of Glasser's system as concerns the following:
   - Effectiveness in curbing inappropriate behavior
   - Effectiveness in improving long-term behavior
   - Ease of implementation
   - Student willingness to cooperate and do the expected work
   - Establishing trust between teacher and student
3. With a group of colleagues, select a grade level and/or subject you enjoy teaching. Outline briefly what you would do to help students improve their work and meet their basic needs for belonging, fun, power, and freedom.

References

Glasser, W. 1969. *Schools without failure.* New York: Harper & Row.

Glasser, W. 1986. *Control theory in the classroom.* New York: HarperCollins.

Glasser, W. 1990. *The quality school: Managing students without coercion.* New York: HarperCollins.

Glasser, W. 1992. The quality school curriculum. *Phi Delta Kappan, 73*(9), 690–694.

Glasser, W. 1993. *The quality school teacher.* New York: HarperCollins.

Glasser, W. 1998a. *Choice theory in the classroom.* New York: HarperCollins.

Glasser, W. 1998b. *The quality school: Managing students without coercion.* New York: HarperCollins.

Glasser, W. 1998c. *The quality school teacher.* New York: HarperCollins.

Glasser, W. 2001. *Every student can succeed.* Chatsworth, CA: William Glasser Incorporated.

9

How Does Spencer Kagan Use Structures and Teacher–Student Same-Side Collaboration to Establish Class Discipline?

Spencer Kagan, originator and principal disseminator of Win-Win Discipline, is a professor of psychology and head of Kagan Publishing and Professional Development. He believes discipline is best established by using **structures**—sets of organized steps—to prevent and redirect misbehavior. The process is enhanced when teachers and students work together from the same side to resolve behavior issues. His ideas are presented in detail in *Win-Win Discipline*, a book he co-authored with Patricia Kyle and Sally Scott. The book presents a parable to introduce his approach to discipline:

> Two women are standing on a bank of a swift river. In the strong current, flailing about, desperately struggling to stay afloat, a man is carried downstream toward them. The women both jump in, pulling the man to safety. While the brave rescuers are tending the victim, a second man, also desperate and screaming for help, is carried by the current toward them. Again the women jump into the river to the rescue. As they are pulling out this second victim, they spot a third man flailing about as he is carried downstream toward them. One woman quickly jumps in to save the latest victim. As she does, she turns to see the other woman resolutely walking upstream. "Why aren't you helping?" she cries. "I am," states the other. "I am going to see who is pushing them in!" (Kagan, 2001)

Kagan's ongoing research focuses on establishing harmonious classrooms, promoting responsible behavior, and improving students' social skills, character qualities, and academic achievement. His structures—which he has aligned with the brain's multiple intelligences and ways of learning—are being used internationally at levels from kindergarten through university, in a wide range of academic subjects. Kagan provides details of his approach in *Win-Win Discipline* and various website articles. Kagan's website address is www.kaganonline.com.

Discipline occurs best when teachers and students work together to establish agreements (rules) concerning acceptable and unacceptable behavior in the classroom. Thereafter, they work on the same side to make decisions, reach collaborative solutions to problems, and develop learned responsibility. In particular, Win-Win Discipline helps teachers deal effectively with classroom disruptions (ineffective behavior choices), categorized as aggression, breaking rules, confrontations, and disengagement (the ABCD of misbehavior). Students who disrupt are said to be coming from one of seven positions—attention seeking, avoiding failure, angry, control seeking, energetic, bored, or uninformed. The ultimate skill of discipline involves selecting and applying intervention strategies (called *structures*) that address misbehavior associated with combinations of misbehavior and student positions. In short, Win-Win Discipline features same-side collaboration, class rules, identifying types of misbehavior and student positions, and applying appropriate structures to ensure appropriate behavior.

WHAT TO LOOK FOR IN THIS CHAPTER

- The primary goals of Win-Win Discipline and how those goals are related to students' lives in general
- The overarching strategies used in Win-Win Discipline to enable students and teachers to work together to find solutions to behavior concerns
- The seven student positions (states of mind/body) that often lead to disruptive behavior
- The structures (plans of action) teachers can use for interacting productively with misbehaving students
- Other specific tactics used in Win-Win Discipline, one example of which is teachers' openly befriending and expressing genuine caring for students

WIN-WIN DISCIPLINE OVERALL

Goal, Elements, and Procedures

Go to the Building Classroom Discipline Video Showcase section of Topic #3: Models of Classroom Management, in the **MyEducationLab** for your course and watch the video entitled "Spencer Kagan— Win-Win Discipline."

The goal of Win-Win Discipline—so called because all participants benefit or "win" from using it—is to help students develop lifelong responsible behavior. It comprises the following elements:

- *Three pillars of Win-Win Discipline.* **Three pillars** comprise the philosophical structure of Win-Win Discipline: (1) *same side,* meaning students, teachers, and parents all work together on the same side to enhance the school experience for everyone; (2) *collaborative solutions,* meaning students and teachers cooperate in proposing workable solutions to discipline problems; and (3) *learned* *responsibility,* the desire to behave appropriately, which students acquire by practicing self-management and the skills of getting along with others.

- *Class rules.* Win-Win Discipline makes use of **class rules,** but they are not formulated solely by the teacher. Rather, they are class agreements worked out cooperatively by teacher and students. Rules (agreements) should be worded simply, limited to about five in number, and posted in the room for easy reference. Students are involved in composing the rules, but after they are posted in the room the teacher goes through them again and directs students to practice the behaviors indicated. In addition, teachers and other adults conscientiously model behavior that is in keeping with the rules. The class also helps identify responsible alternatives to misbehavior, which they might call "The Way We Want Our Class to Be." Those alternatives are posted in the room as well. Because students cooperate in deciding on responsible behavior, they do not feel the rules are imposed on them. Although rules may vary somewhat from class to class, they usually turn out to be quite similar overall. Kagan suggests the following:

  Ready rule: Come to class ready to learn.

  Respect rule: Respect the rights and property of others.

  Request rule: Ask for help when needed.

  Offer rule: Offer help to others.

  Responsibility rule: Strive to act responsibly at all times.

  Kagan says that some teachers prefer to use only one rule, such as: *In our class we agree to foster our own learning, help others learn, and allow the teacher to teach.*

> **?** If at this point you had to select two rules of behavior for your class, what would those two rules be, and why?

- *Attention to types of misbehavior.* Most classroom misbehavior can be categorized into four types—aggression, breaking rules, confrontations, and disengagement. Kagan refers to these as the **ABCD of disruptive behavior.** Misbehavior is considered to be ineffective behavior choices students make when trying to meet specific needs.

> **?** As George and Allen come into the classroom, George shouts an obscenity at Allen. Allen responds in kind. In Kagan's categories of misbehavior, which type or types of misbehavior would this be?

- *Attention to student spositions.* **Student positions** refer to students' physical/emotional states as they exist at any point in time. Seven student positions are involved in most student misbehavior. Kagan calls those particular positions attention seeking, avoiding failure, angry, control seeking, energetic, bored, or uninformed. These positions are neither right nor wrong, neither good nor bad. They indicate individual students' emotional or mental states at the time students misbehave, and they provide teachers a point of departure in addressing misbehavior. Remember: Do not accept misbehavior, but do accept and validate the student's position when he or she misbehaves.

- *Structures.* When misbehavior occurs, teachers identify the position the student is coming from and apply structures that help the student return to responsible behavior. Structures are procedures—steps teachers can take to deal with misbehavior when it occurs. Kagan provides over 200 such structures that are matched to (1) the type of misbehavior and (2) the student position at the time of misbehavior. The structures do more than stifle disruptions; they help students develop autonomous responsibility for their own behavior. Some of the structures can be used proactively to prevent misbehavior, whereas others can be used reactively to deal with misbehavior that occurs.

- *Attention to needs.* Because misbehavior is a manifestation of students' ineffective efforts to meet needs, Kagan urges teachers to help students meet their needs in acceptable ways. For the most part, this can be accomplished by (1) providing a learning environment that is rich with interesting activities and engaging instruction, and (2) establishing a "we" approach that gives teachers and students a joint interest in maintaining responsible behavior. The we approach is part of what Kagan means by *teacher–student same-side collaboration.*

The ABCD of Disruptive Behavior

We saw that Kagan categorizes disruptive behavior as aggression, breaking rules, confrontation, or disengagement. He believes all misbehavior falls into one or more of these categories. Here is how he describes them:

Aggression.   Hostility between students, manifested physically, verbally, and passively, is growing more evident year by year. Physical aggression includes hitting, kicking, biting, pinching, pulling, and slapping. Verbal aggression includes putdowns, swearing, ridiculing, and name-calling. Passive aggression involves stubbornly refusing to comply with reasonable requests.

Breaking Rules.   Students behave in ways that break class rules when they are unable to meet certain needs satisfactorily. Common examples of rule-breaking behavior are talking without permission, making weird noises, chewing gum, passing notes, being out of seat, and not turning in work. Sometimes students break rules just to see what it feels like or to see what happens when they do. Emotions students experience at those times are usually evident in the seven positions—angry, bored, full of energy, desirous of attention, attempting to avoid failure, wanting to control, not understanding what is expected, and not having the ability to follow the rule.

Confrontation.   Power struggles often occur among students or between student and teacher. They usually occur when students attempt to get their way or show dominance over another person. Examples of confrontational behavior are refusing to comply, complaining, arguing, calling names, and giving myriad reasons why things are no good or should be done differently. When students don't get their way in confrontations, they often pout or make disparaging remarks about the task, teacher, or fellow students.

Disengagement.   Students may disengage from lessons for a variety of reasons. They may have something more interesting on their minds, feel incapable of performing the task, or find the task boring or meaningless. Passive disengagement includes inattention, being off task, not finishing work, and acting incapable. Active disengagement includes put-downs, excessive requests for help, and comments such as "I've got better things to do" or "It would be better if . . ."

Student Positions and Their Effects

We saw that Kagan identifies seven student positions (physical/emotional states) that predispose students to behave in certain ways: attention seeking, avoiding failure or embarrassment, angry, control seeking, energetic, bored, and uninformed. He says that when students misbehave, they are coming from one or more of those positions. In order to best help disruptive students, teachers must be able to identify the position the student is coming from and then apply a structure that helps the student return to appropriate behavior.

Win-Win Discipline enables teacher and students to work together to understand the positions, identify the needs associated with them, and learn how to satisfy those needs in responsible ways. Student positions are seen as natural states that all of us experience. But disruptive behavior—which is considered unacceptable—often occurs as students try to meet certain needs. The art of using Win-Win Discipline involves the following:

- Identifying the position from which misbehavior emanates
- Communicating *acceptance* of the position while *refusing to accept* the disruptive behavior associated with it
- Applying an appropriate structure, matched to type of behavior, to help students meet their needs acceptably

All disruptive behavior can be used as an opportunity to help students learn to behave responsibly. The task is made easier if teachers can see things from a student's perspective.

> **?** Mauricio likes to assume a take-charge approach in the classroom. Today, he shouts across the room at Janina and Alicia, "Get over here! You are supposed to be working with us!" Do you consider his behavior to be unacceptable? If so, how do you validate the position he is coming from while indicating his behavior is not acceptable? What would you say to him?

STRUCTURES, APPLICATION, AND TIMING

Kagan, Kyle, and Scott (2004) explain that teachers continually use structures when teaching without recognizing what they are. For example, the structure used most frequently by teachers worldwide (incidentally, one of the least effective) is the "whole-class question–answer." Familiar to teachers and students everywhere, this structure consists of the following steps:

- The teacher asks a question.
- The students raise their hands.
- The teacher calls on one of the students.
- That student answers the question.
- The teacher responds to the student answer.

In the book *Win-Win Discipline* (2004) Kagan, Kyle, and Scott describe in detail a large number of behavior-related structures, which are coordinated with types of misbehavior and student positions. Some of those structures are designed to *prevent misbehavior* and are put in place before misbehavior occurs. Examples of preventive structures are reviewing class rules, having students practice them, and providing lessons students find intriguing and useful.

Other structures are designed for use in *responding to misbehavior* when it occurs. These responsive structures are applied at three different points in time: (1) at *the moment of disruption,* to stop the misbehavior and rechannel it into responsible behavior, (2) during *follow-up,* when students require further assistance in moving beyond a particular misbehavior, and (3) repeatedly over the *long-term,* to help students develop and maintain effective life skills such as self-direction and positive relations with others.

Once the Win-Win philosophy of same-side collaboration has been internalized, students who disrupt usually need only a reminder to get back on track. Teachers can refer to the chart of rules posted in the room and ask, "Are we living up to the way we want our class to be?" If more is required, the teacher might use a structure such as *Picture It Right,* which asks students to picture how they would like the class to be and verbalize what they need to do to make it that way.

More on Structures for the Moment of Disruption

At the moment of disruption, the teacher should intervene in a way that ends the disruption quickly and refocuses attention on the lesson. As necessary, the teacher can acknowledge the student's position, communicate that the disruptive behavior is not acceptable, and enlist the student's cooperation in finding a satisfactory solution. Here are three examples of structures designed for use at the moment of disruption:

- *Picture It Right.* If we were at our very best right now, how would we look?
- *Make a Better Choice.* Try to think of a better choice to make right now.
- *To You . . . To Me.* To you, this lesson may be boring; to me, it is important because . . .

More on Structures for Follow-Up

Follow-up structures are used when students need additional assistance in behaving responsibly. They are applied when moment-of-disruption structures do not bring about a complete or lasting result. Typical follow-up structures include the following:

- Establish a new preventive procedure or reestablish an existing preventive procedure.

- Select a new moment-of-disruption procedure for use the next time the student disrupts.
- Implement a follow-up structure, such as a same-side chat or exploring ways in which one might behave responsibly.
- Provide training in a life skill such as self-control or relating well with others.

Follow-up structures use more highly prescriptive activities such as directly practicing appropriate behavior. They may even call on students to make apologies and restitution, or endure time away from the lesson. If still stronger measures are needed, students may be required to develop a **personal improvement plan** that specifies behavior changes the student needs to make and how those changes will be accomplished. If it is necessary to administer consequences to control disruptive behavior, they should be applied in the following sequence:

1. Warning given to student
2. Reflection time for the student to sit alone and think about the disruptive behavior and how to improve it
3. Personal improvement plan formulated by the disruptive student to develop responsible ways of meeting needs
4. Phone call to parent or guardian
5. Principal's office visit

More on Structures for Long-Term Success

Long-term structures are designed to help students get along with others, be self-directing, and control volatile emotions. As you can see, these outcomes are desirable in the classroom and in all walks of life. Long-term structures are called into play after preventive and moment-of-disruption structures are producing their desired results.

Keep in mind that the major goal of Win-Win Discipline is to help students learn to control themselves responsibly in various situations. Thus, to the extent feasible, teachers should give students an opportunity to resolve problems on their own and display responsible behavior. Different long-term goals come into play for the various student positions, as indicated here.

Student Position	Long-Term Needs and Goals
Attention seeking	Student needs self-validation
Avoiding failure or embarrassment	Student needs self-confidence
Angry	Student needs self-control
Control seeking	Student needs self-determination
Energetic	Student needs self-direction
Bored	Student needs self-motivation
Uninformed	Student needs to self-inform

Win-Win Discipline offers a progression of follow-up structures to help students reach these long-term goals. Here are some of those structures, progressing from less directive to more directive.

Same-Side Chat.   Teacher and student talk together in a friendly manner and in so doing get to know each other better and come to see themselves as working on the same side toward better conditions for all.

Responsible Thinking.   Discussions are used to prompt students to reflect on three considerations: (1) their own and others' needs, (2) how they treat others, and (3) how they conduct themselves. Students can be asked to consider three questions:

1. What if everyone acted that way? (How would our class be if everyone acted that way?)
2. How would I like to be treated? (Did I treat others the way I would like to be treated?)
3. What would be a win-win solution? (What would meet everyone's needs?)

Reestablishing Expectations.   Discuss and if necessary re-teach expectations concerning rules, procedures, and routines.

Identifying Replacement Behavior.   Teachers guide students to generate, accept, and practice responsible behavior that they can use in place of disruptive behavior.

Agreeing on Contracts.   Contracts are written agreements in which the teacher and individual students clarify and formalize agreements they have reached. Contracts sometimes increase the likelihood that the student will remember, identify with, and honor the agreement.

Establishing Consequences.   Consequences are conditions that teacher and students have agreed to invoke when students misbehave. They are held as a last resort and are used only when all other follow-up efforts have failed. Consequences should be aligned with the three pillars of Win-Win Discipline—they begin with same-side orientation; are established through teacher–student collaboration; and are instructive and aimed at helping students learn to conduct themselves with greater personal responsibility.

When misbehavior disrupts or harms others and responsible thinking is not enough, students may need to *apologize* to those they have offended or make *restitution* of some sort. Genuine apologies have three parts: a statement of regret or remorse, a statement of appropriate future behavior, and the request for acceptance of the apology. *Restitution* means making amends for emotional damage that was done or repairing or replacing physical damage. Restitution is a tangible way of taking responsibility and dealing with the consequences of inappropriate choices. As well, it has the potential to "heal the violator."

More on Structures for Promoting Life Skills

As we have noted, the major goal of Win-Win Discipline is to bring about the progressive development of a number of **life skills** that help students live more successfully. Examples of life skills are self-control, anger management, good judgment, impulse control, perseverance, and empathy. Teachers are urged to teach these skills as part of the curriculum and use them when responding to misbehavior. Kagan says that by fostering these life skills, teachers can move beyond interventions that simply end disruptions while leaving students likely to disrupt again in the future. He illustrates his points as follows:

■ A student puts down another student. The recipient of the put-down, having been publicly belittled, has the impulse to retaliate by giving back a put-down or even initiating a fight. To the extent the student has acquired the life skills of self-control, anger management, and/or good judgment, a discipline problem is averted.

■ A student is finding an assignment difficult. She is tempted to avoid a sense of failure by saying to herself and others, "This assignment is stupid." To the extent the student has acquired self-motivation, pride in her work, and perseverance, a discipline problem is averted.

■ A student is placed on a team with another student he does not like. He is tempted to call out, "Yuck! Look who we are stuck with!" To the extent the student has acquired relationship skills, cooperativeness, empathy, and kindness, a discipline problem is averted.

■ Annie is standing in front of her classmates, making a report on how aluminum is obtained from bauxite. William interrupts, asking "What is boxtight?" He laughs and interrupts again. His antics make Annie lose her train of thought and become distraught.

> **?** Into which category would you place William's behavior? What do you consider to be the position from which William's behavior is coming? If you find it necessary to intervene, what structures might you apply to help William at the moment of disruption and for follow-up?

INTERVENTION STRATEGIES FOR TYPES OF MISBEHAVIOR

Interventions—the actions teachers take to deal with misbehavior when it occurs— are used to help students replace their misbehavior with appropriate behavior that continues over time. It is here that teachers select and apply structures that help students behave appropriately. Kagan provides suggestions for many intervention strategies and the time frames in which they should be used in the following sections.

For Attention-Seeking Behavior

Most individuals have a strong need for attention. They want to know others care about them or at least take notice of them. When they feel left out or not cared for, they often behave undesirably in trying to get the attention they crave. They may interrupt, show off, annoy others, work more slowly than others, ask for extra help, or simply goof off. These acts seldom bring the results students hope for—in fact, they are likely to lead to further disruption and increased teacher annoyance.

What Teachers Can Do.   For the *moment of disruption*, teachers can use physical proximity and hand or facial signals to stop the misbehavior, or they can provide additional personal attention, appreciation, and affirmation. If attention seeking becomes chronic, teachers can ask students to identify positive ways to get attention. The teachers can *follow up* by meeting with disruptive students and discussing the need for attention and how it might be obtained in a positive manner. Strategies for *long-term solutions* include helping students strengthen their self-concept and acquire the skills of self-validation.

For Attempts to Avoid Failure or Embarrassment

We have all been in situations where we rationalize our inadequacies in order to soften the pain or embarrassment of failure. No one likes to appear inept. The student who says, "I don't care about the stupid math quiz," knows it is more painful to fail in front of others than not to try at all, and therefore will rationalize failure as lack of caring.

What Teachers Can Do.   Win-win teachers help students find ways to persist and continue to perform without feeling bad if they aren't first or best. For the *moment of disruption*, teachers can encourage students to try to complete the task, assign them partners or helpers, or reorganize and present the information in smaller instructional pieces. For *follow-up* and *long-term strategies,* you can ask students how they think responsible people might deal with fear of failure. Consider providing peer support, reviewing how mistakes are always part of the learning process as people move toward excellence, and using "team pair solo," a structure in which students practice first as a team and then in pairs before doing the assigned activities by themselves.

For Angry Students

Anger is a natural reaction to many situations that involve frustration, humiliation, loss, and pain. Angry students may act out in unacceptable ways because they do not know any other way to deal with the emotions they are experiencing.

Go to the Simulations section of Topic #12: Managing Problem Behaviors, in the **MyEducationLab** for your course and complete the simulation entitled "Dealing with Situations Where Students Are Being Bullied/ Harassed."

What Teachers Can Do.   Teachers don't enjoy interacting with angry students and may experience feelings of hurt or indignation. Often, because they feel personally attacked, their immediate reaction is to retaliate against the students. Obviously, that does nothing to help students manage their anger. Win-Win Discipline provides several structures to help teachers respond positively to angry disruptions. Three of those structures are teaching responsible ways of handling anger, allowing students to cool down and have time to think, and tabling the matter for attention at a later time. *Long-term interventions* include having students practice the skills of self-control and teaching them how to resolve conflicts in a positive manner.

For Control-Seeking Behavior

All of us want to feel we are at least partly in charge of ourselves and able to make our own decisions. When we exercise self-direction, we sometimes try to control others as well. At times students will show this take-charge attitude by disregarding or defying directions from the teacher. Doing so often leads to power struggles between student and teacher. Teachers don't take kindly to noncompliance, arguing, or making excuses, and they often counter in ways that show their dominance, which doesn't benefit the student.

What Teachers Can Do.   For the *moment of disruption*, teachers can acknowledge the student's power, use language of choice (a structure in which the teacher provides students with choice such as, "You may either . . . or . . ."), or provide options for how and when work is to be done. For *follow-up* they may schedule a conference or class meeting at a later time to discuss the situation, ask the class why they think students often struggle against the teacher, and consider how such struggles can be avoided. *Long-term strategies* include involving students in the decision-making process and asking for their help in establishing class agreements about showing respect for teacher and fellow students.

For Overly Energetic Students

At times, humans experience periods of high energy so strong they cannot sit still or concentrate. Some students are in this state a good deal of the time, moving and talking incessantly.

What Teachers Can Do.   If overly energetic behavior becomes troublesome, teachers can, at the *moment of disruption,* take a class break that allows energy to dissipate, provide time for progressive relaxation, remove distracting elements and objects, and channel energy productively. *Follow-up strategies* include teaching a variety of calming strategies and providing activities that allow students to work off energy in positive ways. *Long-term solutions* include managing energy levels during instruction and helping students learn how to channel their energy in ways that bring positive results.

For Bored Students

To say that students are bored is to say they are no longer enjoying given activities sufficiently to continue in them willingly. Their boredom will be evident in their body language, disengagement, and disinclination to participate.

What Teachers Can Do.   To help bored students at the *moment of disruption,* teachers can restructure the learning task, involve students more actively, and inject short activities that energize the students. As *follow-up,* they may talk privately with the students and assign them helping roles such as caretakers for the classroom, materials assistants, or coaches to assist other students. For *long-term solutions,* teachers can provide a rich, relevant, and developmentally appropriate curriculum that actively involves students in the learning process, emphasizes cooperative learning, and calls on students to use their multiple intelligences.

For Uninformed Students

Sometimes students respond or react disruptively because they simply don't know what to do or how to behave responsibly. Disruptions stemming from being uninformed do not occur because of strong emotions, but because of lack of information, skill, or appropriate habit. Even when these disruptions are not emotionally volatile, they are nonetheless frustrating to teachers.

What Teachers Can Do.   To determine whether students know what is expected of them, at the *moment of disruption* the teacher should gently ask if students know what they are supposed to do. If they don't, you can re-teach them at the time. If they only need support, let them work with a buddy. *Follow-up strategies* include more careful attention to giving directions, modeling desired responses, and providing practice in responsible behavior. *Long-term solutions* include encouragement and focusing on the student's strengths.

PARENT AND COMMUNITY ALLIANCES AND SCHOOLWIDE PROGRAMS

Kagan urges teachers to organize collaborative partnerships with parents and the wider community to assist students in making responsible behavior choices. Parents and community citizens usually appreciate and support teachers who handle disruptive behavior in a positive manner. Input, support, follow-through, and backup from parents and other adults strengthen the likelihood of success. Parent–teacher–community cooperation depends largely on teachers reaching out to make contacts—thus, ongoing communication is necessary. Don't give up when parents or community members seem reluctant to participate. Continue inviting them to become actively involved.

Win-Win Discipline provides many helpful suggestions for teacher–parent–community communication and interaction. Contact with potential participants should be made during the first week of school. Phone calls, letters, class newsletters, class websites, and emails are efficient ways to connect with parents. Parent nights and open houses offer opportunities for person-to-person communication, showing parents and others they are valued as allies and even potential mentors and tutors. The broader community can become involved through field trips, guest speakers, apprenticeships, and having students work with day-care and senior centers. Schoolwide efforts in this endeavor usually bring good results.

> **?** The school principal is urging teachers to make better connections with parents and the community, but leaving it up to teachers to decide how they will do so. Miss Able sets up a class website describing class activities that interested people can access. Mr. Beeson sends out personalized invitations to attend a class performance at school. Mrs. Calapari calls 10 parents on the phone and tells them how pleased she is to have their child in class and describes something the child has done unusually well. How do you assess the impact and value of these three different attempts to reach out for support?

ESTABLISHING WIN-WIN DISCIPLINE IN THE CLASSROOM

When you introduce Win-Win Discipline, begin by setting the tone for the class. Let the students know that the class will be built on the three pillars of Win-Win Discipline—same side, collaborative solutions, and learned responsibility. You might say something like this:

> This is our class, and with all of us working together we will create a place where each person feels comfortable and all of us can enjoy the process of learning. As your teacher, I have a responsibility to create an environment where this can happen, but I need your help to make it work. I want each of you to realize you are an important member of this class, with important responsibilities, and that you can help make the class a pleasant place to be. One of your main responsibilities is to help create and maintain a positive learning atmosphere where everybody's needs are met. To accomplish this, we all must work together. I suggest that we begin by creating an agreement about how we will treat each other in this class.

Consider creating class agreements as follows: Begin by constructing a chart with the headings *Disruptive Behavior* and *Responsible Behavior*. Under each heading write two subheadings, *Say* and *Do*. Ask the students to name some of the disruptive things people say and do when they want attention. Record their responses under *Disruptive Behavior*. Then ask the class to name some of the responsible things people say and do for attention. Record their responses under *Responsible Behavior*. Continue this process for each of the seven positions.

When you have reasonable lists, ask students, "How do you feel about these lists? Would you be willing to adopt the responsible behaviors as our class agreement? Can we agree to avoid the disruptive behaviors?" It is essential that students believe their opinions and cooperation are valued. Tell them,

> You and I need to be on the same side and work together to create a classroom we all enjoy where everyone can learn. You will always be included in the decision-making process. You will be able to have your say. We will learn and practice skills that are important for being citizens in a democratic society. Choosing responsible behavior will be one of the most important things we will learn.

During the first weeks, use activities that strengthen the concept of the three pillars. This reassures students that discipline will not be done to them, but will happen with them. In collaboration with the class you might discuss discipline structures and their purposes, develop follow-ups and logical consequences, and solicit student input on some curriculum decisions. You can also show students how you will help them turn disruptive behavior into good learning situations, where reflection, follow-up, and long-term structures come into play. You can do these things in a series of class meetings. Kagan adds that very early in the term you should begin establishing alliances with parents and interested members of the community.

In order to implement Win-Win Discipline as intended, you must do three things. The *first* is to commit yourself to complying with what Kagan calls teaching's **Big Three:**

- Establish an interesting and challenging *curriculum*.
- Provide *cooperative activities* that allow students to work together meaningfully.
- Be an *interesting, stimulating teacher* who adapts the curriculum to student interests and needs.

The *second* is to familiarize yourself with the seven student positions and relate them to the types of misbehavior you are likely to encounter. Remember, you are to accept and validate the seven positions, but not the disruptive behavior associated with them.

The *third* is to select or design structures that help misbehaving students return to responsible conduct. You will put some of these structures in place as preventive measures before classes begin; you will use others to help redirect misbehavior; and you will use still others to help students develop long-term responsibility.

Review with your class the four types of disruptive behavior and the seven student positions associated with them. Explain that (1) misbehavior (which is unacceptable) consists of inappropriate actions people take in trying to meet their needs, (2) when students misbehave, they are coming from a particular natural emotional state that can be identified, and (3) for those emotional states, there are procedures teachers can use to help students meet their needs and return to acceptable behavior.

Continuing to stress collaboration, ask students to think along with you about what could be done to help them behave more appropriately should they misbehave. You might discuss an example such as the following:

During a cooperative group situation, Samuel, a new boy in class, disrupts the class by standing up and calling over to Duwahn in another group. Samuel may or may not know that this behavior is inappropriate, but his action violates one of the class rules that class members have agreed on. What should be done? In accordance with advice from Kagan, Kyle, and Scott (2004), you might describe the following approach and ask for your students' reactions to it:

- Identify the category of misbehavior. Using Kagan's ABCD acronym, we see Samuel's behavior is category B (breaking rules).
- Look beyond the misbehavior to identify the position Samuel is coming from. (Let's suppose you determine that Samuel's position is "being uninformed.")
- Apply a structure for the moment of disruption that is consistent with Samuel's position. You might say, "Samuel, because you are a new member of our class, you may not know, or may not remember, our rule against calling out in class. Do you remember that rule? No? Let's take just a moment to review it so you will remember it in the future."
- It is not likely you will need to say more, but if necessary you could use a follow-up structure to help Samuel make better decisions in the future. For example, you and Samuel might have a private friendly same-side chat to help Samuel understand the rule against calling out and help him identify an alternative behavior that would be acceptable.

Ideally, implementation of Win-Win Discipline should begin before the school year starts, with advance preparation for procedures, routines, and materials associated with each of the seven student positions. But teachers who want to try the approach after the term has begun will find they can put Win-Win Discipline in place at any time. It may take a bit of time to teach your students the fundamental concepts and procedures, but once students are comfortable with them, the program is relatively easy to maintain.

BRIEF REVIEW OF WIN-WIN DISCIPLINE

Many ideas and tactics are included in Win-Win Discipline. The following review is provided to help you tie them together.

- The ultimate goals of Win-Win Discipline are to enable students to manage themselves, meet their needs through responsible choices, and develop life skills that serve well in the future. Win-Win Discipline is more than a strategy for ending disruptions—it has the added strength of fostering autonomous responsibility and other skills that transfer to life situations. Potential discipline problems tend to fade away when students experience an engaging curriculum, interesting instruction, and effective class procedures and management.

- Discipline is not something you do to students. It is something you help students acquire. The aim of discipline is to help students learn to meet their needs in a nondisruptive, responsible manner. Any disruptive behavior in the class can become an important opportunity for developing responsible behavior.

- In developing and implementing Win-Win Discipline, emphasize the three pillars of same side, collaborative solutions, and learned responsibility. For this approach to be effective, teacher and students must be on the same side, working together to create discipline solutions that help students conduct themselves more responsibly now and in the future. In the process, teachers openly express genuine caring for students, validate student positions, and provide support in establishing responsible alternatives to disruptive behavior. Students who participate in the process and help create their own discipline solutions become more likely to make responsible choices in the future.

- Win-Win Discipline proceeds from four types of disruptive behavior, called the ABCD of Disruptive Behavior: aggression, breaking rules, confrontation, and disengagement.

- The four types of misbehavior emanate from one or more of seven student positions, or emotional/physical states the student experiences at any given time. The seven positions are attention seeking, avoiding failure, angry, control seeking, energetic, bored, and uninformed. The teacher should validate the student's position as being natural and understandable, but should not accept the misbehavior. By clarifying the links between student positions and disruptive behavior, teachers are better able to prevent misbehavior, explain the program to students, and select appropriate discipline responses.

- A number of structures are available to help students when they misbehave. Those structures are short procedures the teacher selects and applies to help students return to responsible behavior and increasingly remain there. The structures are matched to the misbehavior and to the student position from which it emanates.

APPLYING WIN-WIN DISCIPLINE IN THE CLASSROOM

- Familiarize yourself with the following principles of Win-Win Discipline:
  1. Do not "do things to students," but help them acquire skills of self-control.
  2. Teach students to meet their needs in a responsible manner.
  3. Use misbehavior as a starting place for developing responsible behavior.
  4. Work together collaboratively with students from the same side to find solutions to behavior concerns.
  5. Involve students in various activities that develop learned responsibility.
- Familiarize yourself and instruct your class about four types of disruptive behavior: aggression, breaking rules, confrontation, and disengagement.
- Familiarize yourself and instruct your class about seven student positions (states of mind) that often lead to disruptive behavior: attention seeking, avoiding failure, angry, control seeking, energetic, bored, and uninformed.
- Validate student positions as being natural and understandable, but do not accept the misbehavior associated with the positions.
- Use selected structures (organized procedures matched to type of behavior and student position) to interact productively with students who misbehave.
- Always endeavor to provide an engaging curriculum, interesting instruction, and effective class procedures and management.
- Using structures, help students create their own responsible discipline solutions and abide by them.

ABCD of disruptive behavior	interventions	structures
Big Three	life skills	student positions
class rules	long-term structures	three pillars
follow-up structures	personal improvement plan	

CASE 1: KRISTINA WILL NOT WORK

Kristina, a student in Mr. Jake's class, is quite docile. She socializes little with other students and never disrupts lessons. However, despite Mr. Jake's best efforts, Kristina will not do her work. She rarely completes an assignment. She is simply there, putting forth no effort at all. *What would Spencer Kagan suggest to help Kristina and Mr. Jake?*

Kagan would advise Mr. Jake to do the following: Mr. Jake would identify Kristina's problematic behavior and ask behavior-specific questions. He also would identify and help Kristina acknowledge her position. Mr. Jake might ask Kristina how she feels about the work, determining if it is too difficult for her (leading to avoidance of failure), or not interesting (leading to boredom). If the work is too difficult for Kristina, and her position is avoiding, or if she doesn't know how to do the work, he might say quietly, "I really want to help you be successful, Kristina. I see this work is not getting finished. None of us wants to tackle something we know will be too hard for us. The best thing to do if something is too hard is to break it into smaller pieces, mastering a part at a time. Another good strategy is to work on the difficult pieces with someone else. What suggestions do you have that will help you be successful?" Together they come up with possible solutions and then, if they agree that Kristina could benefit by working with a partner on smaller pieces, Mr. Jake may ask, "Would you like to work on this section with Danielle before moving on?" Throughout the interaction, Mr. Jake is attempting to help Kristina find a nondisruptive way to meet her needs. But more importantly, Mr. Jake is helping Kristina internalize a process of validating her own needs and seeking responsible rather than disruptive ways to fulfill them. As follow-up, Mr. Jake might focus on her success by saying something like "Kristina, I knew you could do this if we tried making the pieces smaller." His long-term solutions will include further encouragement and individual attention to Kristina's strengths.

CASE 2: SARA WILL NOT STOP TALKING

Sara is a pleasant girl who participates in class activities and does most, though not all, of her assigned work. She cannot seem to refrain from talking to classmates, however. Her teacher, Mr. Gonzales, has to speak to her repeatedly during lessons, to the point that he often becomes exasperated and loses his temper. *What suggestions would Spencer Kagan give Mr. Gonzales for dealing with Sara?*

CASE 3: JOSHUA CLOWNS AND INTIMIDATES

Joshua, larger and louder than his classmates, always wants to be the center of attention, which he accomplishes through a combination of clowning and intimidation. He makes wise remarks, talks back (smilingly) to the teacher, utters a variety of sound-effect noises such as automobile crashes and gunshots, and makes limitless sarcastic comments and put-downs of his classmates. Other students will not stand up to him, apparently fearing his size and verbal aggression. His teacher, Miss Pearl, has come to her wit's end. *Would Joshua's behavior be likely to improve if Win-Win Discipline were used in Miss Pearl's classroom? Explain.*

CASE 4: TOM IS HOSTILE AND DEFIANT

Tom has appeared to be in his usual foul mood ever since arriving in class. On his way to sharpen his pencil, he bumps into Frank, who complains. Tom tells him loudly to shut up. Miss Baines, the teacher, says, "Tom, go back to your seat." Tom wheels around, swears loudly, and says heatedly, "I'll go when I'm damned good and ready!" *How would Tom's behavior be handled in a Win-Win classroom?*

You Are the Teacher

MIDDLE SCHOOL WORLD HISTORY

Your third-period world history class is composed of students whose achievement levels vary from high to well below average. You pace their work accordingly, ask them to work cooperatively, and make sure everyone understands what they are supposed to do. For the most part you enjoy the class, finding the students interesting and refreshing. Your lessons follow a consistent pattern. First, you ask the students to read in groups from the textbook, then you call on students at random to answer selected questions about the material. If a student who is called on is unable to answer a question, the group he or she represents loses a point. If the student answers correctly, the group gains a point. For partially correct answers, the group neither receives nor loses a point. For the second part of the period, the class groups do something productive or creative connected with the material they have read, such as making posters, writing a story, doing a skit, or the like. As appropriate, these efforts are shared with members of the class.

A TYPICAL OCCURRENCE

You call on Hillary to answer a question. Although she has been participating, she shakes her head. This has happened several times before. Not wanting to hurt Hillary's feelings, you simply say, "That costs the group a point," and you call on someone else. Unfortunately, Hillary's group gets upset at her. The other students make comments under their breath. Later, Clarisse also refuses to answer. When you speak with her about it, she says, "You didn't make Hillary do it." You answer, "Look, we are talking about you, not Hillary." However, you let the matter lie and say no more. Just then, Deonne comes into the class late, appearing very angry. He slams his pack down on his desk and sits without opening his textbook. Although you

want to talk with Deonne, you don't know how to approach him at that time. Will is in the opposite mood. Throughout the oral reading portion of the class, he continually giggles at every mispronounced word and at every reply students give to your questions. Will sits at the front of the class and turns around to laugh, seeing if he can get anyone else to laugh with him. He makes some *oooh* and *aaaah* sounds when Hillary and Clarisse decline to respond. Although most students either ignore him or give him disgusted looks, he keeps laughing. You finally ask him what is so funny. He replies, "Nothing in particular," and looks back at the class and laughs. At the end of the period, there is time for sharing three posters students have made. Will makes comments and giggles about each of them. Clarisse, who has not participated, says, "Will, how about shutting up!" As the students leave the room, you take Deonne aside. "Is something wrong, Deonne?" you ask. "No," he replies. His jaw is clenched as he strides past you.

CONCEPTUALIZING A STRATEGY

If you followed the principles of Win-Win Discipline, what would you conclude or do with regard to the following?

- Preventing the problems from occurring in the first place
- Putting an immediate end to the misbehavior
- Involving other or all students in addressing the situation
- Maintaining student dignity and good personal relations.
- Using follow-up procedures to prevent the recurrence of the misbehavior
- Using the situation to help the students develop a sense of greater responsibility and self-control

Activities

1. In your journal, enter notes from Win-Win Discipline that you might wish to include in your own system of discipline.
2. Win-Win Discipline rests on three pillars—same side, collaborative solutions, and learned responsibility. How would you go about communicating these key principles to students?
3. In Kagan's view, how are curriculum, instruction, and management linked to the prevention of discipline problems?
4. To what extent do you feel you could put Win-Win Discipline into effect in your classroom? What portions do you believe you could implement easily? What portions do you believe might present difficulty?

References

Kagan, S. 2001. Teaching for character and community. *Educational Leadership, 59*(2), 50–55.

Kagan, S., Kyle, P., and Scott, S. 2004. *Win-Win Discipline*. San Clemente, CA: Kagan Publishing.

How Does Marvin Marshall Establish Discipline by Activating Internal Motivation and Raising Student Responsibility?

Marvin Marshall believes the best way to ensure good classroom behavior is to help students learn to conduct themselves responsibly. For Marshall, one of today's most influential authorities in discipline, *responsibility* is another word for internal motivation to do the right thing. Teachers can activate that motivation, he says, by (1) articulating clear *behavioral expectations*, (2) *empowering* students to reach them, (3) infusing *positivity* into all aspects of teaching, and (4) promoting a *desire to do the right thing* instead of pushing for obedience.

Dr. Marshall is an experienced teacher, counselor, and administrator who has served at all levels of public education. Currently, he devotes himself to writing, helping with staff development in schools, and speaking nationally and internationally. His views on improving classroom discipline are set forth in his book *Discipline without Stress, Punishments, or Rewards: How Teachers and Parents Promote Responsibility & Learning* (2001, 2007) and his monthly electronic newsletter entitled *Promoting Responsibility & Learning*, which is available free via email from www.marvinmarshall.com.

A PREVIEW OF THIS CHAPTER

Go to the Building Classroom Discipline Video Showcase section of Topic #3: Models of Classroom Management, in the **MyEducationLab** for your course and watch the video entitled "Marvin Marshall—Discipline through Raising Responsibility."

Classroom discipline is best established and maintained by helping students increase their personal level of responsibility—their internal motivation to do the right thing. The most effective teachers know that students will work gladly, with self-control and responsibility, if they find school satisfying (per Theory Y). Ten specific teaching practices hinder learning and lead to misbehavior; they should be replaced with specific practices that facilitate learning and promote responsible behavior. Marshall's hierarchy of social development is powerful in helping students behave appropriately and accept responsibility for the choices they make. Marshall also offers a number of tactics for use in stimulating students to behave responsibly. When students misbehave, teachers should intervene by using authority without punishment and the power of choice, allowing students to choose among two or three acceptable options. In short, establish behavior expectations through the hierarchy, implement Theory Y, and use teaching tactics that call forth internal motivation to do the right thing. When students misbehave, intervene by having them relate their behavior to levels in the hierarchy, identify better behavior, and select among two or three responsible options.

<hr>

WHAT TO LOOK FOR IN THIS CHAPTER

- The 10 practices that damage teaching and how they can be corrected
- Contrasting theories of how to manage people—Theory X and Theory Y
- The nature and power of internal motivation (versus external motivation)
- Marshall's hierarchy of social development, how it is used, and how it is taught
- The 25 tactics teachers can use to stimulate students to behave responsibly
- How you should intervene when students misbehave
- How to evaluate your performance in using Marshall's system

10 PRACTICES THAT DAMAGE TEACHING AND HOW THEY CAN BE CORRECTED

Marshall has noted that most teachers strive to organize meaningful, challenging lessons for their students, hoping the students will control themselves and try to learn. Unfortunately, those hopes are seldom fully realized. Why? One of the reasons, says Marshall, is that teachers unwittingly use 10 practices that are counterproductive to success. Marshall (2008a) says teachers can greatly improve their effectiveness by abandoning those practices and replacing them with practices that bring out the best in students. Here are the 10 damaging practices, each followed by a better practice for teachers.

1. *Being reactive rather than proactive.* Teachers typically wait for misbehavior to occur and then they react to it. Their reactions are often ineffective, especially when teachers are under stress.

Better approach: Teachers would enjoy much better results if, instead of waiting and reacting to misbehavior, they inspired students at the outset to want to behave responsibly. On occasions when students fail to do so, teachers can make nonadversarial responses, such as providing two or three acceptable behaviors from which students can choose.

2. *Relying on rules of behavior.* Rules are meant to control; they do not inspire. Rules are necessary in games, but when used between people, enforcement of rules automatically creates adversarial relationships.

Better approach: Rather than relying on rules, carefully teach students the procedures they are expected to follow and then inspire responsible behavior by emphasizing positive expectations and having students reflect on them.

3. *Aiming for obedience rather than responsibility.* Obedience does not create an internal desire to behave properly.

Better approach: Forget about striving for obedience, per se, and concentrate on promoting responsibility (such as reviewing Marshall's hierarchy of social development). Desirable behavior then follows as a natural byproduct.

4. *Creating negative images.* You create the wrong image when you tell students what they should *not* do instead of what they *should* do. When people tell others what not to do, what follows the "don't" is what the brain visualizes. To illustrate, if you say, "Don't run," you leave a picture of running in the student's brain.

Better approach: The picture you want to leave in students' minds is one that depicts what they should do. For example, instead of saying, "Don't run," it is better to say, "Please walk."

5. *Unknowingly alienating students.* Even the poorest salesperson knows not to alienate a customer, but teachers too often talk to students in ways that prompt negative feelings. That dampens any desire students might have to cooperate with the teacher.

Better approach: People "do good" when they feel positive, not when they feel negative. If you speak with students in a friendly and supportive manner, they are more likely to cooperate with you willingly.

6. *Confusing classroom management with discipline.* Classroom management has to do with classroom organization, student procedures, and the efficient use of materials. It is the teacher's responsibility. Discipline has to do with self-control and appropriate behavior. It is the student's responsibility.

Better approach: Explain to students that it is your responsibility to provide a classroom in which they can learn comfortably and efficiently. Explain that it is *their* responsibility to conduct themselves in a responsible manner, and that you will teach them how to do so.

7. *Assuming students know what is expected of them.* Too often, teachers assume students know, without being taught, how they are expected to conduct themselves in class.

Better approach: Teach your students the procedures and behaviors expected of them and have them practice until they can do those things automatically.

8. *Employing coercion rather than influence.* Although teachers can use coercion to control students temporarily, that process does little to change students or motivate them to learn.

Better approach: Recognize that people change themselves and will do so when inspired and taught, rather than coerced. Most students resist in some degree when *made* to do anything. Therefore, do what you can to inspire and influence students to learn and conduct themselves responsibly.

9. *Imposing consequences rather than eliciting responsible behavior.* When a consequence (an unpleasant aftermath) is imposed on students who fail to meet expectations, ownership of any change in behavior is taken away from the student, which makes the change weak or transitory.

Better approach: A more effective tactic to employ when students misbehave or fail to meet expectations is to **elicit** from the student involved a consequence or a procedure that he or she feels will improve the likelihood of responsible behavior.

10. *Relying on external influences rather than internal processes.* We make a serious mistake when we use reward and punishment to help young people develop self-discipline. Those influences come from outside the individual, rather than from inside. Behavior may seem to change when external influences are applied, but it usually fails the critical test of responsible behavior: Is responsible behavior still in effect when the teacher is not there to watch?

Better approach: True change comes from the self-satisfaction that accrues from one's own efforts, not from threats that induce fear or prizes that reinforce childish values. Therefore, do what you can to help students find pleasure in improvements in learning and personal behavior.

? Which of the foregoing 10 errors is most evident in each of the following?

1. Mrs. Garcia looks at Jamie's work and says, "This is not done correctly. What did you think you were supposed to do?"
2. Mr. Allen says to George, "You broke the no-talking rule again. Go sit at the time-out table until you decide to follow our rules."
3. Miss Smyth says to Maree, "This is a warning: Do not pester Alicia again!"

THE POWER OF INTERNAL MOTIVATION

Marshall emphasizes that although humans are influenced by many factors, all motivation takes place *within* a person. In education, we must learn to use this **internal motivation** to advantage by helping students see how it can bring satisfaction and pleasure. Teachers should stop thinking of themselves as motivators, and instead serve as *stimulators* who activate students' internal motivation in positive ways.

Traditionally, teachers have tried to motivate students by urging, directing, cajoling, admonishing, criticizing, and using rewards and punishments. These pressures, which come from outside the student, are referred to as **external motivation.** The external prompts do not often activate a genuine desire to do well, but rather they cause students to try to avoid discomfort and possibly gain the approval of the teacher. Unfortunately, those external pressures are responsible for most of the stress and poor relations seen in many classrooms.

TWO WAYS OF MANAGING PEOPLE

Marshall says if teachers are to get the best results in their classes, they must inspire students to achieve and ensure they find pleasure in school. In explaining how to accomplish these things, he describes two opposite approaches to managing people, as set forth by Douglas McGregor in 1960. McGregor called the approaches *Theory X* and *Theory Y.* **Theory X** holds that people dislike work, try to avoid it, and must be directed, coerced, controlled, or threatened with punishment before they will do their work. **Theory Y** holds that people will work gladly if their jobs bring satisfaction and will exercise self-direction, self-control, and personal responsibility in doing so. Marshall's approach to discipline is concordant with Theory Y. He says that even though students are generally inclined to behave responsibly, they often don't—either because they don't know how to or because peer pressure or lack of self-control overrides their better judgment.

A proponent of Theory Y, Marshall (2005e) advises teachers to organize classrooms so they promote positive attitudes and good relationships, which make school enjoyable for students and teachers alike. Teachers should endeavor to establish a positive attitude in the classroom, by emphasizing *positivity, choice,* and *reflection* in their daily interactions with students.

Positivity is an emotion of optimism. Being around optimistic people makes us feel better, while being around negative people has the opposite effect. Students will probably like you and be pleased to be in your class if they see you as positive in your outlook and dealings with others, rather than negative and critical. Unfortunately, students often perceive their teachers and schools in a negative light because teachers unwittingly set themselves up as enforcers of rules rather than as encouragers, mentors, and role models. They aim at promoting obedience, without realizing that obedience has no energizing effect on students, but instead fosters apathy, resistance, and defiance.

Choice, on the other hand, empowers students by offering them options. Marshall (2005b) reports the following comments about the **empowerment of choice** he received from a school administrator:

> I began to experiment with giving choices to students. When speaking to students about their behavior at recess, in the lunchroom, or on the bus, I would try to elicit from them what choices they had and how they could make better choices. If a consequence were needed, we would talk together about some of the choices. I would usually start with, "What do you think we should do about the situation?" When I was satisfied with the student's choice, I would say, "I can live with that." The process worked every time and I would wonder at its simplicity.

Reflection is a process of thinking about one's own behavior and judging its merits that plays a major role in changing one's behavior for the better. Teachers must understand they cannot control students by asking for obedience, making demands, or imposing consequences. They cannot force change in how students think, want to behave, or will behave once the teacher's presence is no longer felt. Students do those things for themselves.

What teachers *can* do is establish expectations and empower students to attain them. This process is done in a noncoercive manner by asking **reflective questions** that prompt students to think about how they are behaving. That reflection often sets in motion a positive change in behavior. The way to jumpstart reflection is to prompt students to ask themselves questions such as, "If I wanted to be successful in this class right now, what would I be doing?" In most cases, the answer will be apparent and they begin behaving accordingly.

MARSHALL'S HIERARCHY OF SOCIAL DEVELOPMENT

Marshall has developed a **hierarchy of social development** that has proved very effective in promoting responsible behavior in the classroom. He teaches the hierarchy to students, who move quickly toward responsible behavior as they learn the levels of social development and what those levels entail. Marshall's hierarchy is as follows:

Hierarchy of Social Development

- *Level A—Anarchy (an unacceptable level).* This is the lowest level of social development. When students are functioning at this level, they give no heed to expectations or standards. They have no sense of order or purpose and they seldom accomplish anything worthwhile in class.

- *Level B—Bossing/bullying/bothering (also an unacceptable level).* When functioning at this level, students are bossing, bullying, or bothering others without consideration of the harm they are doing. Here, students obey the teacher or others only when made to do so. In effect they are saying to the teacher, "We are unable to control ourselves. We need you to boss us." Marshall says sharing this concept with students has a profound effect on how they behave.

- *Level C—Cooperation/conformity (an acceptable level).* When functioning at this level, students conform to expectations set by the teacher or others and are willing to cooperate. However, motivation for responsible conduct comes from external influences, such as rules, teacher demands, and peer pressure (which at times may be irresponsible). Discussing and thinking about the nature and effects of external motivation helps students understand and move beyond its influence.

- *Level D—Democracy and taking the initiative to do the right thing (the highest and most desirable level).* When functioning at Level D, students take the initiative to do what they feel is right and proper—they behave responsibly without having to be told to do so. They are prompted to behave in this manner by internal motivation associated with an understanding of what is expected of them and why. Marshall suggests explaining to students that democracy requires citizens to make decisions for themselves, rather than having decisions made for them, as is the case in dictatorships. Democracy expects people do the right thing because they understand it is best for themselves and the people around them. Marshall says that although Level C behavior is acceptable in school, teachers and students should aim for Level D, where students are motivated to make good decisions about their personal behavior, regardless of circumstances, personal urges, or influence from others.

To illustrate how the hierarchy of social development is used to help students reflect on their behavior, suppose two boys are talking together audibly while another student is making a class report. The teacher quietly asks the disruptive boys, "At what level is that behavior?" They think for a moment and answer, "Level B." Their misbehavior typically ceases at that point and their minds turn toward behavior at a higher level.

Value of the Hierarchy

Marshall says that once students understand the hierarchy, their attention turns to self-control and social responsibility. He describes the attributes that give the hierarchy its power (tactics used in association with the hierarchy are described in the next section):

- It enables teachers to separate the act from the actor, the deed from the doer. Without that separation, students become defensive about their behavior when asked to correct it.
- It helps students realize they are constantly making choices, both consciously and unconsciously.
- It helps students understand and deal with peer pressure.
- It fosters internal motivation to behave responsibly.
- It promotes good character development without calling attention to personal values, ethics, or morals.
- It serves as a vehicle for communication that uses the same conceptual vocabulary for youths and adults.
- It encourages students to help keep their classroom conducive to learning, rather than relying solely on the teacher to do so.
- It raises awareness of individual responsibility.
- It empowers students by helping them analyze and correct their own behavior.
- It serves as an inspiration to improve.
- It encourages mature decision making.
- It fosters understanding about internal and external motivation.
- It promotes self-management and doing the right thing, even when no adult is around or when no one else is watching.

Teaching the Hierarchy to Students

Marshall (2001) suggests a number of activities that are useful in teaching students the names and characteristics of the four levels. Examples include visualizing each level and then drawing a picture of it, describing it in writing, describing it orally to others, and listening to others' examples of applying the levels to what goes on in school. He explains that these various modalities turn the four levels into pictures students hold in their minds. He argues that it is the pictures in our minds that drive behavior—toward those activities we believe will bring satisfaction and away from those we believe will bring displeasure. He urges teachers to emphasize that the major difference between the acceptable levels of C and D is the source and nature of the motivation. Level C is behaving responsibly because of adult directions and may involve rewards and punishments. At that level students remain overly susceptible to peer influence, which at times can be counterproductive to responsible behavior. Level D is being responsible without being asked, told, rewarded, or punished. At Level D, students *take the initiative* to do the right thing because they believe it is best for the class, the school, and themselves.

You might wonder how well students can understand these levels and relate them to real life. Brief excerpts from "A Letter Worth Reading" (Figure 10.1) provide commentary on that question. The letter was sent to Marvin Marshall by a teacher using his system.

Figure 10.1   A Letter Worth Reading

Just this week we had a discussion with our students about how they could use their understanding of the four levels of development to help themselves become better readers. We talked about our 30-minute "Whole School Read" time that we participate in each morning. We had the children come up with scenarios of what it would look like if someone were operating at each of the four levels. Students were able to clearly describe conduct at each level.

At Level D, the students described that a person would be using reading time each morning to really practice reading. They wouldn't have to have an adult directly with them at all times; they would keep on task simply because they know what is expected of them. They would read and re-read sections of their book because they know that by doing so they will become better readers. The motivation would be INTERNAL. They wouldn't be wasting any time watching the teacher in hopes of being specially noticed as "someone who was reading," and they wouldn't rely on an adult to keep then on task. Instead they would be reading in an effort to become the best reader that they could be.

The children discussed further that Level D is where people take the initiative to do things that are truly going to pay off for them—what is right or appropriate. People at this level *motivate themselves* to work and achieve. The results are long lasting and powerful. These people put in the necessary effort to become good readers and therefore can get a lot of enjoyment from reading. Because they get enjoyment, they keep reading and therefore become even better readers. People behaving at this level feel good about themselves because they experience improvement and are aware that it is a result of choices that they have consciously made.

It is amazing to see the results of discussions such as these. That night, without any suggestion or prompting on my part, our poorest reader in the class went home and read his reader over and over again. Although his parents are kind people, they haven't understood the importance of nightly reading for their child despite many conversations with us. That night they watched as their little boy independently read and re-read his reader. Both the parents and little boy could see the dramatic improvement in his ability to read. They experienced the powerful impact that internal desire, coupled with one night of true effort, could have on someone's skill at reading. He came back to school the next day bursting with pride and determination to practice more and more so that he could move on to a new, more difficult reader. It only took one more night of practice, and he was able to do that.

Source: A Letter Worth Reading. www.marvinmarshall.com/aletterworthreading.html. Reprinted by permission.

For additional information on how the hierarchy promotes learning in reading, mathematics, spelling, physical education, and other areas, see "Samples of Hierarchies for Promoting Learning" (Marshall, 2005g).

25 TACTICS USEFUL IN STIMULATING STUDENTS TO BEHAVE RESPONSIBLY

Marshall suggests 25 specific tactics that stimulate responsibility in students and help them increase their reliance on internal motivation.

1. *Think and speak with positivity.* If we approach students and situations in a positive manner, we enjoy ourselves more and bring greater pleasure to our students. Students are often put off if they perceive a negative tone in our communications with them. By helping students think in positive terms, we reduce stress, improve relationships, and help them become more successful.

2. *Use the power of choice.* We all have the power to choose our responses and attitudes to situations, events, impulses, and urges. The optimists among us perceive that choices are available; the pessimists perceive a lack of choice. Optimistic thinking engenders responsibility and helps students move away from seeing themselves as victims of life events. Regardless of age, everyone likes to feel they have control over their lives. When we are encouraged to make choices, we become more aware of that control. Consider offering your students choices in school activities, including homework. Doing so noncoercively promotes behavior change and provides hope and feelings of control.

3. *Emphasize the reflective process.* Thinking reflectively increases positivity and choice and, when applied to one's own behavior, can lead to self-evaluation and correction, necessary ingredients for growth and change. Ask students questions and encourage them to ask themselves questions, especially about behavior they have chosen. The questioning process activates the thinking process. When students ask themselves "What?" and "How?" their alertness and interest increase.

4. *Control the conversation by asking questions.* One way for teachers to remain in control of conversations is to ask questions. When you ask someone a question, they have a natural inclination to answer it. If in a discussion or argument you find yourself in a reactive mode and want to move into a proactive mode and regain control, ask a question of your own. For example, a student asks you, "Why do we have to do this assignment?" Instead of answering, redirect the conversation by simply asking, "Do you feel there is another way we can learn this information more easily?" When students complain, you are likely to get good results by asking, "What can I do to improve the situation, and what can you do?"

5. *Create curiosity.* Marshall says curiosity may be the greatest of all motivators for learning. He suggests presenting a problem or a challenge to students and allowing them to grapple with it at the beginning of a lesson. Doing so engenders student curiosity.

6. *Create desire to know.* Allow some time at the beginning of each lesson to talk about what the lesson offers. Students always want to know what's in it for them.

Point out how new knowledge, skills, and insights can help them solve problems, make better decisions, get along better with others, and live life more effectively and enjoyably.

7. *Use acknowledgment and recognition.* Providing acknowledgment and recognition of students' efforts helps them feel affirmed and validated. Such a simple comment as, "I see you did well on that," fosters reflection and feelings of competence, as does a comment such as, "Evelyn raises an interesting question, one that applies to what we've been exploring."

8. *Encourage students.* One of the most effective techniques for stimulating students is to let them know you believe they can accomplish the task before them. For many students, a word of encouragement following a mistake is worth more than a great deal of praise after a success. Emphasize that learning is a process and that no one is perfect. Not being successful at a task is a valuable way of learning. It should be seen as a learning experience, not as failure. (See Marshall, 2005f.)

9. *Use collaboration.* Generally speaking, allowing students to work together cooperatively promotes better learning than does competition. Competing with others is not effective for youngsters who never reach the winner's circle. Students who never feel successful would rather drop out than compete. Instead of competing, allow students to work together, preferably in pairs. Even a very shy student will usually participate with one other person. (See Marshall, 2005d.)

10. *Get yourself excited.* You can't expect others to get excited about what you are teaching if you are not excited about it yourself. Show enthusiasm for the lesson. When lecturing, use a little more animation than when you are conversing, facilitating, or reviewing.

11. *Foster interpersonal relationships in the class.* Connecting with your students one on one is extremely valuable, but helping them connect with each other one on one can be even more valuable. Relationships are extremely important to young people. At the end of a lesson, consider having students participate in *think, pair, and share,* in which they work in pairs and then share their conclusions with the class.

12. *Use variety.* Variety spices up topics that students might otherwise find tedious. A myriad of visual, auditory, and manipulative techniques can be employed in teaching, such as charts, cartoons, models, parts of films, videos, PowerPoint creations, overhead transparencies, listening to music, recording music, rapping, creating verse, creating rhythms, physical movements, enacting the roles of characters in stories or events, large-group discussions, case studies, and working with small groups or buddies.

13. *Stress responsibility rather than rules.* Consider calling behaviors you expect in class *responsibilities* rather than *rules*. For responsibilities that are actually procedures, rather than matters of personal conduct, teach the appropriate procedure and have students practice until they can do it correctly. Every rule, expectation, or responsibility should be stated in positive terms.

14. *See situations as challenges, not problems.* If we help students take a positive approach and view situations as *challenges,* rather than as problems, we help them deal better with what life brings. This also helps students feel they have some control over their lives, rather than being victims of circumstance. Emphasize to stu-

dents that they can use adversity as a catalyst to becoming better, stronger, wiser, and more capable of dealing with life's challenges.

15. *Use listening to influence others.* It is surprising how strongly we can influence students simply by listening to them. The more we are open to students, the greater our influence. One way to develop listening ability is to pretend we are doing the talking for the other person. This can cause us to set aside some of our views and redirect some of our impulsive reactions. Also, we should ask **reflective questions** rather than continually lecturing. Learning to listen and ask evaluative-type questions takes practice, but brings good results.

16. *Be careful about challenging students' ideas.* Very few people like to be put on the defensive by having their ideas and beliefs challenged. Instead of challenging, ask questions such as, "How did you come to that interesting conclusion?" or "An alternative point of view is (such and such). Have you ever considered that viewpoint?"

17. *Avoid telling.* When we tell someone to do something, the message is often perceived as criticism or an attempt to control, regardless of our intentions. Rather than telling, phrase your idea as a suggestion, such as, "You may want to consider doing that later and focusing on the current lesson now." Or use a reflective question stated as if you were curious, such as, "What would be the long-term effect of doing that?" Three more questions you will find useful are: "Is there any other way this could be handled?" "What would a responsible action look like?" and "What do you think a highly responsible person would do in this situation?"

18. *Raise your likeability level.* Most teachers want students to like them. Many believe they can make that happen by trying to be friends with students and may decide, for example, to let students call them by their given name. There is much to be said for friendliness, but personal friendship is not what students need or even want from teachers. If you provide encouragement and empowerment through positivity, choice, and reflection, your students will like you.

19. *Empower by building on successes.* Great teachers know that learning is based on motivation and students are best motivated when they can build on existing interests and strengths. That doesn't mean we should ignore the negative or disregard what needs improvement. But students are more likely to achieve success through their assets than through their shortcomings. The more they are successful, the more they are willing to put effort into areas that need improvement. This is especially true for students at risk who have negative perceptions of their school achievements and, therefore, of school in general.

20. *Nurture students' brains.* Marian Diamond is an internationally known neuroscientist who has studied mammalian brains for decades. She and Janet Hopson are the authors of *Magic Trees of the Mind: How to Nurture Your Child's Intelligence, Creativity, and Healthy Emotions from Birth through Adolescence.* In that book Diamond and Hopson (1998) recommend that teachers provide a steady source of positive emotional support for students, stimulate all the senses (though not necessarily all at the same time), maintain an atmosphere free of undue pressure and stress but suffused with a degree of pleasurable intensity, present a series of novel challenges that are neither too easy nor too difficult for the students, allow students to select many of their own instructional activities, offer opportunities for students to assess the results of their learning and modify it as they think best, provide an enjoyable learning atmosphere that promotes exploration and fun, and allow time for students to reflect and let their brains assimilate new information.

21. *Emphasize the four classical virtues.* The **four classical virtues** are prudence, temperance, justice, and fortitude. *Prudence* is making proper choices without doing anything rash. *Temperance* is remaining moderate in all things, including human passions and emotions. *Justice* refers to ensuring fair outcomes based on honesty. *Fortitude* is showing courage, strength, and conviction in pursuit of the right path. Through the ages, philosophers have contended that these four virtues help people meet challenges effectively and find greater satisfaction in life.

22. *Tutor a few students every day.* Tutoring students one on one is the easiest, quickest, and most effective way of establishing personal relationships with students.

23. *Hold frequent classroom meetings.* Classroom meetings provide excellent opportunities for all members of the class to work together. These meetings are valuable for resolving challenges that confront the whole class and for helping individual students deal with certain problems. (See Marshall, 2005c.)

24. *Resolve conflict in a constructive manner.* When people are involved in conflict, ask each of them what they are willing to do to resolve the situation. Get across the notion that we can't force other people to change, but we can *influence* them to do so through our actions and the changes we are willing to make in ourselves.

25. *Establish trust.* Relationships with others are extremely important to students, especially those who are at risk and those from low-income families. Students who do not value school will be motivated to put forward effort only for a teacher they trust and who cares about them and their interests. Trust in the classroom also depends on emotional and psychological safety. To promote trust, employ the three principles of positivity, choice, and reflection.

HOW TO INTERVENE WHEN STUDENTS MISBEHAVE

Go to the Simulations section of Topic #13: Managing Special Groups, in the **MyEducationLab** for your course and complete the simulation entitled "Understanding the Causes of Unproductive Student Behavior and Preventing This Behavior."

When considering any discipline plan, teachers always want to know the procedures for stopping misbehavior. You have seen how Marshall's hierarchy of social development is used to empower students to move toward more responsible behavior. Let's suppose a student behaves inappropriately and the teacher needs to intervene. The following indicates how the teacher should proceed. It assumes the hierarchy has been taught and students understand how it applies in the classroom.

Step 1: Use an Unobtrusive Tactic.   Suppose Syong is annoying Neri. Before saying anything to Syong, you would prompt her to stop by using an unobtrusive technique, such as facial expression, eye contact, hand signal, moving near Syong, changing voice tone, thanking students for working, saying, "Excuse me," or asking students for help. Marshall (2001) offers 22 unobtrusive visual, verbal, and kinetic techniques that are useful at this juncture.

Step 2: Check for Understanding.   If the unobtrusive tactic doesn't stop Syong's misbehavior, check to see if she understands the level of her chosen behavior. Use a neutral, unemotional tone of voice and phrase the question as, "Syong, which level are you choosing?" or, "Syong, reflect on the level you have chosen." No mention is made of the nature of the behavior or what Syong is doing, only the level of chosen behavior. This helps prevent a natural self-defense that often leads to a confrontation. Without the hierarchy—which separates the student from the student's inappropriate behavior—a teacher may ask, "What are you doing?" This too often leads to a confrontational situation, especially if Syong responds, "Nothing." However, asking, "On what level is that behavior?" prompts not only acknowledgement but also self-evaluation. You are not attacking Syong; you are *separating* her as a person from the inappropriate behavior, something educators often talk about but find difficult to do.

Step 3: Use Guided Choice.   This procedure allows students to choose among two or three options you provide. Marshall says this tactic allows you to use **authority without punishment.** If Syong continues to bother Neri, you can place an essay form on Syong's desk while quietly offering her three *choices*, such as, "Do you prefer to fill out this form in your seat, in the rear of the room, or in the office?" The pre-prepared form contains the following headings Syong is to write about:

> What did I do? (Acknowledgment)
>
> What can I do to prevent it from happening again? (Choice)
>
> What will I do? (Commitment)

Guided choice options should be adjusted in accordance with the grade level, the individual student, and the class. Before responding to the form, the student is asked two more questions: (1) "Do you know the reason the form was given to you?" and (2) "Do you think it is personal?" Students understand that the form was given because, when the student behaves on an unacceptable level, the teacher needs to quickly resolve the disruption and return to the lesson. The form allows you to use teacher authority in a nonpunishing way. Asking a student to reflect is not classified as punishment in the usual sense of the word. After the student responds to the second question, the teacher (of grades 6 and above) asks, "What would you like me to do with the form?" Students generally respond, "Throw it away." Although some teachers might wish to keep the forms, Marshall's approach is to tear up the form and place it in the wastepaper basket right then in front of the student, thus allowing the student to leave the class without negative feelings. Overall, guided choice can effectively stop the disruption, provide the student a responsibility-producing activity to encourage self-reflection, and allow the teacher to return promptly to the lesson. It is crucial to understand that when providing guided choices, the teacher does so by *asking* the student, not *telling*. This reduces confrontation, minimizes stress, and helps preserve student dignity.

It is very unlikely that Syong, having completed the essay form, will continue to bother others, but teachers always want to know what to do in case a student continues to misbehave. Marshall suggests continuing to Step 4.

Step 4: Make a Self-Diagnostic Referral.   Before moving to a more in-depth reflective form, Syong is given the essay form to complete a second time. If this procedure is not effective, then a **self-diagnostic referral** is given. This form contains items such as the following:

- Describe the problem that led to writing this.
- Identify the level of behavior.
- Explain why this level of behavior is not acceptable.
- On what level should a person act in order to be socially responsible?
- If you had acted on an acceptable level, what would have happened?
- List three solutions that would help you act more responsibly.

Marshall advises keeping the completed referrals on file for the entire year, as they might be used in discussions with parents or the administration.

Step 5: Give an Additional Self-Diagnostic Referral.   If Syong continues to bother other students, assign an additional referral to complete, in the same manner as the first. Then mail a copy of the first and second referrals to Syong's parents or guardian, together with a brief note explaining the problem.

Step 6: Give a Final Self-Diagnostic Referral.   If Syong continues to behave on an unacceptable level, assign a third and final self-diagnostic referral. Mail a copy to her parents, along with copies of the first two referrals and both notes. The final note indicates to the parents that you have exhausted all positive means of fostering social responsibility and will refer future disruptions to the administration. Marshall points out that in all these cases, it is the *student who has identified the problem and proposed positive solutions.* All the teacher does is write brief notes to parents and mail them copies of the student's self-diagnostic referrals. The student has done most of the thinking and planning, which gives ownership to the student—a necessary ingredient for lasting change. Marshall says the last few steps rarely, if ever, need to be used.

The Marshall teaching model is summarized in Figure 10.2. Marshall (2008) goes on to emphasize that *having a system to rely on is superior to having a talent for teaching.* Even teachers with a natural talent are challenged by student behaviors that teachers in former generations did not have to deal with. To retain the joy that the teaching profession offers and to reduce one's stress, establish a reliable system for promoting learning and acceptable behavior.

Marshall advises teachers to explain the system to their administrator for approval and prepare communication to send to parents when you are ready to implement the system. Marshall suggests the form letter shown in Figure 10.3 on page 190.

SELF-EVALUATION FOR TEACHERS

Once you decide to use Marshall's *Discipline without Stress,* the following questions will help you evaluate your progress:

- Are you teaching the procedures you expect of your students?
- Are you communicating in a positive manner with your students?

Figure 10.2   The Marvin Marshall Teaching Model

I. Classroom Management vs. Discipline

The key to effective classroom management is teaching and practicing procedures. This is the teacher's responsibility. Discipline, on the other hand, has to do with behavior and is the student's responsibility.

II. Three Principles to Practice

Positivity

Practice changing negatives into positives. "No running" becomes "We walk in the hallways." "Stop talking" becomes "This is quiet time."

Choice

Teach choice–response thinking and impulse control in order to redirect impulsive behavior.

Reflection

Since you cannot actually control or change students, ask reflective questions to actuate change in them.

III. The Discipline without Stress (DWS) System

Teaching the Hierarchy (Teaching)

The hierarchy engenders a desire to behave responsibly and put forth effort to learn. Students differentiate between internal and external motivation— and learn to rise above inappropriate peer influence.

Checking for Understanding (Asking)

Students reflect on the level of chosen behavior. This approach separates the person from the behavior, thereby negating the usual tendency toward self-defense that leads to confrontations between student and teacher.

Guided Choices (Eliciting)

If disruptions continue, a consequence or procedure is elicited to redirect the inappropriate behavior. This approach is in contrast to the usual coercive approach of having a consequence imposed.

IV. Using the System to Increase Academic Performance

Using the hierarchy for review before a lesson and for reflecting after a lesson increases effort and raises academic achievement.

■ Are your students made aware that they continually make choices, consciously and unconsciously, that largely determine their happiness and success in school and life?

■ Do you always give your students choices (preferably three) concerning behavior that shows responsibility?

Figure 10.3   Sample Letter to Parents

Dear Parent(s) or Guardian(s):

Our classroom houses a small society. Each student is a citizen who acts in accordance with expected standards of behavior.

With this in mind, rewards are not given for expected behavior—just as society does not give rewards for behaving properly. Also, irresponsible behavior is seen as an opportunity for growth, rather than for punishment.

Our approach encourages students to exercise self-discipline through reflection and self-evaluation. Students learn to control their own behavior, rather than always relying on the teacher for control.

We want our classroom to be encouraging and conducive to learning at all times. In this way, young people develop positive attitudes and behavioral skills that are so necessary for successful lives.

Sincerely
(Teacher)

Source: Marshall, M. 2008. "The Raise Responsibility System in College Textbooks." http://disciplineforsmartpeople.com/the-raise-responsibility-system-in-college-textbooks. Reprinted by permission.

- Have you carefully taught, and have your students adequately learned, the ABCD levels of social development?
- When disruptions occur, do you ask questions in a noncoercive, nonthreatening manner that prompts student reflection and self-evaluation of behavior?
- If disruptive behavior continues, do you elicit a procedure or consequence from the student for redirecting future impulsive behavior?
- Do you use the hierarchy to promote a desire in students to put forth effort in learning?

You may wish to discuss these questions with your students to get their perspective as well.

Summary Rubric

APPLYING MARSHALL'S SYSTEM IN THE CLASSROOM

- Carefully review the 10 practices that damage teaching. Determine how you will avoid them. Specify the appropriate practices you will use in their place.

- Clarify and differentiate Theory X and Theory Y as approaches to managing students in the classroom. In order to use Marshall's approach effectively, you will need to commit yourself to Theory Y.

■ Place a card on your desk with the following three reminders: *positivity, choice, reflection.*

■ Establish in your mind the nature and power of internal motivation. Think in specific terms how you will call on internal motivation while leaving external motivation aside.

■ Thoroughly familiarize yourself with Marshall's hierarchy of social development. Teach it to your students and put it in effect immediately.

■ Make a chart for reminding yourself of the 25 tactics you can use to stimulate students to behave responsibly. Consciously practice three different ones every day.

■ Write out how you will intervene when any of your students misbehave. Practice with a fellow student or teacher until the sequence of steps becomes automatic.

Terms and Concepts

authority without punishment	four classical values	reflective questions
elicit	hierarchy of social development	self-diagnostic referral
empowerment of choice	internal motivation	Theory X
external motivation	positivity	Theory Y

Concept Cases

CASE 1: KRISTINA WILL NOT WORK

Kristina, a student in Mr. Jake's class, is quite docile. She socializes little with other students and never disrupts lessons. However, despite Mr. Jake's best efforts, Kristina will not do her work. She rarely completes an assignment. She is simply there, putting forth no effort at all. *What would Marvin Marshall suggest to help Kristina and Mr. Jake?*

Marshall would classify this as a *learning challenge,* not as a *behavior problem.* He would tell Mr. Jake not to attempt to force Kristina to learn. Mr. Jake could not force her even if he wanted to: To learn or not to learn is Kristina's choice. Mr. Jake has seen that Kristina is capable of learning and would reassure her of this fact. If she chooses to put forward the effort to learn, she will feel more competent, enjoy herself more, and be happier. But this is her choice. Accordingly, Mr. Jake would attempt to establish a positive relationship by sharing with her his belief in her competency. He would then find out what Kristina likes to do and weave into the assignments some activities that would capitalize on her interests. He would continually check with her to see how she is doing and, thereby, communicate his interest in her. He would suggest that what she chooses to do or not do affects her more than anyone else and that she will not gain any satisfaction if no effort is put forth.

Marshall also would encourage Mr. Jake to employ the hierarchy of social development as follows:

1. Ask Kristina to identify the level of her behavior.
2. Ask her how a responsible person would behave in this circumstance.
3. Positively reiterate the belief that Kristina is capable.
4. Provide Kristina with a few guided choices.
5. Ask her to self-reflect on her subsequent behavior and future decisions.

CASE 2: SARA WILL NOT STOP TALKING

Sara is a pleasant girl who participates in class activities and does most, though not all, of her assigned work. She cannot seem to refrain from talking to classmates, however. Her teacher, Mr. Gonzales, speaks to her repeatedly during lessons, to the point that he often becomes exasperated and loses his temper. *What suggestions would Marvin Marshall give Mr. Gonzales for dealing with Sara?*

CASE 3: JOSHUA CLOWNS AND INTIMIDATES

Joshua, larger and louder than his classmates, always wants to be the center of attention, which he accomplishes through a combination of clowning and intimidation. He makes wisecrack remarks, talks back (smilingly) to the teacher, utters a variety of sound-effect noises such as automobile crashes and gunshots, and makes limitless sarcastic comments and put-downs of his classmates. Other students will not stand up to him, apparently fearing his size and verbal aggression. His teacher, Miss Pearl, has come to her wit's end. *Would Joshua's behavior be likely to improve if Marvin Marshall's techniques of noncoercion and reflection were used in Miss Pearl's classroom? Explain.*

CASE 4: TOM IS HOSTILE AND DEFIANT

Tom has appeared to be in his usual foul mood ever since arriving in class. On his way to sharpen his pencil, he bumps into Frank, who complains. Tom tells him loudly to shut up. Miss Baines, the teacher, says, "Tom, go back to your seat." Tom wheels around, swears loudly, and says heatedly, "I'll go when I'm damned good and ready!" *How would Marvin Marshall have Miss Baines deal with Tom?*

You Are the Teacher

FIFTH-GRADE CLASS

Your new fifth-grade class consists of students from a small, stable community. Because the transiency rate is low, many of your students have been together since first grade, and during those years they have developed certain patterns of interacting and assuming various roles such as clowns and instigators. Unfortunately, their behavior often interferes with teaching and learning. During the first week of school you notice that four or five students enjoy making smart-aleck remarks about most things you want them to do. When such remarks are made, the other students laugh and sometimes join in. Even when you attempt to hold class discussions about serious issues, many of the students make light of the topics and refuse to enter genuinely into an exploration of the issues. Instead of the productive discussion you have hoped for, you find that class behavior often degenerates into flippancy and horseplay.

A TYPICAL OCCURRENCE

You have begun a history lesson that contains a reference to Julius Caesar. You ask if anyone has ever heard of Julius Caesar. Ben shouts out, "Yeah, they named a salad after him!" The class laughs and calls out encouraging remarks such as "Good one, Ben!" You wait for some semblance of order, then say, "Let us go on." From the back of the classroom, Jeremy cries, "Lettuce and cabbage!" The class bursts into laughter and chatter. You ask for their cooperation and no more students

call out or make remarks, but you know several continue to smirk and whisper, with a good deal of barely suppressed giggling. You try to ignore it, but because of the disruptions you are not able to complete the lesson on time or to get the results you hoped for.

CONCEPTUALIZING A STRATEGY

If you followed Marvin Marshall's suggestions, what would you conclude or do with regard to the following?

- Preventing the problem from occurring in the first place
- Putting an immediate end to the misbehavior
- Maintaining student dignity and good personal relations
- Using follow-up procedures to prevent the recurrence of the misbehavior

Activities

1. In your journal, enter ideas from Marshall's *Discipline without Stress* you might want to incorporate into your personal system of discipline.
2. With a classmate or colleague, practice asking the reflective questions Marshall suggests for identifying students' level of behavior.

3. With a classmate or colleague, discuss the meaning and application of the key terms used in Marshall's model.

References

Diamond, M., and Hopson, J. 1998. *Magic trees of the mind: How to nurture your child's intelligence, creativity, and healthy emotions from birth through adolescence.* New York: Dutton.

Marshall, M. 2001. *Discipline without stress, punishments, or rewards: How teachers and parents promote responsibility & learning.* Los Alamitos, CA: Piper Press.

Marshall, M. 2005a. A letter worth reading. www.marvinmarshall.com/aletterworthreading.html

Marshall, M. 2005b. A principal's experience. www.marvinmarshall.com/principal.htm

Marshall, M. 2005c. Classroom meetings. www.disciplinewithoutstress.com/sample_chapters.html

Marshall, M. 2005d. Collaboration for quality learning. www.disciplinewithoutstress.com/sample_chapters.html

Marshall, M. 2005e. Promoting positivity, choice, and reflection. www.marvinmarshall.com/promoting_positivity.htm

Marshall, M. 2005f. Reducing perfectionism. www.disciplinewithoutstress.com/sample_chapters.html.

Marshall, M. 2005g. Samples of hierarchies for promoting learning. www.marvinmarshall.com/hierarchy.htm

Marshall, M. 2008. A system is superior to talent. http://teachers.net/gazette/MAR08/marshall

McGregor, D. 1960. *The human side of enterprise.* New York: McGraw-Hill.

How Does Craig Seganti Use Positive Teacher Leverage and Realistic Student Accountability to Establish Class Discipline?

Today, most teachers accept that their students will misbehave a good deal of the time and are more or less resigned to misbehavior as one of the major downsides to teaching. Teacher Craig Seganti assures us that misbehavior is not an inevitable burden. True, he did experience difficulties with misbehavior when he first began teaching back in 1990. Despite a tough beginning, Seganti survived. He learned from his experiences and before long began to flourish. He describes how he did so in his 2008 book, *Classroom Discipline 101: How to Get Control of Any Classroom*. He believes his approach to behavior management will solve the discipline issue for all teachers and will actually save the careers of teachers who are out of ideas for dealing with resistant, out-of-control students.

Mr. Seganti has taught middle school and high school English and ESL in the Los Angeles Unified School District for more than two decades, working with students from many different backgrounds in schools where students were notoriously difficult to control. He also taught juvenile offenders of both sexes in probation camps and interim schools for Los Angeles County. Seganti says his approach, which focuses on what works with students in the real world, is reality based, not theory based. He presents a recipe you can follow to get the discipline success you always hoped for, freeing you to teach rather than deal endlessly with misbehavior and freeing your students to learn in a positive environment without disruptions and turmoil. To review a broad sampling of Seganti's concepts and procedures, you can access short articles (2008b) he has posted at http://ezinearticles.com/?expert=Craig_Seganti. Those articles address, in a very practical way, topics such as:

How to Get Any Student to Behave Well All of the Time
How to Not Enter into Useless Arguments with Students
Eliminating the Middle Man—The Myth of Giving Warnings
The Role of Accountability in Classroom Management
Stopping Problems Before They Get in the Classroom

In 2009, Mr. Seganti was still teaching in inner-city Los Angeles and reported that he was able to go home relaxed and stress free at the end of every day.

A PREVIEW OF THIS CHAPTER

Adopt and share with students the attitude that the class is for academic learning. Emphasize that disruptions interfere with students' right to a good education. Accordingly, students are held accountable for their behavior in the class, as spelled out clearly in the class rules. The first step to success involves carefully teaching all students to understand and comply with class rules. The leverage that enables teachers to enforce class rules lies in a 15-minute detention that misbehaving students must attend after school. A number of considerate classroom management techniques help students learn comfortably and conduct themselves responsibly. In short, establish and clarify rules, implement leverage as necessary, and manage the classroom for productivity.

WHAT TO LOOK FOR IN THIS CHAPTER

- The teacher attitude that leads to the best results in the classroom
- What Seganti means by *teacher leverage* and *student accountability* and how the two work together to promote learning and desirable behavior
- Specific rules that foster student accountability in the classroom
- The leverage that ensures students will conduct themselves responsibly
- Management efforts that enhance the classroom experience
- Seganti's approach to beginning the class
- The suggested roles of administrators, counselors, and parents in Seganti's approach

KEY ATTITUDES AND SKILLS IN SEGANTI'S APPROACH

Go to the Building Classroom Discipline Video Showcase section of Topic #3: Models of Classroom Management, in the **MyEducationLab** for your course and watch the video entitled "Craig Seganti— Classroom Discipline 101."

Seganti assures teachers his approach will help students be respectful and make a strong effort to learn in class. His procedures may appear strict because he holds students accountable for their actions, but Seganti contends that is exactly what hard-to-manage students need, and further, that the most positive thing you can do for students is give them access to a good education in a classroom focused on learning.

This chapter reviews Seganti's core ideas and suggestions, organized around four elements he features prominently in his approach—teacher attitude, student accountability, leverage for obtaining compliance, and management tactics that support desirable behavior. We will explore these elements in turn. If you wish to reflect on the nuances of Seganti's approach and see how he makes his points, you can view his video and obtain his e-book and other materials at www.classroomdiscipline101.com.

Teacher Attitude That Promotes High-Quality Discipline and Teaching

Your attitude toward discipline sets in motion a dynamic that affects how students behave, for better or worse. The attitude Seganti advocates can be understood through the following four messages he conveys to his students:

- Any student who disrupts the class is interfering with other students' constitutional rights to a good public education.
- We are not equals in the classroom. I am the expert, trained and experienced in how to teach. I make the decisions about how to do that. You are the students who are here to study under my guidance. Your job is to do your best to learn.
- The classroom is for academic learning. Everything we do in class will be aimed at learning. You must do your part, which is to focus and learn. If you are not willing to do that, you will need to end up somewhere else.
- I know you want to feel good about yourselves and I will help you do that. But you need to understand that self-esteem doesn't come from messing around in the classroom. It comes from doing hard work and learning knowledge and skills that will serve you well in life.

The next messages are for teachers. They indicate operating principles that improve your ability to work with students:

- *Actions.* When dealing with students, emphasize actions. They speak far louder than words. It is worse than useless to spend time cajoling, arguing, and continually trying to justify your decisions to students. Just make good rules and enforce them without fail. No explanations are needed. If you don't enforce your rules, students will act as though your rules don't exist.

- *Warnings.* Giving students warnings is self-defeating and only wastes time. Students beyond primary grades know when they are misbehaving, so there is no need to warn them they are misbehaving or that you are thinking of doing something about it. You can spend your day (week, month, career) giving warnings instead of teaching. If you want to avoid students trying to manipulate you, forget the warnings. (Seganti does give students one warning, on the first day of class only, as we will see when we review his rules.)

- *Rewards.* Seganti does not believe in giving students rewards for learning. While he does want students to enjoy his classes, he emphasizes that a good education is the primary reward they get for their efforts and the only one that really counts. He says if you try to motivate students with gimmicks and pep talks, you send a poor message about education—that it is of so little value you need to bribe students to endure it. Seganti says if his students ask what their reward will be for behaving properly, he tells them it is a good education, which is priceless. He does go on to say, however, that he likes to provide students fun activities to do every so often, not so much as a reward for their efforts as to celebrate learning and show there can be (and should be) some fun and enjoyment in the classroom.

■ *Speaking.* Learn how to talk effectively with students. (The suggestions presented here have to do with teaching information and proper behavior. If you were counseling students or commiserating with them, you would speak in a different manner.) Look at the following exchange as an example of what *not* to do.

Teacher: Stop talking, Johnny
Johnny: I wasn't talking.
Teacher: You were talking—I just saw you talking to Henry.
Johnny: Well, Jason was talking. He started it.

(and so forth, on and on)

Seganti comments, "What's your strategy here? Are you going to stand there arguing with Johnny about whether or not he was talking? That only perpetuates the problem." The following shows the proper way of interacting with Johnny.

Teacher: There is no talking in my class, Johnny—stay after school 15 minutes today for detention.
Johnny: But I wasn't talking!
Teacher: Show up for detention. If you don't want another 15 minutes, stop disrupting now.

Student Accountability and 11 Rules That Promote It

Seganti believes in holding students accountable for their behavior, whether good or bad. The basis for accountability consists of class rules of behavior. You must establish effective rules and then make sure students understand them clearly. Compose the rules yourself, before you see your students, and make copies to hand out. Every possible behavior that concerns your class, positive or negative, is to be addressed somewhere in the rules. You are the professional and you know how students should behave. Don't waste time asking students to help you decide what the rules should be.

The first thing you should do when students arrive for class the first day is teach them exactly what the rules mean. There must be no misunderstanding. The students' first assignment in class is to copy the rules neatly, sign them, and hand them in. From that point onward, students are held accountable for their every action in class. They can no longer claim they didn't know. Following are rule topics Seganti advocates. The first two rules are given in Seganti's words, and additional topics for rules are explained briefly. In his book *Classroom Discipline 101* (2008a), you can find his exact wording for 11 rules and his suggestions for teaching them to students.

Seganti's Rule 1 and Rule 2

Rule 1.   You are to enter the classroom calmly and quietly and go immediately to your assigned seat. You are to sit at a 90-degree angle to your desk with your feet on the floor and good posture (spine straight).

How to Teach Rule 1 to Students.   Stand in the door on the first day and teach this rule to each student as he or she enters. This procedure is immediately established as a rule, not an option. A student who enters the room improperly has defied a rule and is subject to the consequence you have established for violating rules, usually a 15-minute detention after school (consequences are explained later in this chapter). Once all students are seated, explain this rule again to the class as a whole.

Rule 2.   Students are to show respect at all times and in all manners toward staff, others, and themselves. This includes all verbal and nonverbal forms of communication, including body language, facial expression, and tone of voice.

How to Teach Rule 2 to Students.   When all students are in the room, read this rule once. Even in the wildest schools there is usually a window of time the first day when students are curious and will listen. Now, read it again, piece by piece. This can become a good lesson on nonverbal communication. Tell the students that most communication is nonverbal. Take your time here. Be a teacher—give examples. Tell the students, "If I give you a direction and you roll your eyes, it is just as disrespectful as if you insult me verbally, and you will get detention." Act it out—"Suppose I say: Juan, open your book to page 134." Pretend to be Juan and roll your eyes. Explain again that eye rolling and other disrespectful actions are just as unacceptable as saying something rude and will be met with the same consequences.

Additional Topics for Rules

Work on Task.   This topic centers on clarifying when students should be on task, how they should be working, what they should do when they have completed their assigned work, and when and how they may talk.

Teachers should begin by clarifying exactly what being on task and paying full attention mean. Seganti suggests that you act out for students what these requirements look like and *do not* look like. Then, have selected students demonstrate behavior that complies with and violates the rule. In addition, help them identify productive and respectful activities they can do when they have completed their work. This heads off the future manipulation technique in which students say "I'm done with my work." Seganti is adamant that students must be trained to get their materials out immediately and be quietly at work by the time the bell rings. He says you will have to insist on this, or else students will begin to dawdle more and more when entering the room.

Distractions.   This topic centers on potential distractions that students might intentionally or inadvertently bring with them to class. Seganti provides a list of potential distractions and carefully explains exactly what he will do if any of those distractions appear in contradiction to the class rule. He explains that class time is devoted entirely to learning and strongly reiterates that nothing will be permitted to interfere with that learning time.

Read the rule aloud to the class and describe what will happen if it is violated. Use examples as necessary. The distractions are not to be brought into the classroom at all—or if they are present, they must be invisible and silent. One of the distractions Seganti highlights is chewing gum. He says he is famous for his "no chewing" rule, which helps make him manipulation-proof. Students sometimes appear to be chewing, but claim they are not, sticking their tongues out to prove it. Seganti says this act can earn three detentions—for chewing gum, for lying, and for making a rude gesture. As Seganti explains it, here is how this situation usually plays out:

Teacher: Spit out the gum, Jane, and come after school for 10 minutes.
Jane: I'm not chewing gum.
Teacher: Well, there's no chewing in my class, even if you aren't chewing any-
thing, so come to detention.
Jane: But I'm not chewing anything!
Teacher: I don't argue with students. You can either spit out the gum or get
suspended for defiance.

(Jane then either spits out the gum or the teacher suspends her.)

Seganti says you won't have to do this for long. Once or twice and everyone gets the idea you are manipulation-proof. Parents or administrators may complain if you suspend a student from class for merely chewing gum. If that happens, you point out that the student has violated two rules—one for chewing gum and another for noncompliance with teacher directions. This point will be addressed again when we explore the roles of administrators, counselors, and parents.

Beginning the Period.   This topic centers on what students must be doing when the bell rings at the beginning of class and what will happen to them if they violate the rule.

Simply explain to students what the rule requires of them when the beginning bell rings. Although Seganti does not say so explicitly, it would be a good idea to have students practice complying with the rule, moving into full compliance at least several seconds before you pretend to ring the tardy bell.

Readiness for Work.   This rule centers on how students should be prepared for class, which includes bringing any materials they need for immediate class partici-pation. It also stipulates what students will not be allowed to do once the bell rings. This admonition covers several matters that might seem trivial, but are serious because they waste learning time.

It is likely that your students will have learned in other classes they can come to class without having at hand all the materials they need for successful learning. They may have the feeling that missing an item or two is not very bad. Seganti says to insist to them they are old enough to take responsibility for this requirement. He advocates firm requirements concerning pencil sharpening in particular, as students often use sharpening as a distraction and manipulation tactic. Unless you are insis-tent on compliance with this rule, your more disruptive students will be asking for various school-related materials all period long.

Miscellaneous Behavior.   This topic centers on matters such as students calling out, leaving their seats, and dealing with the scrap paper and other trash that accumu-lates around desks and elsewhere in the room.

Have students act out the behaviors and procedures associated with speaking out, raising their hands, getting permission, and keeping the classroom environment neat. Show them the wrong way of doing things—such as raising your hand as you start speaking—and the right way—such as raising your hand, waiting for permission, then speaking. Have them practice everything you expect of them. Remind them that you cannot get around to answering each and every question promptly—sometimes they will have to wait a minute when you are busy.

Permissions and Procedures.   This topic centers on permission and procedures for various activities, including leaving the room when necessary. You will be surprised by what Seganti requires of students who request restroom passes, but he says his tactic has worked wonders in stopping the debates between teacher and students on whether or not the student really has to go. If a student begs and squirms to prove the need is real, do the following:

> **Teacher:** Sure, here's the pass—but you have to make up 10 minutes after school.
> **Student:** Huh? Why 10 minutes?
> **Teacher:** (Don't say anything; just hold the hall pass and wait. The procedure has been stated. No need to repeat it.)

Teacher Requests and Directions.   This topic centers on how students are to conduct themselves when the teacher asks them to do anything, such as change seats or pick up trash. Seganti has a steadfast way of interacting with students in these cases—he doesn't argue. Instead, he tells students that if they feel the direction is unreasonable, they may arrange to discuss it with the school counselor, vice principal, or in a conference involving student, parent, and teacher. He does not use class time for arguing with students, insisting the limited time for learning is too valuable to waste in that way.

As before, read the rule aloud, then go back, explain, and have students practice compliant behavior in the manner expected. This rule must make it abundantly clear that you do not argue or debate discipline issues or directions with students. The focus is always directed to actions, not words.

End of Class.   This topic centers on what students are to do when the bell rings at the end of class. Have students practice the procedure you require. Seganti suggests you make a bell noise and have students pack up their materials and then wait for you to say, "Okay, you are dismissed." Don't fall for the old "that's not my paper" retort when it's time to make sure the floor is clean. Students are accountable for their area.

System of Consequences.   This topic centers on what will happen to any student who violates any of the class rules. This system, once it is presented so students understand it, is the only warning Seganti gives. If students who have violated any of the prior rules do not abide by the indicated consequences, they are suspended from class and not allowed to reenter until they have fulfilled the requirement.

By this time, you have carefully gone through how you expect students to conduct themselves in class. You and your students will be tired from reading and talking about them, but rules must be stressed hard the first day so there is no room for doubt about what is expected. The time investment is very effective in helping ensure things go smoothly the rest of the year.

Leverage That Ensures Students Comply with the Rules

Rules for making the class work effectively are no good unless you can enforce them. Therefore, you must create the mindset in every student that breaking the rules in your class is just not worth the effort. To establish that mindset you must have at your disposal some kind of **leverage** that makes students decide to follow the rules. Seganti has determined that the most effective leverage for his classes is "Mr. Seganti's famous **15-minute detention** after school." This detention is only slightly inconvenient: nevertheless, students dislike it. And because they can't get out of it, it works all the better. Seganti calls this detention the "lever that can move boulders." It promotes psychological compliance while causing very little resentment. It doesn't punish teachers, either—they have to stay after school for a while anyway. A student who comes to your detention is tacitly agreeing that you are the authority. Once you have established that point, behavior problems dwindle.

But what if students simply don't appear at detention as directed? That rarely happens, Seganti says, but if it does, you suspend the student from class, in accordance with the class rules, and don't let the student back in until his or her parents have been notified and the detention has been served. Students quickly realize they simply can never get out of complying with detention. In a 2008 personal communication with the author of this book, Mr. Seganti made these further observations about students adjusting to the 15-minute detention:

> Some students who are difficult to manage will not come to detention the first time you assign it, unless they are convinced they cannot get out of complying with the consequence. Therefore, they all must learn very quickly that it is better to show up than not. The whole system depends on the idea that testing the rules will bring more discomfort than simply following them. You must make it clear that if students do not show up for detention when it is assigned, they will be suspended from your class and not allowed to attend until they do so. They must see that you will indeed follow through on this requirement. Once this is clear, you will seldom be tested.

If you suspend a student from class, you will need to inform your administrator and the student's parent or guardian. Preparations for doing so should be made in advance. Figure 11.1 presents Seganti's protocol for calling parents.

Seganti maintains that detention of 10 to 15 minutes is the most effective leverage available to most teachers, but he recognizes that after-school detention is difficult or impossible in many schools because students have to catch buses. He advises teachers who encounter an obstacle to discuss with their administrator ways

Figure 11.1   Craig Seganti's Protocol for Calling Parents

"Hello, Mrs. Smith? I'm Mr. Jones, James's history teacher. James was disrupting my lesson today and I assigned him a 15-minute detention after school, but he didn't come. As he knows, that means he is suspended from my class until he does two things—copy the class rules and come to detention for 15 minutes. Can you make sure he copies the rules for me and comes to detention tomorrow so he can return to class?"

Sometimes the parent will take the student's side and say "What exactly did he do?" Then you can tell them "He was disrupting the lesson talking," or "He defied instructions to change his seat," or whatever. Sometimes a parent will misunderstand and say "You are suspending him for talking in class?" Answer like this: "No. I am suspending him for defiance of my rules and refusing to come to his 15-minute detention. As soon as he makes up his 15 minutes, he can return to class. Can you ensure that he does this and copies the rules for me?" If you get the parent's assurance that James will come to detention the next day, you might delay the suspension until you see if he does.

If James comes to class the next day, you should say in front of the class, "James, as you know I talked to your mother last night and she assured me you are coming to detention today—is that correct?" (James says "yes.") "Okay, then I will hold off the suspension until tomorrow. But let's be clear that if you don't show today you are suspended." This exchange lets the rest of the class know what will happen if they don't show up.

Source: Seganti, C. (2008). *Classroom Discipline 101: How to Get Control of Any Classroom* (pp. 89–90). www.classroomdiscipline101.com. Reprinted by permission.

in which after-school detention can be maintained. If no solution is forthcoming, Seganti suggests three alternatives:

1. Arrange for students to serve detention during school time by going to a fellow teacher's room for 10 or 15 minutes to copy rules—this could be done as a favor or as an exchange.
2. If the whole class is misbehaving, stop and have everyone spend 15 minutes copying the rules. The well-behaved students seldom complain about this because they intuitively realize you are trying to help everyone.
3. In cooperation with four fellow teachers, work out a detention schedule during lunch time. Each teacher can stay 20 minutes or so one day a week. This has the added advantage of establishing a consistent behavior code that involves other classes.

Management Tactics That Support Desirable Behavior

Seganti has identified several tactics teachers can use, both before and after they meet their students, to make this discipline plan more effective. Some of those tactics are presented here:

- *Organize the room arrangement.* The success of your program is affected by how you arrange your room physically. Have your desks in rows and, if you think students might deface the furniture, number each chair and desk so they remain together and students are accountable for them. Have everything in the room, including your materials, neat and organized—a sloppy room encourages sloppy behavior. Place one or two desks adjacent to your desk for students you feel are likely to be most disruptive. Put one desk in the back corner facing the wall, to use for in-class suspensions. If a student doesn't show up for detention, but is not usually disruptive, put him or her in the back of the room facing the wall to copy the rules. Then if they come to detention that afternoon, they can rejoin class the next day.

- *Cultivate quiet.* Cultivate a quiet classroom for a week or two with no group work and minimal talking—give a lot of reading and written work to acclimate the students to the idea that this classroom is quiet. These habits are very powerful. When students get used to them, you can move into more vocal lessons.

- *Be at the ready.* Have your referrals, detention logs, teaching props, and parent phone numbers at the ready.

- *Dress professionally.* In various walks of life, people who are leaders dress differently from those with whom they work. You see this, for example, in the military, religious institutions, and even the workaday world. Seganti believes the way you dress helps determine the impact you have on students by separating you from them psychologically, just as a priest looks different from the congregation or a general from a private. Seganti advises male teachers to wear ties and female teachers to dress in a professional manner. By looking professional, you project a look of authority; if you dress in a way that says, "I am one of you," then students will tend to treat you as one of them. When you establish a psychological separation from your students, you make them less likely to challenge your authority.

- *Make eye contact.* Looking students in the eye and having them look you in the eye reinforces your authority. When you give a direction, and it looks as though your students are not committed to it, get their undivided attention. Say, "Look at me. Did you understand?" Remember, you are looking for full nonverbal and verbal compliance with your directions.

- *Give something back to students.* Teach in a way you can be truly proud of. Teach useful information in an engaging manner that persists all period long. Students are not eager to cooperate with teachers who show little sparkle and assign meaningless tasks. If you teach as though you don't give a darn, students will think you don't care about learning and are using rules as a power trip. But when you combine tight boundaries with teaching that is interesting and valuable, students see that you care enough about them to work hard for their benefit. They will be thankful there is an adult around who can take charge and help them become more competent.

- *Organize procedures.* Good organization is your best friend. Make sure you have procedures for everything—seating charts, labeled desks, referrals, comments to use when students try to manipulate you. Know exactly what the students should be doing from bell to bell.

■ *Listen to students.* Listen attentively to students. Don't listen merely to *what* students say. Listen for the *motivation* behind their words.

■ *Speak in statements.* When speaking with students about discipline matters, use statements, not questions—e.g., "This is work time," rather than "Why aren't you working?"

■ *Educate students.* Recognize that your job is to educate students, not to counsel them or deal with emotional problems they may have. That's what counselors are for.

■ *Hold students accountable for proper behavior.* Recognize that your students already know how to behave properly. You don't have to teach them that. Your rules for the class are simply to make students accountable. Your job with older students is not to teach behavior but to educate. Every student can understand that message.

■ *Prepare.* Know in advance exactly what action you will take every time a student breaks a rule.

■ *Hold the line.* Do not settle for anything less than a quiet, respectful, focused classroom. Repeat all procedures as often as necessary to get it. Make sure students stay on task and complete their work. It is not enough just to be quiet.

■ *Keep 'em busy.* Keep your students busy from bell to bell. Don't have any down time and don't leave any time for talking.

■ *Review the rules.* You can have a near-perfect classroom if you continue having students review the required rules and procedures. Do this every day if necessary until they get it. In a 2008 personal communication with the author of this text, Mr. Seganti commented that feedback he has received from teachers shows the powerful effect of teaching class rules two days in a row. You may say to your students, "Everybody got this yet? No?" (Laughingly) "Okay, we will go over the rules again tomorrow."

■ *Assess yourself.* Review your performance every day. Identify mistakes and figure out what action you can take next time to get a better outcome.

■ *Take care of things.* Do not count on administrative or parental support except to ensure that your established consequences are enforced.

■ *Don't be manipulated.* Students will invariably manipulate you if you allow them to do so. To students, it is a game. They will argue, waste time, cause you to become exasperated, and so forth. Seganti devotes much attention to this matter and shows teachers how to avoid being manipulated. The dialogs that follow indicate what you should do when students try to manipulate you. Notice Seganti responds to students by stating a rule, rather than arguing with students. This tactic keeps attention on the teacher's agenda (in this case, following the rules) instead of moving attention to the student's agenda (such as wasting time, getting the better of the teacher, or trying to get out of detention).

Rule 1. You see Miguel talking.

You: Miguel, that's a 15-minute detention for talking.
Miguel: I wasn't talking.

You: I don't argue with students.

Rule 2. You see Megan chewing gum.

You: Megan, that's a 15-minute detention for chewing gum.
Megan: I'm not chewing gum.
You: Fine, but since giving the appearance of chewing gum is against the rules, you have detention anyway. [Or you might say] If you don't spit it out I will have to send you out for defiance.

Seganti provides more advice on answering manipulators in a piece called "Mr. Seganti's Big Kahuna Manipulation Destroyer" (2008a, p. 126). The manipulation destroyer he describes is *silence*. Seganti explains that when students make manipulative, irrelevant comments like those in the preceding dialogs, you just look at the students and say nothing. After all, *there is no real answer to a manipulative question.* A student is talking. You say, "Stop talking." They say, "I wasn't talking." What good can come of arguing back and forth in a silly exchange? So try just saying nothing. Just look at the student, deadpan, showing that you will not engage in the matter. Silence stops most manipulation in its tracks. The student may make a last feeble protestation such as, "Man, I wasn't even talking," but the matter will usually end there. If the student does continue talking, assign detention if you haven't done so already.

PUTTING SEGANTI'S APPROACH INTO EFFECT

Before you let students through the door of your classroom, you need to make sure they are ready to get down to business. Do not wait inside the room for everyone to enter any way they like, and then try to calm them down and get their attention afterwards. When they approach your room they may be noisy, rude, jumpy, eating, distracted, or doing other things that are not conducive to academics. Don't allow any of this. Instead, make sure that as students walk through your doorway they are moving into a mindset for learning. Be attentive to students' body language, not just their words.

Types of Students to Look For

There are roughly three types of students you should look for on the first day of school:

1. Type A students are polite, prepared, and ready to enter class. Give them their instructions quickly and send them in.
2. Type B students are basically respectful but appear a bit rowdy or distracted. Tell them to stop, take a deep breath, calm down, and then get ready to enter the class in an orderly manner. Make sure they look you in the eye and are clear about your directions—then send them in.
3. Type C students appear disrespectful, arrogant, and/or rowdy. These are the students who are most likely to present problems. Show the class they are not going to be a problem for you. Establish right away that poor behavior in

your presence will not go unchallenged. Have these students stand to the side while the rest of the class enters. Every small thing you do here helps or hurts your cause. You save many problems later on when students see that you are on top of everything from the start. Get compliance from all of these Type C students before you let them enter. Direct them to a specific seat right next to your desk if possible. If they are noncompliant, argumentative, or rude, give them the simple choice of complying or being suspended for defiance. Do this as calmly as possible. You can say, "I don't argue with students. You can follow my directions or be sent out of the room for defiance." This is what sets your authority.

The Doorway and Establishing Expectations

Seganti places great emphasis on what you do when students arrive at your classroom door for the first time. Below is some of his advice on **doorway tactics** (Seganti, 2008a, pp. 21–34).

Stand in your doorway and stop *every* student briefly before they enter. You might have to block the entrance with your body. Hand each student a copy of the class rules and say, "I want you to go directly to the seat I have assigned you without talking and in an orderly manner. You are to sit down quietly, take out your materials and immediately copy these rules onto a separate sheet of paper. Do this without talking. Do you understand?" Point to the exact seat you want them to sit down in. Try to repeat the part about "being quiet" and "not talking" three times before you let them in. Conveying these messages of "strictness" will help your classroom atmosphere enormously.

If any students say they already know how to behave, or if they ask why they need to copy the rules, or if they do or say anything disrespectful, say "I gave you a direction. You need to follow it." Do not enter into a discussion or rationalize your requirements. Don't fool yourself by thinking that copying the rules is a small matter that can just be let go. From the beginning, get students to realize they have to comply with *all* your directions, great and small. Before long, that is what they will do.

If students are disrespectful, do not have their materials, or in any other way appear unprepared for class, do not let them through the door. They can borrow what they need from a friend, but they can't enter the room until they have all of their materials.

If their nonverbal cues say they are not ready to study, have them stand to the side. Tell them what you expect and say honestly, "To me, you don't look ready to study." When they manage to meet your standards of a proper attitude for entry to the class, let them in. Otherwise just wait. There is no hurry.

If any students begin disrupting after entering, call them back to try again. You can say something like, "Now try again—go to your seat quietly, take out your materials without talking, and copy the rules." If the student interrupts while you are speaking, say "Do not interrupt me again. This is not a conversation but a simple direction you can comply with, or else leave the room for defiance." Do this every day until students enter in a manner that meets your standards for entering and getting to work. Repeat this procedure for as long as necessary. Students do not resent it and they soon respond well. They will even start saying your entry rules before you do.

Assigning Seats

Assign seats the first day while students are copying the rules. Because they have not yet been taught the rules, say the following:

> "I'm going to assign seats now. When I tell you where to sit, get up immediately and move to that desk without questioning or complaining. There is no discussion about it, and if you try to engage me in a discussion about your assigned seat you will be sent from the room. Just move to your seat right away. Does everyone understand?"

Then, as you call roll, assign the seats.

Learning Students' Names

Memorize students' names as quickly as possible. Seganti advises doing the following while students are quietly copying the rules:

- Take roll. Call out the first student's name and assign a seat (alphabetical order is easiest at first and least likely to get you a discussion).
- As individual students move to their seats, say their name five times quickly in your head to help memorize it.
- Call the second student's name. Assign a seat. Say the name five times quickly to yourself and memorize it. Then repeat the names of the first and second students (in your head, that is).
- Do this for the first five students. Then review each of their names in your head against the seating chart to see if you have memorized the first five, and put the name to the face.
- Do this with each subsequent group of five students, and review after each group of five—so, after 10 students, you go back to the first and see if you can say all 10 in your head. You should have the names now on the seating chart and can use it for review. After 15, go back to the first again, and so forth. Re-memorize the ones you forgot by checking the seating chart. Their names will come back to you quickly. Seganti says this procedure takes a lot of concentration but is easier than it sounds.

Establishing Leverage

Establishing leverage involves clarifying for students the provisions of the 15-minute detention consequence. This tactic was explained earlier in the chapter.

Excluding Students from Your Class

In Seganti's approach, only three things call for students to get sent from the room—defiance, repeated disruption, and gross disrespect. The following scenarios depict those reasons and are presented in Seganti's words.

Reason 1: Defiance

I tell Judy to change her seat. She says "Why?" I reply that I do not argue with students.

She does not immediately change her seat and I assign her a 15-minute detention and tell her to change her seat. She continues to argue or just doesn't move. I write up a referral, whether or not she moves at this point, and send her from the class for defiance. She goes to the counselor. I have written on the referral that Judy is suspended for defiance until she comes to detention and copies the class rules.

Five minutes later Judy returns from the counselor's office with a note saying "Student counseled—please re-admit student to class." If I re-admit Judy now, I will be making a big mistake. I say to her, "No, you are suspended from my class. Come to detention after school today for 15 minutes, copy the rules, and you may reenter tomorrow."

At my first opportunity, I explain to the counselor once again how my system works, and that the only help I need from him or her is in enforcing my requirement that Judy comes to detention and copies the rules. If Judy does not meet my requirement, I will send her back again for defiance of my detention rule. I don't care if the counselor provides her counseling or not, so long as Judy comes to detention and copies the rules. Judy can copy rules in the counselor's office and she can be moved to somebody else's class, but will not be re-admitted to my class until she copies the rules and does the 15-minute detention. The matter is simply about the necessity that Judy comply with my class rules.

Reason 2: Repeated Disruption

Disruption is anything that interferes with student concentration in class. It might be a little buzz of talk that I have to try to talk over. It might be a student tapping a pencil on the desk, or rumpling papers, or loudly sighing to show disinterest in the class, or turning away from me while I am talking. Those are all disruptions. They are specified in the class rules and are not allowed. Let's say there is a lot of buzz in class, an undercurrent of noise I can't pinpoint. I'm not sure where to start—no one is being really bad, it seems, nothing that would normally call for detention. So, not knowing what else to do, I say "Quiet!" to the whole class.

They quiet down for a minute, like boiling water does when you cut the heat. But then it starts to boil again and you say, "Quiet! Okay, quiet down!" This can go on for quite a while—in some cases for an entire teaching career. What do I do?

- I start with individuals. I pick one student. "Brian, you are disrupting the class. Be quiet or come to detention."
- Brian replies, "Everyone else is talking."
- I ignore his comment, write down his name, and say, "Come 15 minutes after school today. If you continue disrupting I will have to suspend you from the class."

I don't wait for the big disruptions. I make students adjust to the boundary being squeaky tight. My standard is no disruption during my lesson—not even a little. Follow this advice and, tomorrow, count the times you say "quiet" to your class. If it is more than once per class, that adds up to more than five times a day, and from there the incidence is likely to escalate. So, I have the counselor ensure that Brian will come to detention for 15 minutes that day and copy the rules in the meantime. If he doesn't, I won't re-admit him.

Reason 3: Gross Disrespect

If a student swears at you or insults you or engages in any other highly offensive behavior, immediately suspend the student, send him or her from your class, and demand a parent conference as well as the detention and copying the rules or other consequence you use. Any of these things should include your basic consequence of detention because some students would rather have their parents called than have to serve detention. If it looks like a student is going to be a real problem, start a paper trail on him or her right away. You need to minimize the damage they do to your teaching and other students' education.

ROLE OF ADMINISTRATORS AND PARENTS

Go to the IRIS Center Resources section of Topic #7: Working with Families, in the **MyEducationLab** for your course and complete the module entitled "Collaborating with Families."

You should make sure your administrators understand the logic, rules, and procedures of your approach. They don't want to be caught off guard if a parent complains, and they need to know how they can help you make your program work. They will usually be pleased to know you are handling discipline problems on your own and only need their help as backup when students are suspended from your class.

As for parents, Seganti doesn't believe they will be of much help to you in discipline matters. He says he cannot recall a single instance in his career when a parent conference had a significant long-term effect on a student's behavior. Parent conferences are simply not a consequence that students care about. However, they are useful in establishing a paper trail on students who chronically misbehave and defy the teacher. Administrators have no problem if you send a student from your room for defiance, so it is helpful to document your calls to parents when you give detention for serious and repetitive breaches of the rules, especially those rules over which parents have some control, such as having class materials in hand. When you talk with parents, most will listen to the problem and say something like, "Okay, I'll talk to her/him." Occasionally parents will take the student's side and express concern that you are not doing your job properly. When that happens, don't go on the defensive. Explain your rules and ask the parent if they see anything unfair in them (they won't). Explain that their child has not shown up for detention or continually violates the rules, which interferes with your teaching and educational rights of other students.

CLOSING COMMENT FROM MR. SEGANTI

Our schools are currently doing things out of sequence—trying to let students know all their rights and encouraging self-expression and independent thought, and so on, before working to establish basic respect for others and the environment. Schools seem oblivious of the misery they cause students and teachers by emphasizing things in this order. In a more effective sequence, respect must be established first, as a fundamental principle of all classroom interactions (comment provided to author by Craig Seganti, 2008).

APPLYING SEGANTI'S APPROACH IN THE CLASSROOM

- Before classes begin, have your discipline plan carefully organized and be ready to teach it to your students.
- When students first arrive, use Seganti's directions for admitting them to the room, assigning seats, and having students copy the class rules. You might use Seganti's rules or modify them to suit your needs.
- Explain and demonstrate to students the leverage you will use to help them follow the rules. This leverage might be the 15-minute detention or an effective alternative that can be used in your school.
- From the beginning, make your class management procedures evident. Dress and conduct yourself as a professional. Place your desks in rows. Have all

materials organized neatly. Have your referrals, detention logs, teaching props, and parent phone numbers at the ready. Have procedures organized for all class activities and teach the procedures to students. Make sure they know what they should be doing from bell to bell. Speak in statements, not questions—"This is work time," rather than "Why aren't you working?" Know in advance exactly what action you will take every time a student breaks a rule. Hold the line. Keep students busy.

- Take care of discipline matters yourself. No backup is required from administrators, counselors, or parents *except* to support the process students must follow when temporarily suspended from your class.

doorway tactics
15-minute detention
leverage

CASE 1: KRISTINA WILL NOT WORK

Kristina, a student in Mr. Jake's class, is quite docile. She socializes little with other students and never disrupts lessons. However, despite Mr. Jake's best efforts, Kristina will not do her work. She rarely completes an assignment. She is simply there, putting forth no effort at all. *How would Craig Seganti deal with Kristina?*

Mr. Seganti provided the following commentary: Kristina is required by the rules to be on task at all times. Therefore she will be assigned a 15-minute detention if she does not stay on task. At the detention I will try to determine the root of the problem: It is almost always that the work is too challenging, so in this case I might help her with the work after school a bit and/or contact her parents to see if they can help her at home.

CASE 2: SARA WILL NOT STOP TALKING

Sara is a pleasant girl who participates in class activities and does most, though not all, of her assigned work. She cannot seem to refrain from talking to classmates, however. Her teacher, Mr. Gonzales, speaks to her repeatedly during lessons, to the point that he often becomes exasperated and loses his temper. *What suggestions would Craig Seganti give Mr. Gonzales for dealing with Sara?*

CASE 3: JOSHUA CLOWNS AND INTIMIDATES

Joshua, larger and louder than his classmates, always wants to be the center of attention, which he accomplishes through a combination of clowning and intimidation. He makes wisecrack remarks, talks back (smilingly) to the teacher, utters a variety of sound-effect noises such as automobile crashes and gunshots, and makes limitless sarcastic comments and put-downs of his classmates. Other students will not stand up to him, apparently fearing his size and verbal aggression. His teacher, Miss Pearl, cannot control his disruptive behavior. *Would Joshua's behavior be likely to improve if Miss Pearl implemented Craig Seganti's approach in her class? Explain.*

CASE 4: TOM IS HOSTILE AND DEFIANT

Tom has appeared to be in his usual foul mood ever since arriving in class. On his way to sharpen his pencil, he bumps into Frank, who complains. Tom tells him loudly to shut up. Miss Baines, the teacher, says, "Tom, go back to your seat." Tom wheels around, swears loudly, and says heatedly, "I'll go when I'm damned good and ready!" *How would Craig Seganti have Miss Baines deal with Tom?*

You Are the Teacher

NEW FIFTH GRADE

Your new fifth-grade class consists of students from a small, stable community. Because the transiency rate is low, many of your students have been together since first grade, and during those years they have developed certain patterns of interacting and assuming various roles such as clowns and instigators. Unfortunately, their behavior often interferes with teaching and learning. During the first week of school you notice that four or five students enjoy making smart-aleck remarks about most things you want them to do. When such remarks are made, the other students laugh and sometimes join in.

Even when you attempt to hold class discussions about serious issues, many of the students make light of the topics and refuse to enter genuinely into an exploration of the issues. Instead of the productive discussion you have hoped for, you find that class behavior often degenerates into flippancy and horseplay.

A TYPICAL OCCURRENCE

You have begun a history lesson that contains a reference to Julius Caesar. You ask if anyone has ever heard of Julius Caesar. Ben shouts out, "Yeah, they named a salad after him!" The class laughs and calls out encouraging remarks such as "Good one, Ben!" You wait for some semblance of order, then say, "Let us go on." From the back of the classroom, Jeremy cries, "Lettuce and cabbage!" The class bursts into laughter and chatter. You ask for their cooperation and no more students call out or make remarks, but you see several continue to smirk and whisper, with a good deal of barely suppressed giggling. You try to ignore it, but because of the disruptions you are not able to complete the lesson on time or to get the results you hoped for.

CONCEPTUALIZING A STRATEGY

If you followed Craig Seganti's suggestions, what would you conclude or do with regard to the following?

- Preventing the problem from occurring in the first place
- Putting an immediate end to the misbehavior now
- Maintaining student dignity and good personal relations
- Using follow-up procedures that would prevent the recurrence of the misbehavior

Activities

1. What do you see as the major strengths of Seganti's approach? Do you feel it has significant shortcomings? How do you judge it would mesh with your personality and preferred style of teaching?
2. With colleagues or fellow students, practice Seganti's doorway tactics and his method of responding to students who break class rules.

3. In your journal, enter ideas from Seganti's approach that you might wish to incorporate into your personal system of discipline.

References

Seganti, C. 2008a. *Classroom discipline 101: How to get control of any classroom.* www.classroomdiscipline 101.com

Seganti, C. 2008b. *Ezine.* [See articles on the Seganti approach to discipline.] http://ezinearticles.com/ ?expert=Craig_Seganti

What Additional Strategies Might I Use to Enhance My Personal System of Discipline?

This portion of *Building Classroom Discipline* consists of four chapters, each of which presents one or more powerful strategies that help increase the effectiveness of any given approach to discipline.

CHAPTER 12 How Do Top Teachers Establish Personal Influence with Students Who Are Difficult to Manage?

This chapter presents advice from a number of outstanding authorities on how to establish personal influence with students who are difficult to manage. The authorities include Dave Hingsburger (*Power Tools*), Stephen R. Covey (*The 7 Habits of Highly Effective People*), Haim Ginott (*Teacher and Child*), Jane Nelsen and Lynn Lott (*Positive Discipline in the Classroom*), William Glasser (*Every Student Can Succeed*), Tom Daly (*The ADHD Solution for Teachers: How to Turn Any Child into Your Best Student*), Richard Curwin, Allen Mendler, and Brian Mendler (*Discipline with Dignity*), and Ed Ford (*The Responsible Thinking Process*).

CHAPTER 13 How Do Leading Experts Engender Respect and Civility in the Classroom?

This chapter presents key ideas furnished by P. M. Forni, head of the Civility Institute at Johns Hopkins University; Michele Borba, international author and consultant on building moral intelligence; and Diane Gossen, international authority on the role of restitution in bringing about long-term improvement in behavior.

CHAPTER 14 How Do C. M. Charles and Others Energize Their Classes?

This chapter presents strategies for increasing the levels of student involvement and energy through activities that emphasize camaraderie and sense of purpose. The chapter features the contributions of C. M. Charles, author of *The Synergetic*

Classroom, and five teachers at various levels who share efforts they have found effective in energizing their classes.

CHAPTER 15 How Does Eileen Kalberg VanWie Build and Maintain Democratic Learning Communities in Technology-Rich Environments?

This chapter focuses on procedures for establishing democratic communities of learners in technology-rich environments, a topic new to discipline. The lead author of the chapter is professor and researcher Eileen Kalberg VanWie, one of the first to become thoroughly conversant with the process of establishing group purpose and camaraderie in classes that feature high levels of technology use.

12

How Do Top Teachers Establish Personal Influence with Students Who Are Difficult to Manage?

Most teachers say discipline wouldn't be a problem were it not for the very few students in their classes who cause most of the trouble. A familiar refrain: It does seem that within many classes only two to four students cause 90 percent of the disruptions. Those few seem impervious to ordinary discipline tactics, such as isolation, seating next to the teacher's desk, various in-class penalties, trips to the counselor, calling parents, signing contracts promising to behave properly, and so forth.

But in recent years, several influential authorities have identified tactics that seem to bring results the teachers want. The new tactics have much in common, most of them calling for teachers to establish respectful or even caring relationships with the chronic offenders. As those relationships grow, misbehavior declines. Sometimes, those former thorns in teachers' sides become teacher favorites. This chapter explains how to make that happen with eight approaches from respected authorities.

A PREVIEW OF THIS CHAPTER

Teachers have great power over students, but the power is in the form of influence, not force or control. Teachers increase their influence by endeavoring to establish personal relationships with students, which can be done in various ways. Dave Hingsburger advises teachers to open themselves up to the students' points of view. Stephen R. Covey asks teachers to find the frames of reference students use in "seeing" the world, then move into that frame when interacting with them. Haim Ginott explains how we can speak with students in ways that promote confidence and trust. Jane Nelsen and Lynn Lott describe relationship builders teachers can employ with all students. William Glasser shares seven connecting habits to be used with students rather than seven "deadly" habits on which we often fall back. Tom Daly explains how he befriends students who cause the most trouble in his classes. Richard Curwin, Allen Mendler, and Brian Mendler advise teachers to confer dignity and restore students' sense of hope. Finally, Ed Ford shares an effective questioning sequence that establishes mutual respect and leads to an inner sense of self-control.

WHAT TO LOOK FOR IN THIS CHAPTER

- How to grasp students' points of view and enter into their frames of reference
- How to speak with students in ways that earn their confidence and trust
- How to connect with students who cause most of the problems in your classes
- How to confer dignity on students and restore their sense of hope
- How to help students develop an inner sense of self-control

DAVE HINGSBURGER: USE POWER SPARINGLY AND GRASP THE STUDENT'S POINT OF VIEW

Dave Hingsburger, a Canadian psychologist and therapist, provides direct services to people with disabilities and consults with schools, parents, practitioners, and agencies on problematic behavior. He lectures extensively and has given keynote addresses at national and international conferences. He also operates Diverse City Press, a publishing house that specializes in materials for working with the developmentally disabled. He offers important observations concerning teacher power and its use. His suggestions have implications for the treatment of all students.

> You have power over students. Take care that you do not use it to force students to behave in any particular way. Take students as they are and build on that. ■

Hingsburger believes teachers should seriously analyze the attitudes they hold toward troublesome students and their ways of working with them. He points out that teachers and others who work in human care have enormous power over the people they are trying to help and discusses his discomfort with how it can be misused. Too often, he says, teachers use their power to try to force students to behave in "normal" or acceptable ways. Sometimes they do so successfully, but more often that approach only sets up detrimental and unnecessary barriers between teachers and students.

In his book *Power Tools* (2000b), Hingsburger explains that most teachers don't realize or take the following into account:

- They have far greater power than they might think.
- They frequently misuse that power.
- Their misguided behavior is evident to everyone except themselves.
- They are responsible for the unfortunate results that often occur even when they mean well.

He urges teachers and caregivers to "think about what you do on a daily basis with those within your care" (2000b, p. 5) and to understand that students who are difficult to manage have their own perspectives on life and the world. It is usually a waste of time to try to get them to see the "right" way of doing things. Those students benefit more if we help them learn how to disagree with us respectfully.

To do that, we must encourage them to give their points of view, which then gives us an opportunity to learn from them.

Hingsburger stresses that it isn't our job to make people over in our image. Trying to do so will only produce frustration and battles of will, leading to more use of force. The best approach is for teachers to accept students as they are and work from that point, giving them latitude to discover their own way in the world.

It sounds good, but how does one engage with Hingsburger's advice? In his book, *First Contact* (2000a), he urges teachers to see disruptive students simply as individuals with different perspectives on life than their teachers'. Teachers need to realize that even when students' views differ from their own, the two of them can still share emotions, points of view, thoughts, ideas, and ideals. You can move into this understanding with students by talking with them frequently about topics of mutual interest. You must treat them as social equals; strive to understand and acknowledge their points of view, and avoid exerting your power over them. Your role is to understand them and help them open up to you, not to convince them your views are the only correct ones or better than theirs. Students with behavior difficulties do not often encounter teachers who share life views with them, but doing so is likely to bring some good into the lives of both.

STEPHEN R. COVEY: FIND THE STUDENT'S FRAME OF REFERENCE AND LISTEN EMPATHETICALLY

Stephen R. Covey (2004) believes the key to establishing productive relationships lies in empathetic listening, meaning listening sensitively to others. Few of us are good listeners, although we all have the potential to be very good at it. He contends that we can learn to be better listeners if we (1) identify our own frame of reference (our perspectives, values, beliefs, preferences, and so forth) relating to any matter and then (2) try to grasp the frame of reference of the other person, thus putting us more closely in tune with their thoughts.

Recognized as one of *Time* magazine's 25 Most Influential Americans, Covey has dedicated his life to demonstrating how every person can benefit from adopting the habits of truly successful people. He provides guidance for doing so in his books, which have sold over 20 million copies in 38 languages worldwide. His *7 Habits of Highly Effective People* was named the Most Influential Business Book of the Twentieth Century. Among the many other honors he has earned are the International Man of Peace Award, International Entrepreneur of the Year Award, and honorary doctorates from eight universities.

> To work well with troublesome learners, do what you can to understand their view of the world or frame of reference. Then examine your own. Insofar as you can, move from your frame of reference into theirs and communicate from that perspective. ■

Covey explains that for many years he believed others were understanding him accurately when he spoke, especially since he was taking pains to make himself very clear. Finally he realized that what he was trying to convey was framed in his own point of view, not those of the listeners, which were sometimes quite different.

That was when he understood that in order to communicate well, you have to understand both your point of view and that of your listeners. The two, he says, are seldom the same. For teachers, that means understanding students' deeper hopes, fears, realities, and difficulties. When you obtain that understanding, you adjust what you wish to communicate in terms of the student's frame of reference as child or adolescent, rather than from your frame of reference as an adult teacher. What the student sees as reality often differs substantially from what we consider reality, and matters we consider important may be trivial in students' view of the world. If we are to work well with students, we need to know not just their thoughts but what those thoughts mean in their personal existence.

Earlier, Covey wrote that highly successful people attempt to understand their listeners *before* they try to make listeners understand them. As he put it:

> If I were to summarize in one sentence the single most important principle I have learned in the field of interpersonal relations, it would be this: *Seek first to understand, then to be understood.* This principle is the key to effective interpersonal communication. (1989, p. 237)

He further reminds us:

> Empathetic listening takes time, but it doesn't take anywhere near as much time as it takes to back up and correct misunderstandings when you're already miles down the road, to redo, to live with unexpressed and unsolved problems. . . . People want to be understood. And whatever investment of time it takes to do that will bring much greater returns of time as you work from an accurate understanding of [their] problems and issues. (1989, p. 253)

HAIM GINOTT: USE CONGRUENT LANGUAGE THAT CONFERS DIGNITY*

Haim G. Ginott (1922–1973), psychologist, child therapist, parent educator, and author, has explained how teachers can use *congruent language* to develop respectful relationships with students. Ginott began his career as an elementary teacher and then went on to hold professorships in psychology at Adelphi University and New York University Graduate School. He also served as a UNESCO consultant in Israel, was resident psychologist on the *Today* show, and wrote a weekly syndicated column entitled "Between Us" that dealt with interpersonal communication. His books, *Between Parent and Child* (1965), *Between Parent and Teenager* (1967), *and Teacher and Child* (1971), have been translated into over 30 languages and continue to be very popular.

---

*Ginott's ideas were summarized earlier in Chapter 4. They are presented here once more for your convenience.

Ginott's suggestions remain state of the art for showing respect for students' feelings while setting limits on their behavior. His suggestions work especially well with students who are difficult to manage because he does not put students on the defensive, but instead invites their cooperation. In his book *Teacher and Child*, he illuminated the value of congruent communication and provided tactics that continue to resonate with teachers. His suggestions, which were presented in Chapter 4 and are repeated here for emphasis, play to teachers' strength:

> As a teacher I have come to the frightening conclusion that I am the decisive element in the classroom. It is my personal approach that creates the climate. It is my daily mood that makes the weather. As a teacher I possess tremendous power to make a child's life miserable or joyous. I can be a tool of torture or an instrument of inspiration. I can humiliate or humor, hurt or heal. In all situations it is my response that decides whether a crisis will be escalated or de-escalated, and a child humanized or dehumanized. (1971, p. 13)

Ginott reminds us that learning always takes place in the present tense, meaning each moment is a fresh reality in which prejudgments and grudges have no place. Because learning is always a personal matter to students, teachers must remember that each student is an individual who must be treated as such. Good communication is the key to working effectively with students. The style of communication most effective for teachers is *congruent communication,* which addresses *situations* rather than students' character and is harmonious with students' feelings about situations and themselves. Ginott says that *teachers at their best* do not preach, moralize, impose guilt, or demand promises. Instead, they *confer dignity* on their students by treating them as social equals capable of making decisions for themselves. Contrarily, *teachers at their worst* label students, belittle them, and denigrate their character, although seldom intentionally. Ginott urges teachers to conscientiously avoid making certain comments. He is especially adamant about the following (the word "please" that begins each statement has been added by the author of this book to convey Ginott's considerate manner):

- Please don't label students by referring to them as lazy, thoughtless, a bad helper, inconsiderate, a poor citizen, and so on. Instead, say to your students, "I want everybody to happy and successful. What might I do to help you?"
- Please don't ask rhetorical "why" questions ("Why did you write this so poorly?" "Why are you two talking?" "Why am I having to tell you this again?"). Instead, say to your students, "I believe you can do this properly. Let me show you another way. Let's see if it helps."
- Please don't give moralistic lectures ("You are not making an effort to get along with each other," "You will never get anywhere in life if you can't get along with other people"). Instead, say to your students, "We all have our problems. I know I do. Let's see if we can figure out how to make things better."
- Please don't make caustic or sarcastic remarks to students ("I simply don't believe that," "You are not telling the truth. I believe that's the fourth time you have 'lost' your assignment"). Instead, say to your students, "I want to help you get this done. You will feel better if you do, and so will I. Let's try again. Let me give you a hint."

- Please don't deny students' feelings ("You have no reason to be upset," "There is absolutely nothing to worry about"). Instead, say to your students, "We all get worried and afraid at times. It is normal. Let's just do the best we can. If we make mistakes, it doesn't matter. Making mistakes can teach us a lot."
- Please don't demand students' cooperation ("That's enough fooling around. Get back in your seats and get to work, right now!"). Instead, say to your students, "This is work time," or "I'd like to make this more fun for you. Perhaps we might work with partners for the remainder of the assignment."
- Please don't lose your temper and self-control ("Don't you dare speak to me like that again! You will be out of this class once and for all!"). Instead, say to your students, "I truly need your help and cooperation. If you can give me that, I'll definitely help you."

Ginott says teachers should feel free to express anger and other emotions, but when doing so should use *I-messages* rather than *you-messages*. Using an I-message, the teacher might say, "I'm upset about the amount of noise." Using a you-message, the teacher might say, "You are being too noisy." Ginott goes on to say that effective teachers do not dictate to students or boss them around, because those acts too often provoke resistance. Effective teachers have a *hidden asset* on which they can always call, which is to ask themselves, "How can I be most helpful to my students right now?"

As noted in Chapter 4, Ginott says it is wise to use *laconic language,* meaning language that is brief and to the point when responding to or redirecting student misbehavior. He also has a great deal to say about praise. His contentions came as a surprise to teachers in the 1970s who were using praise extensively in behavior modification. *Evaluative praise* is worse than none at all, he said, and should never be used. An example of evaluative praise is "Good boy for raising your hand." Instead of evaluative praise, which speaks to a student's character, teachers should use expressions of *appreciation* for effort, improvement, or accomplishment without evaluating the student's character or talent. For example, the teacher might say, "I enjoyed your story very much," or "I can almost smell those pine trees in your drawing."

Ginott asked teachers to always respect students' privacy, but indicate they are available should students want to talk. As for correcting inappropriate behavior, Ginott simply advised that we stop the misbehavior and teach the student the correct way to behave. Ginott placed strong sanctions on sarcasm and punishment, saying sarcasm is almost always dangerous and should not be used with students. Punishment should not be used at all, as it too often produces hostility, rancor, and vengefulness, while never making students really want to improve.

Teachers, meanwhile, should continually strive for *self-discipline* in their work. They must be very careful not to display the behaviors they are trying to eradicate in students, such as raising their voice to end noise, acting rude toward students who are being impolite, or berating students who have used inappropriate language.

JANE NELSEN AND LYNN LOTT: USE RELATIONSHIP BUILDERS WHILE AVOIDING RELATIONSHIP BARRIERS

Jane Nelsen and co-author Lynn Lott have identified five pairs of teacher behaviors that, depending on how they are used, can either nurture or inhibit relationships

between teacher and students. They call the positive aspect of each pair a *builder* and the negative aspect of each pair a *barrier*. Builders are respectful and encouraging, whereas barriers are disrespectful and discouraging.

Nelsen (left) and Lott (2000) state they can guarantee 100 percent improvement in student–teacher relationships when teachers simply learn to recognize barrier behaviors and stop using them. Where else, they ask, can you get such a generous return for ceasing a behavior? And when the builders are added, the payoff is even greater.

Following are their builders, contrasted with barrier counterparts.

Go to the Building Classroom Discipline Video Showcase section of Topic #3: Models of Classroom Management, in the **MyEducationLab** for your course and watch the video entitled "Jane Nelsen and Lynn Lott—Positive Discipline in the Classroom."

Builder 1: Checking.   Teachers can establish stronger relations with students if they check in advance to see how students think and feel about class expectations and other matters. The *barrier* to avoid is teachers' *assuming* they know how students feel and then proceeding from that basis.

Builder 2: Exploring.   Students relate better to teachers who allow them to explore and perceive situations for themselves and proceed accordingly. The barrier to avoid is *rescuing/explaining*. Teachers erroneously think they are being helpful when they make lengthy explanations, rescue students from difficulties, or do some of students' work for them. What they should do instead is ask students, "What do you need to remember, do, or have in order to take care of yourself?"

Builder 3: Inviting/Encouraging.   To build strong relationships, teachers should invite and encourage students to cooperate, contribute, and be self-directing. For example, they might say, "The bell will ring soon. I would appreciate anything you might do to help get the room straightened up for the next class." The barrier to avoid is *directing*. Teachers do not realize they are being disrespectful when they tell students, "Pick that up." "Put that away." "Straighten up your desk before the bell rings." Such commands build dependency while suppressing initiative and cooperation.

Builder 4: Celebrating.   Teachers should hold high expectations of students and show they believe in students' potential. They should celebrate student progress that is made evident when students take initiative, make an effort, persevere, and improve. The barrier to avoid is *expecting*. Students become easily discouraged when judged negatively because they have fallen short of expectations, as when teachers say, "I really thought you could do that" or "I thought you were more responsible than that."

Builder 5: Respecting.   Respect does much to build teacher–student relationships. Teachers show respect when they speak with students as social equals and without using terms that suggest what students ought to do. The barrier to avoid is the use of *adult-isms*, which are teacher statements that tell students what to do or that sound like parents speaking to naughty children: "How come you never . . . ?" "Why can't you ever . . . ?" "I can't believe you would do such a thing!" These adult-isms foster dependency and guilt rather than initiative and encouragement. If students have not performed up to expectations, the teacher should not admonish them, but ask, "What is your understanding of the requirements for this assignment?"

WILLIAM GLASSER: MAKE ASSIDUOUS USE OF SEVEN CONNECTING HABITS*

Glasser believes if students are misbehaving seriously at school, it is because they are unhappy in your class and probably in school. The question for teachers is, "How do I make my students happy?" Glasser's answer: Providing a useful curriculum that students find enjoyable and establishing relationships with students on a personal basis work wonders for improving behavior in school.

Accordingly, Glasser stresses the fundamental importance of maintaining good personal relationships between teachers and students. Teachers can take a major step toward such relationships simply by consciously avoiding what Glasser calls *the seven deadly habits in teaching* and replacing them with *the seven connecting habits* (Glasser, 2001).

The *seven deadly habits* are teacher acts that inhibit the establishment of caring relationships between teachers and students. Glasser identifies the deadly habits as *criticizing, blaming, complaining, nagging, threatening, punishing,* and *rewarding students to control them.* If teachers are to establish and maintain good relationships with students and gain their willing cooperation, they must eliminate these deadly habits from the interactions they have with students.

? Please take a moment at this point to do the following activities, preferably with a partner:

1. Give an example of criticizing. What might you say in place of the critical comments?
2. Give an example of blaming. What might you say in place of the blaming comments?
3. Give an example of complaining. What might you say in place of complaining?
4. Give an example of nagging. What might you say in place of the nagging comments?
5. Give an example of threatening. What might you say in place of the threatening comments?
6. Give an example of punishing. What might you say or do in place of punishing?
7. Give an example of rewarding students to control them. What might you do instead?

---

*Glasser's suggestions for replacing deadly teacher habits with connecting habits were presented in Chapter 8. They are repeated here for your convenience.

As teachers move away from the seven deadly habits, their relations with students begin to improve. The relations improve still further when teachers use *seven connecting habits*, which Glasser identified as *caring, listening, supporting, contributing, encouraging, trusting,* and *befriending.* Glasser believes—and the success of his quality schools supports his conviction—that all students who come to school can do competent work. In order for this to happen, teachers must strongly connect with their students. This connection is accomplished when teachers use the seven connecting habits and *give up* trying to use external controls in trying to make students behave as they want them to. Glasser makes his point by describing how we relate to friends (and he does indeed urge teachers to befriend their students). He notes that we do not criticize, blame, or speak harshly to our friends. Rather, we use connecting habits when relating with them.

> **?** Please take a moment to do the following exercise, preferably with a partner:
>
> 1. Give an example of a caring comment that would not be construed as an attempt to control.
> 2. Give an example of how you would listen to what students have to say.
> 3. Give an example of something truthful you might say to support a student's efforts.
> 4. Give an example of what you might say to help students contribute to the class.
> 5. Give an example of an honest, encouraging statement you might make to a student.
> 6. Give an example of what you might say or do to show you trust your students.
> 7. Give an example of what you might say or do in an effort to befriend one of your worst-behaved students.

TOM DALY: FIND WAYS TO RELATE WELL WITH YOUR FEW MOST PROBLEMATIC STUDENTS

Tom Daly is a teacher and adjunct professor in San Diego, California, who has worked for many years with students who have serious behavior issues. He has developed and refined a number of tactics for helping his students enjoy greater success. He has shared those ideas with thousands of teachers in more than 10 countries and has helped train hundreds of new teachers. His ideas and suggestions are set forth in his book, *The ADHD Solution for Teachers: How to Turn Any Disruptive Child into Your Best Student* (2004), also available in condensed version on CD. Mr. Daly's website is www.adhdsolution.com.

Daly says that teachers who experience troubling behavioral issues with students should begin by acknowledging that the solution to the problem often lies within themselves, not in their students. Once teachers accept that they may need

Go to the Simulations section of Topic #5: Creating Positive Student–Teacher Relationships, in the **MyEducationLab** for your course and complete the simulation entitled "Developing Positive Teacher–Student Relationships with All Students."

to adopt a different attitude or do things differently, they are ready to begin learning how to change themselves so they influence students in a manner that improves behavior, increases success, promotes respect for authority, and convinces students that education is their ticket to success in life.

One of the efforts Daly features is establishing strong personal relations with the few students in each classroom who cause most of the trouble. He contends that when those students misbehave, they are actually sending teachers a coded message that says "Reach me," meaning they are asking for attention or a personal connection. Daly states that if you can reach your students in a likeable way while holding their respect, you will soon reduce behavior problems by 90 percent. A bonus is that the tactics that are effective with your most troublesome students also have a positive effect on your other students.

To reach out effectively to misbehaving students, he says, teachers must stop thinking of confronting or controlling students' behavior and turn their attention to replacing unacceptable behavior with acceptable behavior. That replacement is best accomplished in a process akin to coaching or personal training—you first establish a personal connection with students and then progressively coach them in how to behave appropriately. The "connect, then coach" approach should be used even when you see students displaying annoying little behaviors such as pencil tapping and blurting out. That is not a time to ignore behavior, Daly says, but a time to *move closer* to the student, literally and figuratively. Daly points out that people become good, responsible adults not because someone demands it or rewards them for being good, but because they have made a real connection with a teacher or other responsible adult. Making that connection, he says, is the key to transforming students' lives.

Your ability to make good connections with your students increases as you endeavor to understand the students' world, including whom they associate with, their chief concerns, and their personal likes and dislikes. This knowledge gives you a foothold in their world and can make the difference between student success and failure.

Daly suggests a number of tactics teachers can use in forging better connections with students. One example of the many he explains is simply to "walk and talk" with your hard-to-manage students as frequently as you can. Walk along with them casually and talk about anything at all. The topic doesn't matter. When students go on casual walks with you, they act differently than they do in a class situation. For one thing, they stop seeing you as an adversary. If you don't try to pry information from them, they open up and divulge more and will often tell you why they misbehave in class. Daly compares the value of this tactic to fishing in a lake where the fish are literally jumping into the boat. For other useful tactics, consult the resources available through Daly's website.

Daly says tactics such as "walk and talk" will definitely work for you, but you have to make them happen, which might require a change in your overall approach to teaching. A good way to begin is to show your enthusiasm for teaching and for the students you are helping. Daly says to think back to your own school days and see if you can remember a teacher who scowled at you and another teacher who seemed happy to see you each day. You can probably remember how much happier you were with the pleasant teacher and how eager you were to cooperate with him or her.

If students with unappealing behavior are to succeed in life, they need to learn how to *be more likeable* and *show respect and appreciation for authority figures.* They not only need to like authority figures, they also need to be liked *by* authority figures—this is very important to students' future success. We should make it clear that we want to like and respect our students, and that it is human nature to try to help those we like. If your students come to like you, they will respect you and follow your lead.

True, it takes some doing to turn one's most disruptive students into models of cooperation, productivity, and good behavior. But Daly has found it can be done, better than we might imagine. Just be sure always to display a positive outlook toward your troublesome students. It won't change their personalities instantaneously, but it will progressively free up their innate desire to do well and encourage them to become more cooperative fairly quickly.

Meanwhile, continue truly believing your most underachieving kids *want* to turn around, even if their behavior doesn't indicate it. Send the message to students, administrators, parents, and, most importantly, *yourself* that you care enough about these kids and your own happiness to roll up your sleeves and find a better way of helping them. When students, colleagues, and parents sense this message emanating from you, they will respect your willingness to go the extra mile. As you move forward, listen to your students and observe their behavior. Make real connections with them—they truly need life-changing relationships with mentors and authority figures such as yourself. Daly says if you can do these things, most of the disruptive behavior in your class will fade away.

RICHARD CURWIN, ALLEN MENDLER, AND BRIAN MENDLER: CONFER DIGNITY AND REESTABLISH HOPE

Richard Curwin (left), Allen Mendler, and Brian Mendler (below) write and consult widely on matters related to discipline and working with challenging youths. Curwin is a professor, consultant, and specialist in school discipline. His articles have appeared in *Educational Leadership, Reclaiming Children and Youth, Instructor, Parenting,* and *Learning.* Allen Mendler, a school psychologist and psychoeducational consultant, has worked extensively with students and teachers at all levels. His articles have appeared in many journals, including *Educational Leadership, Kappan, Learning, Reclaiming Children and Youth,* and *Reaching Today's Youth.* Brian Mendler is a teacher, author, and consultant with Discipline Associates and the Teacher Learning Center. He is co-author of the third edition of *Discipline with Dignity.*

Curwin and Mendler attracted national attention with their 1988 book *Discipline with Dignity,* which has been updated a number of times, most recently in 2008. In 1992 Curwin published *Rediscovering Hope: Our Greatest Teaching Strategy,* in which he explained how to improve the behavior of difficult-to-control students who are otherwise likely to fail in school. Mendler and Curwin followed in 1999 with *Discipline with Dignity for*

Go to the Building Classroom Discipline Video Showcase section of Topic #3: Models of Classroom Management, in the MyEducationLab for your course and watch the video entitled "Richard Curwin and Allen Mendler—Discipline with Dignity."

Challenging Youth, designed to help teachers work productively with students with especially difficult behavioral problems. In 2008, Curwin, Mendler, and Mendler released *Discipline with Dignity: New Challenges, New Solutions*, which emphasizes relationship building, curriculum relevance, and academic success. Curwin, Mendler, and Mendler can be contacted through www.tlc-sems.com.

> To experience success with students who repeatedly misbehave in class, approach them in a manner that preserves their sense of dignity and restores genuine hope that school will be of benefit to them. ∎

Curwin, Mendler, and Mendler say their approach has been notably effective with students who are behaviorally at risk of failure and otherwise likely to drop out of school. The approach offers no magical quick fix, but does provide tools that lead to long-term solutions to chronic problems of misbehavior, including violence.

Students referred to as challenging youth often behave badly in school, and many teachers dread dealing with them. In most interactions with teachers, those students feel their personal dignity is under threat. To make matters worse, they have little faith they will ever be successful in school, or even that school has anything of value for them.

It is those students in particular who Curwin, Mendler, and Mendler say can be reclaimed through tactics that enhance dignity and provide a sense of hope for school success. Their strategy asks teachers always to interact with students in a manner that preserves dignity while ensuring nothing is done to inhibit students' willingness to learn.

While most students misbehave occasionally, some do so in an attempt to regain a bit of control over a system that has damaged their sense of dignity. They refuse to comply with teacher requests, argue and talk back, tap pencils, drop books, withdraw from class activities, and sometimes exhibit hostility and aggression. These students have found they can't be good at learning but can be very good at being bad and, by doing so, can meet their needs for attention and power. These students are often at risk of failure in school, and they find others like themselves with whom to bond, which motivates further misbehavior. Behaviorally at-risk students are difficult to control for several reasons. They usually, though not always, have a history of academic failure. Unable to maintain dignity through achievement, they protect themselves by withdrawing or acting as if they don't care.

To counteract this condition, teachers must make learning attractive and ensure students are successful at it. At-risk students will not persevere unless successful, despite the initial attractiveness of the topic. To ensure success, teachers can redesign the curriculum to promote interest and success. They can encourage students to use different ways of thinking, provide for various learning styles and sensory modalities, allow for creativity and artistic expression, and use grading systems that provide encouraging feedback without damaging students' willingness to try.

ED FORD: EXPOSE STUDENTS TO THE RESPONSIBLE THINKING PROCESS (RTP)*

Ed Ford is president of Responsible Thinking Process, Inc. His organization trains educators and parents in using the Responsible Thinking Process (RTP) to assist the young in conducting themselves more effectively, relating better with others, and becoming more responsible people.

Simply put, the RTP helps students

1. understand what they want for themselves in life and
2. learn how to develop plans for getting what they want, while
3. not infringing on the rights of others.

Ford (2006) does not view behavior as being "caused" by environmental forces, nor does he believe it is possible for one person to control another. He feels it is unfair to expect teachers to change those things over which they have no control. But he does believe teachers should teach students how to understand what they want for themselves in life and how they can develop plans for getting what they want without infringing on the rights of others.

Mr. Ford served in the U.S. Navy, was a newspaper reporter, and later worked in the industrial relations department of a large steel factory. He taught high school for six years, then earned a master's degree in social work and went into private counseling. Not long afterward, he joined the faculty of the Institute for Reality Therapy and began teaching Reality Therapy and consulting in schools and other institutions in Ohio. For the past 30 years, he has taught and consulted in alcohol and drug rehabilitation centers, in mental health centers for residential and outpatients, in approximately 70 school districts, and on the faculty of Arizona State University's School of Social Work. Mr. Ford, a founding member and past president of the Control Systems Group that researches and promotes perceptual control theory, has authored 13 books, including *Discipline for Home and School, Book One* (3rd edition, 2003) and *Book Two* (revised edition, 1999). He recommends his most recently published book be read first: *Discipline for Home and School, Fundamentals* (2004). Currently, he consults and trains extensively with school districts that want to use the Responsible Thinking Process. His website is www.responsiblethinking.com, and he can be contacted through that site.

The Responsible Thinking Process is a school discipline process that does not involve coercion, punishment, or rewards. It is designed to help students develop a sense of responsibility for their own lives and respect for everyone around them. When students have difficulties getting along with others, or when they disrupt in class or other school settings, they are taught how to plan ways to get what they want *without infringing on the rights of others*. This is rarely seen in education, Ford says.

---

*Mr. Ford wishes all readers to recognize that only highly trained and approved people are allowed to teach his system to others. Please understand, therefore, that this section does not purport to teach you the Responsible Thinking Process® (RTP). This presentation is simply to draw your attention to Mr. Ford's ideas. Please check the Responsible Thinking Process website for further information.

Ford insists that "misbehavior" is never truly corrected by reprimands or punishment. It is only corrected when students connect their actions to get what they want with the effects of those actions on others. Students who don't understand this process continue to behave inappropriately, meaning their behavior disturbs others.

> The Responsible Thinking Process is *not* designed to control behavior, "change" students, keep students "in line," or maintain an orderly class. Rather, it is designed to cultivate respect for oneself and others, combined with a pervasive sense of responsibility for one's actions. When these results occur, classrooms acquire a climate of respect, discipline problems decline, and academic learning and positive human relations improve. ■

Teachers want students to learn to think for themselves and deal effectively with their own problems. They typically feel they must tell students what to do and "correct" them when they fail or do the wrong thing. But that effort does not produce the results they want. The Responsible Thinking Process, on the other hand, leads to desirable outcomes because it relies *not* on threatening, directing, and correcting, but on asking key questions that help students learn (when they are willing) to look within themselves and decide how they want to be (Ford and Venetis, 2006). This, in turn, helps them learn how to make more effective plans that will, in the future, provide for them the necessary understanding of how to deal with getting what they want without violating the rights of others.

When students misbehave, the teacher intervenes by asking the following series of questions. The teacher displays a pleasant, matter-of-fact demeanor, with no sign of anger, exasperation, or disappointment:

Question 1: "What Are You Doing?"   This question should be asked first, but always in conjunction with question 2. When students hear this question, they look within themselves and identify their behavior. Telling them what they are doing wrong doesn't help them develop the skill of self-reflection. Neither do you ask them why they are behaving as they are—that only encourages students to make excuses.

Question 2: "What Are the Rules?"   When asked this question, students quickly tie the rules to what they are currently doing and assess their actions in terms of the rights of others. Questions 3, 4, and 5 follow, but as students grow in their understanding of the process, these three questions are no longer needed.

Question 3: "What Happens when You Break the Rules?"   This simply gets students to reflect on the consequences that follow when they break rules and draws attention to how their behavior is affecting others.

Question 4: "Is This What You Want to Happen?"   Now you are asking students to look within themselves and decide how they want to see themselves as persons and how they want to live their lives.

Question 5: "Where Do You Want to Be?" or "What Do You Want to Do Now?"   These questions help students come to closure concerning a plan of action that will resolve the conflict between their behavior and the rights of others.

Question 6: "What Will Happen if You Disrupt Again?"   This question should always be asked, even if students have already reflected and decided to change how they want to be. The reason for asking this question is to make sure students have a clear understanding of school procedures for those who continually disrupt, such as being sent to the Responsible Thinking Classroom where they are helped to make effective plans for resolving their problems.

The foregoing questions should never come across as warnings to students. Warnings imply possible punishment. All they should do is lead students to think about what they are doing in relation to the rules wherever they are and consider, without being prompted, whether there might be a better course of action available to them.

To help illustrate the foregoing points, Ford provides the following scenario, which has been edited and abridged from the website www.responsiblethinking.com:

Mathew, late for class, is running in the hallway. Mrs. Kuhn, a teacher adept in using the RTP questioning process, calls to Mathew in a nonthreatening tone, "Mathew, what are you doing?" She does not scold him or tell him to stop. Mathew looks at her, stops running, and replies, "I'm trying not to be late to class." (Notice Mathew explained his *goal—what he wanted to accomplish.*) Mrs. Kuhn might then ask, "What were you doing to try to get there?" Mathew would probably answer, "I was running." Mrs. Kuhn would then tie the action to the rule by asking, "What's the rule about running in the halls?" Again, the key to RTP is to teach students to think about how they are going to accomplish getting what they want without in any way violating the rights of others. Punishment, rewards, criticism, yelling, constantly correcting—none of these things teach students to think for themselves.

Later, Mrs. Kuhn might ask Mathew if he has managed to figure out a way of getting to his classes on time. If he says "no," then she might ask him if he is interested in learning a way of getting to class on time without violating any rules. If instead he were to say "yes," then she might take an interest in what he has figured out.

Ford explains that Mrs. Kuhn's approach is nonmanipulative and nonpunitive. Her questions and comments lead to Mathew's thinking through what he is doing *in relation to the rules.* Further, it predisposes him toward an action plan that respects the rights of others and gives him personal accountability for his actions. Mrs. Kuhn knows that when she discusses behavior with students, she is far more effective when asking questions than when telling students what to do. She knows that when you tell students what to do, you are doing the thinking for them. When you ask questions (especially "What you are doing?"), and they have to connect their actions to the rules of wherever they are, then the students are encouraged to reflect on their own accountability and think things through. That is the best way to help them learn responsibility.

The fundamental rule of every school, Ford says, should be this: "We do not violate the rights of others." When students are asked the first two RTP questions ("What are you doing?" "What's the rule?"), they must consult their values concerning how others ought to be treated. Ford says that people only begin to change their behavior when they seriously examine their belief systems, assess their own values and standards, and set priorities and standards. When they do so, students usually spend a moment in quiet introspection. It is then that real, permanent change can occur.

As you ask the RTP questions, you are modeling respect for students in three ways: (1) by listening to what they say without trying to control their answers or being critical, (2) by helping them focus on how their actions are breaking rules or disturbing others, and (3) by accepting what students say in response to questions that help them resolve problems *when they are ready* (Ford and Venetis, 2006).

Activities

1. Make notes of authorities' suggestions you find attractive for incorporation later into your personalized system of discipline.
2. This chapter presented contributions from a number of different authorities. Which three of those contributions will you be most likely to incorporate into your discipline system? Explain why.
3. Which two of the contributions do you find most difficult to understand and/or employ in the classroom? Explain why.
4. Rank the eight contributions in terms of value, with 1 being the highest and 8 being the lowest. Working in groups of five or so, obtain composite rankings for your group and share them with the class. Provide for exchange of ideas by allowing groups to exchange reasons for their rankings.
5. Working in pairs, practice the techniques advocated by (1) Ed Ford, (2) Stephen Covey, and (3) Haim Ginott. Arrange for selected students to demonstrate their efforts to the class as a whole.

References

Covey, R. 1989. *The 7 habits of highly effective people.* New York: Simon and Schuster.

Covey, R. 2004. *The 7 habits of highly effective people: Restoring the character ethic.* New York: Free Press.

Curwin, R. 1992. *Rediscovering hope: Our greatest teaching strategy.* Bloomington, IN: National Educational Service.

Curwin, R., and Mendler, A. 1988. *Discipline with dignity.* Alexandria, VA: Association for Supervision and Curriculum Development. Revised editions 1992, 1999, 2002. Upper Saddle River, NJ: Merrill.

Curwin, R., Mendler, A., and Mendler, B. 2008. *Discipline with dignity: New challenges, new solutions.* Alexandria, VA: ASCD.

Daly, T. 2004. *The ADHD solution for teachers: How to turn any disruptive child into your best student.* San Diego, CA: Smarty Pants Publications.

Daly, T. 2006. Eliminate disruptive behavior in your classroom forever. Free 5-part report. www.adhdsolution.com/ref/index.cfm#backgroundreturn

Ford, E. 1999. *Discipline for home and school, book two* (Rev. ed.). Scottsdale, AZ: Brandt Publishing.

Ford, E. 2003. *Discipline for home and school, book one* (3rd ed.). Scottsdale, AZ: Brandt Publishing.

Ford, E. 2004. *Discipline for home and school, fundamentals.* Scottsdale, AZ: Brandt.

Ford, E. 2006. A school discipline program that is radically different from other classroom management programs, traditional classroom discipline programs, or any school behavior management program. www.responsiblethinking.com

Ford, E., and Venetis, G. 2006. Teaching respect using RTP. www.responsiblethinking.com

Ginott, H. 1965. *Between parent and child.* New York: Macmillan.

Ginott, H. 1967. *Between parent and teenager.* New York: Macmillan.

Ginott, H. 1971. *Teacher and child.* New York: Macmillan.

Glasser, W. 2001. *Every student can succeed.* Chatsworth, CA: William Glasser.

Hingsburger, D. 2000a. *First contact.* Eastman, Quebec: Diverse City Press.

Hingsburger, D. 2000b. *Power tools.* Eastman, Quebec: Diverse City Press.

Mendler, A., and Curwin, R. 1999. *Discipline with dignity for challenging youth.* Bloomington, IN: National Education Service.

Nelsen, J., and Lott, L. 2000. *Positive discipline in the classroom.* Rocklin, CA: Prima.

13

How Do Leading Experts Engender Respect and Civility in the Classroom?

In a column in *USA Today*, Chuck Raasch (2003) made reference to a Public Agenda survey that confirmed what most teachers already knew—that lack of student courtesy and civility had become a serious problem in U.S. education. (Public Agenda is a nonprofit public interest group formed in 1975 by social scientist Daniel Yankelovich and former Secretary of State Cyrus Vance. The group regularly obtains and makes available information about matters of concern in the public domain.)

Raasch reported that the 2003 survey found 70 percent of students said disrespectful behavior was common in their schools, and 43 percent of teachers said they spent more time keeping peace in class than actually teaching. A large majority of those teachers blamed parents for not urging their children to study or behave themselves in class. Raasch referred to the finding that some kids today simply don't come to school ready to learn as a "stunning acknowledgment" (no surprise there for teachers). He said if you have seven out of 10 students complaining about behavioral problems in their classrooms, you have to believe that student misconduct is posing a significant problem in today's schools.

The report also relayed teachers' opinion that discourteous or offensive behavior, directed at both teachers and students, was increasingly damaging instruction, learning, and morale. Teachers judged that offensive behavior makes it difficult for students to form beneficial relationships with teachers and fellow students. Concern about this matter is widespread, but notable progress is being made in dealing with it.

A PREVIEW OF THIS CHAPTER

P. M. Forni, director of the Civility Initiative at Johns Hopkins University, laments the ongoing decline of civil behavior in today's classrooms and society as a whole. He provides a number of suggestions to help reverse the decline and restore civility in all aspects of life.

Michele Borba, an international authority on moral intelligence, explains how teachers can help students improve their behavior by understanding and learning to abide by the seven virtues of goodness.

Diane Gossen, an international authority on the nature, value, and application of self-restitution, explains how that process can help students make amends and strengthen themselves following behavior mistakes they make.

WHAT TO LOOK FOR IN THIS CHAPTER

■ P. M. Forni's efforts to improve the level of kind, considerate behavior in the young, in and out of school

■ Michele Borba's concept of moral intelligence and her suggestions for increasing students' levels of moral behavior and positive treatment of others

■ Diane Gossen's efforts to restore a sense of proper behavior among the young

P. M. FORNI: CIVILITY IN THE CLASSROOM

Civility is a way of behaving in which individuals show respect and consideration for others. All teachers would like to promote civil behavior in their classes, but relatively few are well-versed in how to do so. P. M. Forni has directly addressed this concern. Dr. Forni is co-founder and director of the Civility Initiative at Johns Hopkins University, which examines and promotes improvement in civility, manners, and politeness in contemporary society. Professor Forni lectures and conducts workshops on the relevance of civility to the quality of life in the classroom, the workplace, and society at large. Between 2005 and 2007 he was an on-air contributor to the syndicated radio show *The Satellite Sisters*. National and foreign publications have reported his work, including the *New York Times, Times of London, Washington Post, Wall Street Journal, Los Angeles Times,* and *Baltimore Sun.* Professor Forni has appeared on a number of radio and television shows, including ABC's *World News Tonight,* CBS's *Sunday Morning,* and *Oprah.* For additional information on Dr. Forni and the Civility Initiative, consult www.jhu.edu/civility.

Dr. Forni reports that his interest in civility began one day when he realized that his university students would profit more from learning to be kind human beings than from grappling with the works of classical Italian writers. Over time, he compiled his thoughts, experiences, and conclusions, which he has presented in his books *Choosing Civility: The Twenty-Five Rules of Considerate Conduct* (2002) and *The Civility Solution: What to Do When People Are Rude* (2008). Also well worth reading is his 2006 website article, "The Other Side of Civility."

Forni explains that civility encompasses a wide range of values and behaviors, including respect for others and their opinions, consideration, courtesy, the Golden Rule, niceness, politeness, kindness, good manners, fairness, decency, concern for others, justice, tolerance, equality, sincerity, morality, honesty, awareness, trustworthiness, moderation, compassion, friendliness, helpfulness, good citizenship, and abiding by rules.

Forni has formulated some **rules of considerate conduct** to help us understand better ways of relating to and connecting with others. He observes that the rules, which apply in all areas of human interaction, help us establish more enjoyable, companionable, and rewarding relationships with the people we meet. The following is a representative selection from Forni's rules. Each rule provides a fruitful topic for class discussions and role-playing:

- Acknowledge others.
- Think the best of others.
- Listen.
- Speak kindly.
- Accept and give praise.

- Respect others' opinions.
- Respect other people's time.
- Apologize earnestly.
- Refrain from idle complaints.

> **?** What do you think of Forni's rules of considerate conduct? If you wished to help your students follow these rules, how might you do so?

Forni (2006) points out that civility, politeness, and good manners are all things we do *for* other people. They show we consider others' needs for comfort and happiness as valid as our own. At the same time, they work to our advantage in managing our relationships with others. We are social beings, and our happiness and overall well-being depend, in large measure, on the quality of our relationships. Conducting ourselves in a kindly manner allows us to connect more meaningfully with others, and the more considerately we behave, the more likely we are to establish harmonious relationships that increase the quality of our lives.

It is well known that individuals with good relational skills tend to be more successful personally and professionally. Those who have developed the capacity for empathy have the ability to understand and respond thoughtfully to others. Those who know how to listen with compassion and grace attract others. Educators and managers are more successful when they are able to read the feelings of others. In our personal lives, these abilities make us better friends, spouses, and parents.

We all need social support. To obtain it, we must treat others with kindness and consideration, showing we value them as persons. When we do that, others usually want to remain connected to us, sometimes resulting in long continuing relationships. In the past, a large amount of the support we needed came from our extended families. Today, we are more likely to turn to friends, acquaintances, and even strangers for support and care. If we are considerate toward them, people will like and trust us; if they like and trust us, they will let us help them; and by helping them, we help ourselves. It is a powerful truth that social skills strengthen social bonds. They are, therefore, an invaluable asset in establishing quality of life.

Forni (2002) presents a number of interesting quotations that extol the virtues of civility. Among them are the following, which are useful and interesting topics for class discussion:

"Civility is key in learning how to live well with others."—P. M. Forni

"A kind word is like a spring day."—Russian proverb

"We have a choice about how we behave, and that means we have the choice to opt for civility and grace."—Dwight Currie

"The very essence of politeness seems to be to take care that by our words and actions we make other people pleased with us as well as with themselves." —Jean De La Bruyere

"Rudeness is the weak man's imitation of strength."—Eric Hoffer

"Social ties are the cheapest medicine we have."—Shelley E. Taylor

"Every action done in company ought to be with some sign of respect to those that are present."—George Washington

"Behave as if you were in heaven, where there are no third-class carriages, and one soul is as good as another."—George Bernard Shaw

"I can live for two months on a good compliment."—Mark Twain

"The idea is to attract, not to repel."—Peggy and Peter Post

"My right to swing my fist ends at your nose. My right to make noise ought to end at your ear."—Les Blomberg

"[Good manners] must be inspired by the good heart. There is no beautifier of complexion, or form, or behavior, like the wish to scatter joy and not pain around us."—Ralph Waldo Emerson

> **?** If you wanted to discuss three of the foregoing quotations with your students, which would you select, and how would you initiate the discussion?

MICHELE BORBA: DEVELOPING MORAL INTELLIGENCE

Michele Borba is a world leader in understanding and promoting **moral intelligence,** which she considers to be the essential quality in what we call *good character.* She has found that moral intelligence can be taught in school and developed with experience. As students' moral intelligence grows, their behavior improves and they become more self-directing.

Dr. Borba, a former teacher and recipient of the National Educator Award, presents addresses and workshops on moral education and other topics throughout North America, Europe, Asia, and the South Pacific. She writes for a number of popular publications, appears regularly on TV talk shows and National Public Radio, and is the author of 21 books, including *Building Moral Intelligence,* cited by *Publishers' Weekly* as "among the most noteworthy of 2001," and *Parents Do Make a Difference,* selected by *Child Magazine* as Outstanding Parenting Book of 1999. She has also authored *Nobody Likes Me, Everybody Hates Me: The Top 25 Friendship Problems and How to Solve Them* (2005). Information on her publications and seminars can be accessed through her website at www.micheleborba.com.

The Role of Moral Intelligence in Classroom Discipline

Borba believes the schools offer one of the last bastions of hope for developing sound character in our young. She says there are few other places where children can learn the value of responsibility, caring, respect, and cooperation and observe adults displaying those traits consistently. Borba believes good discipline depends on teachers' creating a moral learning community in the classroom, where students feel safe and cared about. In such communities, teachers are better able to connect with students, show care for them, and model the core traits of solid character. Without such a community, she says, no approach to discipline is going to work well.

Borba (2003, 2004) emphasizes that if students persistently misbehave in school, their character invariably diminishes. Teachers should therefore target and address the specific behaviors that damage respectful classrooms and student character—behaviors such as vulgarity, cruelty, bullying, and disrespect. Teachers must help students replace those negative behaviors with positive ones by teaching the desired behaviors explicitly and having students practice them. When students misbehave, teachers should involve them in *responding, reviewing, reflecting,* and *making right.*

To illustrate, suppose Eddie and Juan get in a fight just outside the classroom. The teacher stops them and quickly does the following:

1. *Respond.* Ask Eddie and Juan to tell you what happened. Ask them, "Why did you do it?" "What did you think this would accomplish?" Stay calm and listen to what they say.

2. *Review.* Have Eddie and Juan think about what they have done. Ask them questions such as, "Why do you think I am speaking with you now?" and "What are the rules in class?" Help them review the rules, if necessary. Tell them again, "Fighting is not allowed in this class." "We don't solve our problems by fighting."

3. *Reflect.* Ask questions that cause Eddie and Juan to think about the effects of their behavior, such as: "How do you make each other feel when you fight?" "What do you believe others think of you?" "Do you want to think of yourself as a person who tries to solve problems by fighting, or do you want to think of yourself as someone who can reason things out?" Ask questions that guide each student to empathize with or gain the perspective of the other: "How do you think Juan feels now?" "If you were in his shoes, what do you think he'd like to say to you about what happened?"

4. *Make right.* Help the boys think about atoning for wrongs by making reparation that consists of more than an apology and a promise not to fight again. For example, ask the boys if they would be willing to work together to make a chart for the class that lists alternatives to fighting.

Borba explains that for this intervention process to work successfully, it must be used repeatedly because it builds character over time, rather than providing a quick fix to get through the moment. Both teacher and class must get used to it. Patience is required, and teachers must persist in giving help over and over while tolerating repeated mistakes. They must do this seriously but pleasantly, never showing exasperation and never putting students down. When they do so, students begin to like and trust them.

The Seven Virtues of Goodness

Borba (2001) also urges teachers to teach their students about the seven **essential virtues** of goodness—virtues that are universally accepted by all societies. She identifies those virtues and believes attention to them will help students behave properly and resist pressures that damage their character. The virtues are empathy, conscience, self-control, respect, kindness, tolerance, and fairness. Here is what she has to say about them.

1. *Empathy* is the capacity to relate to the feelings of others. Without empathy, moral intelligence cannot develop fully. A number of societal factors now hinder development of empathy in the young, such as parents who are absent or emotionally unavailable to children, an overabundance of media images of suffering that dull sensitivity, and abuse of children by peers and adults. To counteract these negative influences, Borba urges teachers to do the following:

- Develop caring relationships with students, listen to them with empathy, help them develop stronger emotional vocabularies (words that express feelings), and tell them stories or present scenarios that promote empathetic reaction.
- Create and maintain a caring learning environment.
- Use discipline techniques based on empathy for how students feel.

She also asks teachers to help students become perceptive of others by doing the following:

- Notice when people are hurting. Mirror the facial expressions and try to experience a bit of what they feel.
- Try to console or comfort others who are in pain.

2. *Conscience* refers to the ability to sense the rightness or wrongness of one's actions. Borba points to a decline of conscience in the world today, evident in the rise in youth violence, peer cruelty, stealing, cheating, sexual promiscuity, and substance abuse. She suggests a number of classroom conditions and activities that can help reverse the decline in public and individual conscience, including the following:

- Setting clear class expectations and standards based on the seven virtues
- Creating a context for moral growth, featuring good modeling by the teacher
- Teaching, cultivating, and reinforcing virtues that strengthen conscience and provide a guide for desired behavior
- Increasing students' moral reasoning by having them analyze moral dilemmas presented in context (e.g., historical, scientific, or literary issues; current events; peer interactions)

3. *Self-control* refers to the ability to restrict oneself to behavior that is proper, even when faced with the strong temptation to do otherwise. Borba says self-control is declining due to (1) parents who are overworked and stressed out; (2) child abuse and trauma; (3) glorification of out-of-control behavior in entertainment; and (4) reliance on chemical mollification in place of self-constraint. Borba suggests a number of things that teachers can do to help students develop self-control:

- Give priority to and model personal self-control.
- Encourage students to become their own internal motivators by seeking to do the right thing when met with temptation.
- Show specific ways to control urges and think before acting, including self-control in stress situations, anger management, and the three-part formula of *Think, Stop, Act Right.*

4. *Respect* means showing acceptance and tolerance of others. Respect is declining in most segments of society, as shown by the increase in vulgarity, failure to abide by the Golden Rule, disregard for authority, and lowered willingness to attend to the needs of children. Borba makes a number of suggestions for class activities to increase respect.

- Discuss, model, and teach the differences between respect and disrespect.
- Act respectfully toward students and talk regularly with them about the meaning and practice of respect.
- Target disrespect, rudeness, sassiness, back talk, whining, and vulgarity among students. Teach respectful replacement behaviors.
- Emphasize and expect the good manners and courtesy that enable students to function productively in society. Teach students to say *please* and *thank you*, and otherwise increase their repertoire of respectful behaviors.
- Involve peers in creating a respectful learning environment and reinforcing each other's respectful behaviors.

5. *Kindness* is showing consideration for the well-being of others. The decline in displays of kindness in today's world is due to factors such as lack of good modeling by parents and adults, lack of encouragement for children to behave with kindness, influence of unkind peers, and general desensitization to kindness. To improve this condition, Borba would have teachers do the following:

- Teach the meaning and value of kindness, help students understand that kindness begins with them, and explicitly teach what kind behaviors look and sound like. Ask students to behave with kindness in all situations. Point out observed behavior that shows kindness and ask students to take note of the effect it has on others.
- Establish zero tolerance for cruel, hurtful behavior at school. Put in place specific, spelled-out procedures to stop bullying.
- Provide meaningful activities for students to experience and practice being kind. Ask students to perform random acts of kindness without expecting anything in return.

6. *Tolerance* is showing acceptance for the conditions and behaviors of others. It is declining in society because of a lack of moral monitoring of the young, accessibility of Internet hate sites, racially charged video entertainment aimed at youth, hate music, and stereotypes displayed on television and in motion pictures. To counter this decline, Borba offers these suggestions:

- Model and teach about tolerance.
- Draw attention to and discourage intolerant comments and practices.
- Emphasize the positive aspects of diversity.
- Have students focus on what they have in common with others, not on their differences.

7. *Fairness* is treating others evenhandedly without showing partiality. Today, a sense of fairness is declining because of a breakdown of role models and an overemphasis on competition, so that winning at any cost becomes paramount.

This crisis can be countered by teachers who unfailingly demonstrate and discuss fairness with students, avoid making comparisons among students, help students show respect for their competitors, play by the rules, and limit the all-too-strong emphasis on winning.

Manners in Character Development

In addition to the virtues and ways of teaching them that Borba advocates, she devotes considerable attention to manners, listing and describing "Eighty-Five Important Manners Kids Should Learn" (2001, pp. 152–153). She suggests teaching and practicing these manners in the classroom on a regular basis. Here are a few examples.

- *Essential polite words.* Says *please, thank you, excuse me, I'm sorry, may I?, pardon me, you're welcome*
- *Meeting and greeting others.* Smiles and looks at the person, shakes hands, says *hello*, introduces self, introduces another person
- *Conversation manners.* Starts a conversation, listens without interrupting, uses a pleasant tone of voice, knows how to begin and end a conversation
- *Sports manners.* Plays by the rules, shares equipment, provides encouragement, doesn't brag or show off, doesn't argue with referee, congratulates opponents, doesn't complain or make excuses, cooperates
- *Anywhere and anytime.* Doesn't swear, doesn't belch, doesn't gossip, covers mouth when coughing

Borba presents a number of other suggestions associated with hospitality, table manners, visiting manners, telephone manners, and manners toward older people.

? What do you think of the examples of Borba's "important manners kids should learn"? Which of those listed here could most easily be taught directly to students? If you wished to make them a part of your instructional program, how might you do so?

DIANE GOSSEN: SELF-RESTITUTION IN DISCIPLINE

Self-restitution is a process in which students who have behaved inappropriately (1) reflect on their misbehavior, (2) identify the need or condition that prompted it, and (3) create new ways of behaving that are *in keeping with the kinds of persons they want to be.* This process does not dwell on faults or mistakes, but instead helps students learn how to make things right *within themselves* and with whomever they have offended or whatever they have damaged. The process accomplishes two things that are very important in self-discipline and getting along with others—first, it helps students learn to conduct themselves in harmony with their needs and inner sense of morality, and second, it helps students deal

Go to the Building Classroom Discipline Video Showcase section of Topic #3: Models of Classroom Management, in the **MyEducationLab** for your course and watch the video entitled "Diane Gossen—Discipline through Self-Restitution."

with their behavior shortcomings while committing themselves genuinely to better behavior in the future.

The self-restitution approach to dealing with misbehavior was formulated by Diane Chelsom Gossen, author of *Restitution: Restructuring School Discipline* (1992) and *It's All about We: Rethinking Discipline Using Restitution* (2004). Gossen has worked on Restitution Theory with hundreds of school systems in Canada, the United States, and elsewhere in the world. She has received the YWCA Women of Distinction Award in the Lifetime Achievement category. She served as creative consultant to the award-winning video series on classroom management, *Monday— Marbles and Chalk*, and was featured in the *Journal of Education*'s video entitled *Dealing with Disruptive and Unresponsive Students*. She taught school in Canada and elsewhere for several years, has held faculty positions at two Canadian universities, and for 25 years was a senior faculty member of the Institute for Reality Therapy. Gossen is also author of *Creating the Conditions: Leadership for Quality Schools* (1995, with Judy Anderson). Gossen's website is www.realrestitution.com.

Gossen's Principal Teachings

Gossen says the reward–punish approach to discipline fails for two reasons—it discourages students from reflecting on their personal behavior and it promotes no growth in moral and emotional intelligence. She warns that any system of learning that makes use of heavy authority, threats, rules, punishments, or rewards will, over the long run, only perpetuate the behaviors we are trying to eliminate.

The most effective approach to discipline, she believes, involves self-restitution, a process by which offenders restore themselves, leading to an increased sense of personal responsibility inside and outside the classroom. She credits some of the fundamental concepts in her program to child-rearing practices found among Canadian aboriginal families—practices rooted in internal self-discipline. The restitution process does the following (Gossen, 2004): It provides a means for dealing with root causes of problems and provides a genuine avenue to becoming a better person. It meets the needs of the offended person, but more importantly it is restorative, healing, and thus transformational to the offender. It focuses on solutions and restores and strengthens relationships. It is set in motion through teacher invitation, rather than coercion. It teaches persons who offend to look inside themselves, identify the need that prompts the problematic behavior, visualize the kind of person they want to be, and take action to become more like the person they visualize. It creates solutions to problems and creates conditions for individuals who offend others to repair mistakes and return to the group as stronger persons.

The **Restitution Triangle** in Figure 13.1 illustrates this process. Gossen explains how the Restitution Triangle is used: Beginning at the base of the triangle, the first step is to *stabilize* the offending student by removing fear or anger so learning can take place. This is done by saying things to the student such as "It's okay to make a mistake. You are not the only one. We can solve this problem together."

The next step is illustrated on side 2 (left side) of the triangle. Here we help students understand that people always do things for a reason and usually they are doing the best they know how under the circumstances. To help the student see that the behavior was not the worst possible choice, we ask questions such as "Is there

Figure 13.1   The Restitution Triangle

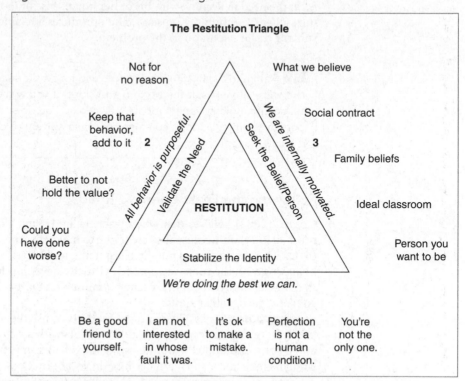

The Restitution Triangle

Not for
no reason

What we believe

Keep that
behavior,
add to it   **2**

Social contract

Validate the Need

Seek the Belief/Person

All behavior is purposeful.

We are internally motivated.

Better to not
hold the value?

Family beliefs

RESTITUTION

3

Could you
have done
worse?

Ideal classroom

Stabilize the Identity

Person you
want to be

We're doing the best we can.

1

| Be a good friend to yourself. | I am not interested in whose fault it was. | It's ok to make a mistake. | Perfection is not a human condition. | You're not the only one. |

Source: Adapted from Gossen, D. 2004. *It's All about We: Rethinking Discipline Using Restitution* (p. 86). Saskatoon, Saskatchewan: Chelsom Consultants. Reprinted by permission.

a worse thing you could have done? Why would that have been worse?" This helps students see their behavior was not as bad as it might have been, and it lifts their guilt so they can think. Then we explain that most behavior occurs when a person feels a need that is not being met. (Previous class discussions have identified needs that often precipitate behavior, such as the need for safety from threat, sense of belonging as a member of the class, love or esteem from others, having fun, a sense of freedom, or having some control over our lives.) We review the list of needs and ask, "Do you think one of those needs might have led you to do what you did?" The student is given time to reflect and reply.

Then we move to the right side of the triangle, where we encourage the student to tap into more ideal pictures of behavior, with comments or questions such as "Think about the kind of person you want to be. What do you and your family believe, as concerns (this problem)? What is our class agreement about this matter?" These questions and comments are always made in a calm tone, never in a confrontational or guilt-producing manner. The student is stimulated to reflect on the behavior and judge it against the image of the person he or she would like to be. The restitution process stabilizes the self-identity of the offending student, validates the behavior as related to a genuine need, and helps the student identify a way to meet the need in keeping with his or her inner sense of morality. It does not shame the student, but brings a sense of relief, produces a feeling of hope, and helps the student create a solution to the problem.

> **?** Return to the Restitution Triangle and follow the sequence it advocates, as shown by numerals at the bottom and sides. If you wished to explain the Restitution Triangle to your students, how would you do so? Practice with another person or simply address comments to an imaginary student who has offended a fellow student.

Following the Least Coercive Road

Gossen (2002) believes that when teachers are having a difficult job in the classroom, it is usually because they are trying to make students do what they don't want to do. Because students naturally resist being made to do anything (as opposed to being enticed), the coercive approach virtually never produces a true inner change in behavior. Moreover, it is extremely draining on teachers, leaving them disheartened, fatigued, and anxious.

For those reasons, Gossen urges teachers to use the least amount of coercion possible, relying instead on engaging students with a rich classroom environment and a curriculum filled with interesting knowledge and enjoyable activities. There, students participate and learn because they want to. Gossen refers to this approach as using the **least coercive road.** The approach is established in discussions with students at the beginning of the year or term. These discussions proceed through four phases: (1) opening up the territory, (2) establishing the social contract, (3) establishing limits, and (4) teaching students how to make self-restitution. The following paragraphs briefly explain these four phases.

Phase 1: Opening up the Territory—Maximizing Freedom

The first step in reducing the level of coercion in the classroom is to reduce the number of interventions you make into students' behavior. Reducing interventions "opens up the territory" so that students have more freedom to explore options, make choices, and learn from the process, which leads toward responsible behavior. Reducing interventions does not mean adopting a permissive approach to teaching. Rather, it encourages teachers to identify and address only what they believe to be truly important in class behavior. Two questions that help open up the territory are (1) "Does it really matter?" and (2) "Yes, if . . ."

Does It Really Matter?   If we find ourselves continually trying to control students, we should ask ourselves, "Does what they are doing really matter?" For example: Does it really matter if he sits with his feet on the floor? She chews gum? Everyone is silent when working? She does her homework? Two students want to exchange seats? Students do not write neatly? He is tardy to class? She hands in assignments late? Students raise their hands before speaking?

Some of these behaviors will be unacceptable to teachers, while others, on reflection, will not seem so important. Gossen says we should not intervene in any of these behaviors unless we can give students a plausible reason for doing so. She says teachers can decide if a behavior really matters by asking themselves the following questions:

- What are my personal and professional beliefs about this sort of behavior?
- What do I believe about how learning occurs?
- How would I like my students to behave long after they have left my class?

Gossen suggests strong limits only on behaviors that pertain to safety, proper function of the class, and other matters about which we have especially strong convictions.

> **?** You might recognize that Gossen's advice concerning maximizing freedom is directly opposite to that given by authorities such as Ronald Morrish and Craig Seganti, both of whom would have you address small misbehaviors to keep them from escalating into more serious ones. In this regard, whose advice do you find more persuasive, and why?

Yes, If . . . When you find yourself too frequently responding to student requests with a "no" or "no, because . . . " consider changing to a positive response that guides the student toward desirable behavior. Suppose a student asks, "Can I sharpen my pencil?" Your normal reply is, "No, because I am talking." A better alternative would be to say, "Yes, if you will wait until I finish my directions." Gossen makes a point of saying *yes* as often as possible. When *no* is the response you need to give, provide a reason and stick to it. Other examples Gossen (1992, p. 79) provides include:

May we listen to the radio?
Instead of: No, because it would be too distracting.
Change to: Yes, if it doesn't bother anyone who is trying to work.

May I go to the bathroom?
Instead of: No, because then everyone will ask to go.
Change to: Yes, if you wait until I've finished my instruction and only one person goes at a time.

Phase 2: Establishing the Social Contract and Building a Sense of Belonging

As you open up the territory, invite and encourage students to work with you to establish a class where learning occurs enjoyably and students are kind to each other. This collaborative effort leads to a *social contract* between you and your students concerning how to be effective members of the group. Virtually all students want to be part of the group, and they easily understand that the class functions better when everyone pulls together. Gossen suggests helping students visualize "internal pictures" in which they get their needs met without interfering with the needs of others. Discussions should focus on two matters: (1) what the class believes in (the group values and beliefs) and (2) establishing class agreements (a social contract) concerning acceptable class goals and the behavior that helps achieve them. Discussions centered on these two issues increase involvement between teacher and students and begin to shift part of the burden for responsible behavior from the teacher to the students.

What We Believe In.   Class members should spend time exploring and discussing their beliefs regarding the kind of person they want to be, individually and as a member of the group. You can begin this process by asking students to think, draw, or write about the kind of friend, student, team member, or individual they want to be. You might ask them to think about a relative or friend they greatly admire and specify what that person does that they appreciate. After allowing them to discuss their ideas, you could next ask them to think about the kind of class they would like to be, including how they would like to work together, conduct themselves, help each other, and enjoy their experience.

The Social Contract.   The foregoing activities will produce a list of qualities the students agree on. Point out that the qualities indicate the values students hold, or what they believe in, then ask them how they think the class could be conducted so they would experience the qualities they have identified. As the students reflect further, ask them if they can suggest ways of conducting themselves that will support the values they have identified—that is, how they can behave in order to enjoy the kind of class they have envisioned. This leads to agreements concerning desirable and undesirable behavior, which can then be formalized as the class social contract.

Phase 3: Establishing Limits and Clarifying Personal Power

Membership in a group requires that individuals give up some personal freedom in exchange for the benefits of group membership. Students need to recognize this fact, along with the duties that accompany membership in social relationships, such as the duty to manage oneself in a manner that does not prevent others from meeting their needs. Each of us wants predictability, enjoyment, and a degree of power in the class. These qualities can be supported through class agreements and individual responsibility, coupled with a bottom line beyond which offensive behavior will not be tolerated.

When the social contract has been established, students inevitably ask, "What if somebody doesn't do what we have agreed to?" In response to that question, we should ask, "What do we believe about this?" When answers are received, we ask,

- "Do you believe it?"
- "If you believe it, do you want to fix it?"
- "If you decide to fix it, what does it say about who you are becoming?"

If a student declines to participate in this process, we draw attention to the class rules and request behavior that complies with them. If that still doesn't work, then we explain that all school personnel have the right, in issues of safety or learning, to restrict the freedom of the offending individual in accordance with schoolwide rules, but we would rather solve the matter in a way that is beneficial to all concerned.

The resulting understandings, guidelines, and limits bring about a shift in student responsibility. As students assume a portion of the load and accept their responsibilities, the class begins to function with more civility and fewer disruptions.

My Job, Your Job.   To strengthen teachers' and students' convictions about how they should function in the class, Gossen suggests specifying the expected roles or jobs of teacher and students. These role expectations should be clarified through teacher–student discussions, with examples that indicate what *is* and is *not* expected of each. This helps students understand who is responsible for what. Originally, Gossen depicted "my job, your job" as shown in Figure 13.2. When students interfere with a job to be done, it is suggested that the teacher ask, "What's the rule?" or "What's your job?" Doing so moves attention from the problem to the solution and avoids debate and excuses. If the student doesn't know the rule or won't say it, state it yourself and ask, "Can you do that?" When the student complies, say, "Thank you, I appreciate it." This type of exchange involves monitoring and redirection of behavior, and is vastly preferable to lecturing or moralizing.

Gossen reports that the "my job, your job" has resonated strongly with teachers, but she believes we also need to explain to students *why* we hold those expectations. It is not reasonable to expect students to support a plan that conflicts with their needs or beliefs. Accordingly, Gossen restated this plan to cause teachers to think in terms of "teacher I want to be" while asking students to think in terms of "student I want to be," as shown in Figure 13.3. These are ideal pictures that go beyond the original "my job," which tended to promote compliance rather than self-analysis and self-direction.

Figure 13.2   My Job/Your Job

My Job Is to . . .	Your Job Is to . . .
Teach	Learn
Answer questions	Ask if you don't understand
Explain different ways	Keep on trying
Go at a pace you can learn	Tell teacher if the pace is too fast
Manage the class	Follow the rules
Enforce rules	Communicate needs
Care	Listen to teacher and other school people
My Job Is *Not* to . . .	**Your Job Is *Not* to . . .**
Take abuse	Do the teacher's job
Baby-sit	Decide for another student
Do students' jobs or work	Discipline other students

Source: Adapted from Gossen, D. 1992. *Restitution: Restructuring School Discipline* (p. 85). Chapel Hill, NC: New View Publications. Reprinted by permission.

Enforcing the Bottom Line.   Teachers are usually expected to apply sanctions for student tardiness, incomplete work, and antisocial behaviors. Usually, we can prevent students from crossing the bottom line by redirecting their attention to role expectations as described above. If our efforts fail, however, and a student still goes beyond the bottom line, we should unemotionally apply the consequences specified in the class rules. We have to accept that a student may decide not to be cooperative or not to learn. We can't change their internal decision. We can only say what we will do if they take this route, while emphasizing that we will do what we can to help them behave more responsibly.

Phase 4: Restitution—Making Things Right and Healing Oneself

While we teachers must enforce bottom-line agreements, what we truly want is improved student behavior based on inner self-control. That goal can be achieved more easily through restitution than through coercion. Self-restitution always takes two things into account—making amends to the victim and helping offenders heal themselves. Forgiveness plays no part in this approach. Gossen points to an important difference in the effects that accrue from restitution versus forgiveness. Forgiveness is bestowed on the offender and offers relief, but it does not build character in the offender. Restitution does build character because it asks of students, "What are you going to do to fix what was done wrong, and how are you going to become more like the person you want to be? Think about it."

Restitution has power to repair an immediate wrong and lead to improved behavior in the future. It stabilizes the offending person with the reassurance it is all right to make a mistake. It meets the needs of the person who is offended, as well as the person who has offended. It strengthens the offender's skills of self-control and humane treatment of others. Teachers, in their role as managers of restitu-

Figure 13.3   Teacher I Want to Be/Student I Want to Be

Teacher I Want to Be	Student I Want to Be
Asks, "How can I best teach you?"	Learns new things and thinks for self
Says and believes, "It's okay to make a mistake—that is how we learn"	Learns self-restitution
Talks about needs of teacher and students	Identifies own needs and recognizes those of others
Models self-restitution and uses the Restitution Triangle	Has fun learning
Seeks to understand others	Thinks about the ideal person to be
Has fun teaching	Helps make and maintain a social contract with the class
Teacher I Don't Want to Be	**Student I Don't Want to Be**
Tells you what to think	Tells you what I think you want to hear
Does your work for you	Says "sorry" just to get off the hook
Criticizes or shames you	Watches the clock

Source: Adapted from Gossen, D. (2004). *It's All about We: Rethinking Discipline Using Restitution* (p. 72). Saskatoon, Saskatchewan: Chelsom Consultants.

tion, ask misbehaving students to work with them to invent solutions to behavior problems. They do not punish or coerce, nor do they remove offending students from the group. Instead, they help them remain in the group with strengthened capability.

Earlier we noted that the restitution process often asks students questions such as "What do we believe?" "Do you believe it?" "If you believe it, do you want to fix it?" "If you fix it, what does it say about you?" When teachers put these questions to offending students, the teachers should say, "No need to answer me. But do answer yourself. We can't change our lives unless there is honesty within." Let the student have time to reflect on these questions. In this manner you do something *with* the student, rather than *to* the student, thus allowing the student to take responsibility for the behavior and correct the causes behind it.

The process of restitution cannot be rushed—students need time to reflect. You can tell it is working when students become able to describe their behavior, evaluate it, make choices related to it, and come up with plans that benefit themselves as well as those they have offended.

To examine other frequently asked questions about restitution and Gossen's replies to them, consult her website at www.realrestitution.com.

Summary Rubric

APPLYING FORNI, BORBA, AND GOSSEN'S SUGGESTIONS IN THE CLASSROOM

- Organize your way of thinking and working with students to emphasize that civility, politeness, and good manners enable us to relate better with others and feel better about ourselves. Explain that civility and manners are things we do *for* other people to make them feel more comfortable and more inclined to associate with us. In turn, we usually benefit from that association.

- Make character building a central part of your discipline system and include it in your curriculum. Establish a moral learning community where students feel safe, respected, and cared about. Discuss the concepts with students and have them practice associated behaviors. Make yourself a living example of solid character for your students.

- Establish a social contract with your class that specifies what the class believes in. Use that contract as the foundation of your discipline system.

- Clarify teacher and student roles in the classroom and expect teachers and students to take responsibility for the roles that apply to them.

- When students misbehave, remind them of class expectations. Ask if they are being the kind of people they want to be. Ask what they plan to do to improve their behavior. Keep students accountable for their behavior so they recognize they have choices over their actions and that actions have consequences.

- Use self-restitution in the more serious instances of classroom misbehavior, as a means of helping students strengthen themselves while making amends to those they have offended.

Terms and Concepts

civility
essential virtues
least coercive road
moral intelligence

Restitution Triangle
rules of considerate conduct
self-restitution

Activities

1. Write notes in your journal concerning ideas from Forni, Borba, and Gossen that you might want to include in your personal system of discipline.
2. By yourself or with others, see if you can combine Forni's civility, Borba's moral intelligence, and Gossen's restitution into a unified approach to class discipline. Share your conclusions with the class.
3. To what extent do you believe Forni's, Borba's, and Gossen's suggestions would work in a class of unruly teenagers? Discuss with class members.

References

Borba, M. 1999. *Parents do make a difference: How to raise kids with solid character, strong minds, and caring hearts.* San Francisco: Jossey-Bass.

Borba, M. 2001. *Building moral intelligence: The seven essential virtues that teach kids to do the right thing.* San Francisco: Jossey-Bass.

Borba, M. 2003. *No more misbehavin': 38 difficult behaviors and how to stop them.* San Francisco. Jossey-Bass.

Borba, M. 2004. *Don't give me that attitude! 24 rude, selfish, insensitive things kids do and how to stop them.* San Francisco: Jossey-Bass.

Borba, M. 2005. *Nobody likes me: everybody hates me: The top 25 friendship problems and how to solve them.* San Francisco: Jossey-Bass.

Forni, P. 2002. *Choosing civility: The twenty-five rules of considerate conduct.* New York: St. Martin's Press.

Forni, P. 2006. The other side of civility. www.jhu.edu

Forni, P. 2008. *The civility solution: What to do when people are rude.* New York: St. Martin's Press.

Gossen, D. 1992. *Restitution: Restructuring school discipline.* Chapel Hill, NC: New View Publications.

Gossen, D. 2002. What do you want? Student behavior. *yA! Magazine for Middle Level Educators, 3*(3), 1–5.

Gossen, D. 2004. *It's all about we: Rethinking discipline using restitution.* Saskatoon, Saskatchewan: Chelsom Consultants.

Gossen, D., and Anderson, J. 1995. *Creating the conditions: Leadership for quality schools.* Chapel Hill, NC: New View Publications.

Raasch, C. 2003. Teachers, parents, outside world are key to classroom civility. *USA Today Online.* www.usatoday.com/news/opinion/columnist/raasch/2003-08-23-raasch_x.htm

14

How Do C. M. Charles and Others Energize Their Classes?

Think back for just a moment on your experiences as a student and try to remember two classes in particular—the most satisfying you can remember, and the least satisfying. Before reading ahead, take a moment to see if you can pinpoint two or three qualities that separated the most satisfying from the least satisfying.

If you are like most people, you probably remember your satisfying class as doing two things: (1) It taught you something you enjoyed or wanted or needed to know, and (2) it did so within an ambience of cooperative goodwill and camaraderie. As for your least satisfying class, you may or may not remember much of what you were supposed to learn, but the impression you retain is probably a dispiriting sense of boredom, uneasiness, or dread.

This chapter has to do with how one organizes classes in which students learn and enjoy themselves while doing so. The benefits of learning with enjoyment are enormous and accrue equally to students and teachers. The greatest pleasure in learning involves acquiring important knowledge and skills through enjoyable experiences. The greatest pleasure in teaching comes from working with students who conduct themselves responsibly and are courteous, helpful, and eager to learn. We know a good deal about bringing these qualities of valuable learning, enjoyment, and courtesy together in the classroom to produce an effect that energizes both students and teachers. The energizing phenomenon is called **synergy**, which often occurs when two or more entities (objects, conditions, or people) are brought together and begin feeding physical or psychic energy to each other. The dynamics are analogous to smoldering logs that, when placed near each other, exchange sufficient heat that both burst into flame.

C. M. Charles, in his book *The Synergetic Classroom: Joyful Teaching and Gentle Discipline* (2000), reflects on the nature and value of synergy in the classroom and how it can be called forth. He identifies synergy as a powerful contributor to making classroom experiences truly satisfying. At school, the synergetic effect is usually most evident in athletic competitions, dramatic productions, and certain activities aimed at achieving a particular purpose, especially if the results are to be recognized by others. In such efforts, teachers and students have a personal stake in what they accomplish and thus are eager to work together. Sense of purpose and cooperation combine to foster creativity and high productivity. The joint effort and its results can leave a sense of satisfaction that endures over time. (Incidentally, as synergy increases, discipline problems usually fade away.)

Charles became aware of the synergetic effect early in his career as a science teacher and athletic coach. Later, as a professor of teacher education, he was able to instill it in innovative programs of teacher education at the credential and graduate levels. Charles has held faculty appointments at the University of New Mexico, Teachers College Columbia University, Pepperdine University, Universidade do Maranhao (Brazil), and San Diego State University, where he is now professor emeritus. He has received five outstanding professor and distinguished teaching awards and served on numerous occasions as advisor in teacher education and curriculum to the governments of Peru and Brazil. He has authored more than 20 books that have attracted wide audiences internationally, with translations into several foreign languages.

A PREVIEW OF THIS CHAPTER

Synergy, a heightened sense of energy that occurs when two or more entities feed energy to each other, often engenders excitement about learning and working with others. You can employ certain factors to increase the energy levels in classes, when it is desirable to do so—among the most effective are compelling topics of instruction, teacher charisma, sensitivity to student needs and wants, and cooperative learning. The Internet provides bountiful advice from teachers concerning topics and activities to which students respond enthusiastically. Five examples are described in this chapter.

WHAT TO LOOK FOR IN THIS CHAPTER

- The nature of classroom synergy and the valuable effects it produces
- Factors that tend to increase levels of synergy in the classroom
- How you can change the levels of synergy to suit class needs
- Selected activities certain teachers use to increase student energy and participation

ESTABLISHING SYNERGETIC TEACHING AND DISCIPLINE IN THE CLASSROOM

Synergetic teaching is an approach that energizes classrooms and makes them more productive and enjoyable. **Synergetic discipline** is the behavior management component of synergetic teaching. It minimizes causes of misbehavior, minimizes mistakes teachers sometimes make in relating with students, and redirects students in positive directions when they misbehave. Synergetic teaching and discipline are

Go to the Building Classroom Discipline Video Showcase section of Topic #3: Models of Classroom Management, in the **MyEducationLab** for your course and watch the video entitled "C. M. Charles—Synergetic Discipline."

compatible with Douglas McGregor's Theory Y of personnel management. As noted in Chapter 10, McGregor contrasted two theories of management—Theory X and Theory Y. Theory X, he said, holds that people dislike work, try to avoid it, and must be directed, coerced, controlled, or threatened with punishment before they will do their work. Theory Y, in contrast, holds that people will work gladly if their jobs bring satisfaction and will exercise self-direction, self-control, and personal responsibility in doing so. McGregor's theories referred to employees in the workplace, but they apply equally to students in school.

Synergetic teaching increases the level of energy in the classroom by involving students in activities they enjoy. Synergy is not important in all activities, especially those that call for calm reflection. But when you feel a higher energy level is desirable, the following suggestions will help you achieve it. The suggestions related to student likes and dislikes are credited in part to Steve Biddulph (1997), Cynthia Mee (1997), and Jean Piaget (2001). Suggestions related to quality in curriculum and teaching are credited in part to William Glasser (2001), and those related to classroom procedures are credited in part to Harry and Rosemary Wong (2007). A number of experienced teachers and administrators also contributed suggestions.

Explain Your Ideas and Invite Cooperation

Sincerely invite your students to work with you in maintaining an interesting, inviting program for learning that is free from fear and based on personal dignity and consideration for others. Share with students your ideas for making the class more enjoyable and productive. Identify your role and their role in the approach. Ask students for input on topics and class activities they find especially appealing. Discuss teacher and student behavior that will be most effective in supporting the program envisioned. Make a list of those behaviors, post them in the class, and conduct practice sessions if necessary to acclimate students to them.

Discuss Student Needs and Take Them into Account in All Activities

Briefly discuss with your class the predominant needs we all share. Go through the following list of needs, emphasizing to students you will be continually mindful of them:

- *Security,* a sense of safety without worry
- *Hope,* the belief that school is worthwhile and success is possible
- *Personal dignity,* feeling respected and worthwhile
- *Belonging,* feeling a part of things, being valued, having a place in the class
- *Power,* having some control of and input into events in the class
- *Enjoyment,* finding pleasure in activities that are stimulating or rewarding
- *Competence,* becoming able to do many things well, including the expected schoolwork

Point out that both students and teachers become uncomfortable when their needs are not being met, and that enjoyment, learning, and effort decline accordingly. Reiterate that you will do your best to ensure everyone's needs are being met in the class.

Emphasize Class Conditions and Activities Students Are Known to Appreciate

Describe what you will do to promote the following qualities in the classroom:

- A teacher who is friendly, interesting, helpful, and supportive
- Camaraderie, or enjoyable associations among members of the class
- Interesting, worthwhile topics to learn about
- Student understanding of the importance of what they are asked to learn
- Opportunity for and likelihood of success and accomplishment
- Attention drawn tactfully to student accomplishments

Also discuss with students some of the things they normally dislike in school and indicate that you will guard against them. Examples include the following:

- Sitting still for long periods
- Keeping quiet for long periods
- Working alone
- Not knowing why something is being taught or learned
- Memorizing facts for tests
- Completing lengthy reading or writing assignments
- Doing repetitive work
- Completing long reading assignments
- Engaging in individual competition where there is little or no chance of winning

Note, however, that some students do not object to all of these activities or conditions—ask their opinions about them and if they can see situations in which some of these conditions might be desirable.

Work to Develop Class Ethics and Trust

Ethics refers to doing what one believes to be the correct and honorable thing in all situations. Ethical student behavior should be emphasized in education, and ethical teacher behavior, needed as a model for students to emulate, is essential for building trust in the class. Students see teachers as ethical and trustworthy if they are invariably kind, considerate, helpful, fair, and tactfully honest. Trust helps teachers and students count on each other for support and fair treatment.

Emphasize and Use Your Personal Charisma

As mentioned earlier, charisma is an aspect of one's personality that others find attractive. It seems to be a blend of talent, experience, personality, and knowledge. Students like charismatic teachers, and teachers like charismatic students. We can all increase our level of charisma and display it through personal charm, friendliness, enthusiasm, and helpfulness.

Improve the Quality of Communication in Your Classroom

Except for trust, no component of human synergy is more important than communication. The type of communication that contributes most in school is verbal give-and-take between teacher and students. It involves listening sensitively, showing genuine interest, and speaking encouragingly, rather than arguing, moralizing, or giving unsolicited advice.

Make Use of Coopetition

Coopetition, pronounced *co-opetition*, refers to members of groups cooperating together in order to compete against other groups. Coopetition is not given a great deal of direct attention in teaching, but it contributes powerfully to synergy. In school, it is exemplified in team athletic events and other performances and competitions. It can be incorporated into almost all areas of the curriculum. Generally speaking, students respond to it enthusiastically.

Resolve Class Problems and Conflicts Amicably and Productively

A class **problem** is a situation or condition that hinders normal class activities enough to require attention, whereas a **conflict** is a strong disagreement between students or between teacher and student.

How to Address Problems.   Suppose students in a high school geometry class are troubled by a heavy load of homework. Or suppose a middle school teacher is greatly embarrassed when the principal visits and finds the room very untidy. When such situations hinder teaching or learning, for any reason, they should be addressed as soon as possible. Sensing the problem, you might say, "Class, something is going on that I think we need to talk about." The problem is then clarified, possible solutions are sought, and a solution is selected and tried.

How to Address Conflicts.   Conflicts are interpersonal situations characterized by strong disagreements or antagonisms, which may or may not include misbehavior. They threaten personal dignity, which is strongly defended. If the individuals involved do not know how to find a peaceful resolution, they tend to fight each other verbally or physically. Examples of conflict situations include disputes over who won a contest, who is entitled to play with a toy, whether work was turned in on time, and whether work has met the standards expected. Conflict is best resolved through a win-win approach that allows both sides to feel most of their concerns are being properly addressed. Here is how to resolve conflicts in your class:

- Make sure all individuals involved have the opportunity to express their concerns.
- Insist that all comments, observations, and suggestions are presented in a courteous manner.
- Encourage both sides to be open and honest, but tactful.
- Encourage each person to try to see things from the other's point of view.
- Keep attention focused on areas of agreement between the disputants.
- Help disputants formulate solutions as joint agreements.
- Do not allow students to argue back and forth, defend themselves, or debate.

Involve Students in Establishing a Behavior Management Plan for the Class

This protocol for involving students in a behavior plan works well if the class is reasonably well-behaved and cooperative. If your students are boisterous or reluctant to cooperate, you might discuss this approach with them and explain that you need their full cooperation before proceeding. As a second option, consider implementing a discipline plan of the types advocated by Ronald Morrish (Chapter 5) or Craig Seganti (Chapter 11).

On the first day of class, begin discussing with your class how the class is to function and how members can conduct themselves for greatest personal and class benefit. For the time being, tell your students that everyone, including yourself, is expected to show consideration for others in the class and avoid saying or doing anything that will hurt feelings or interfere with work. Meanwhile, you should have already thought through a desirable discipline approach, but rather than presenting it as a *fait accompli* on the first day, lead students into it gradually by asking a series of questions adjusted to their maturity level. When done as suggested here, the process requires six short sessions that, ideally, should begin the first day of class and be completed in six consecutive class days. Expect to use about 10 minutes per session for young children and about 15 minutes for older students. If appropriate, you might have your students sit in a circle, especially if you intend to use class meetings for discussing group concerns.

Session 1.   Build further rapport with your students. Smile. Look into their faces. Tell them you are pleased to see them and look forward to working with them. Tell them you want to get their opinions about ways of making the class enjoyable and useful, but first you want to get better acquainted with them. Call their names and ask if you have pronounced them correctly. Tell students just a little bit about yourself, including your special interests and why you became a teacher. Then tell the students you'd like to learn more about them, so you might help them feel comfortable and be successful. Using the class roster, call on a few individual students. As appropriate to their age, ask a question or two about siblings, pets, hobbies, and special interests. Call on as many as time allows and end the session by saying you will get to know all of them very soon.

Session 2.   Tell the students you are dedicated to helping them learn and have an enjoyable time in school. To make sure that happens, you would like to hear their ideas about some matters that might make the school year more enjoyable. Ask the following and take notes on a chart or overhead display:

- Ask what are some of the things they like best about school. List their comments on the left side. They will probably mention playing, associating with friends, sports, art, drama, and music.
- Ask what they like, specifically, about each of the things you've written on the display. Make notes on the right side of the display.
- Ask if they think any of the things they've mentioned might be possible in this class. Circle things they indicate.

Thank them for their contributions and tell them you will do what you can, with their help, to make the class as they would prefer it to be, although there are a few things the school requires that are outside your control.

Session 3.   Give feedback concerning the suggestions students made in session 2. Beforehand, redo the display and indicate the suggestions you consider appropriate for the class. Ask students if they have further thoughts or suggestions. Turn to a fresh page or new transparency and elicit comments about the kind of teacher they prefer.

- Ask them to think of a teacher they really enjoyed or respected. Ask them not to mention names but to indicate what that teacher did that made such a good impression. They will say things such as nice, interesting, helpful, fair, and funny. They may also mention favorite activities and special teacher talents. Write the traits they mention on the left side of your display.
- Review the traits with the class. Ask for examples, such as what is meant by "helpful" or "really fun." Make notes on the right side of the chart.
- Tell students that all teachers are different, but insofar as you can, you will try to be the kind of teacher they prefer. Tell them you will think more about their comments and give them feedback at the next session. Thank them for their helpfulness.

Session 4.   Show students a clean display of the preferred traits they have identified in teachers. Ask if they have additional comments. Tell them you have been thinking about how you can be the kind of teacher they want. If you know you can't do so in every respect, tell them why. Next, draw students out about how they feel they should behave in the class.

- Ask students to think of a classmate who has behaved in class in ways they admired or appreciated. Without names, have them tell what the student was like or what he or she did. List the descriptions on the left side of a clean display page.
- When several behaviors have been listed, go back and ask students *why* they appreciated those behaviors. Make notes accordingly.
- Now ask students how they like other members of a class to treat them. Make notes. Go back and once more ask why.
- Next, ask what kind of behavior they most appreciate from other students when they are working together on assignments. Ask why and make notes.
- Finally, ask students if they understand the meaning of *personal responsibility* and what it involves. Discuss that concept briefly, helping them focus on doing what they know is right and taking care of themselves. Ask if they think it would be possible to have, in this classroom, the kinds of responsible behavior they have discussed. Thank them for their input and tell them you will review their suggestions at the next session.

Session 5.   Provide a review of behaviors the students have indicated they like and appreciate. Ask if they have further comments.

- Now ask what fellow students sometimes do in class that they *dislike*. Ask if they have any ideas *why* students behave in ways others do not like. (If nothing is forthcoming, mention a few causes of misbehavior as presented in Chapter 2.)
- Then ask if they have ideas about what the class can do to keep those unwanted behaviors from occurring—that is, how the class can prevent them.

■ Ask students if they feel they have control over how they behave in the class. Follow with, "What makes you decide whether to behave responsibly or irresponsibly?" Ask if they feel they can almost always behave responsibly in class, for their own sake and for the good of the class.

Thank the students for their input and tell them you will provide feedback later.

Session 6.   Ask students to respond to a summary you have made of their suggestions. Show them a display that lists their contributions concerning (1) things students like best in school, (2) traits appreciated in teachers, (3) behaviors appreciated in classmates, and (4) behaviors disliked in classmates. Once you have done that, show them an outline of the discipline plan you wish to implement in the classroom. Indicate where their suggestions fit into the plan. It is suggested that your plan make specific mention of the following:

■ Desirable and responsible teacher behavior
■ Desirable and responsible student behavior
■ Things that will be done to remove or limit causes of misbehavior
■ What you will do to help students behave responsibly when they have made behavior mistakes

Ask the class what they think of the plan and if they can commit themselves to living with its stipulations. Thank them for their cooperation. By the next day, have the discipline plan outlined and printed. Give a copy to each student and ask them to share the plan with parents or guardians. Also prepare a chart of the plan and post it in the classroom.

Intervene Productively When Students Misbehave

Synergetic Management emphasizes the prevention of misbehavior, but it can also deal effectively with misbehavior when it occurs. For your consideration, four types of interventions are presented here, sequenced from least directive to most directive. You might wish to consider them and think how you would modify them to suit a particular age of students.

Reminders and Body Language.   Subtly remind students of expected behavior. Do this with physical proximity, eye signals, or facial expressions. If these reminders don't work, point to the chart that shows responsible behavior and say, "Class, let's please remember what it means to behave responsibly."

Identifying and Addressing Cause of Misbehavior.   If it seems advisable, identify what you believe is causing the misbehavior. The cause may be apparent, as when students seem to find the lesson boring and therefore disengage from it, or it may be obscure, as when Jason and Nathan continue an emotional dispute that originated outside the classroom. Even if you think you know the cause, check with students to obtain their view. For example, ask, "Is this too boring for you?" "Boys, is there a problem I can help you with?" or "Something is causing us to be inconsiderate of others. What is it? Can we fix it? How can we show greater responsibility." Then address the cause if you can. Doing so is fairly easy if it resides in activities, the classroom, or teacher behavior. You can also minimize its effects when it involves student needs, simply by trying to provide what students are seeking. It is more difficult to limit causes that have to do with egocentric personalities. You can say privately, "Jason, something is causing you to call out and disrupt the lesson. That makes it difficult for me to teach and for other students to learn. Can you help me understand what is causing you to do that so we might make things better for you?"

Having the Student Identify More Responsible Behavior.   Ask the misbehaving student to suggest how he or she might behave in a more responsible manner. If there is any hesitation on the student's part, make a direct suggestion, such as, "Let's keep our hands to ourselves. Will you do that for me, please?" or "Let's start again and find a more responsible way of acting. Will it help if I show you once more what is expected of you? Thank you."

Working Together to Find a Solution.   If the misbehavior involves, or leads to, a confrontational dispute, help those involved identify the cause of the disagreement and work together to find a solution. If the confrontation is between students, as when Jason and Nathan are speaking angrily to each other, say, "Boys, this is disturbing the class. Can you work the problem out between yourselves, or do you need my help?" If they say they can work it out, ask them if they can keep their dispute from affecting the class. If the boys can't resolve the matter, get together with them at a suitable time and in a nonthreatening manner do the following:

- Ask each to tell you calmly what is troubling them. (Explain that you need to hear each person clearly, so please no interrupting or arguing while the other is talking.)
- Ask Jason what he would like for Nathan to do differently. Nathan listens carefully.
- Ask Nathan what he would like for Jason to do differently. Jason listens carefully.
- Ask each of the boys if he feels he could do part, or most, of what the other wants.
- If they agree on a possible solution, thank them and leave it at that. If they cannot reach a solution, ask them if they would mind the class discussing the matter in order to learn more about resolving disputes considerately.
- If they agree to that, bring up the matter at the next class meeting. If they decline permission, say, "Boys, it is not good for any of us in the class when bad feelings exist. How can we resolve this matter so both of you feel all right? What ideas do you have?" If they reach a settlement, thank them. If they don't, say, "I'm disappointed we can't settle this matter so both of you feel all right. But since we can't, I need to ask you to control yourselves, for the sake of the class." It is unlikely that the conflict negotiations will ever reach this point; the boys will agree to a solution earlier in the process.

If the conflict is between you and a student, consider the following: When you are helping a misbehaving student, your efforts will seldom lead to conflict provided you treat the student with consideration. But if conflict should occur, you need to deal with it in a way that brings resolution while preserving positive feelings. Suppose Melissa has once again failed to do her homework. You ask her kindly if there is a problem that is preventing her complying with the class expectation. Your question strikes a nerve and Melissa retorts, "There wouldn't be a problem if you didn't assign this stupid stuff!" What do you do? Consider saying: "Melissa, can you help me understand why you feel the homework is stupid? I'd like your opinion because I want it to be helpful to your progress. What can you suggest that would help you learn this material more easily?" Melissa may apologize, say nothing, come back with another snide remark, or give you a suggestion. If she says nothing or remains uncooperative, consider saying: "Now is not a good time for us to discuss the matter. Perhaps we can do so later, just the two of us. Could you meet with me for a minute or two at (name a time and place)?" When you meet, tell her you are willing to listen if she has something she needs to talk about. If she declines, assure her you are interested in her views and are always ready to help.

If Melissa apologizes, explains her feelings, or talks about some other problem in her life that is probably her real cause of concern, consider saying: "Thank you, Melissa, for informing me. If I can make some changes in the homework or otherwise help with your situation, I'd like to do so. I'll listen to any suggestions you might have."

OTHER VOICES FROM THE RANKS OF TEACHERS

There is widespread interest in techniques that help energize classes and lift spirits. This section presents a sampling of various ideas you can find on the Internet posted by educators who are in classrooms daily.

MARILYN PAGE: MAKING CHANGES IN TEACHER LANGUAGE TO HELP ENERGIZE CLASSES

Marilyn Page (2005) has had extensive experience in observing teachers at work. She reports that these "days of testing" are forcing teachers to focus mainly on teaching factual information, which prevents their doing special things that add excitement in their classes. Page believes teachers can overcome that problem, in part, merely by making changes in the language they use when organizing instruction.

Most teachers, she says, remain stuck in the language that was used by their own teachers, who said they *taught, covered, presented,* and so forth. At the time they were in school, teaching was thought of as passing along information to students or otherwise helping them acquire and memorize it. Today, educators are endeavoring to help students learn to develop and solve problems, raise questions and investigate them, and seek in-depth understanding. The old language has a dampening effect on classroom practice, but is hard to get rid of.

Page identifies five words or expressions teachers can change that will put them on course toward more interesting teaching. The changes shift emphasis away from *teacher and teaching* and focus it on *learner and learning*. Here is what she suggests:

- *Change the word* teaching *to* learning.   Do this with every reference you make to teaching. For example, instead of asking yourself how you can teach Johnnie to do long division, change the question to: "What is the best way for Johnnie to learn long division?" This word substitution causes you to shift thinking so you put the focus on Johnnie and his abilities, talents, and limitations.

- *Change* lesson plan *to* student learning plan.   Here again the idea is to shift the focus from you to your students, and from teaching to learning. Instead of indicating what you will teach, you might say, "Students will be involved in . . ." Specify the activities students will be involved in that promote understanding, not simply recall.

- *Change* unit *to* investigation *or* exploration.   Page asks, "Can you think of a more boring or inactive word than *unit*?" If you are trying to energize your classroom, get rid of that word and replace it with one, such as *investigation*, that conveys learning through action, questioning, problem solving, and critical thinking.

- *Change* cover *to* discover *or* uncover.   Page says *cover* is one of the deadliest words in teaching. It makes one think of putting a lid on a box, rather than lifting a lid and discovering what's inside.

- *Change* presentations *to* interactive learning experiences.   This suggestion has to do not only with activities the teacher provides, but also with presentations students make to classmates. When they are assigned to make reports, tell them they are now the experts and their job is to think of activities that will help class members learn about the topic. Page says this is an awkward struggle for students at first, but they become very creative once they understand what's expected.

Page acknowledges that using new language will not immediately convert dull classes into hives of activity, but insists it will help direct thinking to activities and eventually change the entire approach to helping students learn.

BENNA GOLUBTCHIK: CREATING A MULTISENSORY CLASSROOM

Benna Golubtchik (2008) explains the energizing effect that multisensory activities have on classes. She says allowing students to use various sensory modalities enriches the learning experience while helping students recognize their individual learning strengths and weaknesses. Suppose, for example, you have had your students mold and color a tabletop three-dimensional model of the state in which they live. Afterward, ask them to describe and evaluate the activity, the senses they used in making the model, and which parts of the activity they enjoyed most. Tell them this activity helps them get a better mental picture of how they learn. Help them explore this matter by getting them to reflect on the following questions:

- What did I learn?
- What did I like best about the assignment?
- What senses did I enjoy using the most (touch, sight, hearing, smell, taste)?

- What part did I find most difficult?
- What skills do I still need to improve?

Golubtchik suggests a number of activities that call on various sensory modalities.

Tactual/Kinesthetic Activities

- Making a three-dimensional model such as a physical map
- Demonstrating a process by physically acting it out
- Creating unusual, colorful designs, shapes, and patterns to illustrate a scene from nature or history
- Constructing a timeline and filling in details
- Drawing or painting a picture, poster, chart, graphic representation, or sketch representing learned content
- Constructing props and costumes to dramatize an event or role-play a literary or historical event
- Building a shadow box or diorama
- Creating a dance or movement to tell a story
- Using whole-body learning such as acting out vocabulary words or a sequence of events
- Constructing projects and making diagrams, models, or replicas of systems or procedures
- Building puppets and putting on a show related to content
- Pantomiming a sequence

Auditory Processing Activities

- Identifying rhythmic patterns in music or poetry
- Performing a rap or song that summarizes information
- Writing an original play, rap, jingle, cheer, or song
- Composing music to convey the theme or mood of the lesson

Visual Processing Activities

- Writing a journal
- Creating a real or imagined correspondence between historical or contemporary characters
- Writing newspapers for a different time period, complete with contemporary news, fashion, entertainment, and feature items
- Researching, comparing, and contrasting art of different cultures or time periods
- Rewriting difficult information in a simpler form for an audience of younger students
- Writing poetry, stories, ideas, or thoughts
- Composing scripts to depict historical events
- Utilizing a camera or video camera to create a pictorial report
- Creating a web organizer, Venn diagram, or concept map to convey information to others
- Developing color-coding systems to categorize information

ROSEMARY SHAW: TEACHING STUDENTS
HOW TO DO ONLINE RESEARCH

When Rosemary Shaw (2008) taught her first class in media technology, she had students complete hypermedia projects such as web pages. After a while the usual "bells and whistles" emphasis grew old and dissatisfyingly devoid of content. She found she didn't like the class and neither did her students. She later approached her principal with a suggestion for redesigning the class. Instead of just teaching technology, she wanted to teach students how to do online research on topics that interested them. The new idea was approved and the class turned out to be highly motivating and satisfying for everyone.

Her new approach was organized around six steps in conducting online research—questioning, planning, gathering, sorting and shifting, synthesizing, and evaluating. She introduced those skills to students, told them to identify a topic they'd like to investigate, and they proceeded from that point. Here is what she emphasized in each step.

Step 1: Questioning.   She pointed out that students must understand the assignment clearly before they begin formulating questions for their project. Once they understood what was expected, they brainstormed individual topics for research and began stating questions about the topic they selected. She asked students to talk with parents and friends and possibly other teachers about their topic in order to find out what others think about it. All the while, students were making lists of key words for use in the Internet search engines.

Step 2: Planning.   Once students decided on their topics, they planned things such as the amount of time it would take, the different sources they would consult, whether they needed to work alone or with others, and how experts might be contacted via email.

Step 3: Gathering.   Shaw told students that although it is easy to get quantities of information from the Internet, there is always the chance some of it might be erroneous or misleading. To guard against that eventuality, she asked students to use the library to check books and other sources as well—the more the better.

She also called students' attention to a number of other primary sources of information:

- Memoirs, autobiographies, diaries, journals, speeches, interviews, letters, memos, manuscripts, and other papers in which individuals describe events in which they were participants or observers
- Documents such as birth certificates, death certificates, marriage licenses, permits, other licenses, census data, photographs, audio recordings, films, and video recordings
- Websites that give access to a variety of primary sources

Shaw further urged her students to write to as many experts as feasible. She found that NASA engineers and university professors were especially good about answering correspondence.

Step 4: Sorting and Sifting.   Once information begins coming in, it needs to be put into some sort of order. Shaw advises sorting the information into categorized piles. This helps eliminate information that is repetitious or unneeded.

Step 5: Synthesizing.   When the information is sorted, it is ready to be interpreted and presented in a report. Shaw showed students how to organize information through concept mapping: The main idea is written in the center of the page, then related ideas are placed on branches that fan out from the central idea. She reports that software such as Inspiration and Kidspiration helps with concept mapping.

Students were also taught to organize their material by *clustering*, a type of prewriting that allows one to explore ideas as they occur. The process is akin to brainstorming and free associating. You can begin without a central idea and organize by making outlines of main topics and subtopics.

When the organization is completed, students write up their reports. Shaw reminded them to keep their information organized and to be sure all sources were cited correctly. She advised students to use NoodleTools (www.noodletools.com), which provides a free QuickCite tool for creating MLA and other style citations for books, encyclopedia articles, magazine articles, online magazine articles, newspaper articles, professional web pages, personal web pages, email messages, interviews, and online discussion boards or forums.

Step 6: Evaluation.   After the report is written, students review everything to make sure their work satisfies the requirements of the project.

JUDY JONES: BUILDING A COMMUNITY OF LEARNERS— HIGH SCHOOL STYLE

Judy Jones (2008) writes that the science department in which she teaches has begun collaborating closely in deciding on curricula and activities for engaging students in learning. The effort has produced a heightened level of energy among teachers that has spread to students. She says the results have been amazing. The collaboration makes new teachers feel nurtured and connected, while more experienced teachers are enjoying involvement in cooperative activities with colleagues.

Jones recounts how she and the six other biology teachers decided they needed something creative to energize their classes as students reviewed for an end-of-the-year state test. They came up with a plan for a field day for all 20 biology classes. They planned 14 stations, each teacher responsible for two of them. Activities at the stations involved active processes such as using a dichotomous key to identify a fern, analyzing an autorad to identify a perpetrator, finding the mutation in a strand of DNA, identifying molecular models, matching cell parts with their functions, and the like. The biology classes were organized into five to six groups per class. Each group was given a card with the sequence of stations the students were to follow. The stations were scattered around the campus and each group got a map. They first gathered in the commons, where the principal blew a whistle to start them off. The senior biology students and the advanced placement biology students manned the stations. Each station had a box with the activity, the answer sheet, the key, and an insect stamp with a stamp pad. When a group finished an activity, the older students would quickly grade the activity and stamp the group's card (if they were successful). At the end of the period, the groups turned in their cards and got refreshments and prizes, compliments of the parents' organization.

This day turned out to be exciting for everyone, and the department intends to repeat it. Jones said students were running over the campus, finding stations, engaging in the activities, talking over their answers, and enjoying the competition. All it took was several meetings, a "can do" spirit among the biology teachers, and a supportive principal. Jones acknowledges that time was a concern in organizing the activities, but the benefits made the entire effort highly worthwhile.

NANCY POWELL: KEEPING STUDENTS ENGAGED IN LEARNING WITH MARKER BOARDS

Nancy Powell (2008) reports that one way to maintain a high level of class energy is to keep all students responding actively as you ask questions or pose problems. Under most circumstances this is hard to do. Imagine that in your lesson you are checking for understanding of previous homework, or asking students to name the elements that make up water, or having them spell words on the spelling list. Normally, only one student at a time answers, while the others sit there, chat with each other, or look out the window.

But it is possible to keep all students responding all the time. A good way to do this is to have students use marker boards on which they write their responses and hold them up for you to see.

Powell describes how she obtains, prepares, and uses marker boards. She explains they are available commercially, but are expensive. To get some cheaply, go to your local home improvement center and ask for melamine, tile board, or white board. Usually these boards come in inexpensive four-by-eight-foot sheets. If you have the store cut them into 12-inch squares, you'll get 32 individual white boards. The edges of these boards will need to be smoothed with a little sandpaper. The store might do that for you if you indicate they are for your classroom.

Another good material for marker boards is polyboard, a coated cardboard often used for political signs. If this is not available and you have no other option, try using heavy poster board, file folders, or other cardboard. You can customize these items for single or multiple subjects. Glue a sheet of white paper on them and run them through your school's laminating machine, preferably twice.

Plastic page protectors from office supply stores offer yet another option for marker boards. Just slide in a piece of heavy card stock to make them rigid. If you want lines to write on, add a lined piece of paper. If you want students to use number lines, coordinate graphs, or polar graphs, slide in a paper with these graphs on them. You can make a variety of templates with your copy machine. The sheets can be stored in the page protectors and put in a three-ring notebook.

You will want students to write on the boards with dry-erase markers. Powell suggests each student should have at least two colors. Students can be asked to bring their own markers, but you should keep extras on hand just in case. Many businesses will donate dry-erase markers for your class. In the absence of markers, students can write on a piece of scratch paper.

Marker board erasers are large and expensive, but old clean socks work almost as well. They don't scratch as do paper towels, and so extend the life of the marker board. Drill or punch a hole in the corner of the marker boards. Take a piece of string and tie one end to the sock and the other end to the marker board. That keeps the eraser available at all times. Once or twice a semester, use some glass cleaner and give each marker board an extra cleaning. Have students keep their marker boards in their notebooks or in their desks so you don't waste time passing them out and retrieving them.

Summary Rubric

INCREASING LEVELS OF SYNERGY IN THE CLASSROOM

- Always do what you can to make your class responsive to and compatible with student needs.
- Energize your class through interesting activities, good communication, and your personal charisma.
- Involve students in identifying and reflecting on responsible behavior in the classroom.
- Have a well-organized discipline plan in mind, but obtain input and feedback from students. Doing so gives students a sense of ownership of the rules and responsibilities.
- Keep students active and responsive in the lessons you conduct.
- Place heavy emphasis on developing trust and a sense of ethics in your classes.
- When misbehavior occurs, deal with it in a helpful, nonconfrontational manner and show continual willingness to address whatever is troubling the students.

Terms and Concepts

conflict
coopetition

problem
synergetic discipline

synergetic teaching
synergy

Activities

1. In your journal, add information from this chapter that you might wish to include in your personal system of discipline.
2. To what extent do you feel you could put Synergetic Teaching and Synergetic Management into effect in your classroom? What portions do you believe you could implement easily? What portions do you believe might be difficult?
3. Synergetic Management does not punish students for misbehavior, nor does it apply penalties or other measures to try to force student compliance. Do you think students will take advantage of Synergetic Management's softer nature and disregard the teacher because they have no fear of the consequences? Is there anything in Synergetic Management that would prevent them from doing so?

4. If you introduce Synergetic Management as Charles suggests, a few days might pass before students know exactly what is expected of them in the discipline system. Charles suggests you stress personal consideration until the plan is presented to students. Can you think of two or three other things you might do to keep students from misbehaving during the first days of class?

References

Biddulph, S. 1997. *Raising boys.* Sydney, Australia: Finch Publishing.

Charles, C. M. 2000. *The synergetic classroom: Joyful teaching and gentle discipline.* Boston: Allyn and Bacon.

Golubtchik, B. 2008. Create a multi-sensory classroom. www.teachersnetwork.org/ntol/howto/energize/c13472,.htm

Jones, J. 2008. Collaboration—high school style. www.teachersnetwork.org/ntol/howto/develop/collaborate.htm

Mee, C. 1997. *2,000 voices: Young adolescents' perceptions and curriculum implications.* Columbus, OH: National Middle School Association.

Page, M. 2005. Energizing the classroom with new language: Five steps to dynamic change even in an era of testing. www.redorbit.com/news/education/256444/energizing_the_classroom_with_new_language_five_steps_to_dynamic

Piaget, J. 2001. *The psychology of intelligence.* London: Routledge & Kegan Paul.

Powell, N. 2008. Keep students engaged in learning with marker boards. www.teachersnetwork.org/ntol/howto/energize/c14660.htm

Shaw, R. 2008. Teaching students how to do online research. www.teachnet.org/ntol/howto/energize/onlineresearch.htm

Wong, H., and Wong, R. 2007. *The first days of school: How to be an effective teacher.* Mountain View, CA: Harry K. Wong Publications.

15

How Does Eileen Kalberg VanWie Build and Maintain Democratic Learning Communities in Technology-Rich Environments?

Increasingly, schools are providing learning environments that are especially well equipped with digital technology. Referred to as **technology-rich environments,** those locales vary from portions of libraries to learning centers to classrooms, and in some cases entire schools. In addition, *distance learning,* which supports online learning in sparsely populated areas, uses advanced technology to instruct and interact with students who live far from schools.

These media-intensive environments provide many benefits for students, especially in facilitating communication and access to information. But at the same time, students may be isolated from each other, physically or psychologically, which can greatly reduce interaction. Because interaction is required for certain kinds of learning, teachers in technology-rich environments are advised to incorporate **democratic learning communities** into their media-enhanced programs. Such communities provide participatory activities in critical evaluation, planning, and decision making. This provision allows students to be more directly involved in their own learning by working closely with others who have similar interests, talents, and needs. How can this be done? And how do teachers ensure fruitful student discussions and give and take? These questions are addressed in this chapter.

The lead author of this chapter is Dr. Eileen Kalberg VanWie, a professor at New Mexico State University who is currently conducting research into various aspects of democratic learning communities in technology-rich environments (abbreviated *DLC in TRE*). VanWie taught for several years in elementary and secondary schools before becoming a teacher educator at Southwest Minnesota State University. She values close relationships with schools where she has facilitated professional development, periodically assumed duties as a substitute teacher, and collaborated with teachers investigating learning and teaching environments. Two middle school teachers and a K–12 technology specialist are collaborating with her to research ways of engaging diverse learners in teamwork in media-rich environments.

A PREVIEW OF THIS CHAPTER

Educators are becoming ever more aware of the educational potential of digital technology, which is increasingly available to students in schools. Today's students eagerly embrace this new digital technology. Their familiarity and active involvement may be causing them to think in different ways from students of the past, but educators also know that much valuable learning takes place in social environments that are organized to promote democratic involvement. The question to be answered is: How can, and should, democratic learning communities be organized and used effectively in media-rich environments while integrating digital technology tools for addressing real-world problems?

WHAT TO LOOK FOR IN THIS CHAPTER

- The meaning and nature of technology-rich environments
- The meaning and nature of democratic learning communities in technology-rich environments
- Why democratic learning communities are advocated for use in combination with technology-rich environments
- Procedures useful in establishing democratic learning communities within the context of technology-rich environments
- Four critical aspects of DLC in TRE
- Etiquette and issues in using digital media

TWO FUNDAMENTAL TERMS

Democratic learning communities (DLC) are groups of people (students, families, educators, and the public) who work together to promote meaningful learning. These communities are called *democratic* because they feature freedom of choice, shared responsibility, and self-governance. Such communities provide collaborative opportunities for students to involve themselves in projects they find interesting. When cultural themes that contribute positively to the community are involved, the process draws students into meaningful communication, interaction, conflict resolution, and shared leadership—strengths of democratic learning communities.

Technology-rich environments (TRE) are classrooms, physical spaces, or virtual spaces that use digital technology to engage students in critical and creative thinking, communication, and networking. Electronic tools play key roles in helping students learn content, processes, and social and emotional knowledge and skills.

FOUR PRIMARY QUESTIONS IN ESTABLISHING DLC IN TRE

The goal of DLC in TRE is to enable students to work together and learn from that process as they use digital technology to explore real-world learning. Four questions that teachers face for developing quality in this approach will be addressed in the remainder of this chapter:

1. How do teachers accomplish their multiple roles—researchers, designers, facilitators, leaders, and advocates?
2. How do teachers provide a quality learning environment that emphasizes the use of digital tools?
3. How do teachers establish a learning-centered approach—thus ensuring enhanced learning and interaction among students?
4. How do teachers ensure that participants learn and improve social skills—communication, relationships, collaboration, conflict resolution, and other interpersonal skills and qualities?

Question 1: How Do Teachers Accomplish Their Multiple Roles?

The following vignette illustrates one teacher's efforts in DLC in TRE.

Ms. Morales, adequately versed in digital technology, wished to provide an opportunity for her students to be involved in a worthwhile project that featured the use of technology. She began by discussing the approach first with her school administrator, then with technology specialists and a few selected persons in the wider community. Her purpose was to gain support for her idea and possible collaboration with others.

She was able to obtain that support and so introduced her students to the idea. When they responded favorably, she began guiding them in basic community-building activities related to a code of conduct, working in teams, and using digital etiquette (netiquette). At the same time, she invited students to brainstorm local problems or issues of concern in the school and/or community. They identified some issues they considered important, and she assigned teams to conduct brief Internet and library searches on those issues.

When they had completed their preliminary searches, each team was asked to organize and present a persuasive proposal for investigating their topic further. When that had been done, the class voted on which project they considered most interesting or valuable to the community. Ms. Morales's class voted to study issues concerning water usage in the community.

Before they proceeded further, Ms. Morales guided a discussion about personal responsibility of the members of each team and how the teams might collaborate in undertaking their investigation and making recommendations. She encouraged students to discuss necessary social skills such as negotiation, empathy, conflict resolution, calling each other by respectful names, and respecting public and private digital spaces. The discussions also touched on acceptable use Internet policies and citing references.

Out of those discussions, the class developed search guidelines to follow in their investigation. Students shared the guidelines with their parents to get their permission to participate in the project. (Ms. Morales would have found alternative means for learning these important skills had any parents not given permission.)

Next, the problem was discussed, defined, and developed with different teams assigned to investigate particular aspects of the issue, including local water resources, commercial and private use of water, relevant policies on water use, and regulations that might be in place. Learning goals and assessment processes for the searches were negotiated.

Students then began their assigned searches, using Internet resources, library searches, and interviews with experts using email or Voice over the Internet Protocol (VoIP). One of their goals was to provide their findings and recommendations to the city council or county commissioners and publish them on a community and/or school website. Teams used Excel spreadsheets to organize and analyze data they collected and Google Docs (a wiki) to collaboratively write and edit reports on what they found. Finally, they created a video for informing others of their results. As they worked, they regularly assessed their progress in both content and social skills. Ms. Morales provided guidance by asking questions related to the task and process, suggesting resources, and coaching needed knowledge and skills concerning standards and goals.

The process did not always go smoothly, just as learning and life in any society are not always smooth. But meaningful learning occurred and standards were maintained. Occasional conflicts occurred, which students learned to deal with in an effective manner.

As exemplified by Ms. Morales, teachers first reflect on their philosophy concerning equitable learning for all. They then explain their view to students, parents, educators, and the public. As for media expertise, teachers require a measure of knowledge and skills, but in the early stages it is not necessary that they be expert technicians. If necessary, they can create teams of student or adult technicians whose job it is to help teachers and less-knowledgeable students develop the required technology skills.

For further preparation, teachers might wish to engage in professional development on designing lessons that use technology effectively. They might seek advice on how to negotiate with administrators, parents, and/or the community to obtain help with critical hardware, software, and technical support. In many cases, members of the wider community can provide expert advice on technology practices that increase the likelihood of success. A school technology assistance team can be organized to investigate and resolve technology and support issues. Throughout, teachers display empathy, curiosity, a willingness to take reasonable risks, and a commitment to making learning more effective and engaging.

Question 2: How Do Teachers Provide a Quality Learning Environment That Emphasizes the Use of Digital Tools?

Ordinarily, teachers structure the physical environment to help the class community function. The basic structure should provide flexible room arrangements, careful room color and lighting choices, wireless Internet service, laptop computers, and digital handheld devices. As suggested by Norton and Wiburg (2003), teachers would organize their environments in accordance with how students interact with and respond to materials, tools, each other, and the environment. Standard desks might be removed and replaced with trapezoid-shaped tables that can be arranged in various formations to create small-group computer stations. Or desks and tables might be replaced with stands for laptops and exercise balls for student seating. The environment might also incorporate computer islands, wireless networks, mobile computer carts, handheld devices, and/or technology-enhanced presentation stations. Digital tools might include MP3 players, digital voice recorders, cell and smart phones, palms, "clickers," and tablet computers.

Excellent software supports various types of electronic communication. Synchronous tools (happening at the same time), such as Voice over the Internet Protocol software, video conferencing, and chat rooms, require reliable and strong Internet service for satisfactory use. Asynchronous tools (happening at flexible/convenient/different times), such as discussion boards, blogs, wikis, podcasts, text messaging, and email, also need good Internet service but are more "forgiving" with interruptions to the service.

Online/virtual spaces such as the following can also be helpful in collaborative learning:

- *Learning management systems (BlackBoard, Desire2Learn, or Moodle).* These are password-protected systems that provide structure for the course syllabus, content, assignments, Web links, email, chat rooms, and discussion groups.
- *Classroom management systems (SMART's SynchronEyes, Net Op Tech's Vision6, Vision@Hand, or Apple Remote Desktop).* These systems give teachers the ability to monitor, guide, and control student desktops, as well as provide features of learning management systems.

These systems provide virtual space to share course content, assignments, Web links, email, chat rooms, and discussion groups. Creating small online discussion groups with rotating student facilitators can be used to add interest, encourage critical thinking, understand various perspectives, and practice communication. Keep in mind that the skills for group discussions need to be taught, learned, and assessed whether groups are face to face or online. Teachers or facilitators need to monitor the discussions regularly.

Regarding Assistive Technology Devices

It is common for classrooms to have students with physical and/or learning disabilities. Educators have a responsibility to assure that all students are given fair opportunities to learn and interact with classmates. Assistive technology can greatly support learning for students with disabilities. The federal government defines an *assistive technology device* as "any item, piece of equipment, or product system, whether acquired commercially off the shelf, modified, or customized, that is used to increase, maintain, or improve functional capabilities of a child with a disability" (http://idea.ed.gov/explore/search). Federal law requires that assistive technology must be considered for all students on an individualized education plan (IEP).

These devices can range from low-tech (e.g., pencil grips, card holders, and balls with bells) to high-tech (e.g., talking calculators, text-readers and voice-activated software, or chat PCs). The primary goal is to provide a *least restrictive environment* that allows students to participate as fully as possible in the class. The National Assistive Technology Research Institute (NATRI, http://natri.uky.edu/natri background/topics.html) provides numerous resources to support educators in providing this kind of environment.

Regarding Blogging

Blogs are web-based services that allow users to interact with materials and communicate with people. Schools can set up internal blogs or use password-protected blogs to provide safe environments for the discussions. They can be moderated and individuals who post inappropriate messages can be denied access. *Civility* in blogging and other electronic discourse is critical to constructive learning (Richardson, 2008). Responsible people often disagree, but they do so in respectful ways. Richardson suggested that students examine authentic examples of civil disagreement and guidelines for discourse from the Web. Then they can develop their own set of guidelines and role-play using them for civil discourse in a blog.

Regarding Cell Phones

Middle school students in the Southwest (VanWie et al., 2008) suggested that students can conduct Web searches more reliably with cell phones than with Internet services in schools. Yet some educators are wary of using cell phones for school learning. They cite legitimate concerns such as phone etiquette, students publishing from their phone to the Internet, school security, and persuasive advertising. But any tool can be useful, distracting, or dangerous in a classroom. Teachers and students together can develop guidelines for appropriate use. Parents also need to be involved and give permission for students to use cell phones appropriately.

Kolb (2008) advised that not every student needs to have a cell phone in order to use them successfully for school learning. Center or small-group activities may only require one cell phone per center or group. Kolb also suggested that schools can work with cell phone companies to acquire a bank of inexpensive phones for use in the classroom. Because cell phone use can hinder public safety response to school emergency situations by overloading systems, guidelines for such occasions need to be made clear and role-played during practice for emergency situations. Beneficial uses of cell phones at school can also be role-played.

Kolb (2008) offered many ideas for lessons using cell phones for podcasting, text messaging, researching, conferencing, and as cameras and camcorders. She included listings of free and inexpensive software and services to support the lessons. For example, small groups from two different schools could participate in a virtual science cell phone conference concerning significant issues in science. One student would serve as the moderator of the conference. Each student in the group might research the topic and become a "well-known scientist" in the field. The conference call could be done as homework, so that cell phones would not be needed at school. The conference could be saved as an MP3 for future listening, review, and discussion.

Regarding Digital Cameras and Camcorders

Students usually enjoy working with images, so cameras can be useful for numerous projects. For example, to learn about interdependence, small groups of students could take photos or videos of different organisms and their environments. Then they could investigate how living and nonliving things influence each other. Students could also take photos or videos of something in the classroom or school that they want to see changed. After learning more about the topic, they could take photos of possible changes and predicted consequences to negotiate with appropriate authorities to make the change. Students could prepare images and text giving directions for how to use classroom equipment and/or materials. Having such information available helps students learn to manage themselves in a democratic learning community.

Regarding MP3 Players and Digital Voice Recorders

Digital audio and portable media players are familiar to students, who may not realize that they can make their own podcasts (audio broadcasts where voice messages are recorded, perhaps mixed with music, and downloaded to a portable MP3 player). Students can create radio shows, advertisements, and public service announcements with a partner or in small group of students. Students would need to collaborate in writing a script for the production. Some digital voice recorders have the capability to convert recordings to the MP3 format.

Regarding Video Games

Video games have been viewed more as entertainment than education, but games with educational purposes are now being developed. Squire (2006) described more advantages than disadvantages in learning through video games. For example, students can learn about the real world from simulations, learn about one's own identity by taking on different identities in games, solve problems in games that require understanding of rules, and participate in social organizations with diverse people in diverse locations.

Disadvantages are that simulations may be culturally biased, players may not recognize political agendas, and the games may not represent reality. Well-constructed games usually provide social and collaborative experiences that require critical and creative thinking. It is not necessary to have game consoles in the classroom to use video games for learning. There are many free resources on the Internet, such as PBS Kids (http://pbskids.org), Google (www.google.com/Top/Kids_and_Teens/Games), and Nobelprize.org (http://nobelprize.org/educational_games). Members of the "serious games movement" advocate the development of games that can assess student progress. Teachers still need to reflect on how the games support the learning standards, goals, and assessment of the curriculum as well as the desired social skills of the class.

Regarding WebQuests

WebQuests (www.webquest.org/index.php) are available online and can be created for specific purposes in a democratic learning community. These inquiry-based tasks include websites selected by the teacher for particular learning goals. For example, small groups of students could investigate elements of a story about family relationships or investigate ethical online behavior and netiquette with a defined task and selected websites.

Regarding Wikis

A wiki is a set of web pages designed to allow anyone to edit and contribute to the content (see Google Docs in the "Tools for your classroom" section of Google for Educators). Like blogs, wikis are a Web 2.0 service. Pairs or small groups of students can collaboratively write reports on any subject. Like other Web tools, guidelines for use and social interaction are critical. Regular discussion of the process and social skills development would be part of the group experience. For example, the social skill of "listening to each other" could be assessed with multiple-choice survey items such as "We listened to each other's ideas" and "We used at least one idea from each person."

Regarding Other Technology Tools

In addition to the technology tools described so far, there are many others that can be useful. For example, there are graphing calculators, global positioning systems, Smart Boards, and numerous software programs, with others being invented regularly. Once teachers have made a commitment to integrating digital technology tools, they are likely to continually seek new tools and strategies that assist learning. Integrating digital technology tools requires courage to take reasonable risks in providing meaningful learning experiences. But over time, the process becomes habitual and rewarding.

Question 3: How Do Teachers Establish a Learning-Centered Approach?

Go to the IRIS Center Resources section of Topic #8: Planning, Conducting, and Managing Instruction, in the **MyEducationLab** for your course and complete the module entitled "Using Learning Strategies: Instruction to Enhance Student Learning."

Democratic learning communities in technology-rich environments use a **learning-centered approach,** which places primary focus on using technology for *meaningful learning*—activities that are active, constructive, authentic, and collaborative (Jonassen, 2000). This section addresses design components having to do with democratic core curricula, standards-based curricula, No Child Left Behind, and certain efforts being made nationwide to promote the use of electronic media for meaningful learning.

Designing a Democratic Core Curriculum

A **democratic core curriculum** emphasizes content and processes that bring into play students' beliefs, learning assets, interests, needs, and achievements. It calls for knowledge about the cultural, linguistic, learning, and experiential backgrounds of the students involved. Such a curriculum places great importance on involving students in democratic processes. For example, Beane (2002) suggested beginning by asking students, "What questions or concerns do you have about yourself? What questions or concerns do you have about the world?" That approach is likely to work best within a school culture that values excellent work and mutual concern for all persons involved. In establishing such a culture, schools should reach out to families and neighborhoods for support (Berger, 2003). Berger added further that passion and expectations for quality work are transferred to students in a variety of ways, including sharing examples of excellent work and engaging students in powerful projects.

Designing a Standards-Based Curriculum

At the time of this writing, a standards-based curriculum is considered essential in most public schools, including technology-rich environments. Standards-based curricula, often thought of as government mandates, evaluate student learning in terms of a pre-established set of criteria. The curriculum is then directed at enabling students to meet those criteria. In the past, students were assessed in terms of how they did in comparison to fellow students—an approach called *norm-referenced assessment*. Today, standards-based assessment is called *criterion-referenced assessment*, meaning that students seek to reach certain standards of proficiency established by the school.

Several professional organizations have established criteria for standards-based curricula, especially in language arts, mathematics, and science. Some states have also provided standards for technology usage (e.g., Arizona, Kansas, Wisconsin) and for social–emotional learning (e.g., Illinois, Massachusetts, New York). The democratic learning communities emphasized in this chapter integrate and assess standards related to technology, social skills, and emotional outcomes.

Concerning the No Child Left Behind Act

The No Child Left Behind Act specifies that students must develop certain skills in the use of technology, but it is difficult to meet that requirement and assess its results within the regular curriculum. Help in doing so is available from the International Society for Technology in Education (www.iste.org), the International Technology Education Association (www.iteaconnect.org), and the Partnership for 21st Century Skills (www.21stcenturyskills.org). The six National Education Technology Standards for Students (NETS-S) seem especially appropriate for democratic learning communities in technology-rich environments. The standards are as follows:

1. Creativity and innovation
2. Communication and collaboration
3. Research and information fluency
4. Critical thinking, problem solving, and decision making
5. Digital citizenship
6. Technology operations and concepts

ISTE makes many resources available to help educators address the standards, including Ribble and Bailey's (2007) suggestions for guiding students to learn nine elements of digital citizenship: digital access, commerce, communication, literacy, etiquette, law, rights and responsibilities, health and wellness, and security.

Regarding Standards of Social–Emotional Learning

The state of Illinois has been a leader in developing, teaching, and assessing **social–emotional learning**. The Collaborative for Academic, Social, and Emotional Learning (www.casel.org) provides a wealth of information for helping students learn self-awareness, self-management, social awareness, interpersonal skills, decision-making skills, and responsible behavior. This information is related to the Illinois Social and Emotional Learning Standards (SEL), which appear to have a positive impact on academic learning, safety, and school–family partnerships.

Question 4: How Do Teachers Ensure That Participants Learn and Improve Social Skills?

One of the major components in democratic learning communities is developing and sustaining respectful relationships among group members. Vitto (2003) described the important role that teachers/facilitators play in modeling caring relationships and providing opportunities for students to participate and contribute to learning, with a focus on acquiring resiliency. He stated that the brain does not differentiate emotions and cognition, and for that reason emotions can impede or enhance students' ability to think and plan. Teachers/facilitators can help students to recognize their assets and to provide positive self-talk by asking themselves questions, such as: "What did I do that helped me (us) write this creative story? Does it help or hurt when I lose my temper in class? What are possible consequences of my actions? What are alternative solutions to this problem? What are ways to ask for help?" Encouraging students to monitor their own actions and thoughts in this manner helps them develop self-management.

Many other social and emotional skills can be developed in DLC in TRE, and their value has been well documented (Putnam, 1998; Goleman, 2006; Payton et al., 2008). Putnam (1998) provided resources for collaborative learning that emphasized social skills among diverse groups of students, while Payton and colleagues. (2008) identified numerous studies indicating that social and emotional learning (SEL) raised school grades and standardized achievement test scores among K–8 student populations that are ethnically and socio-economically diverse.

In learning communities there are people with a range of interests, talents, and needs, reflecting diversity in maturity, native language, race, class, gender, ability, disability, sexual orientation, regional membership, and socio-economic realities. If people are to work together constructively and productively, they must be able to trust each other. Trust develops as class members communicate, show help and respect, and begin to understand each other. An important question to consider is, "How can digital technology support equitable opportunities while providing meaningful learning?"

A constructive way to explore that question is to hold group discussions to develop guidelines for working together in respectful ways, whether face to face or online. The guidelines should give attention to facilitating interaction among class members and to using technology tools to advantage. Facilitators/teachers should have clear expectations concerning the social and emotional skills they want students to demonstrate. These expectations provide guidance, but are not imposed on class members. It is hoped that everyone in the community (including the facilitator) will agree to accept and follow the guidelines, which should include dealing with conflict. Conflict is an expected normal part of human interaction. Learning about conflict becomes part of the guidelines and curriculum.

Goal setting and progress monitoring are important functions of the class community. A variety of short- and long-term goals can be addressed in various learning projects, as well as in the classroom guidelines. Students learn skills of goal setting and decision making as part of the democratic curriculum. The goals, with attention to participants' strengths rather than weaknesses, help guide the content of the curricula. An important goal in democratic communities is for all participants to support each other's learning. Having other common goals along with individual ones helps strengthen the learning community. Participants need to have choices but also show responsibility in activities that lead toward their goals.

Student discussions, both asynchronous (different times) and synchronous (specific time), allow students to plan their goals and decisions. Today's young people often enjoy expressing themselves in text, which levels the playing field among students, some of whom are quiet and reflective, whereas others are dominant and aggressive. Written communication allows students to consider their thoughts more carefully before expressing them. Wikis (web pages designed so that anyone who accesses the page can contribute to the written communication) also help students collaborate in goal setting, decision making, and providing support for one another.

Initial community-building activities help participants get to know each other and feel part of the group. Many experienced educators share their creative ideas for developing a group sense of trust and belonging via the Internet. (Go to Google and search for "community-building activities," "energizers," and/or "ice breakers" to find excellent ideas that help students get to know and trust each other.) Posting specific community-building and other activities on a class website can help students who are absent or new to the DLC.

ISSUES TO CONSIDER IN USING DIGITAL MEDIA

Reflecting on various issues related to using digital technology may assist teachers in addressing challenges that may arise. The issues briefly examined here are continuous partial attention, acceptable use policies, netiquette, social networks, cyberbullying, and conflict resolution.

Continuous Partial Attention

Continuous partial attention means giving less than full attention to two or more matters at any given time (Stone, 2008). The goal of continuous partial attention is to feel connected and busy. But if it becomes a regular part of a lifestyle, it leads to distress and pushes individuals into a crisis-management mode. To reduce continuous partial attention in classrooms, teachers can model giving full attention to others, teach students how to block out interruptions, and use a variety of communication tools for engaging attention and doing reflective thinking.

Acceptable Use Policy

Acceptable use policies (AUPs) refer to digital communication behaviors that are considered appropriate for all organizational users. Teachers can create classroom

AUPs that add critical information about the rights and responsibilities students have when using digital communication. These policies communicate what is considered to be fair, ethical, legal, and safe. They should be made an integral part of the democratic core curriculum, not limited merely to a paper the students sign at the beginning of the school year, and should be learning centered, with a focus on what to do rather than on what *not* to do. Some schools have a technology committee that periodically reviews and revises the AUP policies and practices. For suggestions on developing AUPs, see the Virginia Department of Education website at www.doe.virginia.gov/VDOE/Technology/AUP/home.shtml.

Netiquette

Netiquette refers to the use of civility and good manners when communicating via electronic media. Some people think that electronic communication is anonymous, and they may communicate in ways that are less than polite. Online communication differs from face-to-face communication in that body language, emotional expressions, and tone of voice cannot be seen. These realities can sometimes lead to misunderstandings and conflict. It is well to remember that the Golden Rule applies in netiquette just as it does in face-to-face interactions. When conflicts occur, one should ask for clarification and not take things personally. Helping participants acquire an electronic "social presence" and use netiquette will promote more effective electronic communication (Palloff and Pratt, 2007). The Webliography at the end of the chapter includes resources for learning more about netiquette.

Social Networks

Social networks such as MySpace, Facebook, and Flickr were popularized by young people, but nowadays adults of all ages are signing on to connect with lost friends or make new ones. Most popular networks require users to be at least 14 years of age, but it is easy for younger teens and preteens to gain access.

Networks have both benefits and liabilities that need to be considered when designing learning experiences. Researchers at the University of Minnesota (2008) recently found that 16- to 18-year-olds who were surveyed about using social networks had positive attitudes about using technology systems, editing and customizing content, and thinking about online design and layout. They shared creative original work (e.g., poetry and film) and practiced safe and responsible use of information and technology. (For more information, see www.21stcenturyskills.org.)

But safety concerns also exist. Although some tech-wise teens know how to keep themselves safe from scams, bullying, and predators, we should not assume all are able to do so. Therefore, we need to teach them how to keep contact information and passwords private, set the network to allow access only to friends they really know, use photos and text that would be acceptable for the front page of the local newspaper, and understand how sophisticated software is used by scammers to sell products or lure teens into dangerous encounters. Fodeman and Monroe (2008) provide information and lesson ideas for developing safe practices online.

Cyberbullying

Cyberbullying refers to emotional intimidation of others via electronic communication. It often takes the form of inappropriate and hurtful rumors, threats, or photos sent through email, text messaging, blogs, or website posts. Cyberbullying is easy to do and difficult to curtail. Schools and educators need to include clear guidelines on cyberbullying in AUPs, handbooks, classrooms, and curricula. The guidelines must provide information for bullies, victims, and bystanders, including how to prevent bullying and respond to it. In the curriculum, prevention themes should make clear when it is appropriate to stand up to bullies and report bully activity. Discussions should be used to clarify the differences between requesting help and "snitching" or tattling. Schools can begin by surveying students to investigate bullying and then help students treat each other respectfully at all times. Results can be shared with students, educators, and parents/guardians. (For more information on this subject, see Franek, 2005/2006 and Winter and Leneway, 2008.)

Conflict Resolution

As working groups develop, they invariably experience a certain amount of conflict. Tuckman (cited in Palloff and Pratt, 2007) noted this phenomenon in 1965, when he outlined stages of group development he called "forming, norming, storming, performing, and adjourning." Conflict ("storming") among group members is natural and inevitable. Palloff and Pratt (2007) found that online groups go through the same stages as do face-to-face groups, although the destructive effects of conflict may be greater online, due to a lack of verbal, facial, and body cues and difficulty in articulating emotions in a textual format. Online conflict often occurs during social aspects of group study, appearing, for example, as unwillingness to participate and disagreements between group members. Potential conflict should be addressed at the beginning of group work. Guidelines might include the need for all participants to give feedback to each other online and directions on how to proceed when impasses or serious conflicts occur—such as by stopping the discussion, seeking more information, and coming back later for further discussion.

But is conflict always destructive? Johnson and Johnson (cited in Putnam, 1998) stated that certain kinds of conflict are desirable in cooperative/collaborative learning. They recommend intentionally introducing *academic controversies*, in which students' ideas and opinions conflict with those of others. Discussing various perspectives and evaluating the advantages and disadvantages of the proposed ideas resolve the controversies. Properly done, the process calls on students to use online and library resources to investigate the topic, prepare a position statement, and advocate for it. After various perspectives are presented, the group works to reach consensus on the issue—or else agree to disagree.

A CULMINATING SCENARIO

The following scenario shows how democratic learning communities in technology-rich environments can be established collaboratively across various content areas.

Mr. Garcia teaches social studies in a middle school where clusters of students are organized into learning communities representing content areas. He collaborates with fellow teachers who share a common vision for learning in social studies, language arts, mathematics, science/health, art, physical education, world languages, and music. The teachers collaborate in planning and implementing multiage learning experiences for 100 seventh- and eighth-grade students. A special education teacher works with the students, coordinates services, and advises the cluster teachers about the various needs and talents of the students.

The teachers engage students in planning and learning the democratic core curriculum through thematic study. Projects frequently extend, realistically or virtually, the digitized classrooms to "bring in" the community and world.

At the beginning of the school day, students attend one of six advising groups for 30 minutes. Their purpose is to develop and learn to sustain a small learning community. The advising time is co-planned by students and teachers to include learning about each other, social skills, classroom guidelines, netiquette, AUP content, thinking skills, problem solving, celebrations, and more.

This semester the theme of study is "Our Role in Local and Global Economies." A goal for a culminating project is to develop a simulated economy within the middle school. Teachers, during their regular planning time, have identified the following themes for study: (1) money, barter, saving, spending, and credit; (2) goods and services; (3) producers and consumers; (4) jobs and entrepreneurs; (5) scarcity, profit, and trade; (6) stock market and banking; (7) roles of children, women, and men in depressed economies; (8) role of government; and (9) selected world economies.

Teachers assume responsibility for learning themes, standards, and project guidelines related to their areas of expertise. They also identify interdisciplinary standards and means of assessment. Mr. Garcia has supporting roles in each of the themes of the study, but focuses mostly on the last three. Students have common, individual, and small-group opportunities for learning. They are allowed choices in how they will demonstrate what they have learned.

All students learn how to critique and use electronic and printed resources legally. Ethical responsibilities of class members are developed and demonstrated. Students choose among inquiry projects, which have guidelines and assessment standards for all of the content areas, to demonstrate their learning. For example, students can research the role of children in various economies and create news broadcasts with a digital voice recorder or MP3 player. They can research the role of government in the United States and one other country and write a speech to present on a school website, providing their own informed perspective. They can write a letter to a reliable blog stating action, based on their own research, they believe government officials should take to resolve a particular economic situation. They can learn about local producers and take photos (with written permission) to create digital advertisements. Students and teachers can create a class website to share all of the learning projects/products.

The teachers are committed to professional learning through a process called *looking at student work* (www.lasw.org). They also have primary responsibility for coordinating assessment of learning in the small advisory groups. As they collaboratively review samples of students' work, they learn from each other and from their students about assessment of relevant standards of achievement.

Each democratic learning community is unique in its design to meet the needs, talents, and interests of students, while using technology to support the growth of the members.

Terms and Concepts

acceptable use policies

cyberbullying

democratic core curriculum

democratic learning communities

learning-centered approach

netiquette

social–emotional learning

social networks

technology-rich environments

Concept Cases

CASE 1: INTERNET FILTERING SYSTEM DOESN'T ALLOW COLLABORATION

You are a middle school teacher who wants students to collaborate on a research project to learn about civil discourse using Internet resources (e.g., wikis such as Google Docs). The school filtering system does not allow the sites that you believe are important sources of information and/or collaboration for the project. *What do you do?*

CASE 2: CYBERBULLYING

A ninth-grade student who has a difficult home life comes to you, the teacher, to ask for help because someone is sending email messages calling the student gay and ugly. The messages include the phrase "I hate you." *What do you do?*

CASE 3: TECHNOLOGY PARTNER SHARING

As a sixth-grade teacher you regularly have students working with a partner to conduct projects requiring computer tools. A student comes to you saying his partner will not let him use the keyboard. You discover the partner is using the computer for recreational purposes rather than working on the task. *What do you do?*

Activities

1. In your journal, add information from this chapter that you might wish to include in your personal system of discipline.
2. To what extent do you think you could put democratic learning communities in technology-rich environments into effect in your virtual or physical classroom? What portions might be implemented easily? What portions might be difficult?
3. How might you get started in co-designing democratic learning communities with technology-rich environments in your setting?
4. What would you consider to be important democratic core curricula in your setting?

5. How would you set out to build and improve relationships among participants in your learning environment?

6. What specific social–emotional skills might you wish to develop in your learning environment? How would you help students learn them?

References

Beane, J. A. 2002. Beyond self-interest: A democratic core curriculum. *Educational Leadership, 59*(7), 25–28.

Berger, R. 2003. *An ethic of excellence: Building a culture of craftsmanship with students.* Portsmouth, NH: Heinemann.

Fodeman, D., and Monroe, M. 2008. *Safe practices for life online: A guide to middle and high school.* Washington, DC: International Society for Technology in Education.

Franek, M. 2005/2006. Foiling cyberbullies in the new Wild West. *Educational Leadership, 63*(4), 39–43.

Goleman, D. 2006. *Emotional intelligence.* New York: Bantam Books.

Jonassen, D. H. 2000. *Computers as mindtools for schools* (2nd ed.). Upper Saddle River, NJ: Merrill/Prentice Hall.

Kolb, L. 2008. *Toys to tools: Connecting student cell phones to education.* Washington, DC: International Society for Technology in Education.

Norton, P., and Wiburg, K. 2003. *Teaching with technology: Designing opportunities to learn.* Belmont, CA: Wadsworth/Thomson Learning.

Palloff, R. M., and Pratt, K. 2007. *Building online learning communities: Effective strategies for the virtual classroom* (2nd ed.). San Francisco: John Wiley & Sons.

Payton, J., Weissberg, R. P., Durlak, J. A., Dymnicki, A. B., Taylor, R. D., Schellinger, K. B., and Pacham, M. 2008. *The positive impact of social and emotional learning for kindergarten to eighth-grade students: Findings from three scientific reviews.* Chicago: Collaborative for Academic, Social, and Emotional Learning.

Putnam, J. W. (Ed.). 1998. *Cooperative learning and strategies for inclusion* (2nd ed.). Baltimore: Paul H. Brookes Publishing.

Ribble, M., and Bailey, G. 2007. *Digital citizenship in schools.* Washington, DC: International Society for Technology in Education.

Richardson, K. W. 2008. Don't feed the trolls: Using blogs to teach civil discourse. *Learning & Leading with Technology, 35*(7), 12–15.

Squire, K. 2006. From content to context: Videogames as designed experience. *Educational Researcher, 25*(8), 19–29.

Stone, L. 2008. Linda Stone's thoughts on attention and specifically, continuous partial attention. *Jotspot WikiHome.* http://continuouspartialattention.jot.com/WikiHome

University of Minnesota. 2008, June 21. Educational benefits of social networking sites uncovered. *ScienceDaily.* www.sciencedaily.com/releases/2008/06/080620133907.htm

VanWie, E. K., Oxford, M., Martinez, A., and Sabo, K. 2008. Democratic learning communities in technology-rich environments: Survey and focus groups with middle school students. Unpublished data.

Vitto, J. M. 2003. *Relationship-driven classroom management: Strategies that promote student motivation.* Thousand Oaks, CA: Corwin Press.

Winter, R. E., and Leneway, R. J. 2008, March 1. Cyberbullying, part 3—What schools can do. http://techlearning.com/shared/printableArticle.php?articleID=196605055

Webliography

www.ataccess.org/default.html

Alliance for Technology Access is a national network of community-based resource centers, product developers, vendors, service providers, and individuals that provide information and support services to children and adults with disabilities, and work to increase their use of technology. Retrieved January 19, 2009.

www.bucks.edu/online/dlresources/etiquette.htm

Bucks County Community College in Newtown, Pennsylvania, provides an Online Etiquette Quiz. Retrieved January 19, 2009.

http://cct.edc.org/adv_results.asp

Center for Children and Technology investigates ways that technology can make a difference in children's classrooms, schools, and communities through basic, applied, formative, and summative research projects. The goal is to construct a more complete understanding of how to foster greater equity, student achievement, and teacher preparedness in schools. Retrieved January 19, 2009.

www.casel.org

Collaborative for Academic, Social, and Emotional Learning, Chicago, has a goal to make social and emotional learning an essential part of education. Numerous resources are provided. Retrieved January 10, 2009.

www.cyberbullying.org

Cyberbullying.org is Canadian-based and may be the first website specifically dedicated to the issue of cyberbullying. Retrieved January 19, 2009.

www.doe.virginia.gov/VDOE/Technology/AUP/home.shtml

Acceptable Use Policy examples are provided in a handbook by the Virginia Department of Education. Retrieved January 19, 2009.

http://edublogs.org

EduBlogs hosts numerous free blogs for teachers, students, librarians, researchers, and administrators. Retrieved March 27, 2009.

www.fcc.gov/cgb/consumerfacts/cipa.html

Federal Communications Commission (Consumer and Governmental Affairs Bureau) describes the Children's Internet Protection Act. Retrieved January 19, 2009.

www.google.com/educators/index.html

Google for Educators has many free resources for teachers, including GoogleDocs (a wiki used for collaborative writing). Retrieved March 27, 2009.

www.howstuffworks.com

"How Stuff Works" was founded by North Carolina State University President Marshall Brain in 1998. It includes easy-to-understand explanations of how the world actually works, including many technology tools. Retrieved January 18, 2008.

http://idea.ed.gov/explore/search

United States Department of Education provides information about the Individuals with Disabilities Education Act (IDEA), including assistive technology devices. Retrieved March 27, 2009.

www.iste.org

International Society for Technology in Education (ISTE) provides support for advancing the effective use of technology in education. The national technology standards for students and teachers provide a framework for this goal. Retrieved January 10, 2009.

www.lasw.org

Looking at Student Work provides protocols and resources for teachers committed to studying and working together to examine and learn from examples of student work. Retrieved April 25, 2009.

http://natri.uky.edu/natribackground/topics.html

The goal of the National Assistive Technology Research Institute is to research planning, development, implementation, and evaluation of assistive technology services in schools. They identify and disseminate promising practices that may assist schools in developing policies that improve learning opportunities for students with disabilities. Retrieved March 27, 2009.

http://online.uwc.edu/Technology/onlEtiquette.asp

University of Wisconsin provides information about online etiquette that supports more effective communication. Retrieved January 19, 2009.

www.21stcenturyskills.org

Partnership for 21st Century Skills is a collaborative among business, education, community, and government leaders that works to integrate 21st century skills in K–12 schools. Retrieved March 23, 2009.

www.unites.org/html/resource/knowledge/Online_safety.htm

United Nations Information Technology Service provides an article about online safety, security, and ethics. Retrieved January 19, 2009.

www.webquest.org/index.php

WebQuests, inquiry-based lesson design models in which students use selected websites to investigate real-life problems or tasks were developed by Bernie Dodge at San Diego State University. Retrieved March 28, 2009.

www.wiredsafety.org

Wired Safety provides help, education, and information to Internet and mobile device users of all ages. Retrieved January 19, 2009.

PART FOUR

FOUR

What Remains to Be Done?

CHAPTER 16 How Do I Finalize a System of Discipline Designed Especially for Me and My Students?

This chapter presents guidelines for realizing the ultimate goal of this book—a personalized system of discipline that meets your needs and those of the students you teach. To assist you in completing this culminating work, the planning rubric that appeared in Chapter 1 is presented once more, along with numerous possibilities you might wish to address or include. Also provided are suggestions for communicating your discipline plan to students, parents, and administrators. Finally, two prototypical discipline systems, prepared and used by real teachers, are presented for your examination.

16

How Do I Finalize a System of Discipline Designed Especially for Me and My Students?

You are now ready to finalize your personal system of discipline. The planning rubric introduced in Chapter 1 is again presented here, along with notes that clarify and amplify it. By using the rubric as a guide and by referring back to notes you may have taken from chapters you have read, you can easily complete a well-designed personalized system of discipline.

THE PLANNING RUBRIC: PUTTING IT ALL TOGETHER

Professional and Philosophical Considerations

My Philosophy of Discipline

A philosophy of any topic summarizes one's beliefs concerning the overall nature and value of that topic. To state your **philosophy of discipline,** respond succinctly to the following questions. Some reminders are included to help you get started.

Question 1: What Is Classroom Discipline and Why Is It Considered Important? Classroom discipline refers to teachers' efforts to help students conduct themselves responsibly. Discipline is linked to *misbehavior,* defined as any behavior that, through *intent or thoughtlessness,* interferes with teaching or learning, threatens or intimidates others, or oversteps society's standards of moral, ethical, or legal behavior. Misbehavior, when left unchecked, makes classroom life chaotic, hinders teaching, suppresses learning, harms personal relationships, and fosters self-defeating habits.

Question 2: What Is the Purpose of Discipline—That Is, What Do We Want It to Accomplish? You might indicate how you would like your students to conduct themselves, now and in the future, and explain how discipline helps foster that behavior. You might mention its role in such things as a safe environment for students, better environment for learning, habits that enhance students' lives, considerate behavior, positive attitude, productive collaboration, self-control, initiative, self-direction, and personal responsibility.

My Theory of Discipline

Theories are attempts to describe the processes and relationships involved in given events or efforts. You can express your **theory of discipline** by responding to the following questions. Some reminders are included to help get you started.

Question 1: What Are the Necessary Components of an Effective System of Discipline? You might refer to steps taken to develop certain attitudes and behaviors; addressing conditions that often lead to misbehavior; tactics for responding effectively when students misbehave; a style of teaching that engenders purposeful effort; class rules that establish limits on behavior; how to relate positively with students; and procedures that promote student self-control, responsibility, and ability to get along with others.

Question 2: How Do the Various Components Affect Behavior? Generally speaking, discipline components or tactics are intended to suppress misbehavior while fostering responsible behavior that serves students well. Some do so proactively, some supportively, and some reactively, depending on when they are applied. Proactive components are put in place before misbehavior occurs in order to prevent it. They include such things as class rules, engaging activities, teacher charisma, teacher modeling, clear expectations, and clear procedures. Supportive components are put into effect to prolong students' interest or change activities when misbehavior seems imminent. They include such things as circulating among students and interacting with them, using an approach that calls for frequent student responses, or changing the activity. Reactive components exert influence after misbehavior occurs. They are used to stop the misbehavior and help the student regain self-control and behave more responsibly in the future. Tactics include giving students a time-out, practicing correct behavior, redoing an inappropriate behavior in a correct manner, speaking personally with individual students about inappropriate behavior, and demonstrating and practicing proper behavior.

My Professional Demeanor

Include commentary related to your adherence to professionalism, ethics, and legalities in teaching. (For reminders, refer back to Chapter 1.) Also indicate the personal demeanor you will endeavor to maintain and the style of communication you will employ with students. You may wish to use some of the following reminders in explaining how you will conduct yourself in class:

- Learn students' names quickly and chat with each of them as often as feasible.
- Always speak respectfully; don't preach to students, speak derisively, or use sarcasm.
- Use congruent communication and I-messages when discussing problems.
- Use connecting habits in place of "deadly habits" (see Chapter 8).
- Give personal attention to all students and show they are valued members of the class.
- Develop bonds of trust through helpfulness and fair treatment.

- Show students it is all right to make mistakes and use them as excellent opportunities for learning.
- Help students learn how to assume responsibility for the decisions they make.
- Make instructional activities interesting and worthwhile.
- Work to develop a sense of class community, with spirit, camaraderie, and helpful cooperation.
- Be constantly mindful of students' needs for security, hope, enjoyment, and competence.
- Present yourself as enthusiastic, energetic, and eager to help.
- Always model kindness, consideration, and good manners.
- Involve your students in making or approving class agreements about instruction and behavior. Ask students to accept and commit to the agreements as the code that guides class behavior.

Specifics of My Discipline Plan

Go to the Simulations section of Topic #12: Managing Problem Behaviors, in the **MyEducationLab** for your course and complete the simulation entitled "Creating an Effective Classroom 'Discipline' Policy."

Desired Classroom Behavior

Briefly describe the behavior you will try to foster in your class as concerns purposeful effort, respect for others, civility, self-direction, and personal responsibility. Indicate how you will teach these behaviors—through example, direct instruction, discussion, repeated practice, and so forth. (Refer to the Wongs' recommendations in Chapter 6 and Forni, Borba, and Gossen's recommendations in Chapter 13.)

Rules of Behavior

List the rules you will use to formalize behavior expectations and set limits.

Prevention of Misbehavior

Indicate what you will do in advance to reduce the likelihood of misbehavior. It is suggested that you refer back to Chapter 2 and review the section called "Personal and Environmental Factors That Promote Misbehavior." That section reviews 26 conditions that tend to promote misbehavior and what teachers can do to eliminate or soften their effects.

It is also important to reflect on how you will conduct yourself in class. You might wish to indicate what you will *do* and *avoid* as concerns the following:

- Manner of speaking with students
- Helping students do their work and behave themselves
- Showing appreciation for students and their efforts
- Presenting a model of desirable behavior
- Dealing with personal frustration
- Providing communication, directions, and feedback
- Planning and preparation

Support of Proper Behavior

In all classes there are times when students begin to show signs of incipient misbehavior. They become restless, look tired or bored, yawn, look out the window, and so forth. Indicate what you will do at those times to help students stay on task and persevere. Here are some suggestions:

- In advance, clearly demonstrate and practice all the procedures students are expected to follow.
- Communicate clearly and verify that students understand directions.
- Use a charismatic teaching style that enlivens students and holds their attention.
- Give each student personal attention as often as possible.
- Always do what you can to help students be successful.
- Encourage student initiative and responsibility.
- Solicit student feedback on topics and lessons they enjoy as well as things they would like to see changed.

Intervention when Misbehavior Occurs

When intervening in misbehavior, use procedures that have been established and practiced in advance. Encourage students to assume responsibility for correcting their misbehavior. Make sure their dignity is preserved in the process. Here are reminders for dealing with *minor infractions:*

- Show interest in the student's work and ask cheerful questions, make favorable comments, or provide hints.
- Catch students' eyes, send private signals, or move closer to students.
- Issue a light challenge: "Can you finish five problems before we stop?"
- Ask students if they are having difficulty. Ask what you might to do help.
- If the work is boring or too difficult, restructure it or change the activity.

Here are reminders concerning intervention into *more serious infractions:*

- Follow intervention procedures that have been clearly established in advance, with student involvement and approval. Examples include re-teaching correct behavior, having students practice proper behavior, calling on offending students to identify their level or type of behavior, invoking consequences, helping students make restitution and self-restitution, and asking students to write out their plan for proper behavior in the future.
- Talk with offending students calmly and respectfully. Don't lecture, threaten, impugn their dignity, or back them into a corner. Remain pleasant and composed. Don't argue. Remind students they helped make the class rules and agreed to abide by them. Ask them to state how they will conduct themselves responsibly in the future. Make notes of what they say.
- Don't give in to student wheedling or begging. Remind them they can now make a fresh start and everything will be all right as long as they follow the class rules.

- Teach students how to use win-win conflict resolution. If they have disputes, ask them to try to resolve their conflict.
- Use class meetings to address matters that concern the entire class.

Communication with Students

Indicate how you will endeavor to speak with students to best accomplish the following:

- Maintaining student dignity (consult Ginott and Curwin, Mendler, and Mendler in Chapter 12)
- Exerting positive influence on students (consult Glasser and Daly in Chapter 12)
- Establishing and maintaining a sense of "we," or same side with students (consult Kagan in Chapter 9 and Charles in Chapter 14)
- Encouraging personal responsibility (consult Marshall in Chapter 10)
- Redirecting improper behavior (consult Ginott in Chapter 4, Morrish in Chapter 5, Marshall in Chapter 10, and Gossen in Chapter 13)

Communicating My Discipline Plan to Students and Others

Indicate briefly how you will make students, administrators, and parents aware of your discipline plan, including its purpose; nature; and roles of teacher, students, and possibly parents. You might wish to include the following:

- What you will say and show to administrators and parents. (Speak with your administrator before you introduce the plan to students or parents.)
- What you will say, show, demonstrate, explain, and discuss with your students when introducing your system. Have this ready when you first meet your students. You might include how you would like the class to function, how you will relate to students, how you want them to relate to you and each other, and how you would like for them to assume and display personal responsibility so everyone can flourish in safety and comfort. (Consult Morrish, Chapter 5; Glasser, Chapter 8; Marshall, Chapter 10; and Seganti, Chapter 11.)
- Show, on a chart, the headings for jobs or roles the teacher and students are expected to fill in making the class enjoyable and successful. You might wish to ask students to add suggestions. (Consult the Wongs, Chapter 6; and Gossen, Chapter 13.)
- Clarify the behaviors you expect from students and demonstrate the procedures you want them to follow. Indicate that you will ask students to practice sufficiently that they can display the behaviors and follow the rules comfortably. (Consult Morrish, Chapter 5; the Wongs, Chapter 6; Marshall, Chapter 10; and Charles, Chapter 14.) This activity might culminate in a brief set of agreements concerning how teacher and students will conduct themselves in class, together with what will be done to help those who violate the agreements.

TWO PROTOTYPICAL APPROACHES TO DISCIPLINE

For your perusal, here are two discipline approaches constructed and used by experienced teachers. The first places emphasis on rules and consequences that are applied when students misbehave. The second places emphasis on student–teacher cooperation and preventing misbehavior. It is not suggested you emulate these approaches. They simply illustrate highly successful teachers' efforts to help students learn and behave responsibly.

Prototype 1: An Approach That Emphasizes Rules and Consequences

Many teachers use discipline plans that feature rules and consequences. They feel this approach provides stability in the classroom and allows students to learn in a supportive environment. Discipline plans of this type contain (1) a set of *rules* concerning what students are allowed and not allowed to do in class; (2) *consequences*—what happens to students when they behave in certain ways—that may be positive (pleasant) or negative (unpleasant); and (3) *procedures* that are followed in applying the consequences. This approach has served hundreds of thousands of teachers for many years and is still popular today. To see how a present-day teacher uses the rules–consequences procedure protocol, examine the following program developed by third-grade teacher Deborah Sund.

Deborah Sund's Third-Grade Discipline Plan

Deborah Sund, who had been teaching for two years when she devised this program, was seeking a discipline approach that provided structure for her and her students while meeting the needs of all members of the class. Notice that Ms. Sund's plan takes into account students' needs, her own needs, and her particular dislikes.

My Students' Needs

- To learn interesting and useful information, especially that which promotes skills in reading, math, and language
- A learning environment that is attractive, stimulating, free from threat, and conducive to productive work
- A teacher who is helpful, attentive, and kind
- The opportunity to interact and work cooperatively with other students
- To be accepted and feel part of the group
- To learn how to relate to others humanely and helpfully
- To have the opportunity to excel

My Own Needs

- Orderly classroom appearance: good room arrangement; materials neatly stored; interesting, well-thought-out displays
- Structure and routines: a set schedule that allows flexibility and improvisation when needed

- Attention and participation: students pay attention to directions and speakers and participate willingly in all instructional activities
- Situationally appropriate behaviors: quiet attention during instruction; considerate interaction during group activities
- Enthusiasm from me and my students
- Warmth, as reflected in mutual regard among all members of the class
- Positive, relaxed classroom environment reflecting self-control, mutual helpfulness, and assumption of responsibility

My Dislikes

- Inattention to speaker, teacher, other adult, or class member
- Excessive noise: loud voices, inappropriate talking and laughing
- Distractions: toys, unnecessary movement, poking, teasing
- Abuse of property: misusing, wasting, or destroying instructional materials
- Unkind and rude conduct: ridicule, sarcasm, bad manners, and physical abuse

Class Rules.   I ask students on the first day of school to tell me how they would like to be treated by others in the room. I also ask them what they especially dislike. We discuss their contributions at length, making sure through examples that we have a clear understanding of everyone's wishes. By the next day, I have written out some statements that summarize what they have said. I ask them if these ideas seem good ones to live by in the room. They invariably agree and we call the statements our class rules. We spend some time practicing how we will conduct ourselves in accordance with the rules. In the days that follow, I demonstrate the prompts, cues, hints, and other assistance I will give to help my students abide by the behaviors we have agreed on. The following are class rules that typically emerge from discussions with my students:

- Be considerate of others at all times. (Speak kindly. Be helpful. Don't bother others.)
- Do our best work. (Get as much done as possible. Do work neatly, to be proud of it. Don't waste time.)
- Use quiet voices in the classroom. (Use regular speaking voices during class discussions. Speak quietly during cooperative work. Whisper at other times.)
- Use signals to request permission or receive help. (I explain the signals for assistance, movement, and the restroom pass.)

Positive Consequences.   I emphasize that I will always try to show I am pleased in the following ways when students follow the rules we have agreed to:

- Mostly I will give them smiles, winks, nods, and pats when they behave well.
- Sometimes I will say out loud how pleased I am with the way they are working or behaving toward each other.
- Once in a while, when the whole class has behaved especially well, I will give them a special privilege, such as early recess, watching a video, or doing a favorite activity.

- From time to time I will send a complimentary note to their parents or call their parents and comment on how well they are doing.

Negative Consequences. When discussing the class rules, I ask students what they think should happen when someone breaks a rule. They usually suggest punishment. I tell them I don't believe in punishment, but will instead do the following:

- Give them "pirate eyes" (a stern glance with disappointed or puzzled expression).
- Point out that a rule is being broken: "I hear noise." "Some people are not listening."
- Tell them exactly what they have done wrong and ask them to do it properly: "Gordon, you did not use the signal. Ask again and use the signal this time."
- Separate them from the group until they can conduct themselves properly.
- As a last resort, contact their parents and ask for their help.

To Prevent Misbehavior. I discuss with my students a number of things I will do to help them want to behave properly, such as the following:

- Show respect for each student as entitled to the best education I can provide.
- Look for the positive and enjoyable qualities in each student.
- Take time to know each student better on a personal level.
- Take notice of students' feelings and discuss them if necessary.
- Talk with students in ways that imply their own competence, such as, "Okay, you know what to do next."
- Involve them in establishing rules and assuming responsibility for proper behavior.
- Maintain proper lighting, temperature, traffic patterns, and room attractiveness so they won't feel strained, tired, or inconvenienced.
- Emphasize, model, and hold practice sessions on good manners, courtesy, and responsibility.
- Provide a varied, active curriculum with opportunities for physical movement, singing, interaction, and quiet times.
- Keep their parents informed and ask for their support.
- End each day on a positive note, with a fond goodbye and expectations of a happy and productive tomorrow.

Intervening when Students Misbehave. When students begin to misbehave, I will do the following:

- Move close to the student.
- Show interest in the student's work.
- Provide help or modify the activity if it seems to be causing difficulty.
- If necessary, invoke the negative consequences that we have agreed to.

Prototype 2: An Approach That Emphasizes Prevention and Cooperation between Teacher and Students

The following approach emphasizes preventing misbehavior by meeting student needs and building personal relationships. The rationale for this approach is twofold: First, it is difficult to confront misbehavior head-on without producing undesirable side effects such as student resentment and reluctance to cooperate, and second, working with students in this manner promotes greater satisfaction and enjoyment for everyone. When needs are met, students become more inclined to cooperate and less interested in outsmarting or disdaining the teacher, and when causes of misbehavior are addressed rather than the personal character of the student, positive feelings are kept intact. Plans of this sort emphasize the following:

- Attending continually to students' needs for security, hope, acceptance, dignity, power, enjoyment, and competence
- Communicating effectively and regularly with students and their parents
- Making sure to give all students attention, encouragement, and support
- Making class activities consistently enjoyable and worthwhile
- Ensuring that all students experience success and accept responsibility
- Establishing agreements about how class members will interact and behave
- Discussing and practicing manners, courtesy, and responsibility
- Involving all students meaningfully in the operation of the class
- Dealing with incipient misbehavior by attending to its causes

Teachers who adopt this discipline strategy feel it allows them to relate with students in a way that builds positive relationships and produces relatively little stress. Gail Charles uses a discipline plan that incorporates many of these qualities.

Gail Charles's Eighth-Grade English Discipline Plan

The following narration is in Gail Charles's words:

I have been teaching for 25 years. For many of those years, my students misbehaved much more than I thought they should, and I tried to control their misbehavior with scowls, reprimands, lectures, threats, and detentions. My students grudgingly behaved well enough to learn most of what I intended, but I'm sure they felt under siege. I know I did, and the effort it required left me continually frustrated and exhausted.

Seven or eight years ago I began to understand that I am more effective and enjoy my work more when I organize the curriculum to accommodate, even embrace, the needs of my adolescent students and then work cooperatively with them. While I still provide a strong and challenging curriculum, I have switched from a coercive to a collaborative way of teaching. I now try to guide, encourage, and support students' efforts rather than endlessly push and prod. The result has been fewer power struggles, more success, and happier students and teacher.

Winning My Students Over.   My students want to feel accepted and valued by each other and especially by me. They also want to feel safe, so I forbid all ridicule and sarcasm. I've never ridiculed a student, but sorry to say, I have spoken sarcastically many times when struggling against students who disregarded my expectations. I have changed that and no longer use sarcasm or allow students to belittle each other in any way.

I give my students a voice in class matters and listen to them sincerely. I allow them to make decisions about where they sit and with whom they wish to work. I do this as part of trying to make learning enjoyable. They like to work with each other, participate, talk, and cooperate.

Meeting My Needs.   We discuss the importance of making the class enjoyable. I tell the students the class needs to be enjoyable for me, too. I explain up front what I need in order to feel good about the class—that I want the tone to be positive, with everyone showing patience, tolerance, good manners, and mutual respect. I tell them that I want them to be enthusiastic and do the best work they can. I say I need their attention and that I want them to help care for materials and keep the room clean. I promise to treat them with respect, and they usually reciprocate.

Rules and Student Input.   My new approach to discipline has required me to make changes in my curriculum and ways of establishing rules. I have learned to request and make use of student input concerning expectations, operating procedures, and codes of conduct. Formerly, I greeted new students with a printed set of rules and consequences, but often they only saw them as impositions. Now when I meet a new class, I discuss their needs and mine and focus on how we can meet those needs and make our class productive. I give students power to make many decisions and show that I respect what they say.

Together we write a plan for how we will work and behave in the class. Because I want them to make thoughtful suggestions, I ask them, for their first homework assignment, to think back on previous years in school and write brief responses to the following:

- When have you felt most successful in school?
- What did the teacher do to help you feel successful?
- What kinds of class activities have you found most helpful and enjoyable?
- What suggestions do you have for creating a classroom in which all can work, learn, and do their best?

The next day I organize students into small groups to share and discuss what they have written. Volunteers present each group's responses, which I list and project for all to see. Occasionally I add a suggestion of my own. We then streamline, combine, reword, and sometimes negotiate until we reach a set of agreements. Before the next class, I print out copies of the agreements and ask each student and his or her parent or guardian to sign it, indicating their support. I do this for each of my five classes. The agreements turn out to be quite similar from class to class.

Prevention.   In classes of 35 students, distractions abound. It is up to me to keep students successfully engaged in activities they find enjoyable and rewarding. I have had considerable success using reading and writing activities in which students choose books to read and react to them in writing. I present mini-lessons that address common needs I see in the class. Students evaluate their own work and make it the best possible for inclusion in their Showcase Portfolios, which are displayed for parents, teachers, administrators, and others at a Writers' Tea. In addition, students complete at least one project per quarter. They have choices on what they will pursue in their projects and how they will show what they have learned. There is always a high emphasis on quality.

During these efforts, I try to interact personally with every student. It is not easy to forge relationships with over 160 students, but I try to do so in order to show I notice and like them. At the beginning of the year I write a letter to my students introducing myself and telling a bit about my family, hobbies, interests, and goals. I ask them to do the same so I can know them better. I keep a birthday calendar to remember student birthdays. I try to comment on new hairstyles, new outfits, or how great a braces-free set of teeth looks. I chaperone field trips and dances, supervise the computer writing lab after school, and make myself available for conversation before and after school. These little things mean a lot to students.

For their part, many students like to involve themselves in the workings of the classroom. I assign them tasks such as classroom librarian, bulletin board designer, plant caretaker, and class secretary. Their involvement makes them feel important and useful.

More than anything else, I have found that if I want respect from my students, I must show them respect. I want them to enjoy writing, so I write along with them. I want them involved in learning, so I get involved with them. I want them to show good manners, humor, and kindness, so I exemplify those qualities the best I can in my behavior and dealings with them. I make lots of mistakes in these efforts, but the more sincerely I try, the more forgiving my students become.

Interventions.   With the collaborative plan in place, I have relatively few discipline problems and experience little difficulty in dealing with those that occur. Most often, a simple reminder is all that is needed to get students back on track. However, I do use a plan, which I discuss fully with students, for dealing with misbehavior at different levels of seriousness. I explain it to my students as follows:

- *When students begin to become restive.* I am continually alert for signs of disengagement from lessons, as when students begin to fidget, doodle, look out the window, smile or make gestures at each other, whisper, and the like. At those times I will make eye contact with those students or move toward them and ask a question about the work in progress. If several students are losing interest near the end of a lesson, I might make a comment such as, "Class, I'll really appreciate it if you can stick with the lesson for five more minutes." If they begin to lose interest earlier, I say, "Class, I see this activity is not holding your attention. What seems to be the trouble? Any suggestions?" Often they help me resolve the problem.

- *When students violate class agreements.* Most of the time when students violate class agreements they do so unintentionally or without malice—they talk, call out, move about, goof off, or fail to complete their work. But sometimes they misbehave in more troublesome ways, such as showing disrespect for me, treating others abusively, or lying and cheating. That doesn't happen often, but when it does, I have learned to do the following: I say either privately to the individual or to the entire class if all are affected, "This is a serious problem. I'd like us to resolve it together. Let's try. But if we can't, I'll need to ask for help from the vice principal." I do not attack individuals, but instead point out what is occurring and why it is forbidden in the classroom. I ask for their help in keeping the classroom comfortable for everyone. Usually no further action is needed.

But if any individuals continue to cause trouble, I speak with them privately and explain once more why those acts are not permitted in the class or school. I assure them that my goal is not to punish, but to help them develop responsible behavior. Some students will acknowledge what they've done; others will deny it. I don't try to make them admit wrongdoing and I never insist they apologize. What I do is explain my perception of the situation and point out how that disrupts learning and makes others uneasy or afraid. I emphasize that I want to help them to be successful and become the best person they can be. I ask them to think of two better things they might do if the situation occurs again. I ask them if there is anything I can do to help them, and I try sincerely to do so. I feel this is as much as I can realistically do to help them. If that does not work, I inform the school counselor or administrator and let that person take over from there.

I rarely have to face behavior that is threatening, dangerous, or wantonly cruel, such as severe bullying, intimidation, fighting, or possession of weapons or dangerous substances. My procedure in those circumstances is to call for help immediately. That is the policy at my school. At that point, the matter moves out of my hands and into those of persons with special training.

THE FORMULA FOR SUCCESS IS NOW IN YOUR HANDS

When you have accomplished the suggested tasks, you will have developed a system of discipline that will promote success for you and your students. You can confidently gain students' respect and cooperation through establishing personal relations with them, tending to their concerns, supporting their efforts, and helping them overcome obstacles.

As you implement your discipline system and become accustomed to it, both you and your students will make mistakes—perhaps many at first. Point out that mistakes do not necessarily deter learning, but usually help it by providing springboards to higher levels of competence. Ask your students forthrightly to work with you, not against you. Reassure them you will always help them the best you can. The resultant attitude of cooperation will allow you to make full use of your teaching skills in providing an educational experience of high quality for everyone.

Go to the IRIS Center Resources section of Topic #12: Managing Problem Behaviors, in the **MyEducationLab** for your course and complete the module entitled "Who's in Charge? Developing a Comprehensive Behavior Management System."

Go to the IRIS Center Resources section of Topic #12: Managing Problem Behaviors, in the **MyEducationLab** for your course and complete the module entitled "You're in Charge! Developing Your Own Comprehensive Behavior Management System."

Terms and Concepts

philosophy of discipline
theory of discipline

GLOSSARY

The following terms are featured in the models of discipline and supporting chapters in this book. When appropriate, authorities who originated and/or helped popularize the term are indicated.

ABCD of disruptive behavior (Kagan)   Aggression, breaking rules, confrontations, disengagement

Acceptable use policies   Policies (sometimes called Internet use policies) created by schools to define acceptable use of digital communication tools for all users of the system, emphasizing ethical, equitable, safe, social, and legal aspects of electronic communication tools

Accountability   Students being held responsible for making an effort to learn and conduct themselves responsibly

Affective disorders   Disorders that affect mood or feeling, such as bipolar disorder

Anxiety disorders   Emotional disorders that involve fear and extreme uneasiness

Appraising reality (Redl and Wattenberg)   Having students recognize what they are doing wrong

Appreciative praise (Ginott)   Praise that expresses gratitude or admiration for effort

Assertive teachers (the Canters)   Teachers who clearly, confidently, and consistently reiterate class expectations and attempt to build trust with students

Attention-deficit hyperactivity disorder   A mental health issue characterized by short attention span, weak impulse control, and hyperactivity

Attention seeking (Dreikurs)   A mistaken goal of student behavior, involving disruption and showing off to gain attention from the teacher and other students

Authority without punishment   Methods of exerting authority in the classroom without resorting to threat or punishment

Autism spectrum disorder   A range of disorders in which individuals fail to develop normal speech patterns or personal relationships

Autocratic classrooms (Dreikurs)   Classrooms in which teachers command, demand cooperation, dominate, and criticize

Backup system (Jones)   The planned action teachers take when students misbehave seriously and refuse to comply with teacher requests (often means being sent to the principal's office)

Basic needs   Psychological requirements for normal functioning

Basic student needs (Charles)   Security, belonging, hope, dignity, power, enjoyment, and competence

Basic student needs (Dreikurs)   Belonging

Basic student needs (Glasser)   Survival, belonging, control, freedom, and fun

Behavior   The totality of one's physical and mental activities

Behavior as choice (Glasser and others)   The contention that students choose their behavior at any given time.

Behavior difficulties   Generally, student behavior that breaks rules or disrupts learning

Behavior management   Organized efforts to get students to behave in particular ways

Behavior modification   The use of Skinnerian principles of reinforcement to control or shape behavior

Bell work (Jones)   Work students do to begin a class period that does not require instruction from the teacher, such as reading, writing in journals, or completing warm-up activities

Belonging (Dreikurs and Glasser)   A basic human need for legitimate membership in groups, with attendant security and comfort—for Dreikurs, the primary need that motivates social behavior in school

Big Three of discipline (Kagan)   Curriculum, instruction, and management

Bipolar disorder   A mental health diagnosis characterized by alternating cycles of euphoria and depression

Body carriage (Jones)   Posture and movement that indicate to students whether the teacher is well, ill, in charge, tired, disinterested, or intimidated

Body language (Jones)   Nonverbal communication transmitted through posture, eye contact, gestures, and facial expressions.

Boss teachers (Glasser)   Teachers who set the tasks, direct the learning activities, ask for little student input, and grade student work (contrast with *lead teachers*)

Brain injuries, nontraumatic   Cerebral injuries resulting from disrupted blood flow to the brain (as in strokes), or from tumors, infections, drug overdoses, and certain medical conditions

Brain injuries, traumatic Cerebral injuries resulting from blows or other physical damage to the brain, incurred during events such as accidents, sporting events, assaults, or birth

Causes of misbehavior (Charles) The 26 conditions known to foster misbehavior, such as boredom and threat to personal dignity; most can be minimized or eliminated from the classroom

Choice theory (Glasser) Theory that we all choose how to behave at any time and cannot control anyone's behavior but our own, and that all behavior is purposeful in meeting basic needs

Civility Conducting oneself courteously and sensitively, with good manners

Classroom communities (Kohn) Classrooms and schools where students feel cared about and care about each other, are valued and respected, are involved in decision making, and have a sense of *we* rather than *I.*

Class rules Written code that specifies acceptable and unacceptable behavior in the classroom

Conduct disorder A mental health diagnosis in which students strongly violate society's normal standards of behavior

Conferring dignity (Ginott) Showing respect for students by putting aside their past history, treating them considerately, and being concerned only with the present situation

Conflict A problem situation, such as a dispute, that involves a strong clash of wills

Congruent communication (Ginott) A style of communication in which teachers acknowledge and accept students' feelings about situations and themselves

Coopetition (Charles) Cooperation by members in groups that are engaged in competition against other groups—most notable in sports teams

Corrective discipline Steps taken by the teacher to stop student misbehavior

Cyberbullying Misusing technology to harass, intimidate, bully, or terrorize another person

Democratic classrooms (Dreikurs) Classrooms in which teachers give students responsibility and involve them in making decisions

Democratic core curriculum Curriculum that integrates interdisciplinary content, processes, standards, learning experiences, and assessment, supporting the democratic values of freedom of choice, shared responsibility, and self-governance/direction

Democratic learning communities Groups of people (students, families, educators, and the public) who work together to promote meaningful learning

Discipline (Charles) What teachers do to help students conduct themselves appropriately in class

Discipline (Jones) Efforts to engage students in learning, with teachers using the most positive, unobtrusive tactics possible

Discipline, corrective (Charles) Steps teachers take to stop misbehavior and redirect it in a positive manner

Discipline, four-step approach to (Borba) Respond, review, reflect, and make right

Discipline, preventive (Charles) Steps teachers take in advance to prevent or reduce the occurrence of misbehavior

Discipline structures (Kagan) Discipline tactics specially designed for use with different types of disruptive behavior

Discipline, supportive (Charles) Tactics teachers use to help students remain on task when they show signs of incipient misbehavior

Displaying inadequacy (Dreikurs) Student withdrawal and failure to try

Doorway tactics (Seganti) Tactics teachers use as students enter the room to help ensure that they do not misbehave

Dyslexia A mental health diagnosis characterized by difficulties in word recognition, spelling, word decoding, and occasionally with the phonological (sound) component of language

Economically disadvantaged Condition of students living in poverty that may interfere with expected educational progress

Elicit (Marshall) Using tactics that get students to suggest acceptable courses of behavior, rather than imposing teacher demands on them

Empowerment of choice (Marshall) Allowing students to select from acceptable choices how they will conduct themselves—a tactic that empowers students to succeed

Essential virtues (Borba) Empathy, conscience, self-control, respect, kindness, tolerance, and fairness, all of which can and should be taught in school

Ethics of instruction (Charles) A principle of behavior management that stresses morally correct behavior as part of developing trust in the classroom

Evaluative praise (Ginott)   Praise that expresses judgment about students' character or quality of work; considered to be detrimental by Ginott and various other authorities

External motivation   Synonymous with extrinsic motivation—that which comes from outside the individual

Fetal alcohol spectrum disorder   A mental health diagnosis, caused by alcohol consumption by the mother during pregnancy, in which students show poor impulse control, poor judgment, lack of common sense, and learning difficulties

15-minute detention (Seganti)   The requirement that misbehaving students must attend after-school detention for 15 minutes, which provides strong leverage in ensuring that students comply with class rules

Follow-up structures (Kagan)   A discipline tactic used to help students develop proper behavior over the long run

Four classical virtues (Marshall)   Prudence, temperance, justice, and fortitude—these should be emphasized in the process of helping students develop desirable behavior

General rules (Jones)   General rules of behavior that apply at all times, as distinct from specific rules related to certain activities

Genuine discipline   That which leads to student self-control and responsibility

Genuine goal of student behavior (Dreikurs)   Belonging, a fundamental desire to acquire a sense of place and value in a group

Genuine incentives (Jones)   Incentives that truly motivate students to work or behave appropriately, as contrasted with vague incentives such as "become a better person"

Good and bad choices   Choices that result in good or bad behavior, according to theorists who believe behavior results from choices students make

Grandma's rule (Jones)   "First eat your vegetables, then you can have your dessert," or "First finish your work, then you can do something you especially enjoy"

Group alerting (Kounin)   Quickly getting students' attention to advise them of what they should be doing or do next

Group behavior (Redl and Wattenberg)   Behavior that is different from the ways individuals typically behave—more conforming in some ways, combined with more risk taking

Group concern (Jones)   A condition in which every student has a stake in the behavior the group uses to earn preferred activity time

Group dynamics (Redl and Wattenberg)   Psychological forces produced within groups that promote certain kinds of behavior

Helpless handraisers (Jones)   Students who sit with their hands raised, not working unless the teacher is hovering nearby

Hidden asset (Ginott)   Sincerely asking students, "How can I help you?"

Hidden rules   Seldom-recognized values and guidelines that strongly direct behavior in various ethnic and socio-economic groups

Hierarchy of social development (Marshall)   A hierarchy of four levels used to help students reflect on their chosen behaviors; From lowest to highest, the four levels are anarchy, bossing/bullying, cooperation/conformity, and democracy (inseparable from responsibility)

I-messages (Ginott)   Expressing personal feelings and reactions to situations without addressing student behavior or character; for example, "I have trouble teaching when there is so much noise in the room"

Incentive (Jones)   Something outside of the individual that can be anticipated and that entices the individual to act

Influence techniques (Redl and Wattenberg)   Positive influence such as providing attention and support, rather than punishment, to help students conduct themselves appropriately

In loco parentis   Exercising care over students in place of parents

INTASC   The Interstate New Teacher Assessment and Support Consortium, which has described competencies teachers require for professional teaching

Interior loop (Jones)   A classroom seating arrangement with wide aisles to allow teachers to move easily among students at work

Internal motivation (Marshall)   Motivation to behave responsibly without having to be told to do so because of beliefs rooted in ethics and values

Intervention   What teachers do when students misbehave to correct the misbehavior and redirect it in a positive manner

Inviting cooperation (Ginott)   Encouraging and enticing students into activities and giving them choices, rather than demanding their participation

I-statements   See *I-messages*

Laconic language (Ginott)   Brevity of teacher's comments about misbehavior; for example, "This is work time"

Lead teachers (Glasser)   Teachers who involve students in exploring topics and activities for learning, provide necessary help, and encourage students to do quality work

Learning-centered approach   Methodologies and strategies that focus on meaningful learning rather than on teachers or students

Learning communities (Kohn)   See *Classroom communities*

Learning disabilities (LD)   A mental health diagnosis in which students exhibit unusual difficulties in learning certain subjects in school

Least coercive road (Gossen)   A discipline strategy in which teachers use the least amount of coercion (of student behavior) that still allows the class to function effectively

Leverage (Seganti)   Something that teachers can use to ensure student compliance with rules; in Seganti's approach, leverage exists in the form of the 15-minute detention

Life skills   Capabilities such as self-discipline and ability to relate with others that serve one throughout life

Limits   The boundaries that separate acceptable behavior from unacceptable behavior in the classroom

Logical consequences (Dreikurs)   Conditions invoked by the teacher that are logically related to behavior students choose; for example, making amends for what one has done wrong

Long-term structures (Kagan)   Plans for helping students improve their behavior over time

Massive time wasting (Jones)   A condition Jones found prevalent in classrooms where discipline was not efficient

Misbehavior   Behavior that is considered inappropriate for the setting or situation in which it occurs or any behavior that, through intent or thoughtlessness, interferes with teaching or learning; threatens or intimidates others; or oversteps society's standards of moral, ethical, or legal behavior

Misbehavior, causes of (Charles)   The 26 factors that reside in students, the class environment, school personnel, and elsewhere that tend to promote student misbehavior

Mistaken goals (Dreikurs)   Goals of attention, power, revenge, and avoidance of failure that students seek in the mistaken belief they will bring positive recognition and sense of belonging

Momentum (Kounin)   Getting activities started promptly, keeping them moving ahead, and bringing them to efficient transition or closure

Moral intelligence (Borba)   The ability to distinguish right from wrong, the establishment and maintenance of strong ethical convictions, and the willingness to act on those convictions in an honorable way

Netiquette   Complying with standards of courtesy and civility when sending text messages or communicating via the Internet

Neurological-based behavior (NBB)   Behavior associated with compromised neurological functioning, often outside the student's control

Neurological differences   Notable variations in student behavior, believed to be the result of differences in cerebral functioning

Nonassertive teachers (the Canters)   Teachers who fail to take charge and assume a passive, hands-off approach in dealing with students

Noncoercive discipline (Glasser and others)   Discipline in which teachers invite and encourage proper behavior, rather than using demands or threats

Omission training (Jones)   An incentive plan for an individual student who, by cutting down on undesired behavior, can earn preferred activity time for the entire class

Oppositional defiant disorder   A mental health diagnosis in which students regularly oppose and defy the teacher and others

Overlapping (Kounin)   Attending to two or more issues in the classroom at the same time

Permissive classrooms (Dreikurs)   Classrooms in which teachers put few if any limits on student behavior and do not invoke consequences for disruptive behavior

Personal improvement plan (Kagan)   A plan devised cooperatively between teacher and student to help curtail the student's disruptive behavior

Perspective taking (Kohn)   Doing one's best to see and understand a situation from another person's point of view

Philosophy of discipline   The beliefs one has about the nature, purpose, and value of discipline

Physical proximity (Jones)   Moving close to a student who is becoming restive or is misbehaving

Positivity (Marshall)   Maintaining an inclination toward optimism

Post-traumatic stress disorder   A mental health diagnosis in which students have been adversely affected emotionally by witnessing or hearing about traumatic events

Power (Glasser)   A basic student need for control, satisfied when students are given significant duties in the class and are allowed to participate in making decisions about class matters

Power seeking (Dreikurs)   Behaviors such as temper tantrums, back talk, disrespect, and defiance that students use to try to show they have power over the teacher

Preferred activity time (PAT) (Jones)   Time allocated for students to engage in activities of their preference; used as an incentive to encourage responsible behavior

Preventive discipline (Charles)   The aspect of discipline in which one removes or otherwise controls factors likely to lead to misbehavior

Problem   A situation that causes discomfort for someone

Procedures (the Wongs)   Detailed instructions that indicate how students are to perform all activities in class and thus help forestall most discipline problems

Professionalism   Conducting oneself in accordance with the established standards and expectations of a given profession or line of work

Providing help efficiently (Jones)   A technique in which the teacher quickly provides enough help to get a student working again, then moves away in 20 seconds or less

Punishment   Applying strong physical or psychological discomfort to students who misbehave

Quality curriculum (Glasser)   A program of study that emphasizes excellence in learning that students consider useful

Quality teaching (Glasser)   Instruction in which teachers help students become proficient in knowledge and skills the students consider important; usually done via lead teaching

Rage   Extreme behavior, sometimes exhibited by students with NBB, manifested as an explosion of temper that occurs suddenly with no real warning and may turn violent

Rage cycle   Progression of rage through five phases—pre-rage, triggering, escalation, rage, and post-rage

Real Discipline (Morrish)   A three-phase (training, teaching, management) approach to discipline that makes use of teacher insistence and careful teaching of expectations and procedures

Reconciliation (Coloroso)   A human-relations skill in which individuals involved in disputes take steps to resolve and smooth over their differences

Reflective questions (Marshall)   Questions posed to students to help them make better behavioral choices and assume responsibility

Reinforcement (Skinner)   Supplying (or in some cases, removing) stimuli that influence an organism to behave in a particular manner

Reinforcing stimuli (Skinner)   Stimuli received by an organism immediately following a behavior, increasing the likelihood the behavior will be repeated

Resolution (Coloroso)   Identifying and correcting whatever caused a behavior problem; one of the follow-up steps in dealing with misbehavior

Restitution (Gossen, Coloroso)   Repairing or replacing damage done in irresponsible behavior—one of the steps in resolving the problem

Restitution Triangle (Gossen)   A triangle graphic that helps explain and guide the steps involved in the restitution process

Revenge seeking (Dreikurs)   Student behavior intended to be hurtful to the teacher or other students

Right to learn (the Canters)   The contention that students have a right to learn in classrooms that are safe and free from threat

Right to teach (the Canters)   The contention that teachers have a right to teach in classrooms that are free from disruptions, with backing from administrators and parents

Routines (the Wongs)   Detailed instructions that show students how to carry out various tasks in the classroom

Rules of considerate conduct (Forni)   A set of rules that in all areas of human interaction help us establish more enjoyable, companionable, and rewarding relationships with the people we meet

Satiation (Kounin)   Getting all one can tolerate of a given activity, resulting in frustration, boredom, or listlessness

Say, See, Do teaching (Jones)   A teaching method of repeated short cycles of teacher input, each followed by student response, that keeps students attentive and involved

Self-diagnostic referral (Marshall)   A self-diagnosis done by a student who has violated class rules and submitted as a plan for improvement; includes description of what was done wrong and the steps that will be taken to improve

Self-discipline (Ginott)   Self-control, which grows out of freedom to make decisions and having to live by the consequences

Self-restitution (Gossen)   A process of realigning one's behavior, following a transgression, with family or cultural values—helpful in becoming a better person less likely to engage in misconduct

Sensory integration dysfunction (SID)   Irregularities in the process we use to take in information from our senses and organize, interpret, and respond to it

Sensory processing disorder   See *Sensory integration dysfunction (SID)*

Setting limits   Clarifying with members of the class exactly what is expected of them

Seven connecting habits (Glasser)   Caring, listening, supporting, contributing, encouraging, trusting, and befriending; these should replace the seven deadly habits

Seven deadly habits (Glasser)   Criticizing, blaming, complaining, nagging, threatening, punishing, and rewarding students to control them

Shaping behavior (Skinner)   The process of using reinforcement to produce desired behavior in students

SIR (Glasser)   An acronym standing for the process of self-evaluation, improvement, and repetition, used to promote quality

Situational assistance (Redl and Wattenberg)   Providing help to students who, because of the difficulty of the task, are on the verge of misbehaving

Smoothness (Kounin)   Absence of abrupt changes or interruptions by the teacher that interfere with students' activities or thought processes

Social–emotional learning   Learning experiences that promote social and emotional development, including skills of self- and social awareness, self-management, decision making, and responsible actions

Social interest (Dreikurs)   The concept that one's personal well-being is dependent on the well-being of the group, which encourages individuals to behave in ways that benefit the group.

Social networks   Online places where people "meet" to socialize and connect with "friends" near and far

Specific rules   Rules that relate to class procedures and routines

Structures (Kagan)   Discipline approaches designed for use with particular combinations of disruptions and student positions

Student positions (Kagan)   Conglomerates of factors that leave students uninformed or dispose them to seek attention, show anger, avoid failure, become bored, seek control, or be overly energetic

Student roles (Redl and Wattenberg)   Roles students assume in the classroom, such as instigator, clown, leader, and scapegoat

Successive approximations (Skinner)   Behavior that, through reinforcement, moves progressively closer to the desired goal

Support buddies (the Wongs)   Students assigned to help or support each other

Support groups (the Wongs)   Groups of students who help and support each other

Supporting self-control (Redl and Wattenberg)   Doing things that help students maintain self-control when they are on the verge of misbehaving

Supportive discipline (Charles)   Applying tactics when students become restive that prompt them to resume responsible conduct

Survival (Glasser)   A basic need that motivates self-protective behavior

Synergetic discipline (Charles)   Discipline that removes most causes of misbehavior and energizes the class

Synergetic teaching (Charles)   Teaching in a manner that energizes the class by putting in place combinations of elements known to produce heightened classroom energy

Synergy (Charles)   A heightened state of energy that can occur when two or more entities feed energy to each other

Teacher misbehavior (Charles)   Anything teachers do in the classroom that adversely affects learning or human relations, or that is unprofessional in any way

Teacher roles (Redl and Wattenberg)   Various roles students expect teachers to play, such as surrogate parent, arbitrator, disciplinarian, and moral authority

Teachers at their best (Ginott)   Teachers who use congruent communication that addresses situations rather than students' character, invite student cooperation, and accept students as they are

Teachers at their worst (Ginott)   Teachers who name-call, label students, ask rhetorical "why" questions, give long moralistic lectures, and make caustic remarks to their students

Technology-rich environments (VanWie)   Classrooms or virtual spaces with current digital technology tools, such as wireless laptops, handheld devices, and learning management systems

Theory of discipline   An overall explanation of the elements that comprise discipline and how they work together to produce particular outcomes

Theory X (Marshall)   A theory that holds that people must be directed and controlled

Theory Y (Marshall)   A theory that holds that people should be encouraged and given responsibility

Three phases of Real Discipline (Morrish)   (1) Training for compliance, (2) teaching students how to behave, and (3) managing student choice

Three pillars of Win-Win Discipline (Kagan)   Teacher and students on the same side, sharing responsibility, and emphasizing behavior that meets students' needs in a nondisruptive manner

True discipline   Defined by most authorities as inner discipline, self-discipline, and self-control

Useful work (Glasser)   Schoolwork that deals with skills and information that students deem valuable in their lives

Visual instruction plan (VIP) (Jones)   Picture prompts that guide students through the process of the task or performance at hand

Why questions (Ginott)   Counterproductive questions that teachers put to students, asking them to explain or justify their behavior, e.g., "Why did you . . . ?"

Withitness (Kounin)   Knowing what is going on in all parts of the classroom at all times

Working the crowd (Jones)   Moving about the class while teaching and interacting with students

You-messages (Ginott)   Teacher messages that attack students' character, such as "You are acting like barbarians"—these messages are putdowns that can convey heavy blame and guilt

Alkins, K. 2007. AACTE proposal 2008. *Student-teacher relationships: Through the eyes of six beginning teachers.* www.allacademic.com/meta/p_mla_apa_research_citation/2/0/5/4/6/pages205469/p205469-4.php

Amen, D. 2001. *Healing ADD: The breakthrough program that allows you to see and heal the six types of attention deficit disorder.* New York: G.P. Putnam's Sons.

American Academy of Child and Adolescent Psychiatry. 2004a. Child psychiatry facts for families: recommendations, help and guidance from the AACAP. http://pediatrics.about.com/library/bl_psych_policy_statements.htm

American Academy of Child and Adolescent Psychiatry. 2004b. Children with oppositional defiant disorder. www.aacap.org/publications/factsfam/72.htm

American Academy of Child and Adolescent Psychiatry. 2004c. Bipolar disorder in children and teens. www.aacap.org/publications/factsfam/72.htm

American Academy of Child and Adolescent Psychiatry 2008. Teen suicide. www.aacap.org/publications/factsfam/suicide.htm

American Academy of Pediatrics. 2004. Fetal alcohol syndrome. www.aap.org/advocacy/chm98fet.htm

Beane, J. A. 2002. Beyond self-interest: A democratic core curriculum. *Educational Leadership, 59*(7), 25–28.

Berger, R. 2003. *An ethic of excellence: Building a culture of craftsmanship with students.* Portsmouth, NH: Heinemann.

Biddulph, S. 1997. *Raising boys.* Sydney, Australia: Finch Publishing.

Borba, M. 1999. *Parents do make a difference: How to raise kids with solid character, strong minds, and caring hearts.* San Francisco: Jossey-Bass.

Borba, M. 2001. *Building moral intelligence: The seven essential virtues that teach kids to do the right thing.* San Francisco: Jossey-Bass.

Borba, M. 2003. *No more misbehavin': 38 difficult behaviors and how to stop them.* San Francisco. Jossey-Bass.

Borba, M. 2004. *Don't give me that attitude! 24 rude, selfish, insensitive things kids do and how to stop them.* San Francisco: Jossey-Bass.

Borba, M. 2005. *Nobody likes me: everybody hates me: The top 25 friendship problems and how to solve them.* San Francisco: Jossey-Bass.

Brain Injury Society. 2006. *1998 newsletter.* Fall Issue. http://biac-aclc.ca.en

Canter, L., and Canter, M. 1976. *Assertive Discipline: A take-charge approach for today's educator.* Seal Beach, CA: Lee Canter & Associates. The second and third editions of the book, published in 1992 and 2001, are entitled *Assertive Discipline: Positive behavior management for today's classroom.*

CDC. 2004. Alcohol consumption among women who are pregnant or who might become pregnant—United States, 2002. Centers for Disease Control and Prevention. www.acbr.com/fas

Charles, C. M. 1974. *Teachers' petit Piaget.* Belmont, CA: Fearon.

Charles, C. M. 2000. *The synergetic classroom: Joyful teaching and gentle discipline.* Boston: Allyn & Bacon.

Charles, C. M. 2008. *Today's best classroom management strategies: Paths to positive discipline.* Boston: Allyn & Bacon.

Clark, E., Lutke, J., Minnes, P., and Ouellette-Kuntz. 2004. Secondary disabilities among adults with fetal alcohol spectrum disorder in British Columbia. *Journal of FAS International, 2,* 1–12.

Cochran-Smith, M. 1995. Colorblindness and basket making are not the answers: Confronting the dilemmas of race, culture, and language diversity in teacher education. *American Educational Research Journal, 32*(3), 493–522.

Coloroso, B. 2002. *Kids are worth it: Giving your child the gift of inner discipline.* Littleton, CO: Kids Are Worth It!

Cook, P. 2004a. *Behaviour, learning and teaching: Applied studies in FAS/FAE.* (Distance Education Curricula). Winnipeg, Canada: Red River College.

Cook, P. 2004b. *Sensory integration dysfunction: A layperson's guide.* Booklet available from Paula Cook. Internet contact: pcook59@shaw.ca

Cook, P. 2005. *Rage: A layperson's guide to what to do when someone begins to rage.* Booklet available from Paula Cook. Internet contact: pcook59@shaw.ca

Cook, P., Kellie, R., Jones, K., and Goossen, L. 2000. *Tough kids and substance abuse.* Winnipeg, Canada: Addictions Foundation of Manitoba.

Covey, R. 1989. *The 7 habits of highly effective people.* New York: Simon and Schuster.

Covey, R. 2004. *The 7 habits of highly effective people: Restoring the character ethic.* New York: Free Press.

Curwin, R. 1992. *Rediscovering hope: Our greatest teaching strategy.* Bloomington, IN: National Educational Service.

Curwin, R., and Mendler, A. 1988. *Discipline with dignity.* Alexandria, VA: Association for Supervision and Curriculum Development. Revised editions 1992, 1999, 2002. Upper Saddle River, NJ: Merrill.

Curwin, R., Mendler, A., and Mendler, B. 2008. *Discipline with dignity: New challenges, new solutions.* Alexandria, VA: ASCD.

Daly, T. 2004. *The ADHD solution for teachers: How to turn any disruptive child into your best student.* San Diego, CA: Smarty Pants Publications.

Daly, T. 2006. Eliminate disruptive behavior in your classroom forever. Free 5-part report. www.adhdsolution.com/ref/index.cfm#backgroundreturn

Davidson, H. 2002. *Just ask! A handbook for instructors of students being treated for mental disorders.* (2nd ed.). Calgary, Canada: Detselig Enterprises.

DeAngelis, T. 2004. Children's mental health problems seen as "epidemic." *APA Monitor on Psychology, 35*(11), 38.

Diamond, M., and Hopson, J. 1998. *Magic trees of the mind: How to nurture your child's intelligence, creativity, and healthy emotions from birth through adolescence.* New York: Dutton.

Dolphin Education. 2006. Dyslexia research: 4. The incidence of dyslexia. www.dolphinuk.co.uk/education/case_studies/dyslexia_research.htm

Dreikurs, R., and Cassel, P. 1995. *Discipline without tears.* New York: Penguin-NAL. (Original work published 1972.)

Drye, J. 2000. *Tort liability 101: When are teachers liable?* Atlanta, GA: Educator Resources. www.educator-resources.com

Echternach, C., and Cook, P. 2004. *The rage cycle.* Paper available from Paula Cook. Email pcook59@shaw.ca.

Faraone, S. 2003. *Straight talk about your child's mental health.* New York: Guilford Press.

Feldman, E. 2004. *Impact of mental illness on learning.* Keynote address at the 9th Midwest Conference on Child and Adolescent Mental Health, Grand Forks, ND.

Fodeman, D., and Monroe, M. 2008. *Safe practices for life online: A guide to middle and high school.* Washington, DC: International Society for Technology in Education.

Ford, E. 1999. *Discipline for home and school, book two* (Rev. ed.). Scottsdale, AZ: Brandt Publishing.

Ford, E. 2003. *Discipline for home and school, book one* (3rd ed.). Scottsdale, AZ: Brandt Publishing.

Ford, E. 2004. *Discipline for home and school, fundamentals.* Scottsdale, AZ: Brandt.

Ford, E. 2006. A school discipline program that is radically different from other classroom management programs, traditional classroom discipline programs, or any school behavior management program. www.responsiblethinking.com

Ford, E., and Venetis, G. 2006. Teaching respect using RTP. www.responsiblethinking.com

Forni, P. 2002. *Choosing civility: The twenty-five rules of considerate conduct.* New York: St. Martin's Press.

Forni, P. 2006. The other side of civility. www.jhu.edu

Forni, P. 2008. *The civility solution: What to do when people are rude.* New York: St. Martin's Press.

Franek, M. 2005/2006. Foiling cyberbullies in the new Wild West. *Educational Leadership, 63*(4), 39–43.

Gardner, H. 1999. *Intelligence reframed: Multiple intelligences for the 21st century.* New York: Basic Books.

Ginott, H. 1965. *Between parent and child.* New York: Macmillan.

Ginott, H. 1967. *Between parent and teenager.* New York: Macmillan.

Ginott, H. 1971. *Teacher and child.* New York: Macmillan.

Glasser, W. 1965. *Reality therapy.* New York: Harper & Row.

Glasser, W. 1969. *Schools without failure.* New York: Harper & Row.

Glasser, W. 1986. *Control theory in the classroom.* New York: HarperCollins.

Glasser, W. 1990. *The quality school: Managing students without coercion.* New York: HarperCollins.

Glasser, W. 1992. The quality school curriculum. *Phi Delta Kappan, 73*(9), 690–694.

Glasser, W. 1993. *The quality school teacher.* New York: HarperCollins.

Glasser, W. 1998a. *Choice theory in the classroom.* New York: HarperCollins.

Glasser, W. 1998b. *The quality school: Managing students without coercion.* New York: HarperCollins.

Glasser, W. 1998c. *The quality school teacher.* New York: HarperCollins.

Glasser, W. 2001. *Every student can succeed.* Chatsworth, CA: William Glasser.

Glavac, M., 2005. Summary of major concepts covered by Harry K. Wong. *The Busy Educator's Newsletter.* www.glavac.com

Goleman, D. 2006. *Emotional intelligence.* New York: Bantam Books.

Golubtchik, B. 2008. Create a multi-sensory classroom. www.teachersnetwork.org/ntol/howto/energize/c13472,.htm

Goorian, B., and Brown, K. 2002. *Trends and issues: School law.* ERIC Clearinghouse on Educational Management. http://eric.uoregon.edu/trends_issues/law/index.html

Gossen, D. 1992. *Restitution: Restructuring school discipline.* Chapel Hill, NC: New View Publications.

Gossen, D. 2002. What do you want? Student behavior. *yA! Magazine for Middle Level Educators, 3*(3), 1–5.

Gossen, D. 2004. *It's all about we: Rethinking discipline using restitution.* Saskatoon, Saskatchewan: Chelsom Consultants.

Gossen, D., and Anderson, J. 1995. *Creating the conditions: Leadership for quality schools.* Chapel Hill, NC: New View Publications.

Greene, R. 2001. *The explosive child.* New York: Harper Collins.

Hall, P., and Hall, N. 2003. *Educating oppositional and defiant children.* Alexandria, VA: Association for Supervision and Curriculum Development.

Hill, P. 2005. Pharmacological treatment of rage. www.focusproject.org.uk/SITE/UPLOAD/DOCUMENT/Hill

Hingsburger, D. 2000a. *First contact.* Eastman, Quebec: Diverse City Press.

Hingsburger, D. 2000b. *Power tools.* Eastman, Quebec: Diverse City Press.

Institute of Medicine. 1996. Fetal alcohol syndrome: Diagnosis, epidemiology, prevention, and treatment. www.come-over.to/FAS/IOMsummary.htm

Jans, L., Stoddard, S., and Kraus, L. 2004. *Chatbook on mental health and disability in the United States.* An InfoUse report. Washington, DC: U.S. Department of Education, National Institute on Disability and Rehabilitation Research.

Jonassen, D. H. 2000. *Computers as mindtools for schools* (2nd ed.). Upper Saddle River, NJ: Merrill/Prentice Hall.

Jones, F. 1987a. *Positive classroom discipline.* New York: McGraw-Hill.

Jones, F. 1987b. *Positive classroom instruction.* New York: McGraw-Hill.

Jones, F. 2003. Weaning the helpless handraisers, part 2: Teaching to the visual modality. www.educationworld.com/a_curr/columnists/jones/jones004.shtml

Jones, F. 2007. *Tools for teaching.* Santa Cruz, CA: Fredric H. Jones & Associates.

Jones, J. 2008. Collaboration—high school style. www.teachersnetwork.org/ntol/howto/develop/collaborate.htm

Jones, P. 2007. *The video toolbox.* Santa Cruz, CA: Fredric H. Jones & Associates.

Kagan, S. 2001. Teaching for character and community. *Educational Leadership, 59*(2), 50–55.

Kagan, S., Kyle, P., and Scott, S. 2004. *Win-Win Discipline.* San Clemente, CA: Kagan Publishing.

Kellerman, T. 2003. The FAS community resource center. www.come-over.to/FASCRC

Kohn, A. 1993, 1999. *Punished by rewards: The trouble with gold stars, incentive plans, A's, praise, and other bribes.* Boston: Houghton Mifflin.

Kohn, A. 1999. *The schools our children deserve: Moving beyond traditional classrooms and "tougher standards."* Boston: Houghton Mifflin.

Kohn, A. 2001. *Beyond discipline: From compliance to community.* Upper Saddle River, NJ: Merrill/Prentice Hall. 1996 edition published Alexandria, VA: Association for Supervision and Curriculum Development.

Kolb, L. 2008. *Toys to tools: Connecting student cell phones to education.* Washington, DC: International Society for Technology in Education.

Kounin, J. 1971. *Discipline and group management in classrooms.* New York: Holt, Rinehart, and Winston.

Kranowitz, C. 1998. *The out-of-sync child.* New York: Skylight Press.

Kranowitz, C., Szkut, S., Balzer-Martin, L., Haber, E., and Sava, D. 2003. *Answers to questions teachers ask about sensory integration.* Las Vegas, NV: Sensory Resources LLC.

Learning Disabilities Association of America. 2005. Accommodations, techniques, and aids for teaching. www.ldanatl.org/aboutld/teachers/understanding/accommodations.asp

Levinson, H. 2000. *The discovery of cerebellar-vestibular syndromes and therapies: A solution to the riddle—dyslexia* (2nd ed.). Lake Success, NY: Stonebridge Publishing.

Marshall, M. 2001. *Discipline without stress, punishments, or rewards: How teachers and parents promote responsibility & learning.* Los Alamitos, CA: Piper Press.

Marshall, M. 2005a. A letter worth reading. www.marvinmarshall.com/aletterworthreading.html

Marshall, M. 2005b. A principal's experience. www.marvinmarshall.com/principal.htm

Marshall, M. 2005c. Classroom meetings. www.discipline
withoutstress.com/sample_chapters.html

Marshall, M. 2005d. Collaboration for quality learning.
www.disciplinewithoutstress.com/sample_chapters
.html

Marshall, M. 2005e. Promoting positivity, choice, and reflection. www.marvinmarshall.com/promoting_positivity
.htm

Marshall, M. 2005f. Reducing perfectionism. www
.disciplinewithoutstress.com/sample_chapters.html.

Marshall, M. 2005g. Samples of hierarchies for promoting
learning. www.marvinmarshall.com/hierarchy.htm

Marshall, M. 2008. A system is superior to talent. http://
teachers.net/gazette/MAR08/marshall

Maslow, A. 1954. *Motivation and personality.* New York:
Harper.

McGregor, D. 1960. *The human side of enterprise.* New York:
McGraw-Hill.

Mee, C. 1997. *2,000 voices: Young adolescents' perceptions
and curriculum implications.* Columbus, OH: National
Middle School Association.

Mendler, A., and Curwin, R. 1999. *Discipline with dignity
for challenging youth.* Bloomington, IN: National Education Service.

Morrish, R. 1997. *Secrets of discipline: 12 keys for raising
responsible children.* Fonthill, Canada: Woodstream
Publishing.

Morrish, R. 2000. *With all due respect: Keys for building effective school discipline.* Fonthill, Canada: Woodstream
Publishing.

Morrish, R. 2003. *FlipTips.* Fonthill, Canada: Woodstream
Publishing.

Morrish, R. 2005. What is Real Discipline? www.real
discipline.com

Murrell, P. C., Jr. 1991. Cultural politics in teacher education: What's missing in the preparation of African
American teachers? In M. Foster (Ed.), *Readings on
equal education* (Vol. 11, pp. 205–225). New York: AMS
Press.

National Council for Learning Disabilities. 2005. The
ABCs of learning disabilities. www.ncld.org

National Education Association. 1975. *Code of ethics of the
education profession.* www.nea.org/aboutnea/code.html

National Institute of Mental Health. 2005. Health information quick links. www.nimh.nih.gov

National Institute of Mental Health. 2006. Medications.
www.nimh.nih.gov/publicat/medicate.cfm#ptdep1

National Institute of Mental Health. 2008. Health information quick links. www.nimh.nih.gov

Nelsen, J., and Lott, L. 2000. *Positive discipline in the classroom.* Rocklin, CA: Prima.

Norton, P., and Wiburg, K. (2003). *Teaching with technology: Designing opportunities to learn.* Belmont, CA:
Wadsworth/Thomson Learning.

Packer, L. 2005. Overview of rage attacks. www.tourette
syndrome.net/rage_overview.htm

Page, M. 2005. Energizing the classroom with new
language: Five steps to dynamic change even in an era
of testing. www.redorbit.com/news/education/256444/
energizing_the_classroom_with_new_language_five_
steps_to_dynamic

Palloff, R. M., and Pratt, K. (2007). *Building online learning
communities: Effective strategies for the virtual classroom*
(2nd ed.). San Francisco: John Wiley & Sons.

Papolos, D., and Papolos, J. 2002. *The bipolar child.* New
York: Broadway Books.

Payne, R. 2001. *A framework for understanding poverty.* Highlands, TX: Aha! Process.

Payne, R. 2003. Quoted in Claitor, D. 2003. Breaking
through: Interview of Ruby Payne. www.hopemag
.com/issues/ 2003/SeptOct/breakingThrough.pdf

Payton, J., Weissberg, R. P., Durlak, J. A., Dymnicki, A. B.,
Taylor, R. D., Schellinger, K. B., and Pacham, M. 2008.
*The positive impact of social and emotional learning for
kindergarten to eighth-grade students: Findings from three
scientific reviews.* Chicago: Collaborative for Academic,
Social, and Emotional Learning.

Pellegrino, K. 2005. The effects of poverty on teaching and
learning. www.teachnology.com/tutorials/teaching/
poverty/print.htm

Piaget, J. 1951. *Judgment and reasoning in the child.* London:
Routledge & Kegan Paul.

Piaget, J. 2001. *The psychology of intelligence.* London: Routledge & Kegan Paul.

Powell, N. 2008. Keep students engaged in learning with
marker boards. www.teachersnetwork.org/ntol/howto/
energize/c14660,.htm

Putnam, J. W. (Ed.). 1998. *Cooperative learning and strategies for inclusion* (2nd ed.). Baltimore: Paul H. Brookes
Publishing.

Raasch, C. 2003. Teachers, parents, outside world are key
to classroom civility. *USA Today Online.* www.usatoday
.com/news/opinion/columnist/raasch/2003-08-23-
raasch_x.htm

Redl, F., and Wattenberg. W. 1951. *Mental hygiene in teaching.* New York: Harcourt, Brace & World.

Ribble, M., and Bailey, G. 2007. *Digital citizenship in schools.* Washington, DC: International Society for Technology in Education.

Richardson, K. W. 2008. Don't feed the trolls: Using blogs to teach civil discourse. *Learning & Leading with Technology, 35*(7), 12–15.

Schwartz, F. 1981. Supporting or subverting learning: Peer group patterns in four tracked schools. *Anthropology and Education Quarterly, 12*(2), 99–120.

Seganti, C. 2008a. *Classroom discipline 101: How to get control of any classroom.* www.classroomdiscipline101.com

Seganti, C. 2008b. *Ezine.* [See articles on the Seganti approach to discipline.] http://ezinearticles.com/?expert=Craig_Seganti

Shaw, R. 2008. Teaching students how to do online research. www.teachnet.org/ntol/howto/energize/onlineresearch.htm

Shaywitz, S., and Shaywitz, B. 2003. Drs. Sally and Bennett Shaywitz on brain research and reading. www.schwablearning.org/Articles.asp?r=35

Skinner, B. 1953. *Science and human behavior.* New York: Macmillan.

Skinner, B. 1954. The science of learning and the art of teaching. *Harvard Educational Review, 24,* 86–97.

Squire, K. 2006. From content to context: Videogames as designed experience. *Educational Researcher, 25*(8), 19–29.

Starr, L. 1999. Speaking of classroom management—An interview with Harry K. Wong. *Education World.* www.education-world.com/a_curr/curr161.shtml

Stone, L. 2008. Linda Stone's thoughts on attention and specifically, continuous partial attention. *Jotspot WikiHome.* http://continuouspartialattention.jot.com/WikiHome

Streissguth, A., Barr, H., Kogan, J., and Bookstein, F. 1997. Primary and secondary disabilities in fetal alcohol syndrome. In A. Streissguth and J. Kanter (Eds.), *The challenge of fetal alcohol syndrome: Overcoming secondary disabilities* (pp. 23–39). Seattle: University of Washington Press.

The William Glasser Institute. 2009. Reality therapy. http://wglasser.com/index

Traynor, P. 2005. *Got discipline? Research-based practices for managing student behavior.* Mansfield, OH: Bookmasters.

University of Minnesota. 2008, June 21. Educational benefits of social networking sites uncovered. *ScienceDaily.* www.sciencedaily.com/releases/2008/06/080620133907.htm

VanWie, E. K., Oxford, M., Martinez, A., and Sabo, K. 2008. Democratic learning communities in technology-rich environments: Survey and focus groups with middle school students. Unpublished data.

Vitto, J. M. 2003. *Relationship-driven classroom management: Strategies that promote student motivation.* Thousand Oaks, CA: Corwin Press.

Winter, R. E., and Leneway, R. J. 2008, March 1. Cyberbullying, part 3—What schools can do. http://techlearning.com/shared/printableArticle.php?articleID=196605055

Wong, H., and Wong, R. 2000a. The first five minutes are critical. *Teachers.net Gazette.* http://teachers.net/gazette/NOV00/wong.html

Wong, H., and Wong, R. 2000b. The problem is not discipline. *Teachers.net Gazette.* http://teachers.net/gazette/SEP00/wong.html

Wong, H., and Wong, R. 2000c. Your first day. *Teachers.net Gazette.* http://teachers.net/gazette/JUN00/covera.html

Wong, H., and Wong, R. 2004a. A well-oiled learning machine. *Teachers.net Gazette.* http://teachers.net/wong/MAR04

Wong, H., and Wong, R. 2004b. *The first days of school: How to be an effective teacher.* Mountain View, CA: Harry K. Wong Publications.

Wong, H., and Wong, R. 2005. The first ten days of school. *Teachers.net Gazette.* http://teachers.net/wong/JAN05

Wong, H., and Wong, R. 2007. *The first days of school: How to be an effective teacher.* Mountain View, CA: Harry K. Wong Publications.

INDEX

Credits

TEXT CREDITS

INTASC recommendations on pages 9–10 are reprinted by permission from Council of Chief State School Officers. (1996). *Model Standards for Beginning Teacher Licensing, Assessment and Development: A Resource for State Dialogue.* Washington, DC: Author.

Select material in Chapter 5 provided by Ronald Morrish. Morrish is the author of "With All Due Respect: Keys for Building Effective School Discipline" and "Secrets of Discipline." Website: www.realdiscipline.com

Examples of procedures in a fourth-grade classroom on pages 107–111 are adapted with permission from Wong, H., and Wong, R. 2004. "A Well-Oiled Learning Machine." *Teachers.net Gazette.* http://teachers.net/wong/MAR04

The hierarchy of social development on page 180 is adapted with permission from Marshall, M. (2005). "Samples of hierarchies for promoting learning." www.marvinmarshall.com/hierarchy.htm

Select material in Chapter 11 provided by Craig Seganti. Website: www.classroomdiscipline101.com

List of activities for various sensory modalities on page 260 is reprinted by permission, from Golubtchik, B. 2008. "Create a multisensory classroom." www.teachersnetwork.org/ntol/howto/energize/c13472,.htm. Benna Golubtchik is a Senior Faculty Advisor for Teachers Network, www.teachersnetwork.com.

PHOTO CREDITS

p. 23, © Farrell Grehan/Corbis; p. 29, Courtesy of aha! Process, Inc.; p. 41, Courtesy of Paula Cook; pp. 65, 138, 222, Courtesy of The William Glasser Institute; p. 72, Courtesy of Marlene Canter; p. 74, Courtesy of Barbara Coloroso; p. 76, Photo by Jason Threlfall, courtesy of Alfie Kohn; p. 83, Courtesy of Ronald Morrish; p. 101, Courtesy of Harry Wong and Rosemary Wong; p. 120, Courtesy of Fred Jones; p. 156, Courtesy of Spencer Kagan; p. 175, Courtesy of Marvin Marshall; p. 194, Courtesy of Craig Seganti; p. 216, Courtesy of Dave Hingsburger; p. 217, © Najlah Feanny/Corbis; p. 221 (left), Courtesy of Jane Nelsen; p. 221 (right), Courtesy of Lynn Lott; p. 223, Courtesy of Tom Daly; p. 225 (left, right, and bottom), Courtesy of Teacher Learning Center; p. 227, Courtesy of Ed Ford; p. 233, Courtesy of P. M. Forni; p. 235, Courtesy of Michele Borba; p. 239, Courtesy of Diane Gossen; p. 249, Courtesy of C. M. Charles; p. 266, Courtesy of Eileen Kalberg VanWie.